'America': Dream or Nightmare?

Arbeiten zur Amerikanistik

Herausgegeben von Peter Freese

Band 4

Peter Freese

'America'
Dream or Nightmare?

Reflections on a Composite Image

3rd, revised and enlarged edition

Die Deutsche Bibliothek - CIP-Einheitsaufnahme

Freese, Peter:
"America" dream or nightmare? : Reflections on a
composite image / Peter Freese. - 3., rev. and enl. ed. -
Essen : Verl. Die Blaue Eule, 1994

(Arbeiten zur Amerikanistik ; Bd. 4)
ISBN 3-89206-625-6

NE: GT

ISBN 3-89206-625-6
© Copyright Verlag Die Blaue Eule, Essen 1994
Alle Rechte vorbehalten

Nachdruck oder Vervielfältigung, auch auszugsweise,
in allen Formen, wie Mikrofilm, Xerographie, Mikrofiche, Mikrocard,
Offset und allen elektronischen Publikationsformen, verboten

Printed in Germany

Table of Contents

Table of Contents	5
List of Illustrations	7
Preface	11
Preface to the Second Revised Edition	16
Preface to the Third Revised Edition	18

1: Innocents Abroad or Cultural Imperialists? The Power of National 'Images' — 21

My Discovery of 'America'	23
The Spectre of German 'Anti-Americanism'	28
'America' as a Place of the Mind	35
From Kind Uncle to Hateful Big Brother?	66

2: The 'American Dream' and the 'American Nightmare': A Survey — 85

The Sources of the 'Dream' and Its Main Ingredients	94
Success and Progress	109
Frontiers, Real and Imaginary	119
Manifest Destiny: From Continentalism to Imperialism	139
From Melting Pot to Multiculturalism	151
The Other Side of the Coin: The 'Nightmare'	161
The Future of the 'Dream'	174

3: *E pluribus unum*? Growing up in a Multicultural Society as Depicted in the American Short Story — 179

The Relevance of Socialization Patterns in a Multicultural Society	189

From Melting Pot to Multiculturalism: Changing Concepts of American Identity	194
'Growing up in a Multicultural Society' in Selected American Short Stories	236

4: Worshippers of the 'Bitch-Goddess' of Success: Businessmen in American Literature — 273

Calvinism, Social Darwinism, and Capitalism	276
The Commercial Fall as a Prerequisite for the Moral Rise: William Dean Howells, *The Rise of Silas Lapham*	287
Financial Success as a Sign of Spiritual Failure: Abraham Cahan, *The Rise of David Levinsky*	294
From Condemnation to Contempt: The Attitude of Anti-Success from F. Scott Fitzgerald to Kurt Vonnegut	307

5: "America Is West": A Popular Myth and Its Revisionist Interpretations — 320

Owen Wister's *The Virginian*, or the Dubious Politics of the Western	330
E. L. Doctorow's *Welcome to Hard Times*, or the Fraudulence of the Popular Western	355
Bernard Malamud's *A New Life*, or the Mendacity of the Myth of the West	375

Conclusion	395
Bibliography	400
Index	426

List of Illustrations

1:	"German Emigrants Boarding a Steamer Bound for America" (from *Harper's Weekly*, November 7, 1874)	10
2:	"Columbus Landing in America" (woodcut, October 1493)	20
3:	"USA: Land der unbegrenzten Möglichkeiten" (cover of *Der Spiegel*, July 16, 1979)	33
4:	Philippe Galle, "America" (engraving, 1581)	37
5:	"America" (Meissen figurine, 1745)	38
6:	Santa Fe Railway Land Poster (1876)	40
7:	"Hamburg & New York" HAPAG-Poster (1867)	41
8:	"Winona und St. Peter Eisenbahn"-Poster	42
9:	"Auswand'rers Freud" (cartoon from *Neu-Ruppiner Bilderbogen*, around 1838)	48
10:	"Auswand'rers Leid" (cartoon from *Neu-Ruppiner Bilderbogen*, around 1838)	49
11:	'The American Eden' in Theory (illustration by 'Phiz' from *Martin Chuzzlewit*, 1844)	50
12:	'The American Eden' in Practice (illustration by 'Phiz' from *Martin Chuzzlewit*, 1844)	51
13:	"Can the Kaiser" (World War I poster)	53
14:	"Die Welt des Ronald Reagan: Machtzentrum Kalifornien" (cover of *Der Spiegel*, November 7, 1983)	73
15:	"Reagan nach der Wahl: Waffen für den Krieg der Sterne" (cover of *Der Spiegel*, November 12, 1984)	75
16:	"Star Wars-Partner Kohl - Reagan: Reise ins Ungewisse" (cover of *Der Spiegel*, May 6, 1985)	76
17:	"Liste des Proviants" (supply list for steerage passengers to America, 1846)	80
18:	"Dringende Warnung an auswandernde Mädchen" (poster by Otto Goetze, around 1910)	81
19:	'A Log Cabin in the Wilderness'	83
20:	'First Signs of Success'	83
21:	'A Thriving Farm'	84
22:	'The Dream Fulfilled' (the four stages of the growth of a farm as depicted in O. Turner's *History of the Holland Purchase*, 1850)	84
23:	"Hey, I'm Sellin' a Dream Here!" (from *The Guardian*, November 20, 1983)	92
24:	Frederic Remington, "The Fall of the Cowboy" (from *Harper's Monthly Magazine*, September 1895)	122

25:	The Meeting of Union Pacific and Central Pacific at Promontory Point, Utah, May 10, 1869 (photograph by Colonel Charles Savage)	128
26:	"Teddy to the Rescue of Republicanism!" (cover of *The Verdict*, October 30, 1899)	132
27:	Frederic Remington, "In from the Night Herd" (from *Harper's Weekly*, October 9, 1886)	133
28:	John Gast, "Manifest Destiny" or "American Progress" (chromolithograph, 1872)	141
29:	Emanuel Leutze, "Westward the Course of Empire Takes Its Way" (study with oil on canvas, 1861)	146
30:	"'Westward the Course of Empire Takes Its Way' with McCormick Reapers in the Van" (nineteenth-century advertisement)	147
31:	Currier & Ives, "Across the Continent" (engraving, 1868)	149
32:	Joseph Keppler, "Welcome to All!" (cartoon, 1880)	156
33:	Joseph Keppler, "Looking Backward" (cartoon, 1893)	157
34:	"The Melting Pot" (from *Puck*, June 26, 1889)	158
35:	Guy Eurnge, "The Victor's Prize" (1905 colour offset from an undated painting)	173
36:	"Chinese Rathskeller, Cocktails" (New York neon sign, 1975)	181
37:	"A Nation of Nations" (collage of neon signs from the Washington Bicentennial Exhibition, 1981)	182
38:	Emma Lazarus' Sonnet *The New Colossus* (facsimile dated November 2, 1883)	196
39:	"The Great Fear of the Period" (cartoon of the 1870's)	199
40:	Thomas Nast, "The American River Ganges: The Priests and the Children" (from *Harper's Weekly*, September 30, 1871)	202
41:	Thomas Nast, "Every Dog (No Distinction of Color) Has His Day" (from *Harper's Weekly*, February 8, 1879)	203
42:	"New Customers" (from *Puck*, October 3, 1894)	204
43:	"The New Jerusalem" (from *Judge*, January 23, 1892)	206
44:	"Unrestricted Immigration and Its Results - A Possible Curiosity of the Twentieth Century: The Last Yankee" (from *Frank Leslie's Illustrated Newspaper*, September 8, 1882)	208

Illustrations

45	"Well fixed! what more can a Nigger want" (trade card of the St. Louis Beef Canning Co., 1880s)	210
46:	"Nigger Head Tobacco" (trade card, 1880s)	211
47:	"Whistling Rufus" (cover of nineteenth-century sheet music)	212
48:	*Muldoon's Jokes: A Select Collection of the Sayings and Doings of Terrance Muldoon* (cover picture, 1902)	213
49:	"Victory Liberty Loan" (World War I poster)	216
50:	"2nd Liberty Loan" (World War I poster)	217
51:	"3rd Liberty Loan" (World War I poster)	218
52:	"Anti-Chinese Riot in Denver" (drawing, 1880)	226
53:	"Rough on Rats" (nineteenth-century advertisement)	228
54:	"The Missouri Steam Washer" (nineteenth-century trade card)	229
55:	"Be just - even to John Chinaman" (from *Judge*, March 22, 1890)	230
56:	"The Anti-Chinese Wall" (from *Puck*, 1882)	231
57:	"The Argument of Nationality" (late-nineteenth-century cartoon)	232
58:	"Lager Bier" (nineteenth-century advertisement)	233
59:	'Germans on Sunday' (nineteenth-century lithograph)	234
60:	"All of Us Come from Someplace Else" (PAN AM advertisement, 1977)	235
61:	August Riis, "Pell Street Lodging-House" (photograph, around 1890)	239
62:	"Castle Garden Emigrant-Catchers" (late-nineteenth-century cartoon from *Puck*)	272
63:	"Drive Thy Business" (nineteenth-century illustration of adages from *Poor Richard's Almanac*)	279
64:	The "Ladder of Fortune" (lithograph, 1875)	288
65:	"Westward Ho Tobacco" (mid-nineteenth-century advertisement)	319

10   Illustrations

66:	Daniel Boone	
	(nineteenth-century portrait)	322
67:	"Always-on-Hand"	
	(cover of Beadle's Dime Library No. 54)	325
68:	"Lasso Jack"	
	(cover of Munro's Ten Cent Novels, No. 195)	326
69:	"Buffalo Bill's Wild West"	
	(poster)	327
70:	"Roy Rogers Official Flash-Draw Holster Outfit"	
	(about 1950-1955)	328
71:	"Buffalo Bill's Wild West"	
	(poster)	329
72:	Owen Wister, *The Virginian*	
	(a 1902 advertisement)	347
73:	"The Discovery of the New World"	
	(1621 engraving from *Novo Typis Transacta Navigatio*)	394
74:	Hans Rau, *Nützliches Reisebuch für Amerika*	
	(title page of the fourth edition, around 1870)	399

German emigrants boarding a steamer bound for America
(from *Harper's Weekly*, November 7, 1874)

Preface

In almost any American Studies course I have taught during the last decade at both my home university in Paderborn and the American universities at which I have lectured as a guest professor, the complementary notions of the 'American Dream' and the 'American Nightmare' have inadvertently cropped up and on closer scrutiny have often revealed more about the convictions and attitudes of those who introduced them than about the allegedly 'American' traits they were supposed to sum up under a handy label. Frequently, what to some participants seemed a promise which they strove to fulfil - as, for example, the notion of material success in the country of 'unlimited opportunities' - to others was an aberration which they rejected as inhumane, and more than once both German and American groups of students quickly divided into hostile factions, with the same conundrum being simultaneously lauded as a 'Dream' and denounced as a 'Nightmare.'

Confronted with such striking examples of the protean nature of the concept and all too often struck by the lack of factual knowledge and historical perspective of those who precipitately used it, I found it necessary to establish some sort of preliminary definition of the 'American Dream' for my own teaching purposes, and I attempted to do so by dealing with what I took to be its constitutive elements. I published the first result of this dangerous venture, incomplete and subjective as it was bound to be, under the title "The American Dream and the American Nightmare: General Aspects and Literary Examples" in *anglistik & englischunterricht*, 25 (1985), 7-37. In the meantime I have thoroughly reworked and greatly extended this article, and it now forms the central chapter of the book at hand and is meant to serve as a common point of reference for the more specialized investigations.

An essential aspect of the 'Dream' which is still very popular in the German EFL-classroom and figures prominently in the course offerings of German universities is that of the American 'Melting Pot.' This ubiquitous cliché, which has of course never been an appropriate depiction of American social reality, manages to abide in spite of fundamental changes, and in the ongoing discussion about whether the

Federal Republic should be turned into a 'multi-cultural society' it is frequently evoked in ways which betray a deplorable lack of understanding. Some years ago I attempted to offer an alternative to the outdated notion of the 'Melting Pot' and to do so with reference to texts which are suitable for EFL-purposes. This article appeared under the title "Growing up Ethnic in the American Short Story: An Alternative Approach to the 'Melting Pot' Issue in the Advanced EFL-Classroom" in *Englisch-Amerikanische Studien*, 6 (1984), 470-502. I have reworked and enlarged this earlier contribution and made it into a chapter of the book at hand.

At a time in which more students than ever before go in for business and economics and in which the once flourishing *Geisteswissenschaften* face what is commonly called a legitimation crisis, the contradictions between a purely instrumental business ethic - building a poison gas factory in Lybia is all right as long as it boosts the gross national product - and the goal of human self-fulfilment held up by literature and the arts become ever more pronounced. It was against this background that we organized a Paderborn *Ringvorlesung* about "Wirtschaft und Kultur" in the summer semester of 1988 and thus brought together leading managers from the world of commerce and representatives of the humanities with the intention of breaking the silence between two widely unconnected spheres of modern life. It was in this context that I presented a paper on "Das Unternehmerbild in der amerikanischen Literatur," which was published in *Wirtschaft und Kultur*, ed. by Horst Brezinski (Frankfurt: Peter Lang, 1989), pp. 83-106. During the preparation of this paper I was struck by the renewed topicality of the American success myth. Later I offered an English version of this paper at several American universities, and this is how the chapter on "Worshippers of the Bitch-Goddess of 'Success'" gradually came into being. Since one of the novels treated in a little more detail is Abraham Cahan's *The Rise of David Levinsky*, I used some passages from an earlier article which had appeared as "From Talmud Scholar to Millionaire, or a Jewish Variant of 'Making It' in America: Abraham Cahan's *The Rise of David Levinsky*" in the critical anthology *Das Verstehenlehren einer paradoxen Epoche in Schule und Hochschule: The American 1920s*, ed. by Lothar Bredella (Bochum: Kamp, 1985), pp. 114-134.

Besides the notion of the 'Melting Pot' and the myth of 'Success,' it is most certainly the concept of the 'Frontier' which forms a constitutive part of the 'American Dream' and which, as acted out in Hollywood's version of the Wild West and the mendacious Marlboro world, holds a central position in the popular German *Amerikabild*. Since, in the days of President Reagan, I found it ever more imperative to point out the many dangers inherent in the 'cowboy mentality,' I suggested that EFL-teachers should replace *Shane* with *Welcome to Hard Times*, a fundamentally different western still widely unknown in Germany. I offered a reading of this novel, which is an outstanding example of the new revisionist version of the West, in "E. L. Doctorow's *Welcome to Hard Times* and the Mendacity of the Popular Western," an article which formed part of the commemorative issue of *Literatur in Wissenschaft und Unterricht*, 20, 1 (1987), 202-216, that was put together in memory of Paul Gerhard Buchloh. And in the same year I dealt with another highly informative version of the West in an article entitled "'Teaching People How to Write Who Don't Know What to Write': Bernard Malamud's *A New Life* and the Myth of the West," which appeared in *Perspectives on Language in Performance: Studies in Linguistics, Literary Criticism, and Language Teaching and Learning to Honour Werner Hüllen on the Occasion of his Sixtieth Birthday*, ed. by Wolfgang Lörscher and Rainer Schulze (Tübingen: Narr, 1987), vol. I, pp. 642-657. Since I am convinced that both Doctorow's and Malamud's novels offer a welcome antidote to the popular image of the West, I have rewritten both articles and combined them with some general considerations to make another chapter of the book at hand.

In view of the fact that the concept of the 'American Dream' incorporates such intriguing and controversial notions as the 'Melting Pot,' the myth of 'Success' and the idea of an 'Open Frontier,' it is small wonder that, as far as American Studies in the German advanced EFL-classroom are concerned, the 'Dream' is by far the most popular topic. It is, however, rather deplorable that in the available collections of relevant material about the 'Dream' and its historical mutations[1] one

---

1   These readers, put together for the specific needs of the German advanced EFL-classroom, testify to the popularity of the 'American Dream.' They are: *American Dreams, American Nightmares*, ed. by Brian Tracy and Erwin Helms (Paderborn: Schöningh, 1981), accompanied by a comprehensive *Teacher's Book* (Paderborn:

centrally important aspect is usually neglected. This aspect has to do with an essential insight by now firmly established by a branch of comparative literary criticism called imagology, namely, the fact that the 'American Dream' is nothing but an 'image' because as a combination of national foundation myths and collective hopes and aspirations, it is supposed to express peculiarly 'American' traits. Consequently, for Americans it is made up of autostereotypes, that is, of images they have of themselves, whereas for Germans it is composed of heterostereotypes, that is, of images they have of 'others.' This means that Germans, when they talk about the 'American Dream,' inadvertently talk about their *Amerikabild* and thus about themselves. And this means that when they engage in evaluative comments on the feasibility of the 'Dream' or voice the opinion that it has long turned into a 'Nightmare,' they usually say more about themselves than about the real 'America.'

I had to realize that this was my very own predicament when the Claremont Colleges, California, invited me to contribute a paper to an international symposium on "Americans Abroad" and when this paper turned out to deal with a rather particular 'image' of Americans resulting from my own experiences and characteristic of a specific historical constellation. This paper appeared as "'Innocents Abroad' versus 'Coca Cola Conquistadores,' or Contradictory German Images of America" in the *Lock Haven International Review*, 3 (1989), 55-70, and it has become the starting point for a much more detailed investigation of conflicting German *Amerikabilder*. Since these images provide the inevitable filter through which all of us perceive 'America,' I have placed this chapter in front of all the others in order to indicate the unavoidable subjectivity of all my considerations.

Schöningh, 1982); *The American Dream*, ed. by Ulrich Klinge (Düsseldorf: Bagel, 1981); *The American Dream: Advanced Readings in English*, ed. by G. Hocmard, M. Sommers, K. A. Sheram and H. Wolff, with reading strategies by Lyn McLean (New York: Longman, 1982; distributed by Langenscheidt); *The American Dream: Myth and Reality in Contemporary America*, ed. by Gerhard Kirchner, Walter Kühnel and Harald Raykowski (Frankfurt: Diesterweg, 1982); *The American Dream in Literature: A Workbook of Text Analysis*, ed. by Dieter Klaas and Gerd Köhncke (Köln-Porz: Stam, 1982); and *The American Dream*, ed. by Peter Bruck (Stuttgart: Klett, 1986), with a *Teacher's Book* (Stuttgart: Klett, 1986).

From what I have said so far it should be obvious that the present volume is not only a necessarily incomplete but also an unabashedly personal contribution to the protean notion of the 'American Dream.' Whereas I hope that the book as a whole will be found useful as an introduction to some constitutive notions of American intellectual history and as a discussion of numerous literary texts which either endorse or attack these very notions, I felt that, for readers interested in special aspects only, each of the five chapters should be presented as a self-sufficient unit so that it can be studied individually. Consequently, the repetition of certain quotations and references in different contexts is quite intentional. I think that with a subject discussed as endlessly as that of the 'American Dream,' I need not stress that my major aim was not to break new scholarly ground and to impress my colleagues in American Studies. I rather want to contribute to the overdue correction of the faulty notions about America that become so painfully obvious in the current discussions about the alleged growth of German 'Anti-Americanism.' And I especially want to help highschool teachers of English, that is, those who face the difficult task of providing our young people with the necessary knowledge about and the appropriate attitude towards 'others,' by suggesting some appropriate teaching strategies and by offering some suitable material about 'America.'

I am grateful to all the copyright owners of my earlier publications, who kindly allowed me to incorporate smaller or larger parts of previous articles into the present volume. I owe thanks to *Der Spiegel* for kindly permitting me to reprint four of its informative cover pictures, to the Universal Press Syndicate for allowing me to reproduce a relevant cartoon which I found in *The Guardian,* and to *Pan Am* for permitting me to reprint one of their advertisements. With regard to the other and mostly older illustrations I have used, I have made every effort to contact potential copyright owners but had to conclude, and I hope rightly so, that the material is by now in the public domain.

Although this is the first book which I have victoriously composed and done the complete layout of on my own word processor, I am grateful to my secretary Ursula Malitte for her unwavering assistance and her technical expertise. My special thanks are due to my research assistant Michael Porsche, who successfully engaged in many a complicated bibliographical foray and untiringly filled out national and international loan orders, and to Gerry Williams who saw to it that the idiosyncratic English of a non-native did not veer too far from the accepted standard. To my colleagues and students here at Paderborn and at Illinois State University and Claremont McKenna College, with whom I endlessly discussed my ideas and from whom I learned much about both the 'American Dream' and the limitations of my own perspective, I owe gratitude for their interest and their patience; and to the Paderborn *Universitätsgesellschaft* I am indebted for their generous financial support without which the publication of this volume would have been impossible. Finally, I hope that my daughter Martina, who will have to survive on a planet which our grandiose 'dreams' have brought to the brink of destruction, will one day realize that whenever I neglected her during the writing of this book, I also did so for her sake.

Paderborn, December 1989

Preface to the Second Revised Edition

As any author would be, I was pleased to learn that the first edition of the book at hand had been sold out in less than a year after its publication, and when I began revising the manuscript for the second edition, I saw no reason to modify my central thesis. On the contrary, I have meanwhile tested my contention that our shared 'images' of other nations often say more about ourselves than about the nations they are meant to describe and have found this thesis emphatically confirmed at a German-American conference about the other side of the medal, namely, the American *Deutschlandbild*, which I hosted at Paderborn from May 16 to 19, 1990, and the results of which have appeared as *Germany and German Thought in American Literature and Cultural Criticism*, ed. by Peter Freese (Essen: Die Blaue Eule, 1990).

Moreover, the thesis that national hetero-images are more often concerned with the nation describing than with the nation described was strikingly illustrated during the last months on at least two occasions, namely, German unification and the Gulf War. When we miraculously achieved our reunification against the background of a dramatic change in global power structures, commentators in several western countries found it necessary to point out that a larger and stronger Germany might again be a danger to world peace, and, by reverting to the treasure trove of latent national hetero-images, they conjured up the frightening spectre of a *Fourth Reich* - thus, on March 26, 1990, *Time* asked on its cover "The Germans: Should the World Be Worried?" and opened its title story with well-worn references to Tacitus' images of the *Germani* and their *furor Teutonicus*. A little later, however, when a vociferous German peace movement spoke out against war as a means of politics in the Gulf crisis, the same critics who had just accused us of hidden *Großmacht*-strivings denounced us as cowards and dodgers without realizing that it had been their very countries which had for several decades done their best to re-educate militaristic Nazis into peaceful German democrats and that, therefore, instead of complaining they should be glad about the success of their endeavours.

Since I could not increase the number of pages for the second edition, I reformatted the complete text in a smaller type. The forty-odd pages saved by that maneuver I used for the following additions: I almost doubled the number of illustrations and included a list of them for easier reference; I enlarged the chapter "'America' as a Place of the Mind" by using some of the new material which I had collected for my contribution to the 1989 Rauischholzhausen conference on Germany and America, I included numerous new quotations from additional sources which I had discovered since the completion of the original manuscript; I added several references to relevant recent publications; and I corrected a few typographical errors. I hope that, by means of these additions, the book has become more informative for the general reader and more useful for the EFL-teacher.

Paderborn, April 1991

Preface to the Third Revised Edition

Since the publication of the second edition, three more years have gone by, during which American cultural history has been radically rewritten from a new 'race, class, and gender' perspective that replaces the traditional notion of an officially sanctioned 'mainstream' - or 'malestream' - by that of a multicultural 'quilt.' In this context, canon-formation has come to be recognized as a political activity undertaken by the ruling segment of a society with the intention of making its own achievements central and of relegating the work of others to a marginal or trivial status. Consequently - in what is probably the most important influence upon the study of literature in the second half of our century - the traditional canon, which consisted, as the standard joke goes, of "many 'Dead White Males' and Emily Dickinson," has been gradually replaced by a new and more 'hospitable' canon, which incorporates the numerous forgotten female writers whom Hawthorne once denounced as "those damn scribbling women" as well as the long neglected representatives of what the Census calls 'minority populations.' The new approach to American culture past and present has not only resulted in the correction of many a one-sided accentuation, but also unearthed - as, for example, with regard to Asian-American literature - numerous unjustly forgotten texts. Although some of the triumphantly rediscovered writers will probably once more be relegated to minor status when the fervor of single-purpose groups has abated, the 'canon' of American literature has been lastingly altered, and many traditional categories and valuations have been revealed as untenable. A thorough revision of the book at hand in the light of the often revolutionary insights of current cultural and literary research would have demanded nothing less than a complete rewriting. This I could not and did not want to do, but since I was granted some additional pages, I have made two major alterations.

One of these alterations concerns chapter 3, which was updated and partly rewritten in the light of the ongoing 'multiculturalism' controversy and its demand for a radical reconstruction of the country's cultural heritage. Unfortunately, limitations of space forbade the thorough investigation which the new and important developments would deserve, but since I have tried to make them accessible to EFL-students in a recently published topical reader about *From Melting Pot* to *Multiculturalism* and a complementary anthology of nine short stories about *Growing up in a Multicultural Society*, I have been content to limit myself to a few additional pages on the 'multiculturalism' notion and the inclusion of some new primary and secondary material.

In the previous editions, chapter 5 on the myth of the West concentrated on two revisionist novels by Doctorow and Malamud and took it for granted that readers were familiar with the popular concept which both *Welcome to Hard Times* and *A New Life* use as a foil against which to unfold their subversive deconstructions. Having learned that this was an unfounded assumption, I have added a new sub-chapter on "Owen Wister's *The Virginian*, or the Dubious Politics of the Western." This sub-chapter, an earlier and shorter version of which appeared in *Neue Brennpunkte des Englischunterrichts: Festschrift für Helmut Heuer zum 60. Geburtstag*, ed. by Dieter Buttjes, Wolfgang Butzkamm and Friederike Klippel (Frankfurt: Peter Lang, 1992), pp. 64-77, offers a critical reading of the ideological implications of the seminal narrative that inaugurated the genre of the 'cowboy-novel,' and thus it provides the necessary reference for Doctorow's and Malamud's fictional criticism of the popular myth.

Apart from these two major changes, I have added several new illustrations, included references to relevant recent books in the footnotes, and corrected some minor typographical errors. Thus, the book at hand, although it has grown by about forty pages and thereby, hopefully, become a little more informative, has remained substantially the same. Today, of course, I am even more painfully aware than I was in 1989 that my investigation of the 'American Dream' is severely limited with regard to both its methodology and the unlimited nature of its subject. Since, however, I still consider it to be what, in the preface to the first edition, I called "an unabashedly personal contribution to the protean notion of the 'American Dream,'" I am audacious enough to present it in an enlarged third edition and hope that this version will prove as useful to general readers and EFL-teachers and as acceptable to the reviewers as its two predecessors.

Paderborn, October 1994

This woodcut is thought to be the first pictorial representation of Columbus landing in America. It appeared on the cover of an Italian pamphlet dated October 1493, which contains Giuliano di Domenico Dati's poem of sixty-eight stanzas based on Columbus' first letter.

1: Innocents Abroad or Cultural Imperialists? The Power of National 'Images'

> Amerika, du hast es besser
> Als unser Continent, das alte,
> Hast keine verfallene Schlösser
> Und keine Basalte.
> Dich stört nicht im Innern,
> Zu lebendiger Zeit,
> Unnützes Erinnern
> Und vergeblicher Streit.
> [...]
>
> Johann Wolfgang von Goethe,
> *Den Vereinigten Staaten*

> Amerika ist ein Irrtum. Ein gigantischer Irrtum zwar - aber eben doch ein Irrtum.
>
> Sigmund Freud, in conversation with Ernest Jones

> It was wonderful to find America, but it would have been more wonderful to miss it.
>
> Mark Twain, *Pudd'nhead Wilson and Those Extraordinary Twins*[1]

---

1 The three mottoes are taken from *Goethes Werke* [Weimarer Ausgabe], hg. im Auftrag der Großherzogin Sophie von Sachsen (Weimar: Hermann Böhlau, 1887-1920), vol. V, 1, *Gedichte*, p. 137; Ernest Jones, *Das Leben und Werk von Sigmund Freud*, vol. II, *Jahre der Reife 1901 - 1919* (Bern and Stuttgart: Verlag Hans Huber, 1962), p. 81; and Mark Twain, *Pudd'nhead Wilson and Those Extraordinary Twins* (St. Clair Shores, Michigan: Scholarly Press, 1976; reprint of the Author's National Edition, New York and London: Harper and Brothers, 1897-1899), p. 223.

The American novelist Edgar Laurence Doctorow recently said in an interview that "there is no history except as it is composed."² This statement sums up the position of a contemporary writer whose best-selling 'historical novels' dramatize the documented past by having an individual character reconstruct it in the context of his experienced present. Thus, Doctorow's narrative practice convincingly bears out his conviction and makes it a storyteller's variation upon Hayden White's thesis that "the historian performs an essentially *poetic* act, in which he *pre*figures the historical field and constitutes it as a domain upon which to bring to bear the specific theories he will use to explain 'what was really happening' in it."³ Such a position implies that historiography, as many contemporary historians would be the first to agree, is not so much a scientifically objective description of what 'really happened' but an imaginative act of imposing meaning upon the past by emplotting and storifying it according to certain patterns.

The inadvertent 'subjectivity' which is here recognized as determining any reconstruction of bygone historical developments becomes even more pronounced when such processes are part of a foreign nation's history. This is due to the fact that an outside observer's concept of a foreign country is bound to be heavily influenced by the 'images,' that is, by the heterostereotypes of that country and its inhabitants which are prevalent in his own cultural surroundings. Recent work in a branch of comparative literary scholarship that goes by the name of 'imagology' and deals with the "Erforschung literarischer 'Bilder' (d.h. Vorstellungen bzw. 'Stereotypen') vom 'andern Land'"⁴

---

2 E. L. Doctorow, "False Documents," in *E. L. Doctorow: Essays and Conversations*, ed. by Richard Trenner (Princeton, New Jersey: Ontario Review Press, 1983), pp. 16-27; here p. 24.
3 Hayden White, *Metahistory: The Historical Imagination in Nineteenth-Century Europe* (Baltimore and London: Johns Hopkins University Press, 1975), p. x.
4 Hugo Dyserinck, "Komparatistische Imagologie: Zur politischen Tragweite einer europäischen Wissenschaft von der Literatur," in *Europa und das nationale Selbstverständnis: Imagologische Probleme in Literatur, Kunst und Kultur des 19. und 20. Jahrhunderts*, ed. by Hugo Dyserinck and Karl Ulrich Syndram (Bonn: Bouvier, 1988), pp. 13-37; here p. 13. - See also Manfred Fischer, *Nationale Images als Gegenstand Vergleichender Literaturgeschichte: Untersuchungen zur Entstehung der komparatistischen Imagologie* (Bonn: Bouvier, 1981); the detailed research report by Waldemar Zacharasiewicz, "National Stereotypes in Literature in the English Language: A Review of Research," *REAL: The Yearbook of Research in English and American Literature*, 1 (1983), 75-120; and Werner Rieck, "Poetische Bilder von Völkern als literaturwissenschaftliches Problem," *Weimarer Beiträge*, 32 (1986), 48-68.

has quite convincingly shown that among the vehicles for the creation and transmission of such 'images' literary texts are the most influential.[5] Thus, the numerous references to novels, stories, poems and plays in the following chapters are not only due to the fact that literature is my proper field, but they also indicate the important role which these text types play in forming both the auto- and the heterostereotypes of 'America.'

Since I am aware that the following reflections about selected aspects of the 'American Dream' are not only limited by my incomplete knowledge of this protean subject but also conditioned by the fact that I belong to a generation of Germans whose earliest 'image' of 'America' was essentially different from that of my present students, I think it appropriate to make a virtue of necessity by approaching my topic from a personal angle and sketching briefly the experiential background which inadvertently conditions my perspective and helps to define my evaluation of the problems that are presently besetting German-American relations.

My Discovery of 'America'

> Ich habe nie den Fehler gemacht, die Menschen und die Natur eines Landes mit seinem politischen System zu verwechseln.
> Günter Kunert[6]

I met my first American in the spring of 1945. By that time, I was an undernourished child of six; I had never consciously seen my

---

[5] I tried to show that, with regard to the four American hetero-images of German dipsomania, German gluttony-plus-obesity, German cleanliness and love for order, and the German mixture of deep learning and callous immorality, in "Exercises in Boundary-Making: The German as the 'Other' in American Literature," in *Germany and German Thought in American Literature and Cultural Criticism: Proceedings of the German-American Conference in Paderborn May 16-19, 1990*, ed. by Peter Freese (Essen: Die Blaue Eule, 1990), pp. 93-132.

[6] In *Bilder von Amerika: Gespräche mit deutschen Schriftstellern*, ed. by Heinz D. Osterle (Münster: Englisch-Amerikanische Studien, 1987), p. 150.

father, who had been conscripted a few months after my birth and was reported missing in action at the Eastern front; and the recurring experience of my life was the howling of the air-raid sirens and the tense waiting for a bomb to hit the suffocating cellar where my mother and I spent endless hours in frightening darkness. When the war was finally over and one day my friends and I played hide-and-seek in the ruins of a bombed-out street, an American tank rumbled around the corner, the lid opened, and a man stuck out his head and said something incomprehensible. My friends and I stood frozen in horror, but the man laughed and threw something at us - then the lid closed and the tank drove away. After a long time of hesitation we inspected the little parcel and took it home because we could not make out what it was. There we learned it was a bar of chocolate, something we had heard about but never seen. It was judiciously divided between us, and when the chocolate melted in my mouth, I knew two things: Americans were immeasurably rich because they could afford to give away chocolate to strangers; and they were unimaginably kind because they did so. This experience was somehow archetypal for my generation and helped to establish the widespread myth of the American G.I. as liberator and dispenser of unheard-of goods like chewing gum and condensed milk, but it was soon offset by another indelible encounter.

At the end of the war I was suffering from rickets because of a lack of vitamins, and my mother frantically exchanged our possessions bit by bit on the Black Market for something to eat. We knew that these exchanges were strictly forbidden, but when one is starving, one stops worrying about laws. One day, however, somebody must have squealed on us, and two huge M.P.'s entered our apartment and said something which we of course did not understand. They started searching the room and throwing around our scanty furniture, totally disregarding my mother's frantic entreaties. After some minutes, not finding anything, they turned towards the door, but then one came back, moved to our living-room cupboard, a valuable old piece of handmade furniture inherited from my grandparents and carefully guarded through all the war, slowly lifted his huge boot and smashed, with two fast kicks, first the one and then the other door. Then they left. This was my second crucial experience, and from it I gained another insight: Americans were violent and aggressive. This experience, again, was probably representative of similar experiences of most of my generation. Although later we realized that what we had rashly taken to be indicative of national traits was nothing but the general arrogance and aggressiveness of the victors and the frustration of soldiers who wanted to go home, it helped to establish another long-lived stereotype.

Fifteen years later - my father had come back a wreck from a Siberian prison camp, and I was a freshman at Heidelberg University, where I studied English and German - I was looking for a job to finance my studies. I had the good fortune to become a guide at the famous Heidelberg Castle, and since I studied English, I was assigned to American parties. Those were the days when the dollar exchanged for over four Deutschmarks and when, for an American tourist, a night in one of the newly erected Heidelberg hotels cost about half as much as a night in a Best Western Motel in Moscow, Idaho, and when even Americans who at home had never crossed the stateline could afford to live it up in Germany. And those were the days when studying English in Germany meant that one dealt exclusively with British literature, with the emphasis on Old and Middle English and the established 'classics,' and when the contents of our reading lists were defined by that famous taunt of the Reverend Sidney Smith, the editor of the *Edinburgh Review*: "In the four quarters of the globe, who reads an American book?"[7] Consequently, I hardly knew anything about America and had not yet read Mark Twain's *The Innocents Abroad*, a novel which would certainly have prepared me for many an experience.

When I dutifully showed my American tourists round, reeling off my spiel about sieges and duels, dukes and fair ladies, I was time and again struck by their unbelievable lack of historical perspective and their almost hysterical veneration of anything that was old. Hardly a tour went by without somebody taking out his pocket knife and trying to pry a stone out of the castle wall to take home as a souvenir. And one could lay a safe bet that the ancient foxtail in a fancy baroque

---

7   Sidney Smith made this famous remark in his review of Adam Seybert's *Statistical Annals of the United States of America* in the *Edinburgh Review*, 33 (January 1820), 69-80. Here it is quoted from Robert E. Spiller, "The Verdict of Sidney Smith," *American Literature*, 1 (1929/30), 3-13; here p. 6.

jack-in-the-box would be gone after the group had left the building (only to be secretly replaced by another ancient synthetic foxtail made in Taiwan). Three nights a week the owner of a well-known students' pub phoned me asking for a dozen students to come over and sing *gaudeamus igitur* and other students' songs which we had learned for that very purpose. There we sat, getting free beer for our performance, and impersonating to a rapt audience of American tourists a version of German student life which has never existed outside of Sigmund Romberg's *The Student Prince*. And later, when I had read Henry James and other variations of the 'international theme' from Hawthorne's *The Marble Faun* to Bellow's *The Dean's December*, I realized how perfectly we enacted that age-old intercultural motif of the confrontation between the democratic and free but naive and gullible American and the aristocratic and fettered but sophisticated and jaded European, which reaches as far back as the first American comedy, Royall Tyler's *The Contrast*; and how precisely my personal experiences mirrored, in all their contradictoriness, the traditional pattern of American-European heterostereotypes.

My fascination with and curiosity about a country which I had first come to know as an almost mythic place of political freedom and material abundance and which was now represented to me by tourists who fell puzzlingly short of my expectations, was shockingly converted into disbelief, disgust and enraged rejection when I began to learn about America's role in Vietnam and joined my fellow students in endless discussions, day-long assemblies, demonstrations and strikes. 'Vietnam' became the catchword of a painful disillusionment, and the countless reminiscences of members of my age-group amply document that this again was less an individual than a generational experience. When in 1982 I read Peter Schütt's short article "Amerika - jenseits des Ural," I had an uncanny feeling of *déjà vu* because what he said about himself was exactly what I remembered about the painful reversal of my *Amerikabild*:

> Als ich zur Schule ging [...], kam für mich alles Gute aus Amerika. [...]
> Ich bin mit dem amerikanischen Traum großgeworden wie die meisten Kinder meiner Generation. [...]
> Ich hab mir meinen amerikanischen Traum ziemlich lange bewahrt, und auch, als ich Mitte der Sechziger Jahre zum ersten Mal auf die

Straße ging, um gegen den Vietnamkrieg der USA zu protestieren, waren die amerikanischen Ideale von Freiheit, Demokratie und Selbstbestimmung immer noch ein wichtiger Antrieb. Als ich im damaligen SDS, [...], mein politisches ABC lernte, sprachen wir nicht parteichinesisch, sondern amerikanisch miteinander: wir sprachen von sit-ins, go-ins und teach-ins. Darum trafen mich die Knüppelhiebe, mit denen mich am 4. Juni 1966 ein amerikanischer Militärpolizist vom Gelände des US-Konsulats an der Hamburger Alster vertrieb, als ich eine Unterschriftenliste gegen den Vietnamkrieg überreichen wollte, denkbar unvorbereitet, aber sie verfehlten ihre Wirkung nicht. Mein amerikanisches Traumbild zerbrach gründlich, und eine Zeit lang wollte ich wie viele Mitstreiter und Mitläufer der Achtundsechzigerrevolte nichts mehr von den USA wissen. [...][8]

Meanwhile my youthful idealism has been inadvertently replaced by a more distanced pragmatism, and during several extended stays in the United States as student, tourist and guest professor I have gained enough first-hand experience to integrate both the unconditional love of my childhood and the unconditional rejection of my student days into what I hope is a more balanced picture of 'America.' But this picture remains puzzlingly contradictory, with fascinating and infuriating aspects existing irreconcilably side by side. In his poem "Versuch, ein Gefühl zu verstehen," Martin Walser attempts to answer the question "Wer erklärt mir mein Heimweh nach Amerika?" and admits in a later stanza:

> Ich gebe zu: ich bringe nicht zusammen dieses
> kapitalistische Amerika,
> von dem der Globus dröhnt, und das konkrete Amerika,
> das ich erfuhr.[9]

Martin Walser's admission is my own. Consequently, my tentative investigations of selected pieces of that puzzle which is both celebrated as the 'American Dream' and denounced as the 'American Nightmare' are offered as an unabashedly subjective attempt at reconnoitring a treacherous intellectual terrain. Thoroughly aware that my own contradictory 'images' of America lurk behind whatever I

---

8 Peter Schütt, "Amerika - jenseits des Ural: Anmerkungen zum USA-Bild bundesdeutscher Schüler," *Englisch-Amerikanische Studien*, 4, (1982), 397-399; here p. 397.
9 Martin Walser, "Wo viel Schatten ist, ist auch viel Licht. Eindrücke eines verhinderten Einwanderers," in *Bilder von Amerika: Gespräche mit deutschen Schriftstellern*, pp. 219-230; here p. 229.

will say about the 'Dream,' I have assumed, like Daniel Isaacson, the role of a "criminal of perception"[10] and offer the following considerations as my personal variation of his creator's insight that "there is no history except as it is composed."

The Spectre of German 'Anti-Americanism'

> Aber Mut braucht Europa gleichwohl, und zwar den, an sich zu glauben und dem erdrückend übermächtigen transatlantischen Führer - der Partner bleiben mag - beherzt zu raten, was überfällig ist: Ami, go home.
> Rolf Winter, *Die amerikanische Zumutung*[11]

Against the background of my personal experiences, I find it highly deplorable that it has become increasingly impossible to discuss any political disagreement between the United States and the Federal Republic of Germany in a factual and rational manner. When they deal with any German-American disagreement, be it just a passing misunderstanding or a serious difference between the two *governments*, many of our politicians and journalists unfortunately tend to see it in terms of an allegedly growing estrangement between our two *countries* and, depending on their political conviction, they either deplore it as a token of base ingratitude and political naivety or welcome it as a sign of renewed national independence and growing political maturity. Consequently, any quarrel with regard to economic priorities or appropriate defense measures is immediately couched in the loose rhetoric of so-called German 'Anti-Americanism,' and this is not only a dangerously imprecise notion which is quite inappropriate

---

10 E. L. Doctorow, *The Book of Daniel* (Toronto: Bantam Books, 1979), pp. 41; 44; 87; and 291. - See also Peter Freese, "Doctorow's 'Criminals of Perception,' or What Has Happened to the Historical Novel," in *Reconstructing American Literary and Historical Studies*, ed. by Günter H. Lenz, Hartmut Keil, and Sabine Bröck-Sallah (Frankfurt and New York: Campus Verlag and St. Martin's Press, 1990), pp. 345-371.
11 Rolf Winter, *Die amerikanische Zumutung: Plädoyers gegen das Land des real existierenden Kapitalismus* (München: Wilhelm Heyne, 1990), p. 18.

with regard to political disagreements, but it is also all too frequently used with the express, and detrimental, purpose of cashing in on vague stereotypes and conjuring up diffuse emotions.

At present, hardly a week goes by without some commentator either attacking America's arrogance and ignorance and gleefully encouraging hesitant Germans to free themselves from Big Brother's suffocating yoke or praising America's help and concern and threateningly admonishing critical Germans to remain grateful and trustworthy allies of kind Uncle Sam. Ever new opinion polls are released which chart all kinds of alleged changes in the average German's opinion of America; and one popular book after the other is published and advertised as finally providing the definitive explanation of why our 'strange friends' in their role of 'unpredictable super-power' behave the way they do.[12] There is also an ever increasing scholarly literature on German-American relations[13] and a growing number of attempts at gauging the reasons for and the extent of what is diagnosed as a deepening estrangement between the Federal Republic and the United States. These investigations usually, and rather predictably, come to the conclusion that many conflicts are not only blown up out of proportion but that in most of them mutual misconceptions play a crucial role. Recently, for example, a group of German professors of American Studies issued a memorandum in which they deplore that

---

12 See for example Klaus Harpprecht, *Der fremde Freund. Amerika: Eine innere Geschichte* (Stuttgart: Deutsche Verlagsanstalt, 1982); Marion Gräfin Dönhoff, *Amerikanische Wechselbäder: Beobachtungen und Kommentare aus 4 Jahrzehnten* (Stuttgart: Deutsche Verlagsanstalt, 1983); Peter Merseburger, *Die unberechenbare Vormacht: Wohin steuern die USA?* (München: Bertelsmann, 1983). - Among the most recent of these books are Dieter Kronzucker and Klaus Emmerich, *Das amerikanische Jahrhundert* (Düsseldorf: Econ, 1989), and Peter Staisch, *Mein Amerika: Innenansichten aus dem Land der Widersprüche* (München: Piper, 1991).
13 The most comprehensive stock-taking is *Amerika und die Deutschen: Bestandsaufnahme einer 300jährigen Geschichte*, ed. by Frank Trommler (Opladen: Westdeutscher Verlag, 1986), which collects the 47 contributions to the "Tricennial Conference of German-American History, Politics and Culture" held in October 1983 at the University of Pennsylvania in Philadelphia. - See also the thematic issues of *Amerikastudien - American Studies*, 31, 3 (1986), about "Die U.S.A. und Deutschland: Ursprünge und Funktionen gesellschaftlicher und kultureller Stereotypen," and 33, 3 (1988), about "Historische Amerikastudien: Beiträge zur Geschichte der Vereinigten Staaten und der deutsch-amerikanischen Beziehungen," and the thematic issues of *Englisch-Amerikanische Studien*, 6, 1 and 2 (1984) and 10, 2 (1988).

> [...] the amount of teaching and research in American history [at German universities] is in sharp contrast to the eminent importance of the United States for the political life, economy, and culture in the Federal Republic of Germany. Thorough knowledge of the history and culture of the United States is not common in the Federal Republic. [...] this situation is politically and academically irresponsible.[14]

One might feel tempted to reject this complaint as exaggerated and to point out that, after over two decades of mandatory English for almost every German school-child and in a world which international mass media have long turned into McLuhan's global village, more Germans than ever before should know some basic facts about the U.S.A. and that more and more of them have even acquired some first-hand knowledge of America because they have spent their holidays there. The fact, however, that U.S. history is offered at only one out of nine West German universities and that of all the history courses taught at German universities since 1949 less than two per cent were in American history cannot be refuted, and my personal experiences in twenty-five years of teaching American Studies and in hundreds of interviews with German students of subjects other than English conducted for several scholarship organizations convince me that a great educational effort will have to be made in order to enable our young people to replace their home-made misconceptions and prejudices about 'America' with factual and reliable information about the U.S.A.

This is certainly not a new insight. Goethe implied it in his ironic aphorism

> Amerikanerinn [sic!] nennst du das Töchterchen, alter Phantaste, Glücklicher [,] hast du sie nicht hier in Europa gemacht.[15]

---

14 In the U.S.A., this initiative was reported on by Ferdinand Protzman, "To Germans, U.S. Past Is Mostly Blank," *International Herald Tribune*, February 2, 1989, p. 6. - It can hardly be denied that Protzman's title correctly states the facts, but one should not forget that 'To Americans, the European Past Has Traditionally Been Completely Blank.' - See, for example, Kurt H. Stapf, Wolfgang Stroebe and Klaus Jonas, *Amerikaner über Deutschland und die Deutschen: Urteile und Vorurteile* (Opladen: Westdeutscher Verlag, 1986).

15 *Goethes Werke* [Weimarer Ausgabe], vol. I, *Gedichte: Lesarten*, p. 454.

The hero of Ferdinand Kürnberger's novel *Der Amerika-Müde* (1855) came to a similar conclusion when he realized that the *Amerikabild* of his time was built more on hope and projection than on factual knowledge:

> Der Liberalismus der Restaurationsepoche fand in Wort und Schrift über Amerika eines seiner wenigen erlaubten Ausdrucksmittel. Er benutzte es eifrig. Er feierte die Sternbannerrepublik als die praktische Verwirklichung seines geächteten Ideals. Aus dieser Tendenz ging zwar die Wahrheit auf, aber nicht die volle Wahrheit. Er hätte es für politische Unklugheit, ja für Verrat gehalten, die Flecken seiner Sonne zu gestehen.[16]

Visser't Hooft expressed the same idea when he observed in 1931: "[Europa] wird von seinem eigenen Amerikabild stärker beeinflußt als von Amerika selbst."[17] And Hans Hunfeld used this insight in 1984 as the starting point for his exploration of the contemporary German *Amerikabild* in an idiosyncratic book, the blurb of which states: "Was trennt uns vom wirklichen Amerika? Ein Amerika, das wir uns selbst erzeugt haben."[18]

That there exists a curious combination of expectations and projections on the one hand and a lack of factual knowledge about the intellectual, economic and political history of the United States on the other and that the German 'image' of America differs in many respects from the reality of the United States can certainly not be denied. And this state of affairs is corroborated by the statistics recently collected in Sebastian Knauer's study, which is revealingly entitled *Lieben wir die USA? Was die Deutschen über die Amerikaner denken* (1987).[19] Knauer, however, not only provides various statistical proofs of the fact that clichés and prejudices still abound, but he also points to an essential and all too often forgotten distinction, when he observes:

---

16 Ferdinand Kürnberger, *Der Amerikamüde: Amerikanisches Kulturbild* (Wien und Leipzig: R. Löwit, no date), p. 88.
17 Here quoted from Frank Trommler, "Aufstieg und Fall des Amerikanismus in Deutschland," in *Amerika und die Deutschen*, pp. 666-676; here p. 667.
18 See Hans Hunfeld, *Geschichten vom deutschen Amerika* (Bochum: Ferdinand Kamp, 1984).
19 See Sebastian Knauer, *Lieben wir die USA? Was die Deutschen über die Amerikaner denken* (Hamburg: Stern-Bücher, 1987).

> Lieben wir die USA? Ja, wenn es sich um den Lebensstil Amerikas handelt. Nein, wenn es um die Machtpolitik aus dem Weißen Haus geht. Auf diese Kurzformel läßt sich die Auswertung von Meinungsumfragen aus vier Jahrzehnten bringen. Die Bundesbürger wissen zu unterscheiden zwischen dem American way of life, den sie tagtäglich selbst leben, und der Politik der Präsidenten seit 1945, von Harry S. Truman, Dwight D. Eisenhower, John F. Kennedy, Lyndon B. Johnson, Richard M. Nixon, Gerald R. Ford, Jimmy Carter bis hin zu Ronald Reagan. Hier schwankt die Zustimmung mit den Pendelschlägen der amerikanischen Politik.[20]

This distinction is centrally important, and it substantiates my contention that political altercations must not be rashly misunderstood as proof of a general German 'Anti-Americanism.' However, since American political claims and decisions are not generated out of nothing but reflect American history and culture at large, Knauer's clean-cut dichotomy between the alleged German love of the American way of life and the supposed German rejection of certain aspects of American politics is far too simplistic an answer to a complex conundrum. The specific American political claims which are rejected by a growing number of Germans are usually the very ones that most clearly express the basic beliefs and attitudes which have brought forth the American way of life. And when one puts all short-lived political controversies aside and investigates the more general charges which German cultural critics are fond of levelling against the United States and which indignant Americans are bound to reject as unfounded and unfair, one finds that these charges are mostly concerned with the glaring discrepancies between American claims of being a model for the rest of the world on the one hand and American realities which all too often fall short of these claims on the other.[21]

In July 1979, for example, *Der Spiegel* dealt with the current problems caused by the oil crisis in the United States, and it featured a cov-

---

20 Ibid., p. 15.
21 A comprehensive list of relevant contributions would be endless. See, for example, Gerhard Kade, *Die Amerikaner und wir* (Köln: Pahl-Rugenstein, 1983), or Klaus Liedtke, *Cowboys, Gott und Coca Cola: Was unsere Schutzmacht Amerika der Welt zu bieten hat* (Frankfurt: Eichborn, 1984); and especially the two recent bestsellers by Rolf Winter, *Ami Go Home: Plädoyer für den Abschied von einem gewalttätigen Land* (Hamburg: Rasch und Röhring, 1989; no place: Goldmann paperback, 1990), and *Die amerikanische Zumutung: Plädoyers gegen das Land des real existierenden Kapitalismus* (München: Wilhelm Heyne, 1990).

er picture which shows President Carter standing on an empty oil barrel and dutifully correcting the inscription 'U.S.A.: Country of Unlimited Possibilities' by crossing out the 'un.' This picture, which makes a disillusioned president recant his country's constitutive claim, is a witty illustration of the increasingly obvious gulf between the myth of America and the reality of the United States after Vietnam and Watergate. Seven years later, in an article in *The Washington Quarterly*, Gebhard L. Schweigler referred to the same discrepancy between promise and reality when he quite succinctly defined "the buzzwords" of so-called German 'Anti-Americanism' as follows:

- "God's own country": with 35 million living in often abhorrent poverty, with hunger lines, with continued racism?
- "The shining city on the hill": with rotting slums in U.S. center cities as the hotbeds of crime and drug abuse, while the suburbs abound in obscene and wasteful displays of riches?
- "The last best hope of mankind": with a corrupt and stalemated political system that produces as president a peanut-farmer or a Hollywood actor?
- "Only in America": with endless possibilities, from the easy, and deadly, availability of guns to commercially-run prisons, from Bernhard Goetz to whatever the latest horror story may be?[22]

When Schweigler contrasts the contemporary problems of the United States, which politically interested Germans cannot help but know about through newspapers and television, with such charged concepts as 'God's own country,' 'the shining city on the hill,' 'the last best hope of mankind' and 'only in America,' he measures the widely publicized shortcomings of everyday American reality by the exacting yardstick of constitutive 'American' ideals. And it is a familiarity with these very ideals and their complex history which average Germans, quite understandably, lack. Consequently, one of the things we need to teach our young people in school and university in order to enable them to put their often rash assessments of current political problems in a larger cultural context and thus to arrive at a better understanding of the ideological underpinnings of the 'American way of life' in general and American political claims in particular is not so much the - often rather familiar - contemporary reality of the United States but the underlying 'myth' of America and, most importantly, its

---

[22] Gebhard L. Schweigler, "Anti-Americanism in Germany," *The Washington Quarterly*, Winter 1986, pp. 70f.

European roots. Since central aspects of this myth have coalesced into the notion of the 'American Dream,' an examination of this 'Dream' with both its origins full of hope and its sometimes rather nightmarish consequences might contribute to a better understanding of some of the contemporary claims and contradictions which it has helped to generate.

'America' as a Place of the Mind

> Know, then, that, on the right hand of the Indies, there is an island called California very close to the side of the Terrestrial Paradise, [...]
> Garci Rodríguez de Montalvo[23]

From its very discovery, America became the country upon which the European imagination projected its cherished dream of a paradise on earth. When Columbus found what he took to be the "earthly paradise,"[24] the ancient notion of a brave new world had finally found its confirmation in reality, and the New World of America was celebrated as the realization of the Biblical Garden of Eden, the Golden Age of classical antiquity and the Arcadia of the Renaissance. And when the Puritan dissenters fled from their European captivity to erect a new heaven upon earth on the new continent hidden by God's providence till the advent of the Reformation, America became the heaven of millenial promises to a European hell ravaged by the Great Beast of Papacy. Bishop Berkeley and others placed America in the ancient tradition of *translatio imperii*,[25] and generation after generation of

---

[23] Garci Rodríguez de Montalvo, *Las Sergas de Esplandián*, transl. by Edward Everett Hale, *The Atlantic Monthly*, 82 (March 1864), p. 266.

[24] See *The Voyages of Christopher Columbus. Being the Journals of His First and Third, and the Letters Concerning His First and Last Voyages, to Which Is Added the Account of His Second Voyage Written by Andreas Bernaldez*, newly transl. and ed. by Cecil Jane (Amsterdam: N. Israel, and New York: Da Capo Press, 1970; reprint of the edition London: Argonaut Press, 1930), p. 252.

[25] See his famous poem "On the Prospect of Planting Arts and Learning in America," in *The Works of George Berkeley, Bishop of Cloyne*, ed. by A. A. Luce and T. E. Jessop

European emigrants fell prey to the constitutive delusion of American history: the belief that one could start anew, could leave the fetters and the sins of the past behind and begin, an American Adam or an American Eve, a new life in the pristine wilderness of a virgin continent. This, then, has been the one extreme of the European idea of America, and when in the nineteenth century Gottfried Duden and others published their promotional tracts, hundreds of thousands of Germans left their own crowded country and the harsh laws of Metternich's restoration, fleeing from poverty and absolutism towards space and liberty in what Tom Paine had defined as "the asylum for the persecuted lovers of civil and religious liberty from *every part* of Europe"[26] and what the French aristocrat Crèvecoeur had advertized, before he renounced his exalted visions in an Indian wigwam, as a land in which "individuals of all nations are melted into a new race of men, whose labours and posterity will one day cause great changes in the world."[27]

But right from the beginning there had also been sceptical voices, and the earliest horror stories of blood-thirsty Indians and starving settlers and of a continent that was so huge and so wild that it defied the human imagination soon turned into a continuous stream of disparaging reports and remarks. William Bradford's disappointed description of the region around Cape Cod as "a hideous and desolate wilderness, full of wild beasts and wild men"[28] found its continuation in tales of Indian captivity and cannibalism, and the recurring allegorical description of America during the sixteenth and seventeenth centuries in Europe ambiguously combines promises of the good life with tokens of mortal danger. In 1581, for example, the Flemish printmaker Philippe Galle represented 'America' as a naked Amazon

---

(Nendeln: Kraus Reprint, 1979; reprint of the edition London and New York: Thomas Nelson and Sons, 1951), vol. VII, p. 373. - Here the text is reprinted on p. 97.

26 Thomas Paine, *Common Sense*, in *The Life and Works of Thomas Paine*, ed. by William M. Van der Weyde (New Rochelle, N.Y.: Thomas Paine National Historical Association, 1925), vol. II, p. 127.

27 J. Hector St. John de Crèvecoeur, *Letters from an American Farmer* and *Sketches of Eighteenth-Century America*, ed. with an introduction by Albert E. Stone (New York: Viking Penguin, 1981), p. 70.

28 William Bradford, *Of Plymouth Plantation*; quoted from *The Norton Anthology of American Literature*, ed. by Ronald Gottesmann et al. (New York: W. W. Norton, 1979), vol. I, pp. 26-40; here p. 32.

National 'Images'

with a crown of feathers, with a spear in one hand and a human head dangling from the other, and with a severed arm holding a tomahawk beneath her feet. Here, then, cannibalism is America's major trait. By 1750, similar images of the new continent were common all over Europe, and a Meissen figurine of 1745 shows 'America' as a nearly naked woman with a crown of feathers and a scanty skirt of what might be tobacco leaves riding on an alligator as the appropriate animal of the New World. An exotic bird perches on her hand, and an overflowing cornucopia signifies the natural riches of the continent.

In the nineteenth century, numerous promotional books contributed to an immense increase in German emigration to America. The most influential among them was doubtlessly Gottfried Duden's *Bericht über eine Reise nach den westlichen Staaten Nordamerika's und einen mehrjährigen Aufenthalt am Missouri (in den Jahren 1824, 25, 26 und 1827), in Bezug auf Auswanderung und Uebervölkerung, oder: Das Leben im Innern der Vereinigten Staaten und dessen Bedeutung für die häusliche und politische Lage der Europäer, dargestellt a) in einer Sammlung von Briefen, b) in einer besonderen Abhandlung über den politischen Zustand der nordamerikanischen Freistaaten, und c) in einem rathgebenden Nachtrage für auswandernde deutsche Ackerwirthe und Diejenigen, welche auf Handelsunternehmungen denken* (1829). Duden, who started from the assumption that overpopulation was the root of all evil - "daß die meisten Uebel, woran die Bewohner Europa's, und insbesondere Deutschlands, leiden, aus der Übervölkerung entspringen"[29] - painted a glowing image of life in Missouri:

> Welch' ein Ueberfluß und Gedeihen würde hier der Fleiß weniger Hände ganzen Familien bereiten, deren Zustand im Vaterlande, der in Amerika geborene Pflanzer sich nicht als möglich vorstellen kann. Für Millionen schöner Pflanzungen ist am Missouri noch Raum, von den anderen Strömen gar nicht zu reden.
> Die große Fruchtbarkeit des Bodens, dessen ungeheuere Ausdehnung, das milde Klima, die herrlichen Stromverbindungen, der durchaus freie Verkehr in einem Raume von mehreren tausend Meilen, die vollkommene Sicherheit der Personen und des Eigenthumes, bei sehr ge-

---

29 Gottfried Duden, *Bericht über eine Reise [...]* (Elberfeld: Sam. Lucas, 1829), p. iv.

ringen Staatslasten, das ist es, was man als die eigentlichen Pfeiler der glücklichen Lage der Amerikaner zu betrachten hat.[30]

Books like his not only boosted emigration and thus contributed greatly to the success of German shipping lines like the "Hamburg-Amerikanische Packetfahrt-Actien-Gesellschaft" (HAPAG) which brought the emigrants into the New World, but on the other side of the Atlantic the message of such books was taken up and repeated in the advertisements of American railroad companies like the Santa Fe Railway, which, on a Land Poster of 1876, promises German settlers a steady progress on both the prairie and in the forest, or on the poster of the "Winona und St. Peter Eisenbahn-Gesellschaft," which tried to sell land to the newly arrived German immigrants.

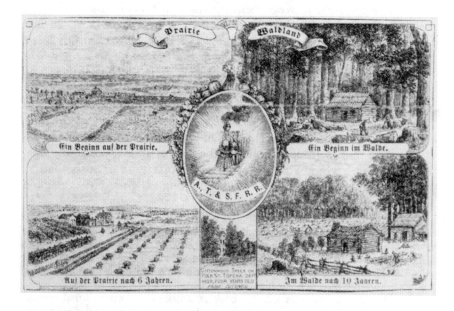

[30] Ibid., p. 181. -It is interesting to note that Duden felt it necessary to correct the fever of expectations his book had aroused. When he published *Die nordamerikanische Demokratie und das von Tocqueville'sche Werk darüber, als Zeichen des Zustandes der theoretischen Politik. Nebst einer Aeusserung über Chevalier's Nordamerikanische Briefe, insbesondere hinsichtlich der wahren Ursachen des Bankstreites und der neuesten Unfälle in dem Handelsleben* (Bonn: E. Weber, 1837), he included, pp. 84-104, an appendix entitled "Duden's Selbst-Anklage wegen seines amerikanischen Reiseberichtes, zur Warnung vor fernerm leichtsinnigen Auswandern."

These promotional tracts, however, also called forth adverse criticism, and thus Duden's praise found its counterpart in Ferdinand Kürnberger's devastating novel *Der Amerika-Müde* (1855), which was meant to rectify the false image of America created by "Dudens Missouri und ähnliche[n] Phantasiewerke[n] über Amerika" (319).[31] Kürnberger's protagonist, who bears certain similarities to Nikolaus Lenau, approaches the New World with high hopes - "Amerika. Es ist der Schlußfall und die große Kadenz im Konzerte der menschlichen Vollkommenheiten. Was unmöglich in Europa, ist möglich in Amerika; was unmöglich in Amerika, das erst ist unmöglich!" (1) - but he returns deeply disappointed: "Und da leugne noch einer die transatlantische Entartung der Rassen! Die geknechteten Europäer sahen wie geistige Menschen, die freien Amerikaner wie verdummte Heloten." (382)

For Kürnberger's poetic protagonist Dr. Moorfeld, the America of 1832 (7) is totally devoid of culture and education, filled with a mendacious and superficial religion, and exclusively given to money-making. Confronted with Benjamin Franklin's "Advice to a Young Tradesman," he coldly observes that this essay reduces man's destiny to the materialistic principle: "Aus dem Rinde macht man Talg, aus dem Menschen Geld." (28) Meeting Dr. Channing, he hears that American critic of America say: "Der Geist unsrer Pädagogik ist nicht der, Menschen zu bilden, sondern Rechenmaschinen zu machen. Der Amerikaner soll baldmöglichst ein Dollar erzeugender Automat werden [...]." (243) And visiting Philadelphia he ironically comments: "Schinderhannes war sehr borniert, sein Wesen am Rhein zu treiben. Er hätte Direktor einer amerikanischen Bank sein müssen." (292) Finally, Kürnberger's deeply disillusioned hero has to admit that the reality of a country characterized by "Sittenroheit" (18) and "kalte, dickhäutige Selbstsucht" (298) cannot come up to his exaggerated idea of 'America,' and he recognizes that "Amerika ist ein Vorurteil" (321).

Kürnberger's novel once more drives home a centrally important insight because both the author's attempt at rectifying what he considered a widespread prejudice about America and his protagonist's well-documented development from glowing admiration to scathing

---

31 All page numbers refer to to the edition given in note 16.

denunciation of the United States demonstrate that one nation's image of another often says more about the nation that harbours it than about the one which is depicted. Hildegard Meyerwas among the first to formulate that insight when she observed in 1929:

> [...] daß nicht nur amerikanische Vorgänge es sind, welche die Wandlung [des deutschen Amerikabildes] bedingen. Sie spielen vielfach sogar nur eine untergeordnete Rolle. Das eigentlich Entscheidende sind die Entwicklungen in Deutschland selber, sind die geistigen Tendenzen und politischen oder wirtschaftlichen Vorgänge, aus denen heraus sich das Urteil über Amerika formt. [...] Nicht Amerika an sich ist es so sehr, was interessiert, sondern die kulturellen, politischen oder wirtschaftlichen Nöte der Heimat und die Sehnsucht nach Besserung lassen den Betrachtenden aus seinem jeweiligen Interessenkreis heraus ein im Sinne dieses Kreises mehr oder weniger einseitiges Bild von dem fernen Lande formen [...][32]

And half a century later, Manfred Durzak arrived at the same conclusion:

> Das Amerika-Bild in der deutschen Literatur sagt mehr über die historische und gesellschaftliche Situierung dieser Literatur und ihrer Autoren aus als über die Realität dieser neuen Wirklichkeit. Dieses Bild ist also enger mit der Bewußtseinsgeschichte der Deutschen verklammert als mit der Sozialgeschichte Amerikas.[33]

This insight is born out by Kürnberger's novel because the crucial change of Dr. Moorfeld's attitude towards America has less to do with the reality of the United States than with a historical change in Germany, namely, the movement from a liberal revolt against the absolutistic oppression of particularism towards a patriotic fight for a politically united Germany on the basis of cultural unity and the con-

---

32 Hildegard Meyer, *Nord-Amerika im Urteil des Deutschen Schrifttums bis zur Mitte des 19. Jahrhunderts. Eine Untersuchung über Kürnbergers "Amerika-Müden"* (Hamburg: Friederichsen, de Gruyter & Co., 1929), p. 5. - See also Theresa Mayer Hammond, *American Paradise: German Travel Literature from Duden to Kisch* (Heidelberg: Carl Winter, 1980).

33 Manfred Durzak, *Das Amerika-Bild in der deutschen Gegenwartsliteratur: Historische Voraussetzungen und aktuelle Beispiele* (Stuttgart: Kohlhammer, 1979), p. 10. - The most recent investigation of the ambivalent German *Amerikabild* as presented in twentieth-century travelogues is Ulrich Ott, *Amerika ist anders: Studien zum Amerika-Bild in deutschen Reiseberichten des 20. Jahrhunderts* (Frankfurt and New York: Peter Lang, 1991).

comitant change of accent from the desire for a constitution like the American one to the rejection of a heterogeneous immigrant country like the United States. This becomes evident when all through the novel the future glory of a united Germany is contrasted with the shortcomings of the present America and when a character poetically declares: "Amerika ist die Baumschule, in welcher die Freiheitsbäume Europas gezogen werden; Amerika ist die große Zisterne, welche die Erde grün erhält in den Hundstagen des Absolutismus." (210)

Quite similar observations can be made with regard to the crucial changes in the *Amerikabild* of the Austro-Hungarian poet whose experiences somehow served as a model for Kürnberger's novel. Initially, Nikolaus Lenau proclaimed his deep enthusiasm for the new nation across the ocean, in which he expected to find the democratic freedom which he so painfully missed in his own country and for whose unspoiled nature he romantically longed. Thus, before he left for what he planned to be a five-year stay in America, he could hymnically contrast his old and his new "Vaterland" in his poem "Abschied, Lied eines Auswandernden":

> Sei mir zum letztenmal gegrüßt,
> Mein Vaterland, das, feige dumm,
> Die Ferse dem Despoten küßt
> Und seinem Wink gehorchet stumm.
> [...]
> Du neue Welt, du freie Welt,
> An deren blütenreichem Strand
> Die Flut der Tyrannei zerschellt,
> Ich grüße dich, mein Vaterland![34]

However, he experienced his short stay as terribly disappointing. Not only did American nature turn out to be far less grandiose than his romantic projections had led him to expect, but the culture of the New World proved to him to be unbearably materialistic and superficial. Thus, ironically, the man who went to America to buy land and

---

34 Nikolaus Lenau, *Sämtliche Werke und Briefe*, ed. by Walter Dietze (Frankfurt: Insel Verlag, 1971), vol. I, *Gedichte und Versepen*, pp. 116 and 117.

to lease it in order to make money,[35] could write angrily to his brother-in-law Anton Schurz:

> Bruder, diese Amerikaner sind himmelanstinkende Krämerseelen. Tot für alles geistige Leben, maustot. Die Nachtigall hat recht, daß sie bei diesen Wichten nicht einkehrt. Das scheint mir von ernster, tiefer Bedeutung zu sein, daß Amerika gar keine Nachtigall hat. Eine Niagarastimme gehört dazu, um diesen Schuften zu predigen, daß es noch höhere Götter gebe, als die im Münzhause geschlagen werden.[36]

And, like Kürnberger's Dr. Moorfeld, he voiced his deep diappointment about the American lack of patriotism, when he wrote to Joseph Klemm:

> Mit dem Ausdrucke 'Bodenlosigkeit' glaub ich überhaupt den Charakter aller amerikanischen Institute bezeichnen zu können, auch der politischen. Man meine ja nicht, der Amerikaner liebe sein Vaterland oder er habe ein Vaterland. Jeder einzelne lebt und wirkt in dem republikanischen Verbande, weil dadurch und *solange* dadurch sein Privatbesitz gesichert ist. Was wir Vaterland nennen, ist hier bloß eine *Vermögensassekuranz*. Der Amerikaner kennt nichts, er sucht nichts als Geld; er hat keine Idee; folglich ist der Staat kein geistiges und sittliches Institut (Vaterland), sondern nur eine materielle Konvention.[37]

But as with Kürnberger, who had no first-hand knowledge of America and whose hero's journey through the New World was primarily a means of commenting on changes in the Old, it can be shown that Lenau's total reversal of hope and praise into disappointment and rejection is only partly a result of his unpleasant personal experiences and to a much larger degree a pose born of prejudice and a comment upon changes within himself and in Germany.

The same could be demonstrated with regard to almost any of the numerous conflicting German *Amerikabilder*. And the confrontation

---

35 On October 16, 1832, he wrote a letter from Baltimore to Anton Schurz, in which he said: "Die Idee, in Amerika Land zu kaufen und durch einen Pächter bearbeiten zu lassen, habe ich nicht aufgegeben; es ist dies auf jeden Fall eine sichere Art, sein Geld anzulegen und sehr gut zu verzinsen." Quoted from Nikolaus Lenau, *Sämtliche Werke und Briefe*, vol. II, *Briefe, Kommentar, Register*, p. 208.
36 This denunciation occurs in the same letter in which he talks about putting out his money at interest; *ibid.*, p. 207.
37 Letter of March 6, 1833, from Lisbon, Ohio, to Joseph Klemm; *ibid.*, p. 216.

between Lenau and Friedrich Gerstäcker, who tried to rectify the Lenau-legend in his novel *Nach Amerika* (1855), and that between Enzensberger and Uwe Johnson, who attacked the condescending attitude of 'travelling German culture critics' in his *Jahrestage* (1970ff.), are only two among many examples which illustrate the crucial fact that our 'America' is more often an image than a reality. And when "Auswand'rers Freud' in Amerika" and "Auswand'rers Leid in Amerika" are humorously juxtaposed in the *Neu-Ruppiner Bilderbogen* of around 1838 and, six years later, the dream and the actuality of the "Eden" to be erected in the New World are accusingly contrasted in two related illustrations done by "Phiz" for Charles Dickens' novel *Martin Chuzzlewit* (1844), the gulf between ideal and reality often says more about the untenability of the ideal than about the shortcomings of the reality. It is obvious that, due to the greater degree of historical distance, such a conclusion is much more easily arrived at in the case of older than in that of contemporary examples.[38] Thus, Sigmund Freud's categorical judgment that America was a gigantic mistake,[39] which was recently so ingeniously incorporated into an invented experiential context in E. L. Doctorow's novel *Ragtime*,[40] says as much about Freud as it says about America. And thus Hitlers reversal of Crèvecoeur's prophecy of the coming American superman into the notion of the American degenerate - "halb verjudet, halb vernegert und alles auf dem Dollar beruhend"[41] - is again not so much a statement about America than one about Hitler's preconceptions.

---

38 Books and articles about German *Amerikabilder* are legion. See, for example, *Amerika in der deutschen Literatur: Neue Welt - Nordamerika - USA*, ed. by Sigrid Bauschinger et al. (Stuttgart: Philipp Reclam, 1975); *Deutschlands literarisches Amerikabild: Neuere Forschungen zur Amerikarezeption der deutschen Literatur*, ed. by Alexander Ritter (Hildesheim and New York: Georg Olms, 1977); or *Amerikanisches Deutschlandbild und deutsches Amerikabild in Medien und Erziehung*, ed. by Frank Krampikowski (Baltmannsweiler: Burgbücherei Schneider, 1990).
39 See the second motto on p. 21.
40 See E. L. Doctorow, *Ragtime* (London: Pan Books, 1976), pp. 34-36, where Freud visits the Lower East Side and Coney Island with his disciples Jung and Ferenczi, is oppressed by the noise of New York, cannot get used to American food and suffers from the scarcity of public facilities. Appalled by American rudeness and convinced that "the trip had ruined both his stomach and his bladder," Freud concludes that "America is a mistake, a gigantic mistake."
41 James V. Compton, *Hitler und die USA: Die Amerikapolitik des Dritten Reiches und die Ursprünge des Zweiten Weltkrieges* (Oldenburg and Hamburg: Stalling, 1968), p. 33.

National 'Images'

Throughout the course of history, then, the European image of America has constantly, and for reasons which lay in the beholder, oscillated between an extreme of hope and admiration on the one hand and an extreme of disgust and disparagement on the other. Consequently, to unravel the reasons for these contradictory attitudes requires a careful investigation, and such investigation must be based on the crucial insight of social psychology into the genesis of prejudices and stereotypes, namely, that any attitude towards another group, be it ethnically, religiously, or politically defined, has as much to do with the value system of the subject who harbours the stereotype as with the object it is directed against.

Those American World War I posters, for example, that admonished Americans to "Can the Kaiser" or to "Stop the Huns" from raping little girls and bayonetting helpless pensioners revealed more about American attempts at boundary making during an emotionally charged period of history than about German reality. Similarly, the simplistic attitude of the present-day German bourgeois who rejects loud pop music and fast-food chains, inane TV serials and commercialized athletics as a hateful Americanization of good old Teutonic customs says less about actual American reality than about the prejudiced person's image of 'America.' One way of explaining the formation of such images is to see them as an attempt at relief through projection. An 'other,' in this case America as the worldwide purveyor of mass culture, is made the scapegoat upon whom the faults and shortcomings of one's own reality are projected and thus exorcized. This is how, for example, Hans-Ulrich Wehler explains the current German 'Anti-Americanism,' when he says:

> Der Antiamerikanismus bietet nun all diesen Frustrationen ein bequemes Ventil. Mit Hilfe eines schlichten Projektionsmechanismus wird die Kritik an der Bundesrepublik auf Amerika als Inkarnation des westlichen Kapitalismus: als Gipfel der Konsumvergottung und des Wachstumsfetischismus, des krassesten Materialismus und einer unerhörten Arroganz der Macht fugenlos übertragen. Tiefe Unzufriedenheit mit der eigenen Gesellschaft ist jedoch eine wesentliche Triebkraft

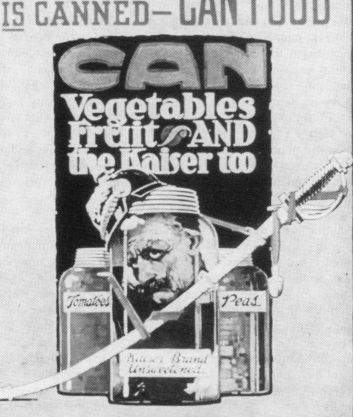

dieses deutschen Antiamerikanismus. Seine Giftigkeit wird dadurch noch verschärft, daß eigene Amerikaerfahrungen weithin fehlen.[42]

Another traditional explanation, which hardly seems convincing any longer in the face of American economic problems, is that a negative *Amerikabild* results from the mixture of feelings of economic inferiority as compensated by complementary feelings of cultural superiority. In former times this may have made a lot of sense: Europeans grudgingly had to admit that Americans could build better cars, higher skyscrapers and faster locomotives, and to compensate for that they insisted that they had better table manners, knew more about painting and music and had culture instead of mere civilization. At first glance one might argue that the old European cliché of 'You've got the money, but we've got the culture'[43] was recently revived by such TV series as *Dallas* and *Dynasty*, which present to the awed German viewer a world of wealth and abundance. But as the Ewings and the Carringtons flaunt their riches by driving Mercedes and shaving with Brauns, latent German inferiority complexes can safely remain dormant and need not blossom into compensatory 'Anti-Americanism.'

A third and related theory holds that when Europe lost its erstwhile importance in terms of global politics to the American superpower, it needed to insist that it was at least morally superior. This, again, seems quite convincing. Up to some years ago, for example, a standard topic in the German advanced EFL-classroom was the so-called American 'Negro-problem.' First - to put the matter rather cynically - it was much easier to talk about the oppression of Blacks in Harlem or Watts than about the problems of 'guestworkers' in Germany because there was no danger that one's moral indignation would have to be translated into practice. And secondly, it did a person good to remind those uppity Americans who had come to reeducate us for democracy that they had their own problems in that field.

---

42 Hans-Ulrich Wehler, "Zum dritten Mal: Deutscher Antiamerikanismus," in his *Preußen ist wieder chic ... Politik und Polemik in zwanzig Essays* (Frankfurt: edition suhrkamp, 1983), pp. 37-46; here p. 43.
43 See Beniamino Placido, "Die Erfindung Amerikas," in Gian Paolo Ceserani, Umberto Eco, and Beniamino Placido, *Modell Amerika: Die Wiederentdeckung eines Way of Life* (Münster: Englisch-Amerikanische Studien, 1985), pp. 95-141; here p. 116.

Together with a lot of other, and more acceptable motives, then, this feeling of righteous indignation mixed with a little *Schadenfreude* is certainly one ingredient of the widespread German criticism that accompanied such recent accidents in the great American experiment as Watergate and My Lai, Grenada, the bombing of Tripoli, and the Iranian arms deal.

Gerd Raeithel has recently sorted out the objections which are raised most frequently in Germany against the American way of life under three headings.[44] According to him, the first type of criticism argues that Americans are rootless and totally lack a sense of shared values. This charge, which is somehow related to our inability to come to terms with the gigantic extension of the American continent and the mobility of its heterogeneous inhabitants, had its heyday during the blood and soil ideology of the Third Reich. Thus, Oswald Spengler asked "Was ist der 'hundertprozentige' Amerikanismus? Ein nach dem unteren Durchschnitt genormtes Massendasein, eine primitive Pose oder ein Versprechen der Zukunft?" And he answered that America is neither a real nation nor a real state but only a conglomerate of men intent upon making money: "Das Leben ist ausschließlich wirtschaftlich gestaltet und entbehrt deshalb der Tiefe, um so mehr als ihm das Element der echten geschichtlichen Tragik, das große Schicksal fehlt, das die Seele der abendländischen Völker durch Jahrhunderte vertieft und erzogen hat."[45] And, to add a beautifully absurd example, the Austrian essayist Arthur Holitscher gleefully prophesied that soon many Americans would turn into constitutional idiots because their frequent movements up and down in the elevators of their skyscrapers were a violation of the human body and would inevitably result in genetic degeneration:

> Es ist undenkbar, daß diese ewige, unerhörte Auf- und Nieder-Fahrerei auf die Dauer die Struktur des menschlichen Körpers, des fahrenden Menschen nicht verändern sollte. Das Herz, das Gehirn müssen sich verändern, der liebe Gott hat diesen Zustand des Hinauf- und

---

44 See Gert Raeithel, "Antiamerikanismus als Funktion unterschiedlicher Objektbeziehungen," *Englisch-Amerikanische Studien*, 6,1 (1984), 8-21. - See also Gert Raithel et al., "Projektvorschlag: Europäische Amerika-Urteile im 20. Jahrhundert," *Sprache im technischen Zeitalter*, 56 (1975), 333-341.

45 Oswald Spengler, *Jahre der Entscheidung*, Erster Teil, *Deutschland und die weltgeschichtliche Entwicklung* (München: C. H. Beck, 1933), p. 48.

Hinabfahrens im Tierreich nicht vorgesehen. Es wird zu den anderen Typen des amerikanischen Menschen ein neuer, der Wolkenkratzertypus hinzukommen, das wird der nationale Kretin sein.[46]

This is as extreme as Reinhard Lettau's scathing comment on the simultaneity of atrocities in Vietnam with the alleged technical triumph of the "Mondtorkelei irgendwelcher Apollostrolche."[47] But the criticism of American superficiality and thoughtlessness is a recurring aspect of our fumbling attempts at evaluating the American way of life. And it is, of course, all too often confirmed and reinforced by Americans.

A second type of criticism holds that Americans are heartless and utterly lack any deeper feeling. Thus, in Kürnberger's *Der Amerika-Müde* the following dialogue occurs:

> [...] Amerikas Schönheit ist Amerikas *Idee!*
> Das sagt' ich mir auch, als ich herfuhr, [...], aber ich komme hinter den Fehler meiner Definition. Die Schönheit ist nicht eine Idee, sie ist eine sinnliche Form. Wie existiert hier das *Herz?*
> Das Herz existiert nicht in Amerika [...][48]

A. E. Johann entitled one of his American novels *Land ohne Herz,*[49] and Joachim Fernau, in his extremely critical and very successful book *Halleluja - die Geschichte der USA,* in which he scathingly concluded: "Gewinnt der Amerikanismus, so wird er in 150 Jahren die Menschheit zugrunde richten,"[50] observed that Americans are unable to enjoy themselves because they are too restless.[51] This observation, which is suspiciously close to the insistence of many American writers that becoming is much more important than being, is specified in such recurring diagnoses as the one that marriage as the true harmony of two

---

46 Arthur Holitscher, *Amerika: Heute und morgen - Reiseerlebnisse* (Berlin: S. Fischer, 1912), p. 61.
47 Reinhard Lettau, "Über Kollaboration," in his *Zerstreutes Hinausschaun: Vom Schreiben über Vorgänge in direkter Nähe oder in der Entfernung von Schreibtischen* (München: Carl Hanser, 1980), pp. 151-155; here p. 152.
48 Ferdinand Kürnberger, *Der Amerikamüde,* p. 174.
49 See A. E. Johann [i.e. Alfred Wollschläger], *Das Land ohne Herz: Eine Reise ins unbekannte Amerika* (Berlin: Deutscher Verlag, 1942).
50 Joachim Fernau, *Halleluja - Die Geschichte der USA* (München: Herbig, 1977), p. 319.
51 See *ibid.,* pp. 124; 141; 196; and especially 316.

souls is impossible in America because the wife is just a possession on the same level as the house and the car. American children are time and again characterized as precocious heartless brats, but especially the American woman has repeatedly come under fire. Thus, the syndrome of 'momism' has been lovingly dissected by German critics in the wake of Philip Wylie's *Generation of Vipers*,[52] and Kurt Tucholsky, for example, nastily observed that below the navel the American woman is made of celluloid.[53]

But more than anything else, German critics have elevated the eating habits of the Americans into a standard emblem of their tastelessness, superficiality, unrest, and, in short, their general lack of culture. Thus, in 1832 Nikolaus Lenau commented in a letter home:

> Man darf die Kerle nur im Wirtshause sehen, um sie auf immer zu hassen. Eine lange Tafel, auf beiden Seiten fünfzig Stühle (so ist es da, wo ich wohne); Speisen, meist Fleisch, bedecken den ganzen Tisch. Da erschallt die Freßglocke, und hundert Amerikaner stürzen herein, keiner sieht den andern an, keiner spricht ein Wort, jeder stürzt auf eine Schüssel, frißt hastig hinein, springt dann auf, wirft den Stuhl hin und eilt davon, Dollars zu verdienen.[54]

Two decades later a character observed in Kürnberger's *Der Amerika-Müde*: "Deutsch zu hungern wird mir leichter, als amerikanisch zu essen."[55] And in 1964 Fritz Raddatz offered a contemporary variation of Lenau's complaint when he depicted lunch in an American coffee shop in the following way: "Kein Mann sieht eine Frau, keine Frau sieht einen Mann, man sagt zur Kellnerin zwar 'Baby,' 'Honey' oder 'My Love' - aber das scheppert wie die flinken Teller auf dem Kunststoffbüffett."[56]

---

52 See Philip Wylie, *Generation of Vipers* (New York and Toronto: Farrar & Rinehart, 1942).
53 See Gert Raeithel, "Antiamerikanismus als Funktion unterschiedlicher Objektbeziehungen," p. 16.
54 Nikolaus Lenau, *Sämtliche Werke und Briefe*, vol. II, p. 207.
55 Ferdinand Kürnberger, *Der Amerikamüde*, p. 148.
56 Fritz Raddatz, "Amerikanisches Alphabet," *Süddeutsche Zeitung*, December 5/6, 1964. Here quoted from Gert Raeithel, "Antiamerikanismus als Funktion unterschiedlicher Objektbeziehungen," p. 17.

A third type of criticism argues that Americans lack bonds and lasting relationships. Thus, for German observers up to about twenty years ago, the American throwaway society with its incredible concept of built-in obsolescence came under repeated fire as an indication of the lack of bonds and deeply felt connections. Americans, they observed, have no feelings for either subjects or objects. In the same way in which they have exterminated the buffaloes and killed the Indians, they heartlessly hire and fire their employees, divorce their marriage partners, and throw away whatever they do not need any longer. Hegel characterized the United States as "ein Gemeinwesen, das von den Atomen der Individuen ausging, so daß der Staat nur ein Äußerliches zum Schutze des Eigentums war," and he detected an "Überwiegen des partikulären Interesses, das sich dem Allgemeinen nur zum Behufe des eigenen Genusses zuwendet."[57] Ortega y Gasset observed in *The Revolt of the Masses* that it is no accident that lynching is an American invention.[58] And in the Cooper chapter of his *Studies in Classic American Literature*, D. H. Lawrence used Deerslayer to define "the myth of the essential white America" and concluded : "The essential American soul is hard, isolate, stoic, and a killer. It has never yet melted."[59]

These sketchy remarks about the historical mutations of the German and, as far as that goes, the general European image of 'America,' about some traditional explanations of the Old World's criticism of the New, and about the most frequent German charges levelled against the American way of life might suffice to sketch the historical background which is all too often neglected today, when topical political altercations between the Federal Republic and the United States are prematurely diagnosed as tokens of a general German 'Anti-Americanism.' But a widespread lack of historical awareness and the inability to put current news into its wider cultural context is not the only deficit of the ongoing debate. The very term 'Anti-Americanism' itself

---

57 Georg Wilhelm Friedrich Hegel, *Die Vernunft in der Geschichte*. Vol. XVIII A, Part I of *Sämtliche Werke: Neue kritische Ausgabe*, ed. by Johannes Hoffmeister (Hamburg: Felix Meiner, 5th ed., 1955), pp. 205f.
58 José Ortega y Gasset, *Der Aufstand der Massen* (Hamburg: Rowohlts Deutsche Enzyklopädie, 1956), p. 86: "Es ist nicht ganz zufällig, daß das Lynchrecht amerikanisch ist, denn Amerika ist in gewisser Weise das Paradies der Massen [...]."
59 D. H. Lawrence, *Studies in Classic American Literature* (New York: Viking Press, rpt. 1969), p. 62.

is a highly questionable concept. On the one hand it is an empty and finally meaningless term because, as Günter C. Behrmann rightly observes:

> Als Sammelbegriff für alle Aussagen, die nicht zu einer positiven Einstellung gegenüber den Vereinigten Staaten und ihrer Politik beitragen, ist 'Antiamerikanismus' ein nur politisch brauchbarer, weil fast beliebig einsetzbarer Begriff. Wer ihn verwendet, baut darauf, daß er den politischen Gegner in einem vorbehaltlos proamerikanisch gestimmten Publikum schon mit der Kritik an nicht uneingeschränkt positiven Urteilen über die amerikanische Politik oder mit dem pauschalen Vorwurf des Antiamerikanismus mattsetzen kann.[60]

On the other hand the concept is dangerously misleading for two rather obvious reasons. In analogy to such parallel terms as 'Anti-Communism' or 'Anti-Semitism,' the notion of 'Anti-Americanism' denotes an antagonistic and hostile attitude towards *everything* that is characteristically 'American,' and this is quite evidently not what most commentators mean when they talk about what they take to be either a deplorable or a welcome change in the climate of opinion. Moreover, in contemporary German the notion of 'Anti-Americanism' lacks its necessary counterpart because, in contrast to 'Anti-Communism' and 'Anti-Semitism' which denote the respective opposites of 'Communism' and 'Semitism,' the once powerful notion of *Amerikanismus* has almost completely disappeared from the German language. This is borne out by the fact that the respective entry in the most recent *Duden* offers 'American way of living and working' only as a secondary and somehow archaic meaning which has been widely superseded by a new meaning, namely, 'a peculiarity of American English as used in another language.' And this change is even more obvious with regard to the *Brockhaus Enzyklopädie* of 1986, which only knows the plural *Amerikanismen* as linguistic borrowings and defines the singular *Amerikanismus* as 'a development in the American Catholic church of the nineteenth century which led to an adaptation of belief to social surrounding and was condemned by Pope Leo XIII in 1899.'[61]

---

60 Günter C. Behrmann, "Antiamerikanismus in der Bundesrepublik: 1966 - 1984," *Amerikastudien - American Studies*, 31 (1986), 341-349; here p. 342.
61 See *Brockhaus Enzyklopädie* (Mannheim, 19th, completely rev. ed., 1986), s.v. "Amerikanismen" and "Amerikanismus."

According to Otto Basler, the German neologism *Amerikanisierung* was first used by Emil Du Bois-Reymond in a speech given in 1877, in which he talked about "die gefürchtete Überwucherung und Durchdringung der europäischen Kultur mit Realismus und das reißend wachsende Übergewicht der Technik als Amerikanisierung," whereas the related and more recent neologism *Amerikanismus* became generally known in Germany by 1926.[62] It was in the years after World War I, and especially in the twenties, when America came to exert an ever increasing influence throughout Europe, that the phenomenon of *Amerikanismus* became a much discussed issue in Germany. In these years, numerous cultural critics and political commentators tried to define the genuinely American way of living, working, and doing business and attempted to answer the crucial question whether Europe should resist all transatlantic influences or adopt them in order to be able to compete.

As early as 1912, Arthur Holitscher, in his contradictory and rather influential travelogue *Amerika: Heute und morgen*, had decreed that Europe would have to come to terms with American claims:

> Amerika ist das Schicksal und die Erfüllung des Menschengeschlechts. Amerikas Energie, die das absurde Wachstum einiger weniger Mächtigen verursacht hat, besinnt sich heutigentages schon und sucht sich die Bahn zu dem Rechte Aller. Die Weltordnung, unter der wir heute leben, wird dieser Sturmflut des siegreichen Menschheitsgewissens nicht standhalten können. Sie wird zerstört werden und untergehen wie Atlantis und Lemuria zerstört wurden und untergegangen sind.[63]

After World War I, in a Germany which had lost the war and, as a consequence, many of its old certainties, the question of the future relationship between Europe and America became especially pertinent.

---

62 Otto Basler, "Amerikanismus: Geschichte des Schlagwortes," *Deutsche Rundschau*, 56 (August 1930), 142-146; here pp. 144. See also p. 146: "Auf das Jahr 1926 mag der Beginn des allgemeinen Bekanntwerdens des Schlagwortes Amerikanismus in seiner Anwendung auf Deutschland festgelegt werden [...]." - Gert Raeithel, "What's Anti-Americanism Anyway?" *Englisch-Amerikanische Studien*, 10 (1988), 171-178, is right when he argues that individual instances of the term can be found much earlier, and Arthur Holitscher, *Amerika: Heute und morgen - Reiseerlebnisse*, pp. 293f., provides a pertinent example in 1912 when he defines Chicago as "schrecklichste Stadt des Erdballs" and then admonishes himself not to make the mistake, "daß ich den Amerikanismus mit diesem Chicagoer Tempo verwechsle."
63 Arthur Holitscher, *Amerika: Heute und morgen - Reiseerlebnisse*, p. 429.

There was a group of forward-looking critics who came to the conclusion that the economic power of the New World and the democratic education provided for its citizens were far superior to the antiquated ways of Europe and that therefore the Old World's only chance to remain competitive would be to adopt such much-discussed American methods as Taylorism[64] and Fordism[65] and to imitate the new 'unity' which was coming into being on the other side of the Atlantic. Thus, in his study *Das wirtschaftliche Amerika* (1925), Carl Köttgen summed up his empirical and statistical comparisons of the German and the American economy by saying:

> Der gewöhnliche Mann in den Vereinigten Staaten hat ein Realeinkommen, das um 70% größer ist wie bei uns. [Und dieser Unterschied hat im wesentlichen] zwei Gründe: bessere, wirtschaftliche Organisation in Richtung der Vereinfachung, der Erzeugung in Mengen und dadurch möglich gewordene Verwendung von maschinellen Verfahren und Einrichtungen und zweitens größere Arbeitsintensität, auch längere Arbeitsdauer des Einzelnen.[66]

And since he felt that the United States were setting the pace for future developments, he concluded that Germany's only chance would be to adopt the American trend towards standardization and rationalization.

In his book on *Demokratie und Erziehung in Amerika* (1926), Carl Brinkmann attempted to go beyond Köttgen's statistics and to achieve an unprejudiced understanding of the new culture that was emerging in America, and what he discovered were the vague outlines of a still indistinct but promising unity:

---

64 The term goes back to Frederick Winslow Taylor (1856-1915), an American industrial engineer, whose books on *The Principle of Scientific Management* (1911) and *Shop Management* (1911) introduced new management methods for shops, offices, and industrial plants and made him the 'father of scientific management.' - Arthur Holitscher, *Amerika: Heute und morgen*, p. 307, rather sceptically defines the "System Taylor" as "das System der 'wissenschaftlichen Ausnutzung der menschlichen Kraft im Dienste der Fabrikarbeit,' das System des 'Speeding-up,' der Aufpulverung, wie ich es nennen möchte, das System der Anspannung und des Verbrauches der menschlichen Energie bis an die äußerste Grenze der natürlichen Bedingungen."

65 The term refers to the revolutionary method of assembly line production as introduced and perfected by Henry Ford (1863-1947), whom Europeans either lauded or rejected as the apostle of mass production.

66 Carl Köttgen, *Das wirtschaftliche Amerika* (Berlin: VDI-Verlag, 1925), pp. 70f.

> Nicht der Amerikaner zeigt es, aber am Amerikaner zeigt es sich, nicht er verwirklicht es schon, aber er läßt uns innewerden, daß es so etwas geben könnte. Was? Eine Umlagerung von Kulturwerten, die weder eine bloße Umkehrung ist (wie in der Legende von Zivilisation und Kultur) noch eine bloße Verjüngung. Vielmehr: Während (durchaus nicht allein in Deutschland) europäischer Idealismus aus Überständigkeit auf der einen Seite verzärtelt und untätig, auf der anderen verwildert und barbarisch wird, taucht hier etwas empor, das neue geistige Reihen bildet, wo nur Gegensätze zu sein schienen. 'Theoretische' und 'praktische,' 'ästhetische' und 'ethische,' 'spiritualistische' und 'materialistische' Haltungen versöhnen sich in einem Realismus und Aktivismus, dessen Naivität ungefähr da steht, wohin die neuen europäischen Philosophien der 'Wirklichkeit' und des 'Konkreten' streben: Welt nicht zu zerdenken, sondern erst einmal zu leben, schöpferisch nicht nur in Ekstasen, sondern zunächst im Einfachen zu sein, im Erkennen und Handeln keine Rollen zu spielen, sondern den Ernst und die Schönheit der Dinge außer und in uns zu fassen. Amerika ist fern davon, das alles schon zu können, und weiß es, deshalb verlangt es nach uns. Aber auch wir können es nicht allein, wenn wir das auch meist nicht wissen und deshalb überheblich den Untergang tragieren. Nur wenn wir den Ruf von drüben hören, können wir hoffen, nicht beim Worte genommen zu werden. (43f.)[67]

Praising the American university, in spite of all its shortcomings, as a "Vorbereitungsort für den Staatsbürger schlechthin, der den intellektuellen Anforderungen und den ethischen Traditionen der von der Peripherie zum Zentrum vielfach geschichteten Parlamente und Wahlämter gewachsen sein soll" (45), and admiring the close link between theory and practice in American schools and colleges, Brinkmann decreed: "das tatsachenfreudige Amerika ist gerade auch, was die Wertbeurteilung und die danach orientierte Reform gegebener Zustände anlangt, auf sehr vielen Gebieten aktiver oder doch einheitlicher und stetiger aktiv gewesen als das in Beharrung und Umsturz zerissene Europa." (97) And what his positive estimation of the New World finally came to was this recognition:

> Zwischen Natur und Geist, Ding und Vorstellung ist nicht die europäische, von europäischen Naturalismen und Idealismen verschieden überbrückte Kluft. Zwischen ihnen ist eine unauflösliche Beziehung des gegenseitigen Sichermöglichens, vor welcher Überheblichkeit des Geistes, Leere oder Drohung der Natur, Gegensatz des Machens und

---

[67] All page numbers in brackets refer to Carl Brinkmann, *Demokratie und Erziehung in Amerika* (Berlin: S. Fischer, 1927).

Wachsens, der Kühnheit und Frömmigkeit gleichmäßig in die höhere Einheit des Göttlich-Menschlich-Natürlichen aufgehen. (104f.)

Whereas Köttgen and Brinkmann spoke for numerous others who felt that a worn-out Europe could and should learn from America, there was also an opposed school of cultural critics who were morally appalled by what they understood as American standardization and superficiality. Thus Adolf Halfeld, in his influential book *Amerika und der Amerikanismus* (1927), postulated, "Wir müssen uns klar werden, welches die geistigen und seelischen Kräfte sind, die das Phänomen des Amerikanismus bewegen (x),"[68] and he then set out to examine the conundrum of *Amerikanismus* and to explode, on the basis of his personal experience, "die undeutlichen und von naiver Bewunderung zeugenden Vorstellungen, die der Durchschnittseuropäer heute von Amerika besitzt" (xiii). By contrasting European culture as organically grown with American civilization as planned from scratch and by looking at various aspects of American life, he arrived at such definitions of *Amerikanismus* as "eigenartige Mischung von blinder Tatsachengläubigkeit, fanatischer Rechthaberei und moralischer Selbstgerechtigkeit" (11) or "Verachtung des Menschen und seiner geistigen Rechte, Verkümmerung des Herzens, Barbarismus der größten Zahl [...] und Tod der Landschaft" (112).

Halfeld recognized: "Im Erfolgsgedanken und nicht in Kulturwerten gipfelt der Inhalt des Amerikanismus" (25), and he observed with moral revulsion: "Es blieb dem Amerikanismus vorbehalten, seiner Jugend eine Art von neuem Idealismus einzupflanzen, der als 'Business Idealism' eine sonderbare Dreieinigkeit von Gott, Money Making und bürgerlichen Erfolgstugenden zustande bringt." (25) He characterized Americans as "Maschinenmenschen" (37) and defined "Drug Store, Automatenrestaurant, Lunch Room, Benzinstation, Woolworthladen und Kino" as the "nachgerade klassisch gewordenen Zwingburgen der amerikanischen Seele" (37). Standardization and superficiality, Fordism and Taylorism are the war cries of his critical dissection of the American "Dollardiktatur" (54), which he saw as obsessed with success, in which he found no place for the "geistige Lei-

---

68 All page numbers in brackets refer to Adolf Halfeld, *Amerika und der Amerikanismus: Kritische Betrachtungen eines Deutschen und Europäers* (Jena: Eugen Diederichs, 1928).

stung als Gradmesser menschlichen Könnens" (65), and which according to him for the first time in human history had built a society upon a single value: money. Dealing in great detail with such facets as the excrescences of fundamentalism, the omnipotence of the success ideal, the limitations of a mass culture, and what he called "Kulturfeminismus" (209), namely the fact that the American woman had the "unumschränkte Herrschaft im Reiche der menschlichen Kulturwerte" (209), Halfeld expressed his certainty that the much discussed Americanization of European culture would never take place since it is

> [...] die Bild- und Ideenwelt der Gemeinschaft selbst, die sich dem geschichtlich wurzellosen Normenideal des Amerikanismus widersetzt. Sie sind sich wesensfremd und schließen einander aus: Amerikanismus läßt sich nicht importieren, und Neues säen - auch das Unbegrenzte und Allgemeine - kann man nur auf dem lebendigen Boden des Volkstums. (50)

And finally there were those who, like Theodor Lüddecke, understood the contrast between Europe and America in Spengler's terms as that between 'culture' and 'civilization' and therefore argued, "daß sich Europa gleichfalls 'amerikanisiert' hätte - selbst wenn es überhaupt kein Amerika gäbe," and concluded that a certain degree of 'Americanization' was an inevitable prerequisite for economic survival: "Wir haben keine absolute Wahl mehr, hier abzulehnen oder anzunehmen - die amerikanischen Lebensformen werden uns von der Seite der Wirtschaft her einfach aufgezwungen."[69] In the heated discussion of the twenties,[70] then, *Amerikanismus* was an economically and culturally charged concept which could denote both the enthusiastic acceptance and the indignant rejection of new and challenging 'American' ways, and this is fittingly illustrated by the respective entry in *Der Große Herder* of 1931.

There one reads under *Amerikanismus* that in Europe this notion serves as "Schlagwort entweder der kritiklosen Amerika-Begeisterung oder der ebenso unkritischen Amerika-Verdammung." It is then duti-

---

69 Theodor Lüddecke, "Amerikanismus als Schlagwort und als Tatsache," *Deutsche Rundschau*, 56 (March 1930), 214-221; here pp. 216 and 215.
70 For a detailed discussion see the chapter "Der Amerikanismus" in Peter Berg, *Deutschland und Amerika 1918 - 1929: Über das deutsche Amerikabild der zwanziger Jahre* (Lübeck and Hamburg: Matthiesen Verlag, 1963), pp. 132-153.

fully stressed that America possesses "Oberfläche und Tiefen, Tugenden und Laster wie Europa auch," but this is followed by the observation that in the New World every new development has been "schneller, energischer, hemmungsloser, massiger und äußerlich erfolgreicher" than in the Old. When the essence of "Amerikanertum" is then defined with the help of such categories as efficiency, prosperity, mass production, standardization, mass advertising, the lust for records, and "Erfolgsreligion," the writer's conservative scepticism becomes rather obvious. And this is confirmed when one reads:

> Das Schlagwort kommt auf, als sich Europa besonders nach dem Weltkrieg durch das Vordringen von Amerikas überwältigender Wirtschafts- und Finanzmacht bedroht fühlt. Insbesondere befürchtet man eine finanzielle und politische Überfremdung, außerdem einen Niedergang des eigenen Geisteslebens (Massenzivilisation, Kulturfeminismus, Mechanisierung und Veräußerlichung, Versportlichung, usw.).
> [...]
> Ein gewisses Maß von Amerikanismus erträgt Europa wohl: den gesunden Optimismus, die Befreiung von historisch-nationalen Vorurteilen und Fanatismen, im Wirtschaftsleben ein mehr aufs Ganze gehendes Planen und Handeln. Den schädlichen Einflüssen hat Europa seine geschichtliche Sendung entgegenzusetzen, seine Kulturwerte und die Fülle seiner nationalen Formen: deutschen Idealismus, englischen Konservatismus, nordischen Geist, die Seele des Ostens und die durch Jahrhunderte bewährten Traditionen der romanischen Länder. Den Kern des Widerstandes aber bildet das sakramentale Christentum der katholischen Kirche mit seiner unbeirrbaren Überzeugungsgrundlage und seiner bindenden Moral.[71]

The revealing fact that the attached bibliography contains seven titles "Für Amerika," two titles "Gegen Amerika," and four titles "Für und Wider," plainly shows that there was a time when the ambiguous notion of 'Americanism' could stand for either an 'uncritical enthusiasm for America' or an 'uncritical condemnation of America' and when it was taken for granted that the Janus-faced New World could

---

71 *Der Große Herder: Nachschlagewerk für Wissen und Leben* (Freiburg: Herder & Co., 1931), vol. I, s.v. "Amerikanismus." - For another recent discussion of "wie vielschichtig der Begriff des Antiamerikanismus ist und wie mißverständlich er gebraucht werden kann" (pp. 11f.) see Emil-Peter Müller, *Antiamerikanismus in Deutschland: Zwischen Care-Paket und Cruise Missile* (Köln: Deutscher Instituts-Verlag, 1986).

call forth diametrically opposed evaluations. But what had been a highly controversial issue after World War I was no longer so in the wake of World War II. After 1945, against the background of both the atrocities of the Third Reich and the threat of communist world dominion, 'America' was no longer seen as a threateningly different transatlantic power which might infiltrate and control native German culture, but as a welcome liberator. Therefore a general pro-American attitude was simply taken for granted, and consequently the original concept of *Amerikanismus* became quite superfluous, whereas the opposite notion of 'Anti-Americanism' was turned into a political weapon against those wo did not show the 'right' attitude. This development, then, provides another caveat against the loose and precipitate use of a questionable concept.

From Kind Uncle to Hateful Big Brother?

> Being an American means never having to say you're sorry.
> Kurt Vonnegut, *Hocus Pocus*[72]

Members of my generation, who got their first oranges out of Carepackages, who found their first jobs in factories and offices which would never have come into being without the help of the Marshall-Plan, and who greatly admired the American airlift to Berlin, were bound to love America almost unconditionally. And whenever anything occurred that might provide a reason for criticism, our bad conscience and our sense of collective guilt easily stifled the impetus to speak up: Who were we, with the atrocious history of the holocaust just behind us, to dare criticize our American friends? Thus we had a rather one-sided partnership that functioned beautifully, and every new American invention from bobby socks to petticoats, from Bill Haley's rock n' roll to Elvis Presley's songs was immediately taken over and imitated. Uncle Sam was the benevolent elder brother who

---

[72] Kurt Vonnegut, *Hocus Pocus* (New York: G. P. Putnam's Sons, 1990), p. 95.

had liberated us from the perversities of National Socialism and reeducated us for democracy, had taken up the burden of rescuing us, in our precarious borderline existence, from being swallowed by the detestable Communists behind the Iron Curtain.

But by and by things changed: a new generation grew up that was no longer numbed by the nightmare of recent history - my present students, for example, born more than twenty years after the end of the Third Reich, flatly refuse to be held personally responsible for Hitler's atrocities of which, alas, they often know very little; and in contrast to us they need no longer worry about their fathers' potential implications in Nazi activities because their fathers, like me, were small children during the Third Reich. The Iron Curtain was partially raised by the politics of détente, and now it has completely vanished and the two Germanies are finally reunited. In short, young Germans no longer feel obliged to apologize for being German, and their growing self-confidence has, naturally, led to their wish that Germany should have a say in the formulation and enactment of her foreign policy. Thus, American demands and priorities are no longer automatically accepted as the last word. This change becomes dramatically evident if one compares two presidential visits. When, in 1963, President Kennedy came to Berlin and announced, from the balcony of the Schöneberg Rathaus, "Ich bin ein Berliner," thousands of young Germans cheered and fervently believed in that charismatic figure as the herald of a new beginning and a move towards a better world. When, more than twenty years later, President Reagan came on his ill-starred visit to the Bitburg cemetery, thousands of young Germans staged demonstrations against both him and Chancellor Kohl and against the Strategic Defense Initiative. This indicates that, for a number of reasons, the overall situation has changed, and the French critic Brigitte Sauzay makes this very point when she observes:

> Will man sich die Gefühle vorstellen, welche die Deutschen diese ganzen Jahre hindurch den Amerikanern entgegenbrachten, genügt es, den Film über Kennedys Berlin-Reise im Juni 1963 anzusehen. Gewaltige Volksmengen jubeln ihm zu und rasen vor Begeisterung, als er erklärt: "Ich bin ein Berliner." Zwanzig Jahre später ist Reagan in Bonn Beschimpfungen ausgesetzt. Der Polizei gelingt es nur mit Mühe, den gigantischen Aufmarsch von fünfhunderttausend Demonstranten gegen seine Teilnahme am NATO-Gipfel unter Kontrolle zu halten. [...]

Was ist im Zeitraum von zwanzig Jahren geschehen? [Eine neue Generation ist herangewachsen] Diese erinnert sich nicht mehr an die Care-Pakete. Ihre neuen Universitäten sind nicht mehr aus Geldern des Marshall-Plans gebaut, die Gedenkstätte für die Toten der Berliner Luftbrücke bedeutet ihnen nichts. Ihre Kindheitseindrücke sind anderer Art: Demonstrationen gegen den von den Amerikanern unterstützten Schah, Protest gegen die materialistische Konsumgesellschaft nach amerikanischem Vorbild und vor allem, Abend für Abend im häuslichen Fernsehen, das Bild amerikanischer Soldaten, die in Vietnam kämpfen - kämpfen oder bloß töten?[73]

This change explains why both Americans, unused to opposition from their most faithful ally, and certain German politicians, afraid of antagonizing the tutelary power, are worried. Worry they might, but the critical voices that irk them must not be rashly misunderstood as signs of German 'Anti-Americanism.'

In the strict meaning of the term, contemporary German youth simply cannot be 'Anti-American' because it is certainly the most Americanized we have ever had. Levi's and MacDonald's provide their standard uniform and their standard cuisine, if cuisine one can call it. *Dallas* and *Dynasty, The Streets of San Francisco, Falcon Crest, Kojak, Starsky and Hutch, Charlie's Angels, Fame, Magnum, Hill Street Blues,* and *Miami Vice* are among the most successful TV series in Germany. American pop stars rank high in the German charts and dominate German discos, Mickey Mouse and E.T., Superman, Luke Skywalker and Alf are the venerated heroes of German adolescents, and contemporary German juvenile slang is so Americanized that older Germans rightly worry about what is happening to our language. But the very youngsters who unthinkingly adopt every fad invented in Southern California or the Black ghettos of the north find their leading bogeyman - as long as they are politically interested at all, and not too many of them are - in Uncle Sam. The beloved elder brother of only two decades ago has become the hateful Big Brother of Orwellian connotations, who practises a 'daily fascism'[74] and is responsible for Vietnam and Watergate as well as for Cruise Missiles and Pershing-2s; who in-

---

73 Brigitte Sauzay, *Die rätselhaften Deutschen: Die Bundesrepublik von außen gesehen* (Stuttgart: Bonn Aktuell, 1986), pp. 113-115.
74 See Reinhard Lettau, *Täglicher Faschismus: Amerikanische Evidenz aus 6 Monaten* (München: Carl Hanser, 1971).

vaded Grenada, supported the Contras in Nicaragua, and answered terrorist bomb attacks by bombing the civilian population of Tripoli; who engaged in undercover arms deals with the Iranian ayatollahs, and who might have derived a new and dangerous sense of being "Globo-Cop"[75] from his success in the Gulf War. To me, this curious contradiction between an almost slavish imitation of the American way of life and an impassioned rejection of American politics is an additional argument against the undifferentiated thesis of a growing German 'Anti-Americanism,' and this is why I feel that Bernhard Katsch's ironic little poem makes an important point:

> In Farmerhose
> Saß er und schimpfte
> Auf die Amerikaner.
> Im Hintergrund
> Röhrte Rock-and-Roll.
> Ich sagte: Nimm
> den Kaugummi
> Aus dem Mund,
> Dann versteht man
> Dich besser.
> Er sagte: "Okay!"[76]

Moreover, the articulate - and often quite justified - youthful denunciation of America as being most 'advanced' in such aberrations as the destruction of the environment through over-industrialization and the thoughtless waste of a consumer society, as the inhumanity and injustice bred by the relentless competition for material possessions, as the exploitation of Third World countries, or as the mind-boggling excrescences of an armaments race based on the power of overkill is unfortunately not at all representative of German youth as a whole. On the contrary, and quite deplorably so, young Germans who silently adjust to the insane complacency and the pragmatic mores of the ruling adult establishment still greatly outnumber their peers who

---

75 See "Global Beat," *Time*, April 1, 1991, pp. 20-25, where the much touted idea of "a new world order" as proclaimed by President Bush on March 5 is investigated with reference to the widespread fear that the role of the U.S. in this 'NWO' will be that of a militaristic "Globo-Cop."
76 Quoted from Kurt Tudyka, "Anti-Amerikanismus - Was ist das?" in *Amerika: Der Riskante Partner*, ed. by Anton-Andreas Guha and Sven Papcke (Königstein: Athenäum, 1984), pp. 117-130; here p. 129.

protest against the accumulated absurdities of our everyday reality, and as in America, the majority are rather apolitical and career-oriented: on both sides of the Atlantic the hippies have been ousted by the yuppies. Thus, with regard to German youth, what is wrongly called German 'Anti-Americanism' is a minority phenomenon, and with regard to the total population, all the available statistics indicate that no major change in attitude has occurred:

> [Der] politische Vertrauensverlust der USA hat die starken affektiven Bindungen der Bundesbürger an die Amerikaner aber nicht beeinträchtigen können. Nichts deutet auf einen zunehmenden Antiamerikanismus [...]. Mehrheiten der Bundesbürger aller Gruppierungen - mit Ausnahme der GRÜNEN - mögen die Amerikaner auch nach dem Nachrüstungsbeschluß und trotz Reagan; wenn nicht Deutscher, dann wäre man am liebsten Amerikaner.[77]

'Anti-Americanism,' then, is a notion which is both too undifferentiated and too charged with diffuse emotions to be a useful concept for a discussion of the changes which have undoubtedly taken place within German-American relationships and which have recently become glaringly obvious in the reaction of many Germans to the Gulf War. And for the benefit of those shrill American commentators who have gleefully used the scandal of German participation in building a chemical plant in Lybia and the conflict about the modernization of short-range rockets within NATO to unearth the old stereotypes of German megalomania and unreliability and to chastise us for our alleged ingratitude, a crucial fact needs to be pointed out which I find unduly neglected in the ongoing discussion.

The main sources from which the average German gets his or her information about the U.S.A. are the mass media; and the overwhelming majority of films, features, reviews, and talk shows dealing with America on German TV are synchronized versions of American productions. That means that, ironically enough, by far the greatest part of criticism of America disseminated in Germany is of American origin. After all, it was James Baldwin, a bestselling author in Germany and a classic in the German EFL-classroom, who told us about

---

[77] Harro Honolka, *Schwarzrotgrün: Die Bundesrepublik auf der Suche nach ihrer Identität* (München: C. H. Beck, 1987), p. 160. - See also table 34, p. 234, for the results of relevant pools from 1957 to July 1986.

the squalor of Harlem; it was Alex Haley's immensely successful *Roots* that informed us about the perversities of the 'peculiar institution' of slavery. It is the Nobel-Prize-winning Saul Bellow, a well-loved author in Germany, who complains in novel after novel about the emptiness of contemporary American existence. It was John Updike's *Couples* that gave us the idea that wife-swapping is common in American suburbs; and it is Kurt Vonnegut's devastating criticism of the 'American Dream' gone sour that is part of our literary fare. Week after week, *Dallas* and *Dynasty* present us with money-grabbing tycoons and insinuate that J. R. Ewing is the epitome of the successful American businessman, that women can be bought for money, and that you can do anything as long as you can afford good lawyers. Our children learn from *Kojak* and from *The Streets of San Francisco* that American cities are crime-ridden warrens filled with drug-pushers, rapists and murderers barely held at bay by trigger-happy and underpaid policemen who are easily bought. That between New York and San Francisco there are what jaded Californians call 'the fly-over states,' namely a large rural America with a totally different set of values and life styles, is blotted out by the exotic criminality of *Miami Vice*; and I know from my own teaching experience that if one tells German high school students, whose image of an American classroom is that of Evan Hunter's *Blackboard Jungle*, that the question of school prayer is a burning issue in the U.S.A., they show only surprise and disbelief.

Is it not logical, then, that German children who receive their image of America from the *Star Wars* films and from *Rambo*, from *Platoon* and *Full-Metal Jacket*, to name just a few recent box-office hits of the German cinema scene, and who, lacking the first-hand experience of American reality which would enable them to recognize the limited representativeness of most of the films and TV serials they are daily exposed to, will hardly arrive at that view of the U.S.A. which Americans would understandably like them to have? To condense this observation into a consciously oversimplified thesis: what certain American commentators deplore as the critical and lopsided image many Germans have of contemporary American life is the logical result of what America has exported as her self-portrayal in her literature, her TV productions, her popsongs, and her movies. And one need only compare the relevant *Spiegel* editorials, which are frequently accused of an 'Anti-American' bias, with the American material investigated in

Lloyd DeMause's psycho-history *Reagan's America*[78] to realize that there is hardly any German criticism of America raised which has not been much more emphatically voiced in the United States themselves.

But, again, it is not the German scepticism about certain aspects of the American way of life, mainly created by American mass culture as exported into the Federal Republic, which really worries certain observers. What these observers, who have popularized the notion of German 'Anti-Americanism' as fitting their political intentions, are essentially concerned about is the unwillingness of a sizeable percentage of German youth and the allegedly 'left' German intelligentsia to accept the new political conservatism in the U.S.A. and the actual political decisions through which it is expressed. Consequently, what these critics mean when they wrongly talk about 'Anti-Americanism' is not the - non-existent - rejection of America and the Americans in general, but the unwillingness to accept the goals of the moral majority, the scepticism about the frightening excrescences of televangelism, the indignation about a world picture that defines the Soviet Union as 'the realm of evil,' the worrying about Reaganomics and increasing deficit spending, and the resentment of a policy which claims for America the right to decide what will be good for her allies.

The necessity of such a distinction can be illustrated by three representative cover pictures of *Der Spiegel*. In November 1983 the magazine devoted its cover story to "The World of Ronald Reagan: Power Centre California" and investigated the alleged shift of the American power centre from the East to the West Coast. The composite cover picture shows Reagan as a sunburnt, Stetson-wearing Westerner, with cowboys on horseback, threatening Indians on table mountains and covered waggons suggesting the myth of the Wild West; with a glamorous starlet and 'Hollywood' associating the Californian dream factory; with Mickey Mouse representing the Disney world of popular culture; with skyscrapers and computer screens conjuring up both modern technology in general and Silicon Valley in particular; and with ominous rockets and assault craft from which marines swarm out implying the possibility of actual warfare. In November 1984 *Der*

---

78 See Lloyd DeMause, *Reagan's America* (New York and London: Creative Roots, Inc., 1984).

Spiegel featured an article about the risks of the SDI project, and the controversial cover picture showed President Reagan, after his reelection and with his SDI programme accepted, as Darth Vader, the evil representative of the Galactic Empire from George Lucas' *Star Wars* films. And in May 1985 it was SDI again that got front coverage, with Reagan and Kohl as "Star War Partners" riding on a U.S. rocket and embarking upon a "Journey into the Unknown." All three covers, which, by the way, provide excellent material for the advanced EFL-classroom, have been wrongly accused of being 'Anti-American.' This, however, they are not because what they speak out against is not 'America' in general but specific aspects of the policy of a particular president. Moreover, when they critically relate President Reagan to the inanities of popular culture they take him up on his very own terms, and when they express scepticism concerning the feasibility of the adolescent mentality of the popular western as a guideline for practical politics, they only repeat, in a rather subdued way, what has been said much more aggressively by numerous American commentators.[79]

Even after its reunification, Germany is still a small country, but it has one of the greatest accumulations of conventional, nuclear and - until very recently - chemical weapons per square mile in the world. Many of these weapons are not under our own jurisdiction, and they are stationed in densely populated areas. When there is an accident with a nuclear rocket, the worried people who ask their government about what really happened receive the answer that the government does not know because the investigation is undertaken by the Allied Forces and declared top secret. But on the same day on which the people get this infuriating reply they might read in their local newspaper another article about the alarming rate of drug abuse in the American Army, and they are left to worry about what might happen when addicts are allowed to service the most complicated death-dealing machinery. Many such examples could be adduced to drive home the point that most of the current issues that lead to controversies have absolutely nothing to do with a general 'Anti-Americanism' but

---

79 See, for example, the extremely revealing collection of newspaper cuttings in *The Clothes Have No Emperor: A Chronicle of the American 80s*, ed. by Paul Slansky (New York: Simon and Schuster, 1989).

with specific aspects of German-American relations. Situated at the cutting edge between the Western super power and a crumbling Soviet Union and trying to come to terms with the new role of their country without waking the ugly spectres of the past, more and more politically aware Germans begin to see certain things in a way that cannot but differ from the American majority point of view.

In his novel *Cat's Cradle* (1963), Kurt Vonnegut introduces the American ambassador Minton, who has lost his job because of a subversive statement made by his wife and who is transferred for disciplinary reasons to the utterly unimportant Caribbean island of San Lorenzo where he will have no chance of doing any harm. When John, the protagonist, asks him what this subversive statement consisted of, Minton says that his wife had written that "Americans are forever searching for love in forms it never takes, in places it can never be [...] The highest possible form of treason [for an American] is to say that Americans aren't loved wherever they go, whatever they do."[80] Taking this - American - criticism of an American attitude as a cue, I feel that both the American desire to be loved and the German worry about coming up to that expectation - Knauer's book is revealingly entitled *Lieben wir die USA?* - are a decidedly wrong approach. It is obvious that the great majority of contemporary Germans respect and accept America as a tutelary power, know full well about the historical debt they owe her, and realize that, the global situation being what it is, they will have to remain her ally.[81] But by now the more articulate and independent among Germany's young people have become self-confident enough to dare criticize certain American actions and to resent certain American attitudes. Since mutual criticism is a necessary part of a good and open partnership and since political alliances are not built on love but on common interest, the present worry about an alleged German 'Anti-Americanism' seems greatly exaggerated.

Since I believe with James Baldwin "that the past is all that makes the present coherent,"[82] I would suggest that instead of blowing up contemporary misunderstandings out of all proportion, we should try

---

80 Kurt Vonnegut, *Cat's Cradle* (New York: Dell Books, rpt. 1970), pp. 71f.
81 See the detailed statistics in Sebastian Knauer, *op. cit.*
82 James Baldwin, "Autobiographical Notes," in his *Notes of a Native Son* (London: Corgi Books, 1969), p. 4.

to put them into an historical perspective. If we do so, we will recognize that there is hardly anything exceptional going on but that what we observe are simply political, economic, and, increasingly so, ideological differences between two nations of vastly different size and influence and with radically different histories to shape their present-day expectations and aspirations. Therefore, it is neither Mark Twain's cynical quip from *Pudd'nhead Wilson's Calendar* that "it was wonderful to find America, but it would have been more wonderful to miss it"[83] nor Joachim Fernau's scathing statement "Wissen ist bekanntlich Macht, aber Nichtwissen erleichtert oft das Leben. Der zweite Teil des Satzes ist der berühmte 'american way of life'"[84] which can serve as illustrations of the present situation. Much more appropriate is an observation made by a character in Alain Resnais' film *Mon Oncle d'Amérique*. This character says that 'America doesn't exist,' and he confirms his statement by adding 'I know for certain because I've been there.' Thus he once more drives home the point that for many Europeans 'America' is still a place of the mind, a utopia upon which they project their unfulfilled desires;[85] and thereby he implies that when these Europeans discover the discrepancy between their ideal of 'America' and the reality of American life and politics, they tend to blame the United States for not coming up to their exaggerated expectations.

In his poem "America Is Hard to See," Robert Frost ironically observes, with reference to Columbus, that

> America is hard to see.
> Less partial witnesses than he
> In book on book have testified
> They could not see it from outside -
> Or inside either for that matter.
> We know the literary chatter.[86]

---

83 See the third motto on p. 21.
84 Joachim Fernau, *Halleluja - Die Geschichte der USA*, p. 62.
85 This is also the thesis of Peter Mason's new book, *Deconstructing America* (London: Routledge, 1990), which is advertized as an attempt "to show how European representations of America constitute a cultural monologue which tells us more about the Old World than the New."
86 Robert Frost, *In the Clearing* (New York: Holt, Rinehart and Winston, 15th pr., 1979), p. 22.

National 'Images' 79

How right Frostis with regard to those who attempt to evaluate 'America' from "inside," is not only confirmed by Thomas Berger's ironical observation that "America has never really existed except as a product of the will,"[87] but also by the heroine of Erica Jong's novel *Any Woman's Blues* (1990), who has this to say about her contradictory country:

> America is my home, and so I love and hate it equally, as one loves and hates one's parents. I know it too well. I know its great energy, its pragmatism, but I also know its crazy evangelists, its corrupt politicians, its mad addiction to money. What I love about America is its boundless optimism; what I hate is the way it fetters that optimism in a straightjacket of puritanism. If you have X, you can't have Y. If you have Q, you can't have Z. If you have mind, your body must pay. If you have body, your mind must pay. What I hate about America is its belief in dualism - its belief in retribution - when the truth is that the more you have the more you have, the more you grab the *less* you have, and the more you give the more you have. For life on its deepest level is a potlach, not a stock market: only by giving do we become rich. Only by nurturing the mind do we nurture body. Only by loving the body do we really love the mind. They are indivisible, united, one. The heart of America knows this, the body politic of America does not.[88]

And the appropriateness of Frost's laconic observation that one can neither "see [America] from outside" should have become evident from the preceding chapters, in which assorted transatlantic definitions of 'America' have time and again been revealed as the biased results of attempts at 'boundary-making' and thus as images of an 'other' which usually say more about the subjects who harbour them than about the object they are meant to depict. Consequently, we should not while away our time with solving the impossible task of

---

87 Zulfikar Ghose, "Observations from a Correspondence: From Thomas Berger's Letters," *Studies in American Humor*, new series 2 (1983), 5-19; here p. 13.
88 Erica Jong, *Any Woman's Blues* (London: Arrow Books, 1990), pp. 258f.

Liste des Proviants,

wie solche
gewöhnlich den Zwischendecks- und Stearage-Passagieren,
von

Bremen

nach

Newyork, Baltimore, Philadelphia oder New-Orleans und Galveston

gehend, verabreicht wird, wobei es indessen dem Capitain des Schiffes überlassen bleibt eine etwaige Abänderung zu treffen.

Sonntag: Fleisch oder Speck und Pudding mit Kartoffeln.
Montag: Fleisch oder Speck und Bohnen oder Erbsen mit Kartoffeln.
Dienstag: Fleisch oder Speck und Bohnen oder Erbsen mit Kartoffeln.
Mittwoch: Speck und Sauerkraut mit Kartoffeln.
Donnerstag: Fleisch oder Speck und Erbsen oder Bohnen mit Kartoffeln.
Freitag: Fleisch und Reissuppe oder Hafergrützsuppe mit Kartoffeln.
Sonnabend: Reis oder Scheldegerste mit Pflaumen und Syrub.

Portion
per Woche für jeden Passagier an Bord:

3 Pfund Schwarzbrod.
2 „ Weißbrod.
3/8 „ Butter.
2½ „ Fleisch.
1 „ gesalzenes oder 3/4 Pfund geräuchertes Speck.

Jeden Morgen Caffee und jeden Nachmittag Thee oder Caffee.
Gemüse und Trinkwasser hinreichend.

developing a 'correct' image of 'America,'[89] and instead of worrying about whether to love Americans as Mark Twain's innocents abroad[90] or to loathe them as Rolf Hochhuth's cultural imperialists,[91] we should concentrate upon acquiring a better knowledge and a more adequate understanding of the complex cultural contexts within which our contradictory images of 'America' could come into being.

The dangers and hardships which hundreds of thousands of European immigrants had to endure when they embarked upon their hopeful voyage to the promised land are difficult to imagine in these days of comfortable and fast air travel. But when one studies an 1846 list of supplies for steerage-passengers or ponders the implications of a 1910 poster alerting single women to the moral dangers they faced when they emigrated on their own, one might get an idea of the 'American Nightmare' which many emigrants had to live through. On the other hand, the 'American Dream' that lured these emigrants across the Atlantic and that made them run such risks is graphically illustrated in the four pictures from Turner's *History of the Holland Purchase* (1850) which show the development of a New York farm in its successive stages. These pictures impressively convey the promise which America offers to any hard-working pioneer. After his humble beginnings in a primitive log cabin with only a few acres of cleared

---

89 Recently, in two bestselling books, Rolf Winter has attempted to replace the still predominantly positive German *Amerikabild* by what he thinks to be the 'correct' version. In *Ami Go Home: Plädoyer für den Abschied von einem gewalttätigen Land*, p. 32, he rejects the United States as "ein habituell friedensunfähiges, beständig auf dem Kreuzzug befindliches Land;" and in *Die amerikanische Zumutung: Plädoyers gegen das Land des real existierenden Kapitalismus*, p. 129, he argues: "Die Sicherheit der Erde ist in den Vereinigten Staaten ebenso garantiert wie die Unversehrtheit des Porzellanladens beim Eintritt des Elefanten; das belegt die amerikanische Geschichte. Sie sind zwanghafte Triebtäter beim Bruch internationalen Rechts. Kein anderes Land hat in dem nun ausklingenden Jahrhundert, in dem es die Vereinigten Staaten zur alleinigen Weltführerschaft brachten, internationale Vereinbarungen häufiger gebrochen. Zur Gewalt, die sie immer auch gegen sich selbst wandten, paßt fugenlos die Gewalt, mit der sie, gewandet als Weltpolizist, nach außen vorgingen. Die Vereinigten Staaten können nicht anders als in Gewalt agieren; die Gewalt ist ihr Schicksal."
90 See Mark Twain's travel narrative *The Innocents Abroad; or, The New Pilgrims' Progress* (Hartford: American Publishing Company, 1869).
91 See Rolf Hochhuth's three 'American tragedies' *Guerillas, Tod eines Jägers*, and *Judith* (Reinbek: Rowohlt, 1970, 1976, and 1984 respectively).

land wrested from the unchartered wilderness, he will gradually increase his possessions, until he finally becomes the happy owner of an impressive farm house, which is surrounded by fertile fields extending towards the horizon.

84   National 'Images'

The following chapters offer some tentative considerations of central aspects of that complex and contradictory conundrum which is alternately called the 'American Dream' and the 'American Nightmare.'

2: The 'American Dream' and the 'American Nightmare': A Survey

I guess I'm still looking for the American Dream. To me, it's people having control over their lives.

The American Dream is to be better off than you are.

The American Dream is really money.

Maybe the American Dream is in the past, understanding who you are instead of looking to the future.

The American Dream? I think: for whites only.

I worry about our young people. Do they have the dreams, the guts, the sinews, the red-blooded ability, to preserve our way of life? The thing our grandparents came over here to find. They found a nation founded, if you'll pardon the expression, under God and a Divine Constitution. Every youngster should have the dream of becoming president of the United States. Of course, I believe in Horatio Alger, and I love it.

> Answers given to Studs Terkel in the interviews in his *American Dreams Lost and Found*[1]

---

1   Studs Terkel, *American Dreams Lost and Found* (New York: Ballantine Books, 1981), pp. 73; 42; 63; 56; 178; and 316f.

Whoever attempts to understand the complexities of American life and literature or to come to terms with American popular culture as exported to Europe will time and again run up against certain enduring beliefs and convictions. These beliefs, which can be traced back to central American foundation myths, coalesce - in ever changing patterns - in the central vision of the 'American Dream.' Because this comprehensive vision is necessarily diffuse, any attempt at defining what it stands for is bound to remain subjective and imcomplete,[2] and because this vision changes with the times, a tolerably representative working definition of the 'Dream' can only be deduced from a detailed survey of American intellectual history.[3]

---

[2] In his detailed examination of "Die Funktion des 'American Dream' in der amerikanischen Gesellschaft" (Phil. Diss., München, 1968), pp. 4f., Hartmut Keil observes: "Der 'American Dream' wird gleichgesetzt mit 'individual success,' 'advancement,' 'materialism,' 'personal success,' 'neighborliness,' 'naturalness,' 'individuality,' 'freedom,' 'equality,' 'equal opportunity,' 'search for identity,' 'national purpose,' 'American consciousness,' 'democratic dream,' 'dream of paradise,' 'verwirklichte Utopie,' 'moving force,' 'liberation of humanity,' 'world's salvation,'" and rightly concludes: "Eine Definition aufgrund aller bisherigen Erklärungsversuche wäre also recht sinnlos; denn das Ergebnis wäre eine Aufzählung beinahe aller Aspekte der amerikanischen Gesellschaft."

[3] Books on the 'Dream' are legion, ranging from Kenneth S. Davis, *The Hero: Charles A. Lindbergh and the American Dream* (Garden City, N. Y.: Doubleday, 1959), and William R. Brown, *Image Maker: Will Rogers and the American Dream* (Columbia: University of Missouri Press, 1970), to Charles Hearn, *The American Dream in the Great Depression* (Westport, Conn.: Greenwood Press, 1977), and Allan D. Heskin, *Tenants and the American Dream* (New York: Praeger, 1983). - Among the less specialized studies, the most informative is *American Dreams, American Nightmares*, ed. by David Madden (Carbondale, Ill.: Southern Illinois University Press, 1970), an excellent collection of essays. A short but helpful introduction to the topic is provided by Robert H. Fossum and Joseph K. Roth, *The American Dream* (no place: BAAS Pamphlets in American Studies, 1981). Recommendable studies of specific aspects are Frederick I. Carpenter, *American Literature and the Dream* (New York: Philosophical Library, 1955), which is especially good on the nineteenth century; and Daniel J. Boorstin, *The Image or What Happened to the American Dream* (New York: Atheneum, 1961), which investigates the changes of the 'Dream' due to the graphic revolution. - Helpful collections put together for use in American schools and colleges are *In Search of the American Dream*, ed. by Jane L. Scheiber and Robert C. Elliott (New York: North American Library, 1974); *The American Dream: Vision and Reality*, ed. by J. Derek Harrison and Alan B. Shaw (San Francisco: Canfield Press, 1975); *Pursuing the American Dream*, ed. by Kenneth S. Knodt (Englewood Cliffs, N.J.: Prentice-Hall, 1976); and *The American Dream*, ed. by Lew Smith (Glenview, Ill.: Scott, Foresman and Co., 1977). - Among the more recent contributions are Shinji Takuwa, *The American Dream and Self-Examination* (Tokyo: Eihosha, 1978); Ann-Janine Morey-Gaines, *Apples and Ashes: Culture, Metaphor, and Morality in the American Dream* (Chicago: Scholars Press, 1982); and *The Frontier Experience and the American Dream: Essays on*

How centrally important the 'Dream' still is and how easily the fundamental values and promises that constitute it can be related to the respective requirements of a given historical situation becomes most easily obvious when one looks at selected instances of political rhetoric. Thus, the following quotations from the speeches which American presidential candidates and presidents have delivered in recent years when they accepted their nominations and when they outlined their political programmes at their inaugurations can provide a first inkling of what the 'American Dream' is all about:

On January 20, 1969, Richard Milhous Nixon said in his Inaugural Address:

> [...] In pursuing our goals of full employment, better housing, excellence in education; in rebuilding our cities and improving our rural areas; in protecting our environment and enhancing the quality of life - in all these and more, we will and must press urgently forward.
> We shall plan now for the day when our wealth can be transferred from the destruction of war abroad to the urgent needs of our people at home.
> The American dream does not come to those who fall asleep.
> [...]
> As we measure what can be done, we shall promise only what we know we can produce, but as we chart our goals we shall be lifted by our dreams.

Four years later, on January 20, 1973, he referred again to the 'Dream' when he said in his Second Inaugural Address:

> [...] Above all else, the time has come for us to renew our faith in ourselves and in America.
> In recent years, that faith has been challenged.
> Our children have been taught to be ashamed of their country, ashamed of their parents, ashamed of America's record at home and of its role in the world.
> [...]
> As I stand in this place, so hallowed by history, I think of others who have stood here before me. I think of the dreams they had for America, and I think of how each recognized that he needed help far beyond himself in order to make those dreams come true.

American Literature, ed. by David Mogen, Paul Bryant, and Marle Busby (College Station: Texas A & M University Press, 1989).

On January 20, 1977, Jimmy Carter joined his predecessor in conjuring up the lasting importance of the 'Dream':

> [...] Two centuries ago our nation's birth was a milestone in the long quest for freedom, but the bold and brilliant dream which excited the founders of this nation still awaits its consummation. I have no new dream to set forth today, but rather urge a fresh faith in the old dream.
> [...]
> The American dream endures. We must once again have full faith in our country - and in one another. I believe America can be better. We can be even stronger than before.
> [...]
> These are not just my goals. And they will not be my accomplishments, but the affirmation of our nation's continuing moral strength and our belief in an undiminished, ever-expanding American dream.

Carter's successor Ronald Reagan had this to say in his Inaugural Address on January 20, 1981:

> [...] If we look to the answer as to why for so many years we achieved so much, prospered as no other people on Earth, it was because here in this land we unleashed the energy and individual genius of man to a greater extent than has ever been done before.
> [...]
> It is no coincidence that our present troubles parallel and are proportionate to the intervention and intrusion in our lives that result from unnecessary and excessive growth of government. It is time for us to realize that we're too great a nation to limit ourselves to small dreams. We're not, as some would have us believe, doomed to an inevitable decline. I do not believe in a fate that will fall on us no matter what we do. I do believe in a fate that will fall on us if we do nothing. So, with all the creative energy at our command, let us begin an era of national renewal. Let us renew our determination, our courage, and our strength. And let us renew our faith and our hope.
> We have every right to dream heroic dreams.
> Your dreams, your hopes, your goals are going to be the dreams, the hopes, and the goals of this administration, so help me God.

On July 17, 1984, Reverend Jesse Jackson addressed the Democratic National Convention in San Francisco and said:

> I just want young America to do me one favor. Exercise the right to dream. You must face reality - that which is. But then dream of the reality that ought to be, that must be. Live beyond the pain of reality

with the dream of a bright tomorrow. Use hope and imagination as weapons of survival and progress. [...]
Young America, dream.

On August 23 of the same year, Ronald Reagan delivered his acceptance speech in Dallas and predicted for his second term:

[...] Four years ago we raised a banner of bold colors - no pale pastels. We proclaimed a dream of an America that would be 'a shining city on a hill.' [...] Now, it's all coming together. With our beloved nation at peace, we are in the midst of a springtime of hope for America. Greatness lies ahead of us.

And having won again, he declared in his Second Inaugural Address on January 21, 1985:

[...] But we, the present-day Americans, are not given to looking backward. In this blessed land, there is always a better tomorrow.
[...]
We believed then and now: There are no limits to growth and human progress when men and women are free to follow their dreams. And we were right to believe that.
[...]
Two of our Founding Fathers, a Boston lawyer named Adams and a Virginia planter named Jefferson, members of that remarkable group who met in Independence Hall and dared to think they could start the world over again.
There's no story more heartening in our history than the progress that we've made toward the brotherhood of man that God intended for us. Let us resolve there will be no turning back or hesitation on the road to an America rich in dignity and abundant with opportunity for all our citizens.
Let us resolve that we, the people, will build an American Opportunity Society in which all of us - white and black, rich and poor, young and old - will go forward together, arm in arm. Again, let us remember that though our heritage is one of blood lines from every corner of the Earth, we are all Americans, pledged to carry on this last, best hope of man on Earth.
[...]
It is the American sound. It is hopeful, big-hearted, idealistic, daring, decent, and fair. That's our heritage, that's our song. [We are] one people under God, dedicated to the dream of freedom that He has placed in the human heart, called upon now to pass that dream on to a waiting and hopeful world.

On July 21, 1988, finally, Governeur Michael S. Dukakis delivered his nomination acceptance speech to the Democratic Convention in Atlanta and assured the delegates:

> [...] We're going to win because we are the party that believes in the American dream.
> A dream so powerful that no distance of ground, no expanse of ocean, no barrier of language, no distinction of race or creed or color can weaken its hold on the human heart.
> And I know, because my friends, I'm a product of that dream and I'm proud of it. A dream that brought my father to this country 76 years ago, that brought my mother and her family here one year later - poor, unable to speak English but with a burning desire to succeed in their new land of opportunity.
> And tonight in the presence of that marvelous woman who is my mother and who came here 75 years ago; with the memory in my heart of the young man who arrived at Ellis Island with only $25 in his pocket, but with a deep and abiding faith in the promise of America -
> [...]
> My friends, the dream that carried me to this platform is alive tonight in every part of the country - and it's what the Democratic Party is all about.
> [...] to every American, you are a full shareholder in our dream.
> And my friends, if anyone tells you that the American dream belongs to the privileged few and not to all of us, you tell them that the Reagan era is over, you tell them that the Reagan era is over and that a new era is about to begin.
> [...]
> It's time to meet the challenge of the next American frontier - the challenge of building an economic future for our country that will create good jobs at good wages for every citizen in this land [...]
> [...]
> [...] we believe that there are no limits to what America can do.
> [...]
> But my friends, maintaining the status quo - running in place - standing still - isn't good enough for America. Opportunity for some isn't good enough for America. Because working together, we're going to forge a new era of greatness for America.
> [...]
> My friends, the dream that began in Philadelphia 200 years ago; the spirit that survived that terrible winter at Valley Forge and triumphed on the beaches at Normandy; the courage that looked Khrushchev in the eye during the Cuban missile crisis - is as strong and as vibrant today as it has ever been.
> [...]
> A new era of greatness for America.

And when we leave here tonight, we will leave to build that future together.
To build the future so that when our children and our grand-children look back in their time on what we did in our time; they will say that we had the wisdom to carry on the dreams of those who came before us; the courage to make our own dreams come true; and the foresight to blaze a trail for generations yet to come.

Depending on their political convictions, readers of these statements[4] with their grand rhetorical flourishes and their pathetic incantations of a sublime vision of greatness will either be elated or appalled. And they will easily recognize that there is a deep gulf between the idealistic concepts which constitute the 'Dream' and the flawed reality within which it is constantly conjured up. This gulf becomes immediately obvious when the inflated rhetoric of public speech is contrasted with the narratives of average American citizens who view history 'from the bottom up;'[5] and the contradictions between ideal and reality are glaringly depicted in a cartoon that appeared in the English *Guardian* of November 20, 1983, which laconically contrasts the high-flown promises of the 'Dream' with the lack of the bare necessities for survival and which sarcastically concludes that "dreams don't go well on an empty stomach."

---

4   All quotations are taken from the speeches as reprinted in either the annual *Historic Documents* or in the *Weekly Compilation of Residential Documents* or in *Vital Speeches of the Day* (all easily available from the German *Amerikahäuser*). Useful background information is provided by the critical anthology *Die Rhetorik amerikanischer Präsidenten seit F. D. Roosevelt*, ed. by Paul Goetsch and Gerd Hurm (Tübingen: Narr, 1993).
5   See Studs Terkel, *American Dreams Lost and Found*, as quoted in note 1. This collection of about 100 statements by Americans of all ranks about their dreams and aspirations, their failures and frustrations is a veritable treasure trove for any EFL-teacher. Its sequel, *The Great Divide: Second Thoughts on the American Dream* (New York: Avon Books, 1989), provides another gathering of personal narratives, which betray a growing mood of disappointment and despair; and the most recent volume, *Race: How Blacks and Whites Think and Feel about the American Obsession* (New York: Anchor Books, 1993), collects personal statements that show how the 'Dream' has been tainted from the very beginning by America's interracial dilemma. - In spring 1983, *Newsweek* dedicated its fiftieth anniversary issue to *The American Dream*. Reconstructing twentieth-century American history through the experience of "five heartland families" from "Springfield, a city of 73,000 on the banks of Buck Creek in central Ohio," the magazine brought "to life generations of people who dreamed very American dreams, and who found that many of them came true." This richly illustrated issue is an excellent example of history from the bottom up and would provide any EFL-teacher with a valuable antidote against precipitate generalizations.

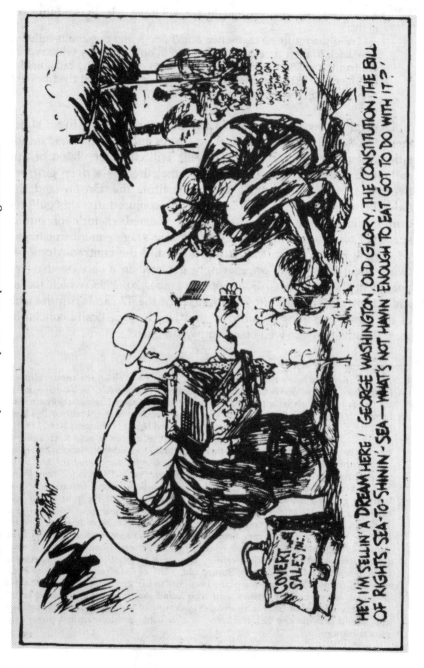

As a German, one is inevitably reminded of the crucial differences in the estimation of the 'Dream' brought about by the political developments of the last few decades. To young post-war Germans in the days of the Marshall-Plan, the Berlin Airlift and Care packages, for example, the concept of the 'American Dream' conjured up a fantastic vision of material plenitude, political liberty and individual self-fulfilment. In our post-Vietnam, post-Watergate days of Cruise Missiles and Pershing-2s, however, many young Germans have come to denounce this concept as a mendacious label for chauvinistic strivings, unwarranted feelings of superiority and thoughtless crimes against nature in the name of unbridled progress. Consequently, for them the 'Dream' has become a 'Nightmare.'

These contradictory appraisals of the 'Dream' within different historical constellations show that whoever attempts to discover what the 'American Dream' is all about is faced with two formidable tasks: coming to terms with one of the most elusive aspects of American intellectual history and having to take sides in the ongoing discussion about the discrepancies between the promises of a breathtaking vision and the shortcomings of a flawed reality. Because so many rash and incorrect opinions are voiced within the heated debate of what is loosely, and for the most part wrongly, dubbed the growing German 'Anti-Americanism,' it might be helpful to undertake a little foray into the American history of ideas: after all, as Germans we should know better than others that only a sounder knowledge of the past will enable us to achieve an adequate understanding of the present.

Before I undertake such an attempt, however, let me briefly outline its unavoidable limitations. The 'American Dream' is a concept which was given its name as late as 1931 when James Truslow Adams, in his influential study *The Epic of America*, used the term right in the middle of the Depression to define "that American dream of a better, richer, and happier life for all our citizens of every rank" and praised such a vision as "the greatest contribution we have as yet made to the thought and welfare of the world."[6] Since Adams introduced the term,

---

6   James Truslow Adams, *The Epic of America* (Boston: Little, Brown, and Company, 25th ed., 1943), p. viii. - Relevant excerpts from this book are reprinted in the EFL-reader *American Dreams, American Nightmares*, ed. by Brian Tracy and Erwin Helms (Paderborn: Schöningh, 1981), pp. 19-21.

it has been used by playwrights, poets and novelists, invoked by historians, sociologists and philosophers, exploited by the advertising industry, and - as can be seen from the preceding quotations - touted by politicians in almost every conceivable context.

Predictively, any attempt at abstracting from the plethora of relevant publications something even faintly resembling a definition of the 'Dream' is doomed to failure. Therefore I will limit myself to a discussion of some of the roots of the 'Dream' and to a survey of what I consider its most important elements.

The Sources of the 'Dream' and Its Main Ingredients

> In conclusion, the admiral says that the sacred theologians and wise philosophers have well said that the earthly paradise is in the end of the east, because it is a very temperate place, so those lands which he had now discovered are, he says, 'the end of the east.'
> *Journal of the First Voyage of Columbus*[7]

Long before 'America' became a country, it was a continent, and long before it was known to exist as a continent, it was a vision and a dream. America, then, was invented before it was discovered, and long before Americans ever began to dream their national 'Dream,' Europeans of all nations used to dream their dreams about an America of the mind and, later, about an America which slowly emerged from the reports of the first discoverers, exploiters and settlers. The earliest comment in German literature on Columbus' first voyage, for example, can be found in Sebastian Brant's *Narrenschiff*, which was published in Basel in 1494 and in which one reads:

---

[7] *The Voyages of Christopher Columbus. Being the Journals of His First and Third, and the Letters Concerning His First and Last Voyages, to Which Is Added the Account of His Second Voyage Written by Andreas Bernaldez*, newly transl. and ed. by Cecil Jane (Amsterdam: N. Israel, and New York: Da Capo Press; reprint of the edition London: Argonaut Press, 1930), p. 252.

> Ouch hat man sydt jnn Portigal
> Vnd jnn hispanyen vberall
> Golt, jnslen funden, vnd nacket lüt
> Von den man vor wust sagen nüt.[8]

Here, 'islands rich with gold and hitherto unknown naked people' are deemed worth mentioning, and Brant's reference is just one of many examples which demonstrate that the newly discovered continent almost immediately became the country on to which the European imagination projected its cherished notions of a paradise on earth.

Such diverse traditions as Plato's idea of the miraculous island of Atlantis, the Irish monk Brendan's myth of a fabulous Edenic island in the western sea, or the dream of an immensely rich country called El Dorado, spurring the Spanish *conquistadores*, coalesced around America, which Columbus himself took to be "the earthly paradise."[9] The age-old metaphor of a "brave new world" - to use the term from Shakespeare's *The Tempest* which Aldous Huxley would later adopt as the ironic label for his dystopian nightmare[10] - suddenly found its confirmation in reality, and such outstanding men as Erasmus of Rotterdam, Sir Thomas More and John Donne set out upon imaginary voyages and blended Biblical accounts of the Garden of Eden, classical fables of the Golden Age, and the Renaissance concept of Arcadia into fantastic visions of the New World of America.[11]

---

8 Sebastian Brant, *Narrenschiff*, ed. by Friedrich Zarncke (Darmstadt: Wissenschaftliche Buchgesellschaft; 1973; reprint of the edition Leipzig 1854), p. 66, ll. 53-56.
9 See note 7. - With his belief that the Biblical Garden of Eden could be located at the easternmost verge of the known world, Columbus stood in an ancient tradition. - See Appendix No. XXXV, "Of the Situation of the Terrestrial Paradise," in Washington Irving, *Life and Voyages of Christopher Columbus* (New York: G. P. Putnam's Sons, 1892), vol. V, pp. 361-371.
10 See William Shakespeare, *The Tempest*, V, 1: 181ff., where Miranda exclaims; "O, wonder! / How many goodly creatures are there here! / How beauteous mankind is! O brave new world, / That has such people in't!" - See Aldous Huxley, *Brave New World* (London: Chatto & Windus, 1932).
11 Among the many books on early European ideas of America and on the interplay between the Old and the New World, I have found the following most helpful: Hugh Honour, *The New Golden Land: European Images of America from the Discoveries to the Present Time* (New York: Pantheon Books, 1975), is a lavishly illustrated volume presenting a wealth of material; *First Images of America: The Impact of the New World on the Old*, ed. by Fredi Chiappelli (Berkeley: University of California Press, 1976), deals with diverse aspects in two volumes of collected essays. - An extensive

When, in 1606, Christopher Newport sailed forth from England to bring 120 settlers to Virginia to found Jamestown, the poet Michael Drayton celebrated the event in his ode "To the Virginian Voyage." He described the new colony as "Earth's onely paradise" and glowingly spoke of it as a realm

> Where nature has in store,
> Fowle, venison, and fish,
> And the fruitfull'st soyle,
> Without your toyle,
> Three harvests more,
> All greater than you wish.
>
> [...]
>
> To whose, the golden age
> Still natures lawes doth give,
> No other cares that tend,
> But them to defend
> From winters age,
> That long there doth not live.[12]

This widespread concept of America as an innocent and pastoral country providing a stark contrast to a sinful and urbanized Europe - a concept which the Jamestown settlers would soon find many good reasons to doubt - was connected with a specific topos of historiography. There had existed a venerable tradition dedicated to the idea that the rise of civilization followed the course of the sun from east to west. Thus, when Columbus discovered America, it was generally believed that the western-most country had finally been found and that it was destined to become the seat of the most highly advanced civilization and of mankind's greatest achievements.

Later, this idea lent itself both to theories of colonization and empire building and to the belief of Protestant dissenters who felt called upon to overcome the sins of papacy and to rejuvenate the world by erecting a New Jerusalem. The first of these variations found its most

---

bibliography of relevant titles is provided by David B. Quinn, *North America from Earliest Discovery to First Settlements: The Norse Voyages to 1612* (New York: Harper & Row, 1977), pp. 569ff.

12 *The Poems of Michael Drayton*, ed. with an introduction by John Buxton (London: Routledge and Kegan Paul, 1953), p. 123-125.

obvious expression in Bishop George Berkeley's poem "On the Prospect of Planting Arts and Learning in America." Berkeley had stayed in America from September 1728 to September 1731 in connection with his abortive scheme for a missionary college in Bermuda,[13] and his poem outlines the course of history from east to west and celebrates the westernmost country, America, as the place of fulfilment.

> The Muse, disgusted at an Age and Clime,
> Barren of every glorious Theme,
> In distant Lands now waits a better Time,
> Producing Subjects worthy Fame:
>
> In happy Climes, where from the genial Sun
> And virgin Earth such Scenes ensue,
> The Force of Art by Nature seems outdone,
> And fancied Beauties by the true:
>
> In happy Climes the Seat of Innocence,
> Where Nature guides and Virtue rules,
> Where Men shall not impose for Truth and Sense,
> The Pedantry of Courts and Schools:
>
> There shall be sung another golden Age,
> The rise of Empire and of Arts,
> The Good and Great inspiring epic Rage,
> The wisest Heads and noblest Hearts.
>
> Not such as *Europe* breeds in her decay;
> Such as she bred when fresh and young,
> When heav'nly Flame did animate her Clay,
> By future Poets shall be sung.
>
> Westward the Course of Empire takes its Way;
> The four first Acts already past,
> A fifth shall close the Drama with the Day;
> Time's noblest Offspring is the last.[14]

---

[13] For details see Berkeley's "A PROPOSAL for the better Supplying of CHURCHES in our Foreign Plantations, and for Converting the Savage Americans, to Christianity, by a College to be erected in the *Summer Islands*, otherwise called *The Isles of Bermuda*," London, 1725; in *The Works of George Berkeley, Bishop of Cloyne*, ed. by A. A. Luce and T. E. Jessop (Nendeln: Kraus Reprint, 1979; reprint of the edition London and New York: Thomas Nelson and Sons, 1951), vol. VII, pp. 345-362.

[14] *The Works of George Berkeley, Bishop of Cloyne*, vol. VII, p. 373.

Berkeley, then, celebrates the coming of another "golden age" on the "virgin earth" and in the "happy climes" of America, which will supersede the puny attempts of "Europe [...] in her decay." That such ideas not only preoccupied the first settlers but were also still very popular at the beginning of the nineteenth century becomes obvious from the letters of John Adams, the Second President of the United States. In a letter of May 23, 1807, to Benjamin Rush, Adams reports that he had asked his brother

> [whether] he recollected the first line of a couplet whose second line was, "and empire rises where the sun descends." He paused a moment and said, -
> "The eastern nations sink, their glory ends,
> And empire rises where the sun descends."
> I asked him, if Dean Berkeley was the author of them. He answered no. The tradition was, as he had heard it for sixty years, that these lines were inscribed, or rather drilled, into a rock on the shore of Monument Bay in our old colony of Plymouth, and were supposed to have been written and engraved there by some of the first emigrants from Leyden, who landed at Plymouth. [...] I conjecture that Berkeley became connected with them, in my head, by some report that the bishop had copied them into some publication. There is nothing, in my little reading, more ancient in my memory than the observation that arts, sciences, and empire had travelled westward; and in conversation it was always added since I was a child, that their next leap would be over the Atlantic into America.[15]

"The tradition" to which Adams' brother refers was a combination of three popular notions, namely, the belief that some pre-Columbian explorers of America had left a record of their visit in the form of a message carved on a rock, the popular but factually wrong belief that the Pilgrim Fathers had first stepped ashore at Plymouth Rock, and the riddle of the Indian petroglyphs on Dighton Rock at Taunton, Massachusetts, which Cotton Mather had written about in 1690. These traditions were combined by an anonymous author, who obviously composed the couplet remembered by Adams' brother and published it - at the time of Bishop Berkeley's residence in Newport, Rhode

---

15 *The Works of John Adams, Second President of the United States: with A Life of the Author, Notes and Illustrations,* by His Grandson Charles Francis Adams (Boston: Little, Brown and Company, 1854), vol. IX, pp. 599f. - For an early investigation of this tradition see John Fiske, "Prophetic Voices About America: A Monograph," *Atlantic Monthly,* 20 (September 1867), 275-306.

Island - in the following letter to the *Boston Newsletter* of September 3, 1730:

> Plimouth, Massachusetts
> SIR,
> As there hath been discovered in this our Town a very wonderful Phanomena [sic], I have sent you an Account thereof for the perusal of your curious Readers,
> Walking last Week with a Friend by a Place where they were about to dig a Cellar, we discovered a Stone, on which there seemed to be Engraven certain Letters, which when we had cleared from the Dirt, we read to our great Astonishment engraven very deep the ensuing Lines,
>
> > *The Eastern World enslav'd, it's Glory ends;*
> > *And Empire rises where the Sun descends.*
>
> It seemeth to have been buried long in the Earth; but as I intend to bring it with me to Boston so soon as the Distemper is past, and shew it to the curious and learned Gentlemen in that Place, it seemeth unnecessary to give any further Description thereof at Present.
> Your assured friend, &c.[16]

About three decades later, Nathaniel Ames, the well-known almanac maker from Denham, Massachusetts, included a comment on the future of America in his *An Astronomical Diary: or an Almanack for 1758* and there took up the notion of *translatio imperii, studii et religii*:

> The Curious have observ'd that the Progress of Humane Literature (like the Sun) is from the East to the West; thus has it travelled thro' *Asia* and *Europe*, and now is arrived at the Eastern Shore of *America*. As the Coelestial Light of the Gospel was directed here by the Finger of GOD, it will doubtless, finally drive the long! long! Night of Heathenish Darkness from *America*: - So Arts and Sciences will change the Face of Nature in their Tour from Hence over the Appalachian Mountains to the Western Ocean; and as they march thro' the vast Desert, the Residence of Wild Beasts will be broken up, and their obscene Howl cease for ever; [...][17]

---

16 *An Early American Reader*, ed. by J. A. Leo Lemay (Washington: United States Information Agency, 1988), p. 40.
17 *Ibid.*, pp. 42f.

When one reflects on the often quoted final stanza of Berkeley's poem of 1726, the couplet in the anonymous letter of 1730, Ames's prophecy of 1758 and Adams' comment of 1807, it becomes evident that such ideas as the westward movement towards ever new frontiers and the conviction that it is America's 'Manifest Destiny' to missionarize and pacify the world, which are supposed to be indigenously American, go back to ancient European traditions. In the same way, J. Hector St. John de Crèvecour's belief that "Americans are the western pilgrims who are carrying along with them that great mass of arts, sciences, vigour, and industry which began long since in the East; they will finish the great circle,"[18] and Walt Whitman's reference to "the circle almost circled"[19] in "Facing West from California's Shores" prove to be American variations upon the ancient solar analogy of the European imagination.

While Drayton's and Berkeley's poems represent the widespread European belief in America as a singular chance for mankind to begin anew and perfect itself, it was the Protestant Reformation which gave a new and momentous twist to this concept because the hopeful adventurers who had left their European countries of their own volition to explore and exploit the New World were now replaced by desperate emigrants who fled from religious persecution and sailed to America to find a place where they could live according to their convictions. The lasting heritage of the early Puritan settlers made America, in the words of Charles L. Sanford, "more than almost any other modern nation [...] a product of the Protestant Reformation, seeking an earthly paradise in which to perfect a reformation of the Church."[20] For them, America became the land provided by God and concealed by his providence from unworthy European eyes until the advent of the Reformation when his chosen people were to erect a New Jerusa-

---

18 J. Hector St. John de Crèvecoeur, *Letters from an American Farmer* and *Sketches of Eighteenth-Century America*, ed. with an introduction by Albert E. Stone (New York: Viking Penguin, 1981), p. 70.
19 "Facing West from California's Shore," in *The Complete Writings of Walt Whitman*, issued under the editorial supervision of His Literary Executors, Richard Maurice Bucke, Thomas B. Harned, and Horace L. Traubel (St. Clair Shores, Michigan: Scholarly Press, 1977; reprint of the edition New York: G. P. Putnam's Sons, 1902), vol. I, p. 135.
20 Charles L. Sanford, *The Quest for Paradise: Europe and the American Moral Imagination* (Urbana, Ill.: University of Illinois Press, 1961), p. 74.

lem and thus to fulfil the promise of millennial thinking.[21] This is why John Winthrop, preaching his famous sermon aboard the *Arbella* in 1630, could admonish his fellow believers to "consider that wee shall be as a Citty vpon a Hill, the Eies of all people are vppon vs"[22] and why Captain Edward Johnson in his *Wonder-Working Providence* could define Massachusetts as the place "where the Lord will create a new Heaven, and a new Earth in new Churches, and a new Commonwealth together."[23]

In Puritan typological thinking, the concept of America as a mythic El Dorado where Ponce de Leon searched for that Fountain of Youth which Nathaniel Hawthorne ironically revived in "Dr. Heidegger's Experiment" was replaced by the idea of America as a New Canaan where God's own people were called upon to found their commonwealth. Thus Thomas Morton, who annoyed the strict Puritans of Plymouth Plantation by setting up his maypole of Merry Mount, made immortal by Hawthorne in his story of the same name, entitled the history of his settlement on Mount Wollaston *New English Canaan*. Published in Amsterdam in 1637, this history suggests an analogy between the Israelites, to whom God had said: "I am the Lord your God, which brought you forth out of the land of Egypt, to give you the land of Canaan,"[24] and the New England colonists who left their English captivity, crossed their Red Sea, namely the dangerous Atlantic, and found their religious freedom in their promised land, the

---

21 As late as 1866, in his *Oration Delivered before the City Authorities of Boston, July 4, 1866*, Samuel K. Lathrop expressed this widespread conviction that the discovery of America had been precisely timed by God when he said that if "the discovery [had] been made a few centuries earlier, the semi-barbarous institutions and feudalism of the Old World would have been transplanted in their vigor to the New [...] Had the discovery been delayed a few centuries, the new ideas and and principles [...] which the Reformation called forth, would in all human probability have had but a short-lived, struggling existence. Confined to Europe, they would have been strangled, [...]." Thus, "civil and religious liberty" could only flourish in America, "because at the hour of its utmost need God gave it opportunity to plant itself on this new continent." - Quoted from *Nationalism and Religion in America: Concepts of American Identity and Mission*, ed. by Winthrop S. Hudson (Gloucester, Massachusetts: Peter Smith, 1978), p. 54.
22 John Winthrop, "A Modell of Christian Charity," in *An American Primer*, ed. by Daniel J. Boorstin (New York: New American Library, 1985), pp. 26-43; here p. 40.
23 Edward Johnson, *Johnson's Wonder-Working Providence, 1628 - 1651*, ed. by J. Franklin Jameson (New York: Barnes & Noble, rpt. 1959), pp. 24f.
24 Leviticus 25:38.

'New Canaan' of America. Thus Cotton Mather could begin his *Magnalia Christi Americana* by stating that he would "write the Wonders of the Christian Religion, flying from the Depravations of Europe, to the American Strand."[25] Moreover, he could say about William Bradford, the first governor of Plymouth Plantation, that "the Leader of a People in a Wilderness had need be a Moses."[26] From John Cotton and Thomas Goodwin, who believed the last reckoning would occur in 1655 and around 1700 respectively,[27] to Jonathan Edwards, who wrote in his *Some Thoughts Concerning the Present Revival of Religion in New England* "that the beginning of this great work of God must be near" and found it "probable that this work will begin in America,"[28] numerous examples could be quoted to show that many of the early American settlers and their descendants fervently believed that America had been chosen by God as the site of Christ's Second Coming. Such typological thinking has deeply influenced many later and outwardly secularized developments which can hardly be understood outside such a context. Here are just two examples:

The New World paradise to be brought about by millennial Protestantism was conceived of as the counterpart of an old world ravaged by the accumulated sins of papacy. Hence, as Sanford succinctly puts it, "Europe has ever since, in one way or another, played the role of Hell in the American imagination."[29] In the opinion of the early settlers, therefore, their saintly enterprise of regaining paradise on the virgin soil of the American continent stood in continual danger of being thwarted by the machinations of the Antichrist, and it was not only John Cotton who feared the interference of "Principalities from Hell, or the Great Beast, the Catholic Church."[30] This old idea of

---

25 *Selections from Cotton Mather*, ed. by Kenneth B. Murdock (New York: Hafner Press, 1973; reprint of the edition New York: Harcourt, Brace, and Company, 1926), p. 1.
26 *Ibid.*, p. 49.
27 See R. W. B. Lewis, "Days of Wrath and Laughter," in his *Trials of the Word: American Literature and the Humanistic Tradition* (New Haven and London: Yale University Press, 1965), pp. 184-235; here p. 202.
28 *The Works of Jonathan Edwards*, general editor John E. Smith (New Haven and London: Yale University Press, 1957ff.); vol. IV, *The Great Awakening*, ed. by C. C. Goen (1972), p. 353.
29 Charles L. Sanford, *op. cit.*, pp. 95f.
30 John Cotton, *An Exposition upon the Thirteenth Chapter of Revelation* (London: printed for Livewel Chapman, 1656), p. 111; here quoted from Charles L. Sanford, *op. cit.*, p. 90.

Europe as a fallen world continually threatening to contaminate the purity of America resurfaces in new guise in secular literature when in the first American comedy, Royall Tyler's *The Contrast* (1790), the innocent Jonathan with his homely American shrewdness is elevated above foppish and infamous Englishmen. The same 'contrast' can be detected behind the numerous variations of the encounter between American innocence and naivety and European experience and sophistication popularized by Mark Twain in *The Innocents Abroad* (1869), brought to perfection by Henry James in his narratives about the 'international theme,' and used by contemporary writers like Bernard Malamud, John Updike and Saul Bellow as a backbone for their plots.

On another level, the early Puritans' fear of the intervention of some mysterious evil in their godly American experiment contributed to a conspiratorial notion of history, demonstrated in the early Salem witchcraft trials as well as in Senator McCarthy's hysterical persecution of communists and fellow travellers. And it is this idea of history as a battle of the good against the bad forces which baffled Europeans need to know about in order to understand why, for example, President Reagan could speak of the Soviet Union as the 'realm of evil' and thus discuss political issues in theological terms.

While the first, the mythic tradition envisaged America as the pastoral country in which a new golden age would flourish and where westward-bound mankind would establish its most advanced form of civilization, the second, the religious tradition of millennial Protestantism took America to be the New Canaan where God's chosen people were to create a new earthly paradise. But a third tradition must be added to the composite picture. This line of thinking, which goes as far back as Sir Thomas More's *Utopia* (1516), reached its epitome in the political thinking of the Enlightenment and found its lasting expression in the Declaration of Independence. But it is not only this cherished document that needs to be mentioned in this context, because the third tradition also led to countless utopian experiments on American soil. The earliest of such experiments were, of course, of entirely religious origin. But a second phase of American utopianism began when, on a January afternoon in 1825, the British industrialist Robert Owen purchased the *Harmonie* colony of George Rapp and his pietist sect on the Wabash River in Indiana and reopened it as *New Harmony*, a self-supporting community, without any religious implications, meant to turn into an ideal miniature state. After the numerous experiments in Owenism, all of which failed conspicuously, came the experiments in Fourierism, among which the Transcendentalist utopia at Brook Farm, which forms the backdrop for Hawthorne's *The Blithedale Romance*, was the best known. But Fourierism, too, had spent itself by the time of the Civil War, and it was Edward Bellamy's *Looking Backward* (1888) which triggered off a third wave of communal experiments. But most of the more than three-hundred practical attempts at establishing an ideal society in America were short-lived, and this is a fate they share with the communal experiments of the youthful American counter-culture in the sixties, of which Kurt Vonnegut's son Mark provides an impressive example in his novel *The Eden Express* (1975).

The lasting heritage of enlightened thinking, however, lives on, and the Declaration of Independence is a centrally important document in which Thomas Jefferson converted rationalistic philosophical theories into a momentous political statement of intention when he made John Locke's philosophy of natural laws the basis of American government. Locke had used the ethnological knowledge of his time about the life of the Indians in his theory of the 'state of nature' and the 'laws of nature.' And since he found that the Indians did not know money and therefore had no reason whatsoever to make any attempt at enlarging their possessions beyond what they needed for survival, he concluded: "Thus in the beginning all the World was *America*, and more so than that is now."[31] Jefferson adopted Locke's arguments concerning the laws of nature and integrated them into his position that all men were created equal and endowed with certain inalienable rights, that any government was instituted for the purpose of protecting these rights, and that a government which would violate these rights could be rightfully altered or abolished. These promises certainly marked a milestone in the development of democratic ideas when they were given legal force.

---

31 John Locke, *Two Treatises of Government*, ed. by Peter Laslett (Cambridge: Cambridge University Press, 1970), p. 319.

It is tempting to point out the discrepancies between the Declaration's promise of "life, liberty and the pursuit of happiness" and the reality of Indian ethnocide and Black slavery or to stress the fact that the author of the Declaration was himself a slaveholder. Such deplorable contradictions between theory and practice cannot be denied, but one must not forget that Jefferson's belief that "the equal rights of man and the happiness of every individual are [...] the only legitimate object of government"[32] led to a Constitution which is not only the oldest constitution applying to a nation as a whole, but which incorporates a detailed Bill of Rights. This Bill, consisting of the first ten Amendments, grants freedom of religion, speech, press and assembly and protection against unreasonable searches and seizures, excessive bails and fines and imprisonments without charges; and - two hundred years ago - it must have impressed many a contemporary European *Untertan* as a dream turned into unbelievable reality.

Simplifying a many-faceted matter, one might say, then, that it was the combination of

- the mythic projection of America as a land of milk and honey and an El Dorado in which the Fountain of Youth bubbled forth in a pastoral landscape,
- the religious concept of America as the site of the New Jerusalem and a land in which Christ's Second Coming would establish a new paradise on earth, and of
- the political promise of America as a country in which the tyrannical restraints of the Old World would be replaced by human equality, liberty and brotherhood,

which laid the ground for the 'American Dream.' The New World figured in the European imagination as what Crèvecoeur had called "this great American asylum" for "the poor of Europe"[33] and what Thomas Paine defined as "an asylum for mankind."[34] And when in the nine-

---

32 In a letter to A. Coray of October 31, 1823. Here quoted from *The Political Writings of Thomas Jefferson: Representative Selections*, ed. by Edward Dumbauld (New York: The Liberal Arts Press, 1955), p. xxv.
33 J. Hector St. John de Crèvecoeur, *op. cit.*, p. 68.
34 Thomas Paine, *Common Sense*, in *The Life and Works of Thomas Paine*, ed. by William M. Van der Weyde (New Rochelle, N.Y.: Thomas Paine National Historical Association, 1925), vol. II, p. 150. - See also *ibid.*, p. 127: "This new world hath been the

teenth century an ever-growing wave of immigrants set forth for America, they were guided by these sentiments as rephrased in the hundreds of promotional books and tracts which recommended the New World as the country in which the poor and underprivileged masses of Europe would find a chance to improve their conditions and to achieve the desired self-fulfilment.

To mention just one of these books, let me point to Gottfried Duden's enormously influential *Bericht über eine Reise nach den westlichen Staaten Nordamerika's und einen mehrjährigen Aufenthalt am Missouri (in den Jahren 1824, 25, 26 und 1827), in Bezug auf Auswanderung und Übervölkerung, oder: Das Leben im Innern der Vereinigten Staaten und dessen Bedeutung für die häusliche und politische Lage der Europäer, dargestellt a) in einer Sammlung von Briefen, b) in einer besonderen Abhandlung über den politischen Zustand der nordamerikanischen Freistaaten, und c) in einem rathgebenden Nachtrage für auswandernde deutsche Ackerwirthe und Diejenigen, welche auf Handelsunternehmungen denken* (1829). This report, which skilfully and convincingly contrasts the vast spaces and the democratic life of America with the cramped narrowness and the political oppression of Germany, quickly began to exert its influence and greatly contributed to the growing exodus of Germans fleeing from the repressive measures of a Metternich.

There were, of course, critical voices as well. Alexis de Tocqueville, that clear-sighted observer, had his rather prophetic reservations about American mass democracy, and Duden's praise of American opportunities was rejected as wrong in Ferdinand Kürnberger's novel *Der Amerika-Müde* (1857). Thomas Moore, an Irishman who lived in America during Jefferson's second administration, rhymed

> Take Christians, Mohawks, democrats, and all
> From the rude wig-wam to the congress-hall,
> From man the savage, whether slav'd or free,
> To man the civiliz'd, less tame than he, -
> 'Tis one dull chaos, one unfertile strife
> Betwixt half-polish'd and half-barbarous life;

---

asylum for the persecuted lovers of civil and religious liberty from *every part* of Europe."

> Where every ill the ancient world could brew
> Is mix'd with every grossness of the new.[35]

And Mrs. Frances Milton Trollope, in her notorious book on *Domestic Manners of America* (1832), flatly stated that she could not stomach the citizens of the New World: "I do not like them. I do not like their principles, I do not like their manners, I do not like their opinions."[36] Such voices were not new, and Crèvecoeur for example, who once had so enthusiastically endorsed the idea of civilization's movement from east to west and asserted that Americans would "finish the great circle," was severely disappointed by the roughness and savagery of the frontier, deserted his family to seek refuge with an Indian tribe, and tried to fulfil his transatlantic utopia in a wigwam. Even earlier, the religious enthusiasm of many a Puritan settler was subdued by the unbelievable hardship of pioneer existence. One need only think of the infamous 'starving time' in the Jamestown of 1609, where the settlers whom Drayton's ode had accompanied on their voyage into "Earths onely paradise," dug up Indian corpses to eat and one man killed his wife and pickled her to last him through the winter, or read William Bradford's account of the arrival of the *Mayflower* at Cape Cod (1620) in order to realize the painful discrepancies between the ideal and a reality described as "a hideous and desolate wilderness, full of wild beasts and wild men."[37]

Despite such disappointments and setbacks, however, America remained a hope and a vision. The encounter of the mythic and religious promises and the political and social expectations with the actual geographical reality of the New World bred, in an endless series of interpenetrations, the complex pattern of convictions and aspirations known as the 'American Dream.' And I would argue that the constitutive elements of this 'Dream' are

---

35 Thomas Moore, "To the Honourable W. R. Spencer," in *The Poetical Works of Thomas Moore, Collected by Himself* (London: Longman, Brown, Green, and Longmans, 1853), vol. II, p. 315.
36 Quoted from *Travelers to the New Nation 1776 - 1914: An American Studies Reader*, ed. by Marc Pachter (Washington: United States International Communication Agency, 1982), p. 11.
37 William Bradford, *Of Plymouth Plantation*; quoted from *The Norton Anthology of American Literature*, ed. by Ronald Gottesman et al. (New York and London: W. W. Norton, 1979) vol. I, pp. 26-40; here p. 31.

- the future-orientated belief in a steady improvement of individual, communal and societal conditions of existence, that is, the belief in PROGRESS;
- the conviction that everybody can realize his highest ambitions by means of his own endeavours, that is, the belief in the general attainability of SUCCESS;
- the certainty that God has singled out America as his chosen country and has appointed the Americans to convert the rest of the world to true American-style democracy, that is, the belief in MANIFEST DESTINY;
- the assurance that, in the context of civilization's irresistible westward movement, ever new borderlines are to be crossed and ever new obstacles are to be surmounted, that is, the idea of the continual challenge of respective FRONTIERS;
- the belief in the American form of government of the people, by the people and for the people as the sole guarantor of LIBERTY and EQUALITY; and
- the idea that immigrants of different nationalities, different ethnic stock and different religious affiliations can be fused into a new nation, that is, the conviction expressed in the notion of the MELTING POT; or the hope that they can live peacefully together without abandoning their diverse cultures, that is, the belief in CULTURAL PLURALISM, MULTI-ETHNICITY, or MULTICULTURALISM.

Other observers might put the accent on other aspects, and such facets as the cult of NEWNESS, the glorification of YOUTH, the belief in unhampered MOBILITY and the chances for ever NEW BEGINNINGS certainly deserve equal stress. But they can be subsumed under the seven elements which I will now briefly discuss.

Success and Progress

> Were we really brought up to believe in one another? We were brought up to succeed, weren't we?
> Arthur Miller, *The Price*[38]

One of the central doctrines of Puritanism is that of predestination: that is, the idea that certain individuals, in Calvin's words, are predestined for salvation from eternity through God's "gratuitous mercy, totally irrespective of human merit,"[39] and that the remainder are condemned to eternal damnation. Consequently, man - deprived of the mediating agencies of a hierarchically ordered church - can contribute nothing to his deliverance and cannot know his destination. At the same time he is called upon to glorify God, not through prayer and contemplation only, but through strife and labour. Haunted by the insecurity about his status as an elected or a damned soul, the incredibly lonely Puritan establishes a connection between his temporal and his spiritual calling, devotes all his strength to his professional success, and reasons that God's permission to become successful in this life might be taken as a sign of salvation in the life thereafter. Professional success thus becomes a 'proof' of salvation previously and independently granted. Since the Puritan is not only obliged to do continual hard work but also forbidden to enjoy the fruits of his labour and admonished to keep up a strict inner-worldly asceticism, his theologically founded economic virtues lead to the amassing of capital which, instead of being spent upon living well or in support of the arts, is brought to the bank to earn interest. Thus the complex conundrum which Max Weber analyses in his famous and controversial study *Die protestantische Ethik und der Geist des Kapitalismus* is set in motion.[40]

---

38 Arthur Miller, *The Price*; here quoted from his *Collected Plays* (London: Secker & Warburg, 1981), p. 368.
39 Calvin, *Institutes of the Christian Religion*, book III, chapter xxi, paragraph 7. - Here quoted from Richard Henry Tawney, *Religion and the Rise of Capitalism: A Historical Study* (Harmondsworth: Penguin Books, rpt., 1964), p. 117.
40 Max Weber's seminal study and a representative selection of scholarly reactions to it are most easily accessible in Max Weber, *Die protestantische Ethik I: Eine Aufsatzsammlung*, ed. by Johannes Winckelmann (München and Hamburg: Siebenstern,

Soon, however, the original Calvinist impetus weakened, and the capitalist spirit continued to flourish in a secularized version. A good example of this momentous mutation is provided by Benjamin Franklin, the exemplary American go-getter and self-made man. When Franklin expostulates, in his "Advice to a Young Tradesman" (1748), that "Time is Money,"[41] when he writes his "The Way to Wealth" (1758), when he reports in his *Autobiography* about his "bold and arduous project of arriving at moral perfection,"[42] or when he espouses Industry, Frugality and Prudence as what Richard Weiss calls "the great trinity of the Protestant ethic,"[43] the end has become the means. Worldly success is desirable no longer as an indication of spiritual salvation, but in its own right, and the high degree of purely utilitarian thinking that characterizes Franklin becomes obvious in the many adages from *Poor Richard's Almanac*, which still belong to the core of homespun American wisdom. The secure conviction that anyone can pull himself up by his own bootstrings and 'make it' by observing the rules of the game and working hard enough infuses such Franklinesque sayings as "God helps them that help themselves" or "Early to Bed, and early to rise, makes a Man healthy, wealthy and wise."[44] And the knowledge that one need not be good as long as one manages to seem to be good, defines the beginning of a success ethic which identifies the good with the useful, holds that being successful can be learnt, and is a philosophy of practicality with a rather thin veneer of moralizing. America, this doctrine says, provides equal opportunity for everybody, and it is entirely up to the individual to make the best of his chances and to rise 'from rags to riches.'[45]

2nd rev. ed., 1969); and *Die protestantische Ethik II: Kritiken und Antikritiken*, ed. by Johannes Winckelmann (München and Hamburg: Siebenstern, 1968).
41 Benjamin Franklin, *The Autobiography and Other Writings*, ed. with an introduction by L. Jesse Lemisch (New York: New American Library, 1961), p. 186.
42 *Ibid.*, p. 94.
43 Richard Weiss, *The American Myth of Success: From Horatio Alger to Norman Vincent Peale* (New York: Basic Books, 1969), p. 28.
44 Benjamin Franklin, *op. cit.*, pp. 189 and 190.
45 The standard books on the American myth of success are Irvin G. Wyllie, *The Self-Made Man in America: The Myth of Rags to Riches* (New Brunswick, N.J.: Rutgers University Press, 1954); Kenneth S. Lynn, *The Dream of Success: A Study of the Modern American Imagination* (Boston: Little, Brown & Co., 1955); John G. Cawelti, *Apostles of the Self-Made Man* (Chicago and London: University of Chicago Press, 1965); Richard Weiss, *The American Myth of Success: From Horatio Alger to Norman Vincent Peale* (New York: Basic Books, 1969); and Richard M. Huber, *The American Idea of*

The man who popularized this message and whose more than one-hundred novels offered the standard recipe for achieving the success promised by the 'American Dream' was Horatio Alger Jr., who graduated from Harvard in 1852, finished his studies at the Divinity School in Cambridge in 1860, and was offered his first pulpit in Brewster, Massachusetts, in 1865. When he was expelled by a shocked congregation because he had been found guilty of the "abominable and revolting crime of unnatural familiarity with *boys*,"[46] the shamed closet homosexual went to New York where he attempted to sublimate his homosexuality into a concern for homeless boys by serving as chaplain to the Newsboys' Lodge and where he launched his career as a children's author. In 1868, his most successful novel, *Ragged Dick*, appeared in book form and established him as a popular author. In this and the countless other books he had written by 1890, he combined the Puritan concept of the individual's self-responsibility for a proper exercise of his temporal calling with the Calvinist doctrine of inner-worldly asceticism, the Emersonian idea of self-reliance and the belief in America as a country of unlimited opportunities where every individual was rated according to merit and not to birth and rank. But to this well-established mixture he added the first inkling of a new ingredient.

In 1859, Charles Darwin had published his seminal work *On the Origin of Species by Means of Natural Selection*, and soon afterwards Herbert Spencer had transferred Darwin's revolutionary theory of biological evolution to sociology and taught that economic competi-

---

Success (New York: McGraw-Hill, 1971). A book of much wider scope which should be consulted is Martha Banta, *Failure and Success in America: A Literary Debate* (Princeton, N.J.: Princeton University Press, 1978); two recent and very informative studies are Lawrence Chenoweth, *The American Dream of Success: The Search for the Self in the Twentieth Century* (North Scituate, Mass.: Duxbury Press, 1974), and Joseph Epstein, *Ambition: The Secret Passion* (New York: E. P. Dutton, 1980; and Harmondsworth: Penguin Books, 1982); and the Paderborn dissertation by Bernd Rasche, *Der Zwang zum Erfolg: Kulturgeschichtliche Untersuchungen eines modernen Leidens an amerikanischer Kurzprosa des 20. Jahrhunderts* (Stuttgart: M & P, 1991), deals with the depiction of the success myth in the modern short story.

46 Quoted from Carl Bode, "Introduction" to *Ragged Dick and Struggling Upward*, ed. by him (New York: Viking Penguin, 1985), p. xiv. - Among the studies of Horatio Alger see especially John Tebbel, *From Rags to Riches: Horatio Alger, Jr., and the American Dream* (New York: Macmillan, 1963); Ralph D. Gardner, *Horatio Alger, or The American Hero Era* (Mendota, Ill.: Wayside Press, 1964); and Gary Scharnhorst with Jack Bales, *The Lost Life of Horatio Alger, Jr.* (Bloomington: Indiana University Press, 1985).

tion was dominated by what he so famously defined as the law of "the survival of the fittest."⁴⁷ Spencer's theory of 'Social Darwinism' became enormously influential in America because it served as a welcome justification for the shirt-sleeved ruthlessness of self-made millionaires such as the Carnegies, the Vanderbilts or the Rockefellers, and John D. Rockefeller could revealingly declare in one of his Sunday-School speeches that "the growth of a large business is merely a survival of the fittest."⁴⁸ Jack London's Captain Larsen in *The Sea Wolf* (1904) summed up the new world view when he laconically stated:

> I believe that life is a mess. It is like yeast, a ferment, a thing that moves and may move for a minute, an hour, a year, or a hundred years, but that in the end will cease to move. The big eat the little that they may continue to move, the strong eat the weak that they may retain their strength. The lucky eat the most and move the longest, that is all.⁴⁹

And Theodore Dreiser translated this attitude into the famous symbol of the lobster and the squid in his novel *The Financier* (1912).⁵⁰

These examples, however, belong to a later period, and Horatio Alger, who published most of his novels in the 1860s and 1870s, kept to the boundaries of the genteel tradition and preached a doctrine of frugality, hard work and prudence which was already rather outdated even in his day. Alger knew that constant work and a prudent abstention from every vice was hardly enough to guarantee the desired success in a highly competitive society, and so he added an emphasis on luck and introduced into all his books the *deus ex machina* of the lucky coincidence. His heroes never make a fortune but they always find or inherit it, and the intriguing gospel which their stories preach is no longer that of virtue resulting in material reward but that of luck never coming to the wicked. By showing, in such immensely popular

---

47 The famous phrase, which is often wrongly ascribed to Darwin, was coined by Spencer, seven years before *The Origin of Species*, in his essay on "A Theory of Population, Deduced from the General Law of Animal Fertility," *Westminster Review*, 57 (1852), 468-501.
48 Quoted from Richard Hofstadter, *Social Darwinism in American Thought* (New York: George Braziller, rev. ed. 1959), p. 45.
49 Jack London, *The Sea Wolf* (New York: Bantam Books, 1963), p. 35.
50 See Theodore Dreiser, *The Financier*, chapter I. - The relevant excerpt, which is very suitable for EFL-purposes, is reprinted in *American Dreams, American Nightmares*, pp. 78-82.

books as *Mark, the Match-Boy* or *Ragged Dick*, that unceasing work and manful struggle against temptation - don't smoke, don't drink, don't consort with loose women - would inevitably lead a boy to some happy event resulting in wealth and fame, Alger made the myth of individual success a central ingredient of the popular American imagination and thus helped to give the 'American Dream' a decidedly materialistic twist which faithfully mirrored the spirit of an age no longer referred to as the "golden age" which Drayton and Berkeley had envisaged on the new continent, but fittingly dubbed *The Gilded Age* in Mark Twain's and Charles Dudley Warner's novel of that title (1873).

Alger's 'from rags to riches' formula and the concomitant belief in the attainability of individual success as measured in terms of money and social recognition certainly define that aspect of the 'Dream' which has been most often criticized by foreign observers - and by Americans - as an indication of shallow materialism. Such cynical quips as 'A man is a success if he can make more money than his wife can spend' or 'A woman is a success if she can find such a man' or the famous and rather revealing advice of a well-known coach to his players that 'Nice guys finish last,' all exemplify an obsession with public recognition and betray a willingness to achieve such recognition even by foul play.

Those who doubt that William James was right when he rejected the "squalid cash interpretation" of success as a national disease and contemptuously spoke of it as "the bitch-goddess"[51] of America, and those who have difficulty believing that one of the roots of the 'worship' of money is really of a religious nature might read Norman Vincent Peale's influential self-help manual *The Power of Positive Thinking* (1952), in which texts from the Old and the New Testament are combined into "a simple yet scientific system of practical techniques of successful living that works" and "scientific procedures for the release of spiritual energy through the mechanism of prayer"[52] are outlined in

---

51 James used this phrase in a letter of September 11, 1906 to H. G. Wells. Quoted from *The Letters of William James*, ed. by his son Henry James (New York: Kraus Reprint Co., 1969; reprint of the edition Boston: Little, Brown & Co., 1926), vol. II, p. 260.
52 Norman Vincent Peale, *The Power of Positive Thinking* (Kingswood: Cedar Books, rpt. 1968), pp. x and 57. - Excerpts from Peale's book are reprinted in the EFL-reader

detail. In the Reagan era, in the context of a gradual reduction of social welfare in the name of individual responsibility and self-reliance, there was a new wave of such self-help books. This tendency is perhaps best exemplified by Robert Schuller's bestseller *Tough Times Never Last, But Tough People Do!* (1983). In this book, Schuller, who is the founder and senior minister of the famous Crystal Cathedral in Garden Grove, California, and whose telecast, *The Hour of Power*, is one of the most widely viewed programmes, preaches the "Ten Commandments of Possibility Thinking" and argues that there is nothing "worse than the no-risk mentality we have in America," because "if Jesus Christ had operated that way, He would never have died on the cross."[53]

The development of the success myth went hand in hand with a belief in general progress representing, to use Ekirch's definition, "a measurable growth in the pursuit of knowledge and in the achievements of science as well as an advance in the ability of men to control for good their own lives and destinies."[54] It is difficult to retrace the American belief in progress, which is part of a phase of Western thought in general, to specific roots. But one need only imagine a country which has successfully secured its independence against all odds, which has enjoyed an immense expansion in population, territory and wealth, which has before its continually advancing frontiers a vast continent full of inexhaustible resources, and whose inhabitants are convinced that they are destined to show a worn-out Europe what they can achieve, and one will realize that here the ideas of European philosophers fell upon the most fruitful soil. In 1788, for example, Benjamin Franklin could praise "the improvements in philosophy, morals, politics, and even the conveniences of common living" in a letter to the Reverend John Lathrop and continue:

God's Own Country: Religion in America, ed. by Donald Lloyd Turner (Paderborn: Schöningh, 1987), pp. 93-96.

53 Robert H. Schuller, *Tough Times Never Last, But Tough People Do!* (Toronto: Bantam Books, 1984), p. 123. - For a detailed study of recent self-help literature and its ideology see Birgitta Koch-Linde, *Amerikanische Tagträume: Success und Self-Help Literatur der USA* (Frankfurt and New York: Campus Verlag, 1984).

54 Arthur Alphonse Ekirch, Jr., *The Idea of Progress in America, 1815-1860* (New York: Columbia University Press, 1944), p. 11. - For a more recent study of the theme see Robert Nisbet, *History of the Idea of Progress* (New York: Basic Books, 1980).

> [...] I have sometimes almost wished it had been my destiny to be born two or three centuries hence. For invention and improvement are prolific, and beget more of their kind. The present progress is rapid. Many of great importance, now unthought of, will before that period be produced; [...] if the art of physic shall be improved in proportion with other arts, we may then be able to avoid diseases, and live as long as the patriarchs in Genesis; to which I suppose we should make little objection.[55]

And three years later Thomas Paine could observe in "Rights of Man" that the revolutions in America and France had thrown "a beam of light over the world":

> I see in America, the generality of the people living in a style of plenty unknown in monarchial countries; and I see that the principle of its government, which is that of the *equal Rights of Man*, is making a rapid progress in the world.
> [...]
> From the rapid progress which America makes in every species of improvement, it is rational to conclude, that if the governments of Asia, Africa, and Europe, had begun on a principle similar to that of America, or had not been very early corrupted therefrom, that those countries must, by this time, have been in a far superior condition to what they are.[56]

Philip Freneau, who expressed his glowing confidence in the future of the New World in such patriotic poems as "America Independent" or "The Rising Glory of America," in 1798 could compose his "Ode to the Americans" in order to advance the argument "that the progress of liberty and reason in the world is slow and gradual; but, considering the present state of things, and the light of science universally spreading, that it cannot be long impeded, or its complete establishment prevented."[57] And in 1807, Paine's friend Joel Barlow could say, in his preface to *The Columbiad*, that "the future progress of society

---

55 *The Writings of Benjamin Franklin*, coll. and ed. with a Life and Introduction by Albert Henry Smyth (New York: Haskell House, 1970; reprint of the edition New York and London: Macmillan, 1905-1907), vol. IX, p. 651.
56 Thomas Paine, "Rights of Man," in *The Life and Works of Thomas Paine*, vol. VI, pp. 161f.; 175; 233.
57 Philip Freneau, "Ode to the Americans," in *A Collection of Poems on American Affairs and a Variety of Other Subjects Chiefly Moral and Political* (Delmar, N.Y.: Scholars' Facsimiles & Reprints, 1976; reprint of the edition New York: D. Longworth, 1815), p. 39.

and the civilization of states" was not only "desirable" but "that to believe it practicable [was] one step towards rendering it so."[58] In 1818 Thomas Jefferson could write in a letter to Dr. Benjamin Waterhouse:

> When I contemplate the immense advances in science and discoveries in the arts which have been made within the period of my life, I look forward with confidence to equal advances by the present generation, and have no doubt they will consequently be as much wiser than we have been as we than our fathers were, and they than the burners of witches.[59]

In 1839 John L. O'Sullivan could pathetically proclaim that "we are the nation of human progress" and defiantly ask "who will, what can, set limits to our onward march?"[60] In 1846 Walt Whitman could declare in a newspaper editorial that "Thirty years from this date, America will be confessed the *first nation* on the earth."[61] And in 1885 the Congregational minister Josiah Strong, in his influential bestseller *Our Country*, could extoll "all the progress in civilization made by the race" and observe with deep satisfaction:

> But this has not been simply a mechanical era of marvelous material progress. With the exception of astronomy, modern science, as we now know it, is almost wholly the creation of the nineteenth century. In this century, too, have the glorious fruits of modern missions all been gathered. Another evidence of progress which, if less obvious than material results, is more conclusive, is found in the *great ideas* which have become the fixed possession of man within the past hundred years. Among them is that of individual liberty [...] Another idea, which, like that of individual liberty, finds its root in the teachings of Christ, and has grown up slowly through the ages to blossom in our own, is that of honor to womanhood, whose fruitage is woman's elevation. [...] Another striking evidence of progress is found in the en-

---

58 *The Works of Joel Barlow*, intr. by William K. Bottorff and Arthur L. Ford (Gainesville, Florida: Scholars' Facsimiles & Reprints, 1970), vol. II, p. 383.
59 Thomas Jefferson, *Writings*, ed. by Paul L. Ford (New York and London: Putnam, 1892-1899), vol. X, p. 103; here quoted from Arthur Alphonse Ekirch, Jr., *op. cit.*, p. 32.
60 John L. O'Sullivan, "The Great Nation of Futurity," *Democratic Review*, 6 (November 1839), 426-430; here quoted from the reprint in *Manifest Destiny*, ed. by Norman Graebner (Indianapolis: Bobbs-Merrill, 1968), pp. 15-21; here p. 17.
61 Walt Whitman, "American Futurity" (November 24, 1846); here quoted from Arthur Alphonse Ekirch, Jr., *op. cit.*, p. 52.

hanced valuation of human life, which has served to humanize law and mitigate "man's inhumanity to man."[62]

These are just a few representative examples from an almost endless reservoir of statements by writers and politicians, educators and theologians who share a deep belief in a specifically 'American' form of progress and who base this belief on one or several of the following factors: the American form of democratic government, the vast extension of the territory available for settlement, the inexhaustible material resources provided by the American continent, and the inevitable advance of science and technology. A quotation from President James K. Polk's 1846 annual message to Congress might appropriately sum up this many-faceted belief:

> The progress of our country in her career of greatness, not only in the vast extension of our territorial limits and the rapid increase of our population, but in the resources and wealth and in the happy condition of our people, is without an example in the history of nations.[63]

While these two central ingredients of the 'Dream,' the belief in individual success and the concomitant belief in societal progress, helped to make the newly founded nation, within the shortest of times, into an industrial and technological power of the first order, right from the beginning both beliefs found fervent critics who warned that the heedless pursuit of material success would exact the price of spiritual failure, that unchecked scientific progress would turn against mankind, and that instead of realizing their dreams the adherents of success and progress would finally find themselves caught in a nightmare.

As early as 1820 Washington Irving presented a subtle criticism of the 'American Dream' in his tale "The Legend of Sleepy Hollow." Here the scheming Yankee Ichabod Crane is ousted by the cunning backwoodsman Brom Bones, and consequently Sleepy Hollow, the dreamy

---

[62] Josiah Strong, *Our Country : Its Possible Future* and *Its Present Crisis* (New York: Baker and Taylor, 1885); here quoted from the reprint of the revised edition 1891, *Our Country*, ed. by Jurgen Herbst (Cambridge, Mass.: The Belknap Press of Harvard University Press, 1963), pp. 15 and 16f.

[63] President James K. Polk, "Second Annual Message," December 8, 1846; here quoted from Arthur Alphonse Ekirch, Jr., *op. cit.*, p. 49.

enclave of stability and order, is spared the onslaught of questionable 'progress.' In 1832, another cautionary tale appeared, when Nathaniel Hawthorne published his warning contrafactum upon Benjamin Franklin's optimistic story about his arrival in Philadelphia in his ambiguous story "My Kinsman, Major Molineux," in which Franklin's superficial belief in the possibility of new beginnings is contrasted with Hawthorne's deeper knowledge of man's sinfulness and imperfection. Later, right in the middle of the industrial boom of the Gilded Age, William Dean Howells published his novel *The Rise of Silas Lapham* (1885), in which he made the financial fall of the self-made millionaire the prerequisite for his moral rise; and four years later Mark Twain, the erstwhile optimistic humorist gradually turning misanthropist, denounced his period's facile belief in progress in his pessimistic novel *A Connecticut Yankee in King Arthur's Court* (1889), in which he presented a worthy descendant of Irving's "native of Connecticut: a State which supplies the Union with pioneers for the mind as well as for the forest."[64] Mark Twain's Yankee, who sets out to convert King Arthur's Britain into an industrialized and 'enlightened' country, gradually loses his superficial belief in "the march of civilization" and "the magic of science,"[65] and the final battle between medieval superstition and backwardness and the supposedly superior nineteenth-century technology and Yankee practicality ends with the pathetic self-defeat of the latter.

Further examples are legion. Nathanael West, in his satirical novel *A Cool Million* (1934), brilliantly testified to the phoniness of the 'from rags to riches' myth; Budd Schulberg, in his novel *What Makes Sammy Run?* (1941), portrayed Sam Glickstein's ruthless rise from poor copy boy to powerful Hollywood tycoon as the pathological case history of a deeply disturbed individual for whom the world is a rat race and who works by the motto that "going through life with a conscience is like driving your car with the brakes on."[66] And Henry Miller, in his programmatically entitled travelogue *The Air-Conditioned Nightmare*

---

64 Washington Irving, *The Sketch-Book of Geoffrey Crayon, Gent.* (New York: G. P. Putnam's Sons, 1894), vol. II, p. 253.
65 In *The Works of Mark Twain*, ed. by Frederick Anderson, vol IX, *A Connecticut Yankee in King Arthur's Court*, ed. by Bernard L. Stein (Berkeley: University of California Press, 1979), p. 439.
66 Budd Schulberg, *What Makes Sammy Run?* (London: Corgi Books, rpt. 1967), p. 56.

(1945), derided "the land of opportunity" as "the land of senseless sweat and struggle" and as "a world suited for monomaniacs obsessed with the idea of progress - but a false progress, a progress which stinks" and contemptuously decreed that there is only "one thing America has to give [...] MONEY."[67] Throughout serious American literature there is a rich vein of severe criticism of the ideas of progress and success, which runs counter to the facile optimism of the popular self-help manuals and the dreams conjured up by political propaganda.

Frontiers, Real and Imaginary

> We wonder whether the great American dream
> Was the singing of locusts out of the grass to the west and the
> West is behind us now:
> The west wind's away from us
> We wonder if the liberty is done:
> The dreaming is finished
> We can't say
> We aren't sure
> Or if there's something different men can dream
> Or if there's something different men can mean by
> Liberty ...
> Or if there's liberty a man can mean that's
> Men: not land
> We wonder
> We don't know
> We're asking
>   Archibald MacLeish, *Land of the Free*[68]

---

67 Henry Miller, *The Air-Conditioned Nightmare* (London: Panther Books, rpt. 1973), pp. 16, 19 and 35.
68 Archibald MacLeish, *Land of the Free* (New York: Da Capo Press, 1977), pp. 83-88. Parts of the poem are reprinted in the EFL-reader *The Frontier and the American West*, ed. by Peter Bruck (Paderborn: Schöningh, 1980), pp. 37-39. - MacLeish wrote this poem in July and August 1937 as a running commentary on a series of photographs taken for the Resettlement Administration, and he called the unusual combination "a book of photographs illustrated by a poem." The photographs and the poem grew out of the trauma of the Depression and the years in which droughts and dust-storms drove people from their land and made them realize that the 'American

When the ancient European idea of the westward movement of civilization was transplanted to America, it was daily corroborated by the reality of life on the new continent. Beginning along the eastern seaboard, the original thirteen states soon began to extend westward, and the frontier, that is, the borderline between the permanently settled areas and the virgin wilderness of the seemingly endless continent, was continuously pushed further to the west. When the legendary frontiersman Daniel Boone led a group of pioneers through the Cumberland Gap in 1775, Kentucky was opened up and the first great natural obstacle, the Appalachian Mountains, was surmounted. When, in the momentous Louisiana Purchase of 1803, Jefferson bought all the French possessions west of the Mississippi from Napoleon and more than doubled the national territory at one go, Meriwether Lewis and William Clark set out on their famous expedition and found a land route to the Pacific.

From decade to decade the frontier advanced further to the west, and an endless stream of pioneers followed in the steps of Cooper's archetypal Leatherstocking and blazed their laborious trails across the vast prairies, inhospitable mountains and desolate deserts. After the disaster at the Alamo, where another famous frontiersman, Davy Crockett, found his death, Texas was annexed in 1845; and in the treaty of Guadelupe-Hidalgo in 1848, Mexico was forced to cede two-fifth of her territory, which later became California, Nevada, Utah and most of Colorado, New Mexico and Arizona. A year earlier Brigham Young had safely brought his Mormons across the great Salt Lake Desert and settled in the Salt Lake Valley, which he praised as a gathering place for Israel. And a year later, President Polk's announcement that gold had been discovered at Sutter's Fort near Sacramento started the California Gold Rush, brought more than 100,000 'Forty-Niners' to the new El Dorado, and changed the dreamy village of Yerba Buena into the flourishing city of San Francisco, which grew from 812 inhabitants in March 1848 to about 25,000 in 1850.

Dream' could no longer be grounded in the possession of land and the self-sufficiency implied by land-ownership.

Soon all over the west the buffalo's and the Indian's trail became the trader's 'trace,' was turned into a road and finally into a bed for a railway line. Indian villages became trading posts, evolved into military forts and then into settlements. Thus what had been the trader's or the miner's frontier became the rancher's and finally the farmer's frontier. The two great inventions of the repeating rifle, which spelt death for the Indians, and the barbed wire, which converted the open ranges into fenced-in fields and signalled the demise of the cowboy, became the emblems of advancing civilization; and the 'Iron Horse,' the puffing locomotive, functioned - to vary the title of Leo Marx's seminal study - as the irresistible machine which destroyed the 'garden' of the west.[69]

As far as the EFL-classroom is concerned, the momentous effect of Joseph Farwell Glidden's invention of barbed wire on life in the Great Plains is usually, and deplorably, neglected. But barbed wire was "an important factor in the decline of the cattle kingdom. It brought about the disappearance of the open range and turned 'range country' into 'big-pasture country.'"[70] Consequently, Frederic Remington's famous painting, *The Fall of the Cowboy*, which appeared in *Harper's Monthly Magazine*, September 1895, as an illustration of Owen Wister's article "The Evolution of the Cow-Puncher" and which shows the newly developed barbed wire and rail gaps as obstacles to free passage over the plains and as inventions which symbolize the end of cowboy life, should be combined with the lyrics of Cole Porter's famous song "Don't Fence Me In." Together these two 'texts' constitute a highly significant mini-unit on the end of the Old and the beginning of the Wild West.

---

[69] See Leo Marx, *The Machine in the Garden: Technology and the Pastoral Ideal in America* (New York: Oxford University Press, 1964), which is still the definitive study of the encroachment of technology upon the 'garden' of the West. - For the earlier dream of a paradisiacal reconciliation between culture and nature to be achieved in the New World, see Jochen Achilles, "Die Paradiesvorstellung von der Versöhnung des Menschen mit der Natur: Literaturgeschichtliche Betrachtungen zu einem Aspekt des amerikanischen Traumes," *Amerikastudien - American Studies*, 35 (1990), 203-218.

[70] *The Reader's Encyclopedia of the American West*, ed. by Howard R. Lamar (New York: Thomas Y. Crowell, 1977), s.v. "barbed wire." - For a detailed account see for example Henry D. McCallum and Frances T. McCallum, *The Wire That Fenced the West* (Norman: University of Oklahoma Press, 1965).

Dream and Nightmare 123

DON'T FENCE ME IN

Wild Cat Kelly, looking mighty pale,
was standing by the sheriff's side
and when that sheriff said: "I'm sending you to jail,"
Wild Cat raised his head and cried:

Wild Cat Kelly, back again in town,
was sitting by his sweetheart's side
and when his sweetheart said: "Come on, let's settle down,"
Wild Cat raised his head and cried:

Refrain:

Oh, give me land, lots of land under starry skies above
DON'T FENCE ME IN
Let me ride thru the wide open country that I love,
DON'T FENCE ME IN.
Let me be by myself in the evening breeze
Listen to the murmur of the cottonwood trees.
Send me off forever, but I ask you please
DON'T FENCE ME IN;
just turn me loose,
Let me straddle my old saddle underneath the western skies.
On my cayuse, let me wander over yonder till I see the mountains rise.
I want to ride to the ridge where the West commences
Gaze at the moon till I lose my senses
Can't look at hobbles and I can't stand fences,
DON'T FENCE ME IN.

Songs by ... Cole Porter (New York: Harms Inc., 1954), pp. 32f.

In the early nineteenth century, American Christians alternately regarded the gradually opening West as a replica of either the 'howling wilderness' which the Pilgrim Fathers had to face when they went ashore in Massachusetts or the 'Garden of Eden' which God had promised his chosen people on the new continent; and for them the central task which the new territory posed was the urgent problem of Christian education. The gospel had to be spread among the rough pioneers to save them from barbarism, and this task was all the more important since more and more Americans believed that their country's destiny would be decided west of the Alleghenies. In 1832, for example, Lyman Beecher, the father of Henry Ward Beecher and Harriet Beecher-Stowe, went from New England to Cincinnati to become the first president of Lane Theological Seminary; and his famous speech *A Plea for the West* represents a widespread attitude. Beecher refers to "the opinion of Edwards, that the millennium would commence in America" and agrees with it because "where shall the central energy be found, and from what nation shall the renovating power go forth," if not from America? Then he argues:

> [...] if this nation is, in the providence of God, destined to lead the way in the moral and political emancipation of the world, it is time she understood her high calling, and were harnessed to the work. [...]
> It's equally plain that the religious and political destiny of our nation is to be decided in the West. There is the territory, and there soon will be the population, the wealth, and the political power. [...] the West is destined to be the great central power of the nation, and under heaven, must affect powerfully the cause of free institutions and the liberty of the world.
> The West is a young empire of mind, and power, and wealth, and free institutions, rushing up to a giant manhood, with a rapidity and a power never before witnessed below the sun. And if she carries with her the elements of her preservation, the experiment will be glorious - the joy of the nation - the joy of the whole earth, as she rises in the majesty of her intelligence and benevolence, and enterprise, for the emancipation of the world.

The success of the Western "experiment," however, will depend on the education and Christianization of the pioneers. Therefore - and this is his major concern - Beecher calls for an "all-pervading influence of schools, and colleges, and seminaries, and pastors, and churches,"[71] and in the rest of his speech he passionately pleads for the necessity of a Protestant Christian education in the West, which alone will make this region capable of joining in the great experiment of American democracy and which is necessary to counterbalance the detrimental influence of the growing number of European Catholic immigrants with their alleged ignorance of democratic responsibilities.

About half a century later, Beecher's concern was still very much alive among Eastern Christians, and when Josiah Strong summed up the state of affairs for the American Home Missionary Society in his bestselling book *Our Country*, he eloquently argued that American destiny would be fulfilled in the West. Modifying another critic's observation that ten years in the history of America equal half a century of European progress into the insight that "ten years in the New West are, in their results, fully equal to half a century east of the Mississippi," he advances his thesis of western supremacy and conjures up the whole history of *translatio imperii* to make his argument more convincing:

> Since prehistoric times, populations have moved steadily westward, as De Tocqueville said, "as if driven by the mighty hand of God." And following their migrations, the course of empire, which Bishop Berkeley sang, has westward taken its way. The world's scepter passed from Persia to Greece, from Greece to Italy, from Italy to Great Britain, and from Great Britain the scepter is to-day departing. It is passing on to "Greater Britain," to our Mighty West, there to remain, for there is no further West; beyond is the Orient. Like the star in the East which guided the three kings with their treasures westward until at length it stood still over the cradle of the young Christ, so the star of empire, rising in the East, has ever beckoned the wealth and power of the nations westward, until to-day it stands still over the cradle of the young empire of the West, to which the nations are bringing their offerings. The West is to-day an infant, but shall one day be a giant, in each of whose limbs shall unite the strength of many nations.

---

71 Lyman Beecher, *A Plea for the West* (Cincinnati: Truman and Smith, 2nd ed., 1835); here quoted from the partial reprint in *God's New Israel: Religious Interpretations of American Destiny*, ed. Conrad Cherry (Englewood Cliffs, New Jersey: Prentice-Hall, 1971), pp. 119-127; here pp. 120f.

In order to alert his countrymen to the harmful influences which might taint the coming glory of the West, Strong then discusses in great detail the perils which have to be warded off, namely, unrestrained immigration of unwanted elements, the spread of 'Romanism' as a denomination in conflict with the fundamental principles of American government, the threat of 'Romanism' and Secularism to the public schools as prime agencies of Americanization, the vile teachings of Mormonism, the perils of intemperance, the threat of socialism, the dangers of 'Mammonism,' and the detrimental influence of cities upon morals and religion. Since, as Strong pervasively argues, the as yet unformed society of the West is "peculiarly exposed" to all these dangers and since it is the West "which holds the key to the nation's future," he passionately pleads for money for the Home Missionary Society to bring the right morals and the true Christianity to the West.[72]

Whereas Lyman Beecher and Josiah Strong concentrated on the religious implications of western expansion, others simply were concerned with the unheard-of opportunities provided by the vast stretches of available land. One year after Beecher's speech was published, the journalist Horace Greeley sounded the battlecry of the westward movement most clearly when, in the editorial for August 25, 1836, in his weekly journal *The New Yorker*, he stated:

> If any young man is about to commence the world, with little in his circumstances to prepossess him in favor of one section more than another, we say to him, publicly and privately, Go to the West; there your capacities are sure to be appreciated, and your industry and energy rewarded. Those who possess facilities for doing well where they are, should never remove to a strange country in the hope of doing better; but those who emigrate at all ought to go where there is room for them, and where they will not be less than welcome. We have so much faith in this doctrine that we shall most certainly put it in practice if it shall ever become advisable to change our location. The West is the land of promise and of hope: let all who are else hopeless, turn their eyes and, when able, their steps toward it.[73]

---

72 Josiah Strong, *Our Country: Its Possible Future and Its Present Crisis*, pp. 18, 39f., 192, and 194.
73 This is the most famous of Greeley's many editorials which helped to pave the way for the *Homestead Act* of 1862. It is reprinted in *The Frontier and the American West*, pp. 27-29; here p. 27f.

Greeley's injunction has become proverbial in the form 'Go west, young man,' and it is interesting to note that as late as 1984 Lee Iacocca, the former president of Ford and legendary 'saviour' of Chrysler, uses it in his record-breaking bestseller *Iacocca: An Autobiography* to put his personal success story in a historical context. There he reports that after finishing his university studies he had successfully applied for a job with Ford and that, after an all-night railway journey he arrived, like a latter-day Ben Franklin, in unfamiliar Detroit with "a duffel bag on my shoulder and fifty bucks in my pocket." Since he had to travel on to the Ford Headquarters, he asked a stranger for the way to Dearborn and got the answer "Go west, young man - go west about ten miles!"[74]

The conquering of the west was of course anything but a pure success story, and the greatest tragedy was certainly the systematic displacement and finally the almost total extermination of the Indians. But the price in white lives was also high. Numerous parties of hopeful settlers - as, for example, the ill-starred Donner Party, half of whose members starved to death in the Sierra Nevada - never reached their destination; and the famous saying "In God we trusted, in Kansas we busted" or the well-known song about "Starving to Death on My Government Claim" are telling comments on the less fortunate consequences of the *Homestead Act* of 1862.

Naturally, there was to come a time when the available land would be used up and when the open frontier would have to be declared closed. It was on May 10, 1869, in the little wilderness settlement of Promontory Point in Utah that a silver sledge drove a golden nail into a railroad tie and that an exultant voice announced over the telegraph, "The last rail is laid! The last spike is driven! The Pacific Railroad is completed!" After many years of unbelievably hard work, 1,775 miles of rails across endless prairies and through steep mountains were laid, the Union Pacific and the Central Pacific met, the first transcontinental railroad was completed, and henceforth one could travel in relative ease and luxury from coast to coast. The replacement of the waggon trail and the stagecoach by the Pullman car was a decisive step in the

---

74 Lee Iacocca, *Iacocca: An Autobiography* (Toronto: Bantam Books, rpt. 1988), p. 27.

This famous and widely reprinted photograph was taken by Colonel Charles Savage on May 10, 1869 at Promontory Point, Utah, where the Central Pacific's *Jupiter* and the Union Pacific's 119 met and where the completion of the transcontinental railroad was celebrated.

Dream and Nightmare

conquest of the west, and in 1890 the Superintendent of the Census could declare the frontier closed.[75]

Three years later, an unknown young historian named Frederick Jackson Turner read a paper on "The Significance of the Frontier in American History" before the American Historical Association in Chicago and inaugurated a new interpretation of the recently closed frontier, which he defined as "the meeting point between savagery and civilization," when he stated:

> American social development has been continually beginning over again on the frontier. This perennial rebirth, this fluidity of American life, this expansion westward with its new opportunities, its continuous touch with the simplicity of primitive society, furnish the forces dominating American character. The true point of view in the history of this nation is not the Atlantic coast, it is the Great West.

And he argued that the frontier had not only shaped American history but also decisively helped to form the American national character:

> [...] to the frontier the American intellect owes its striking characteristics. That coarseness and strength combined with acuteness and inquisitiveness, that practical, inventive turn of mind, quick to find expedients, that masterful grasp of material things, lacking in the artistic but powerful to effect great ends, that restless, nervous energy, that dominant individualism, working for good and for evil, and withal

---

[75] The standard book on the West in American intellectual history is still Henry Nash Smith, *Virgin Land: The American West as Symbol and Myth* (Cambridge, Mass.: Harvard University Press, 1950); two important studies of the 'frontier' in American literature are Edwin Fussell, *Frontier: American Literature and the American West* (Princeton, N.J.: Princeton University Press, 1965), which analyses the influence of the West in the works of Cooper, Hawthorne, Poe, Thoreau, Melville, and Whitman; and Richard Slotkin, *Regeneration Through Violence: The Mythology of the American Frontier, 1600 - 1860* (Middletown, Conn.: Wesleyan University Press, 1973), which is a comprehensive study of the frontier in American literature, with the accent on the motif of violence. - An informative pocketbook anthology of both fictional and expository texts about the West is *Looking Far West: The Search for the American West in History, Myth, and Literature*, ed. by Frank Bergon and Zeese Papanikolas (New York: New American Library, 1978). - The indispensable reference guide on the history, literature and film of the West is *The Reader's Encyclopedia of the American West*. - Among more recent publications, I found Robert V. Hine, *The American West: An Interpretive History* (Glenview, Ill., and London: Scott, Foresman and Company, 2nd ed., 1984); and Robert G. Athearn, *The Mythic West in Twentieth-Century America* (Lawrence: University Press of Kansas, 1986) especially helpful.

that buoyancy and exuberance which comes with freedom, these are traits of the frontier, or traits called out elsewhere because of the existence of the frontier. Since the days when the fleet of Columbus sailed into the waters of the New World, America has been another name for opportunity, and the people of the United States have taken their tone from the incessant expansion which has not only been open but has even been forced upon them.[76]

The Turner-thesis, as influential and as controversial as Max Weber's thesis about the affinities between Calvinism and capitalism, has had a considerable influence on American historiography, and the major arguments advanced against it are that, in concentrating exclusively on the frontier, it neglects such important factors as Southern agrarianism or Eastern capitalism, that its concept of a 'composite nationality' wrongly presupposes that the same environment will shape all people in the same way, and that American democracy is not born from scratch on the frontier but is deeply indebted to European 'germs.' Here the many controversies surrounding Turner's thesis cannot be discussed in detail,[77] but it is important to point out that when the real Old West went out of existence the imaginary Wild West came into being, and a mythical world of the mind began to replace a bygone world of reality. Thus, at least with regard to the tenacity of the imaginary west with its roaming cowboys, its sinister bandits, its law-enforcing marshals and its strict code of honour Turner's claim that "to the frontier the American intellect owes its striking characteristics" seems to be substantiated.

That the myth of the Wild West is a centrally important aspect of the 'American Dream' can be shown by a brief look at three exemplary figures. In 1880 a young man from a distinguished family, who had almost died of asthma, graduated from Harvard and made some first attempts at a political career. But soon he withdrew to his farm in the Dakota Badlands, where he led the rough life of a cowboy and began writing his historical study *The Winning of the West* (1889-96). Back in

---

76 Frederick Jackson Turner, "The Significance of the Frontier in American History," in *An American Primer*, pp. 542-570; here pp. 545 and 566f.
77 See, for example, Ray Allen Billington, *Westward Expansion: A History of the American Frontier* (New York: Macmillan, 1949), chapter XI; and *The Frontier Thesis: Valid Interpretation of American History?* ed. by Ray Allen Billington (Huntington, N.Y.: R. E. Krieger, 1977).

New York, he quickly climbed the ladder of political success, and when in 1898 the Spanish-American War broke out, he organized the famous Rough Riders, who gained fame when they seized San Juan Hill in Cuba. In 1901, upon McKinley's assassination, this man became the 26th President of the United States. His name was Theodore Roosevelt, he dreamed of a rebirth of the revolutionary American virtues on the vast prairies of the open west, and his famous political maxim 'Speak softly and carry a big stick' is reminiscent of the Westerner's proverbial taciturnity and his solution of problems by means of personal strength and direct action. These associations are very obvious in a contemporary cartoon by Horace Taylor. It appeared on October 30, 1899 on the title page of *The Verdict* and depicted the presidential candidate Theodore Roosevelt with Stetson hat and bandanna, lasso and pistol. By showing him riding recklessly towards political success, the cartoon quite clearly implied that Roosevelt's impulsive political style was thought to reflect the mentality of the cowboy.

Another young Easterner, this time a student at the Yale School of Fine Arts, also left the effete East for a period of strenuous adventure in Kansas, and when he came back turned into the most famous illustrator of western life. One of the earliest of his cowboy pictures, "In from the Night Herd," appeared in *Harper's Weekly* on October 9, 1886, and it is the forerunner of almost 3,000 paintings and drawings, in which he captured Indians and cowboys in spirited action. His name was Frederic Remington. The third, a Harvard graduate in music named Owen Wister and a fellow-student and friend of Roosevelt, suffered a nervous breakdown and travelled west on his doctor's orders to recuperate in the healthy atmosphere of a Wyoming cattle ranch. Coming back, he settled down as a lawyer in Philadelphia, and in 1902 he published a novel entitled *The Virginian: A Horseman of the Plains*, which became an instant success. This novel, dedicated to Roosevelt, is the first 'cowboy novel' and thus the ancestor of thousands of western tales, Hollywood westerns and TV serials. That Roosevelt incorporated the western notions of manliness, self-reliance and strength into his political credo; that Remington made the daily life of the West his artistic subject; that Wister invented his heroic southern-born cowboy who married a northern schoolmarm from Vermont and established law and order on the prairies of the West;

TEDDY TO THE RESCUE OF REPUBLICANISM!

Dream and Nightmare

and that all three did so at a time when the real Old West was on the point of vanishing and when the traditional East was undergoing basic changes brought about by the new corporate structures bred by industrialization and by the millions of 'new immigrants' milling in the slums of the rapidly growing cities, shows that these men dreamt the same dream,[78] summed up in 1930 by Archibald MacLeish in the hymnic statement that "America is West [...] A shining thing in the mind."[79] Only in the West could the Virginian and Molly Stark be united in matrimony and thus heal the rift between North and South which the Civil War had caused; only in the West, in an open and simple land devoid of the complexities of industrial trusts and the misery of urban slums, could the old revolutionary virtues of Virginia and Vermont resurface; only in the West could good and bad be easily distinguished; and only in the West could a man still be a man.

This dream, which came into being when the reality it glorified went out of existence, has been kept alive by the Gene Autreys and the Ken Maynards, the Paul Newmans and the John Waynes, and it combines the ideals of mobility and simplicity, of life in accordance with a majestic landscape and of freedom from the fetters of advanced civilization. It presents a world where there are no complex shades of gray but where there is only black or white and where one lives according to a simple code of honour, relies on the precision of one's gun and - perhaps most important - where man can be free of the 'civilizing' influence of woman.[80]

---

78 See G. Edward White, *The Eastern Establishment and the Western Experience: The West of Frederic Remington, Theodore Roosevelt, and Owen Wister* (New Haven and London: Yale University Press, 1968).
79 Archibald MacLeish, "American Letter," in *The Collected Poems of Archibald MacLeish* (Boston: Houghton Mifflin, no date [1962]), p. 73.
80 Among the growing number of books on the western I would recommend: John G. Cawelti, *The Six-Gun Mystique* (Bowling Green, Ohio: Bowling Green University Popular Press, no date [1971]), an attempt at defining the formula of the western, with nine useful appendices on western novels, films, directors, etc.; John G. Cawelti, *Adventure, Mystery, and Romance: Formula Stories as Art and Popular Culture* (Chicago and London: University of Chicago Press, 1976), with an excellent chapter on the history of the western; Jenni Calder, *There Must Be a Lone Ranger: The Myth and Reality of the American Wild West* (London: Sphere Books, 1976), an informative investigation of the myth of the West; Charles Leland Sonnichsen, *From Hopalong to Hud* (College Station and London: Texas A&M University Press, 1978); and Christine Bold, *Selling the Wild West: Popular Western Fiction 1860 to 1960* (Bloomington: Indiana University Press, 1987). - Two good collections of articles are *Focus on the*

In his article on "The Evolution of the Cow-Puncher," Owen Wister compares the cowboy to the medieval knight-errant when he says that "in personal daring and in skill as to the horse, the knight and the cowboy are nothing but the same Saxon of different environments" and when he rhapsodizes that "no hoof in Sir Thomas Malory shakes the crumbling plains with quadruped sound more valiant than the galloping that has echoed from the Rio Grande to the Big Horn Mountains."[81] Such an analogy points to the simplicity of the western world view in which the unfathomable complexity of modern life is replaced by the simple dichotomy between the 'goodies' and the 'baddies.' But when *Time* celebrates the western as "an allegory of freedom, a memory and a vision of the deepest meaning of America"[82] and Fishwick argues that "the cowboy symbol quickens young America's belief in personal guts, integrity, and ingenuity, and the movies about him are a never-ending course in citizenship and the American way of life,"[83] one has to add that the escapist vision also reveals a decidedly adolescent cast of mind. The repercussions of the cowboy myth on contemporary everyday existence are not limited to an evocation of pastoral landscapes and manly resourcefulness as conjured up in the Marlboro advertisements. They also include the highly controversial issue of the private possession of guns and the resulting problems of violence and self-justice, and they have contributed to an attitude which was wittily exposed by the Swedish critic Harry Schein, when he laconically declared that the famous western *High Noon* is "the most honest explanation of American foreign policy."[84]

Western, ed. by Jack Nachbar (Englewood Cliffs, N.J.: Prentice-Hall, 1974); and *The Western: A Collection of Critical Essays*, ed. by James K. Folsom (Englewood Cliffs, N.J.: Prentice-Hall, 1979).

81 Owen Wister, "The Evolution of the Cow-Puncher," in *The Writings of Owen Wister* (New York: Macmillan, 1928), vol. VI, pp. xix-li; here p. xxvii. - An excellent introduction to the real life of the cowboy is provided by the catalogue of the 1983 exhibition at the Library of Congress: Lonn Taylor and Ingrid Maar, *The American Cowboy* (Washington: Library of Congress, 1983), a large-format book which includes a wealth of original material, well-researched interpretive essays, and a helpful bibliography.
82 "Westerns: The Six-Gun Galahad," *Time*, March 30, 1959, pp. 36-43; here p. 43.
83 Marshall W. Fishwick, "The Cowboy: America's Contribution to the World's Mythology," *Western Folklore*, 11 (April 1952), 77-92; here p. 92.
84 Harry Schein, "The Olympian Cowboy" [transl. from the Swedish by Ida M. Alcock], *The American Scholar*, 24 (1955), 309-320, here p. 316.

While the vanished West is immortalized by the myth of the cowboy, which expresses the traditional values, ethics and dreams of a large part of white America, the closed geographical frontier was soon resurrected as a newly opened social frontier, namely, the 'open frontier of opportunity.' Thus, the challenge implicit in crossing the rim of settlement and conquering an unknown territory was kept alive; latent energies were rechannelled; and the pioneer moving westward across an open continent was replaced by the self-made man moving upward through the strata of an open society.[85] But there came a time when this frontier, too, was closed, when the social structure solidified, and when Horatio Alger's 'from rags to riches' formula and its Social Darwinist mutations lost their original appeal. A new challenge, a new frontier was needed, and it was an ingenious stroke of President John F. Kennedy when, on July 15, 1960 in Los Angeles, he picked up the myth of the frontier and declared in his nomination acceptance speech:

> [...] I stand tonight facing west on what was once the last frontier. From the lands that stretch 3,000 miles behind me, the pioneers of old gave up their safety, their comfort and sometimes their lives to build a new world here in the West. [...]
> Today some would say that those struggles are all over, that all the horizons have been explored, that all the battles have been won, that there is no longer an American frontier.
> But I trust that no one in this vast assemblage will agree with those sentiments. For the problems are not all solved and the battles are not all won, and we stand today on the edge of a new frontier - the frontier of the 1960s, a frontier of unknown opportunities and perils, a frontier of unfulfilled hopes and threats.
> [...]
> But I tell you the new frontier is here, whether we seek it or not. Beyond that frontier are uncharted areas of science and space, unsolved problems of peace and war, unconquered pockets of ignorance and prejudice, unanswered questions of poverty and surplus. [...][86]

This was an electrifying promise that the cold-war inertia would be replaced by vigorous action and adventure, that the old virtues of

---

85 See Richard Slotkin, *The Fatal Environment: The Myth of the Frontier in the Age of Industrialization, 1800 - 1890* (Middletown, Conn. : Wesleyan University Press, 1985).
86 Quoted from *U.S. News & World Report*, July 25, 1960, pp. 100-102; here p. 102. - Excerpts are reprinted in the EFL-reader *American Dreams, American Nightmares*, pp. 100f.

Dream and Nightmare

pioneer days would be revived for the solution of contemporary problems. And Kennedy went even further when he specified the frontier image by setting the nation the task of facing the challenge of Russian cosmonauts and of conquering the 'open frontier of space.' In this context it turns out to be no accident that American rockets and space capsules frequently bear names which refer to the conquering of the West: *Ranger, Eagle, Intrepid, Pioneer, Columbia, Challenger.*

With regard to literature, the western hero who helps frontier settlers to survive on the precarious borderline between civilization and savagery by protecting them from the forces of evil and by exterminating the 'baddies,' soon exchanges his horse for a car and, in the new guise of big-city sleuth, begins to roam the dangerous streets and alleys of the nocturnal city instead of riding across the lonely stretches of desert and prairie. Raymond Chandler's and Dashiell Hammett's 'hard-boiled' private eyes Philip Marlowe and Sam Spade are outstanding examples of this mutation, and at present it is especially Elmore Leonard who is keeping up this tradition. This writer, who began his career with such offbeat Westerns as *Hombre*, now writes big-city crime novels patterned on the formulas of the classic Western.

In *City Primeval* (1980), for example, which bears the programmatic subtitle *High Noon in Detroit*, both the protagonist, the self-assured city cop Raymond Cruz, and his immoral antagonist, the multiple murderer Clement Mansell, who is known as the Oklahoma Wildman and reminds the reader of Billy the Kid, come across as *alter egos* locked in a deadly personal battle to be fought according to some ancient code. The observation that Mansell was "born somewhere between fifty and one hundred years too late" (199),[87] the frequent references to Wyatt Earp (14) and Buck Rogers (38), to "the no-bullshit Old West lawman" (15), to films like *The Gunfighter* (33) and to such prominent Western actors as John Wayne (15), Clint Eastwood (15) and Gregory Peck (33) establish a net of parallels between the 'Wild West' and the metropolitan 'frontier,' and a female lawyer who acts as the contemporary version of the educated schoolmarm drives home the point when she describes the conflict between policeman and criminal as "Mano a mano.

---

87 All page numbers in brackets refer to Elmore Leonard, *City Primeval* (Harmondsworth: Penguin Books, 1988).

No - more like High Noon. Gunfight at the O. K. Corral. You have to go back a hundred years and out west to find an analogy" (139). To make things even more obvious, the Anglo-Saxon code of the cowboy is contrasted with the Albanian concept of the vendetta which leaves no room for fair play. In the final shootout, however, it becomes obvious that the code of the West is no longer operative in the crime-ridden metropolis because the detective, having carefully staged a duel with his antagonist, kills him in cold blood.

After the metropolitan 'frontier,' which the mayor of New York in Tom Wolfe's *The Bonfire of the Vanities* (1987) envisages as a pattern of precisely defined "frontiers" between the First World of Manhattan and "the Third World" (13)[88] of Harlem and the Bronx, at which he keeps "his Custer's command post" (14), American literature develops still another 'frontier' by projecting, like John F. Kennedy in his nomination acceptance speech, the 'Wild West' into outer space. One need only read a book like Ray Bradbury's *The Martian Chronicles* (1950) to realize that a large part of American science fiction depicts the imaginary exploration and exploitation of alien planets and galaxies as if they were variations of the Old West with its arid plains, its sun-drenched deserts, its towering mountains, and its green valleys. Against such a well-established and symbolically charged background, the traditional Indian companion of the Anglo-Saxon Western hero turns into a knowledgeable extraterrestrial 'other' such as Spock in *Star Trek*; and the unbelievable success of George Lucas' *Star Wars* is explained by the fact that Luke Skywalker's galactic adventures are nothing but a variation upon the western myth of the lone hero's single-handed combat with the forces of evil.

---

88 All page numbers in brackets refer to Tom Wolfe, *The Bonfire of the Vanities* (London: Pan Books, 1988).

Manifest Destiny:
From Continentalism to Imperialism

> And of all our race He has marked the American people as His chosen nation to finally lead in the regeneration of the world.
> Senator Albert J. Beveridge in the United States Senate on January 9, 1900[89]

The process of secularization not only changed the idea of success from an indication of man's spiritual salvation into a concept denoting the self-serving quest for money and status; it not only contributed to the mutations of the idea of progress from a millennial belief in man's advancement toward God to the enlightened belief in man's innate perfectibility and then into the modern belief in the ever greater achievements of science and technology; but it also helped to change the early Puritan settlers' conviction that America was chosen by God to supersede a depraved and effete Europe into the nineteenth-century political claim that America was meant to rule the world. When the westward movement came to a halt at the Pacific coast, it was only natural to look beyond the horizon towards other lands to be cultivated, liberated and Christianized. H. Richard Niebuhr sums up this shift in the American interpretation of her election when he says: "The old idea of American Christians as a chosen people who had been called to a special task was turned into the notion of a chosen nation especially favored [...]. As the nineteenth century went on, the note of divine favoritism was increasingly sounded."[90]

In an article by John L. O'Sullivan in the *Democratic Review* of 1839, the new expansionist implications of American self-understanding became quite obvious when he said that "the far-reaching, the boundless future will be the era of American greatness. In its magnificent domain of space and time, the nation of many nations is destined to manifest to mankind the excellence of divine principles," and when he

---

89 Here quoted from Albert K. Weinberg, *Manifest Destiny: A Study of Nationalistic Expansionism in American History* (Chicago: Quadrangle Books, no date [originally 1935]), p. 308.
90 H. Richard Niebuhr, *The Kingdom of God in America* (Chicago and New York: Willett, Clark & Company, 1937), p. 179.

continued that "its floor shall be a hemisphere."[91] It was a few years later, with regard to the Texas question, that the same writer provided the new watchword of expansionism. In the July 1845 issue of the *Democratic Review* he declared all legal questions to be of secondary importance and claimed continental dominion for the U.S.A. by virtue of her "manifest destiny":

> Why, were other reasons wanting, in favor of now elevating this question of the reception of Texas into the Union, out of the lower region of our past party dissensions, up to its proper level of a high and broad nationality, it surely is to be found, found abundantly, in the manner in which other nations have undertaken to intrude themselves into it, between us and the proper parties to the case, in a spirit of hostile interference against us, for the avowed object of thwarting our policy and hampering our power, limiting our greatness and checking the fulfilment of our manifest destiny to overspread the continent allotted by Providence for the free development of our yearly multiplying millions.[92]

The new concept of America's "manifest destiny" is most revealingly illustrated in John Gast's 1872 painting of the same title. This famous painting depicts the irresistible westward progress of civilization, with the cowboy on horseback, the gold-digger, the pioneer in his covered waggon, the stagecoach, and the transcontinental railroad driving both the Indian and the buffalo ever further west, and with the 'goddess' of civilization sailing benevolently over the prairies. The notion of 'manifest destiny' was soon applied to the Oregon question as well, and it became the clarion call for a dogma which combined the older theological idea of election with a theory which Weinberg defines as "geographical destination"[93] - America needed the whole continent to fulfil her duty -, with a belief in the superiority of the

---

[91] John L. O'Sullivan, "The Great Nation of Futurity;" here quoted from the reprint in *Manifest Destiny*, ed. by Norman A. Graebner, p. 17.

[92] "Annexation," *Democratic Review*, 17 (1845), 5. Here quoted from Albert K. Weinberg, *Manifest Destiny: A Study of Nationalistic Expansionism in American History*, p. 112. - The article is unsigned, but Julius W. Pratt, "The Origin of 'Manifest Destiny,'" *American Historical Review*, 32 (1927), 795-798, has attributed it, on grounds of internal evidence, to John L. O'Sullivan, the editor of the *Democratic Review* and the *New York Morning News*.

[93] See Albert K. Weinberg, *op. cit.*, chapter II, "Geographical Predestination." - See also Frederick Merk, *Manifest Destiny and Mission in American History* (New York: Alfred A. Knopf, 1963).

Dream and Nightmare

When the New York firm of George A. Crofutt published Gast's picture as a 12 x 16 chromolithograph for $ 10, the 'chromo' bore this lengthy explanation of the painting's symbolism on the reverse side:

American Progress!
Subject, *The United States of America*

This rich and wonderful country - the progress of which at the present time, is the wonder of the old world - was, until recently, inhabited exclusively by the lurking savage and wild beasts of prey. If the rapid progress of the "Great West" has surprised our people, what will those of other countries think of the *"Far* West," which is destined, at an early day, to be the vast granary, as it is now the great treasure chamber of our country? How this change has been wrought, and by whom, is illustrated by our Chromo,
"American Progress."

Purely National in design, this beautiful painting represents the United States' portion of the American continent in its beauty and variety, from the Atlantic to the Pacific Ocean, illustrating at a glance the grand drama of Progress in the civilization, settlement and history of our own happy land.

In the foreground the central and principal figure, a beautiful and charming Female, is floating Westward through the air bearing on her forehead the "Star of Empire." She has left the cities of the East far behind, crossed the Alleghanies and the "Father of Waters," and still her march is Westward. In her right hand she carries a book - Common schools - the emblem of Education and the testimonial of our National enlightenment, while with the left hand she unfolds and stretches the slender wires of the Telegraph, that are to flash intelligence throughout the land. On the right of the picture is a city, steamships, manufactories, schools and churches, over which beams of light are streaming and filling the air - indicative of civilization. The general tone of the picture on the left declares darkness, waste and confusion. From the city proceed the three great continental lines of railway, passing the frontier settler's rude cabin, and extending toward the Western Ocean. Next to these are the transportation wagons, overland stage, hunters, gold seekers, pony express, the pioneer emigrant and the war-dance of the "noble red man." Fleeing from "Progress," and towards the Pacific, which shows itself on the left of the picture beyond the snow-capped summits of the Sierra Nevadas, are the Indians, buffaloes, wild horses, bears, and other game, moving Westward, ever Westward the Indians with their squaws, papooses, and "pony lodges," turn their despairing faces towards, as they flee from the presence of, the wonderous vision. The "Star" is *too much for them.*

What American man, woman or child does not feel a heartthrob of exultation as they think of the glorious achievements of *Progress* since the landing of the Pilgrim Fathers, on staunch old Plymouth Rock! What home, from the miner's humble cabin to the stately marble mansion of the capitalist, should be without this *Great* National Picture, which illustrates in the most artistic manner all the gigantic results of American Brains and Hands! Who would not have such a beautiful token to remind them of our country's grandeur and enterprise which have caused the mighty wilderness to blossom like the rose!!! One of the best art critics has pronounced this picture *"one of the grandest conceptions of the age."*

American form of government - America was destined to bring liberty and equality to the world -, and with a conviction that the Anglo-Saxons were of superior racial stock - the Congregational minister Josiah Strong in his 1885 bestseller *Our Country* stated that "the Anglo-Saxon is the representative of two great ideas," namely, that of "civil liberty" and that of "a pure *spiritual* Christianity," and expressed his confidence that "on this continent God is training the Anglo-Saxon race for its mission."[94] Thus, theological, geographical, political and racial ideas combined to change the old idea of American destiny, in which the ultimate reason for God's selection remained a divine mystery, into a new variation in which America was chosen for clear or *manifest* reasons. It need hardly be added that this new idea provided a welcome justification for the young world power's imperialistic and hegemonic claims, and one example must suffice to demonstrate the political consequences of this new sense of mission.

O'Sullivan, in 1845, had still been content with demanding that it was "our manifest destiny to overspread the continent allotted by Providence for the free development of our yearly multiplying millions." A contemporary young reporter named Walter Whitman, who would later write free verse, had chimed in with idealistic editorials for the Brooklyn *Eagle* about the sacred right of 'Yankeedoodledom,' and Herman Melville, in his semi-autobigraphical novel *White-Jacket* (1850), had combined the Puritans' millenarian view of history with the contemporary enthusiasm for westward pioneering and the belief in American democracy into a hymnic observation, which also implies a reference to 1 Peter 2: 9.

> Escaped from the house of bondage, Israel of old did not follow after the ways of the Egyptians. To her was given an express dispensation; to her were given new things under the sun. And we Americans are the peculiar, chosen people - the Israel of our time; we bear the ark of the liberties of the world. Seventy years ago we escaped from thrall; and, besides our first birth-right - embracing one continent of earth - God has given to us, for a future inheritance, the broad domains of the political pagans, that shall yet come and lie down under the shade of our ark, without bloody hands being lifted. God has predestinated, mankind expects, great things from our race; and great things we feel

---

94 Josiah Strong, *Our Country: Its Possible Future and Its Present Crisis*, pp. 200, 201, and 216.

in our souls. The rest of the nations must soon be in our rear. We are the pioneers of the world; the advance-guard, sent on through the wilderness of untried things, to break a new path in the New World that is ours.[95]

That Melville here expressed a conviction that was widely shared became quite obvious a decade after *White-Jacket*. In 1861, the German-born painter Emanuel Leutze, who had learned his craft at the Royal Academy in Düsseldorf, was commissioned by the U.S. Congress to decorate the wall of the west staircase of the House of Representatives, and he set out to paint a grandiose twenty by thirty feet mural that was to illustrate the settlement of the Far West and to bear the title *Westward the Course of Empire Takes Its Way*, but that is also known as *Westward Ho!*. In 1862, Leutze, who had gone West to sketch the Rocky Mountains and experience overland travel and who had made two elaborate studies (one with oil on canvas, which is reproduced on p. 146), finished his monumental painting, which, in his own words, was meant

> to represent as near and truthfully as the artist was able the grand peaceful conquest of the great west [...] Without a wish to date or localize, or to represent a particular event, it is intended to give in a condensed form a picture of western emigration, the conquest of the Pacific slope [...].[96]

Leutze quite obviously considered the conquest of the West not to be the result of diplomatic negotiations or military victories, but understood it as the achievement of America's common people. In view of the complexity of the theme, he was not content with a single picture, but in his composite visualization of Berkeley's notion he combined a central tableau showing, again in his own words, "a party of Emigrants hav[ing] arrived near sunset on the *divide* (watershed) from whence they have the first view of the pacific slope, their 'promised land' 'Eldorado,' having passed the troubles of the plains, 'The valley

---

95 Herman Melville, *White-Jacket; or, The World in a Man-of-War*, ed. by Harrison Hayford, Hershel Parker, and G. Thomas Tanselle, in *The Writings of Herman Melville*, vol. V (Evanston and Chicago: Northwestern University Press and Newberry Library, 1970), pp. 150f.
96 All quotations are from Leutze's notes as published in Justin G. Turner, "Emanuel Leutze's Mural *Westward the Course of Empire Takes Its Way*," *Manuscripts*, 18, No. 2 (September 1966), 4-16.

of darkness' &c.," with a realistic landscape picture that serves as the predella along the bottom and shows San Francisco Bay seen from the Golden Gate. In his notes, Leutze quotes the two relevant lines from Berkeley's poem and comments that "the drama of the Pacific ocean closes our Emigration to the West," and in view of the tradition set in motion by Berkeley's poem, the Golden Gate turns out to be an especially adequate choice, since it conjures up a western Eldorado, a 'golden land' for a new 'golden age.' Across the top Leutze put an elaborate border, in the center of which a bald eagle (the U.S. heraldic bird) holds an unfurling scroll on which is written "Westward the Course of Empire Takes Its Way," while Indians attempt to escape from the scroll and a maze of winding plant tendrils. Two frames to the right and the left concatenate iconographical motifs from both classical and Biblical literature, which Leutze's notes describe as "a playful introduction from earlier history as a prelude to the subject of the large picture" and which constitute a kind of typology of westward movement. Finally, in the right and the left bottom corners, there are two medaillion portraits of Daniel Boone, the archetypal frontiersman, and of William Clark, the co-commander of the Lewis and Clark expedition (1803-1806) that explored a land route to the Pacific. Leutze's painting, then, combines a quasi-realistic picture of a pioneer group on their way West with diverse iconographical motifs into an allegorically charged depiction of the 'westward course of empire,' and the religious overtones make it quite obvious that

> like the expansionists of the 1840s, Leutze saw westward emigration as a divinely impelled phenomenon. The program of his painting reiterates a theme familiar from an earlier decade: the American people, a new Israel, fulfilling their historical and moral destiny by entering their Promised Land in the West.[97]

Thus, the mural elevates the related notions of *translatio imperii* and 'manifest destiny' into recurring elements of world history by not only relating the contemporary settlement of the American West to the geographical extension of the huge continent (with San Francisco as the westernmost part) and to such 'timeless' icons of peace and progress as the dove with a branch and the raven with manna, but by also

---

97 Dawn Glanz, *How the West Was Drawn: American Art and the Settling of the Frontier* (Ann Arbor: UMI Research Press, 1982), p. 79.

Dream and Nightmare

"WESTWARD THE COURSE OF EMPIRE TAKES ITS WAY" WITH McCORMICK REAPERS IN THE VAN.

seeing it as a repetition of a continually recurring process that extends from classical antiquity (Hercules and the Argonauts) and Biblical history (Moses, the spies of Eshcoll, and the Three Magi) through modern European history (Columbus) to American national history (the Lewis and Clark expedition and Daniel Boone).

Leutze's picture became so well known that at some time in the second half of the nineteenth century the producers of McCormick Reapers appropriated it, cut away the allegorical frame, erased a few of the details of the centerpiece to create space for their product and thus turned the painting into an advertisement for an agricultural implement that would play a central role in the development of midwestern farming. They gave the new picture the title "'Westward the Course of Empire Takes Its Way' with McCormick Reapers in the Van," and thus changed the vision of the Irish philosopher and the German painter into an advertising slogan that takes the westward movement for granted and praises a particular product as one of its prerequisites. And the immense popularity of this concept is also illustrated by the famous and often anthologized Currier & Ives engraving of 1868, which presents the whole range of relevant motifs under the triumphant title "Across the Continent."

Later, however, the notion of 'manifest destiny' would acquire new connotations, and on January 9, 1900, when the Senate was still considering the future of the Philippines ceded by the beaten Spain, Senator Albert J. Beveridge of Indiana delivered a startling speech which epitomized a new imperialism:

> God has not been preparing the English-speaking and Teutonic peoples for a thousand years for nothing but vain and idle self-contemplation and self-admiration. No. He made us master-organizers of the world to establish system where chaos reigns. [...] He has marked the American people as His chosen nation to finally lead in the redemption of the world.[98]

---

98 Quoted in Ernest Lee Tuveson, *Redeemer Nation: The Idea of America's Millennial Role* (Chicago and London: University of Chicago Press, 1968), p. vii.

Dream and Nightmare

On September 25 of the same year, in a Republican campaign speech in Chicago, Senator Beveridge took up this line of thought and declared that America was

> [...] the "empire" of which the prophetic voice declared "Westward the Star of Empire takes its Way" - the star of the empire of liberty and law, of commerce and communication, of social order and the Gospel of our Lord - the star of the empire of the civilization of the world. Westward *that* star of empire takes its course.[99]

Thus the historiographic vision of a Bishop Berkeley became the political maxim of Senator Beveridge; a mythic ingredient of the ancient dream dreamt by an eighteenth-century Irish philosopher who had envisaged America as a refuge for the arts and the home of a new golden age was used as a poetic endorsement of nineteenth-century American imperialism justifying its power politics by recourse to some God-given 'manifest destiny.'

This is not the place to follow in detail the further development of the concept through the ensuing alterations between missionary interventionism and disappointed isolationism, but the few examples provided will warrant the observation that whoever wants to understand the American engagement in Vietnam, the Middle East or Grenada needs to know about the unique mixture of America's belief in her spiritual election and moral superiority on the one hand and straight American *Realpolitik* on the other, between Walt Whitman's romantic "Passage to India" of 1871 with its hymnic praise of

> [...], thou born America,
> For purpose vast, man's long probation fill'd,
> Thou rondure of the world at last accomplish'd[100]

and Captain Alfred T. Mahan's expansionistic *Interest of America in Sea Power* of 1897 with its call for a strong navy.

---

99 Albert J. Beveridge, " The Star of Empire" in his *The Meaning of the Times and Other Speeches* (Indianapolis: Bobbs-Merill, 1908), pp. 118-143; here quoted from the reprint in *God's New Israel: Religious Interpretations of American Destiny*, pp. 140-153; here p. 140. - Another of Beveridge's immensely successful speeches, "The March of the Flag," first delivered in Indianapolis on September 16, 1898, is reprinted in *An American Primer*, pp. 644-653.
100 *The Complete Writings of Walt Whitman*, vol. II, p. 189.

A contemporary literary treatment of the complex issue of 'manifest destiny' and its role in post-war America, by the way, can be found in Robert Coover's outrageous mixture of historiography and fiction on the Rosenberg case, *The Public Burning* (1977), in which a personified Uncle Sam alias Sam Slick figures as the cunning archetype of the nation's unconscious beliefs and values and sneeringly talks about "our manifest dust-in-yer-eye," and where a scheming politician named Tricky Dick Nixon unctuously says:

> And what's most important, I have the faith: I believe in the American dream, I believe in it because I have seen it come true in my own life. TIME has said that I've had 'a Horatio Alger-like career,' but not even Horatio Alger could have dreamed up a life so American - in the best sense - as mine.[101]

From Melting Pot to Multiculturalism

> Potato salad has always seemed to me to be a particularly apt dish for 4 July, representing an ingenious conglomeration of unlikely elements to make something fairly tasty. That these vegetables are able to get along all in one dish is a miracle to me akin to the ostensible melting pot we have all come together today to make a lot of noise about.
> This, of course, is a myth. There is no more a melting pot here in America than a dish without lettuce and tomatoes is a salad.
> Jeremy Leven, *Creator*[102]

In his *Letters from an American Farmer*, published in London in 1782, J. Hector St. John de Crèvecoeur tried to define the new breed when he asked "What, then, is the American, this new man?" and when he gave this answer:

---

101 Robert Coover, *The Public Burning* (New York: Viking Press, 1977), pp. 8 and 295.
102 Jeremy Leven, *Creator* (Harmondsworth: Penguin Books, 1981), p. 309.

> *He* is an American, who, leaving behind him all his ancient prejudices and manners, receives new ones from the new mode of life he has embraced, the new government he obeys, and the new rank he holds. He becomes an American by being received in the broad lap of our great Alma Mater. Here individuals of all nations are melted into a new race of men, whose labours and posterity will one day cause great changes in the world.[103]

This famous passage, which can also be typologically understood as a reference to "the new man" whom St. Paul admonished the Colossians to "put on" and whose coming would end all ethnic diversion,[104] marks the birth of a concept which has since occupied the American imagination and which has brought forth a rhetoric that has dominated American talk about ethnic matters and been used by proponents and opponents of assimilation alike. The many-faceted metaphor of 'melting' is not only related to such mythological notions of regeneration as Ponce de Leon's Fountain of Youth and to the Pauline concept of trans-ethnic rebirth and redemption through Christ, but the melting pot as 'crucible' is also connected with the imagery of alchemy. This becomes evident from a notebook entry made by Ralph Waldo Emerson in 1845 in response to the contemporaneous movement of Know-Nothingism with its militant xenophobia:

> I hate the narrowness of the Native American party. It is <a> the dog in the manger. It is precisely opposite to all the dictates of love & magnanimity: & therefore, of course, opposite to true wisdom. [...] Man is the most composite of all creatures, the wheel-insect, *volvox globator*, is at the beginning. Well, as in the old burning of the Temple at Corinth, by the melting & intermixture of silver & gold & other metals, a new compound more precious than any, called the Corinthian Brass, was formed so in this Continent, - asylum of all nations, the energy of Irish,

---

103 J. Hector St. John de Crèvecoeur, *op. cit.*, pp. 69 and 70. - The central passage from the Third Letter is now available in an annotated EFL-reader, *From Melting Pot to Multiculturalism: 'E pluribus unum'?*, ed. by Peter Freese (München: Langenscheidt-Longman, 1994), pp. 4f., with detailed explanatory material in the accompanying *Resource Book*.

104 See Colossians 3: 9-11: "Lie not one to another, seeing that ye have put off the old man with his deeds; And have put on the new man, which is renewed in knowledge after the image of him that created him: Where there is neither Greek nor Jew, circumcision nor uncircumcision, Barbarian, Scythian, bond nor free: but Christ is all, and in all." - See the convincing interpretation by Werner Sollors, *Beyond Ethnicity: Consent and Descent in American Culture* (New York and Oxford: Oxford University Press, 1986), pp. 81-86.

Germans, Swedes, Poles & <the> Cossacks, & all the European tribes, - of the Africans, & of the Polynesians, will construct a new race, a new religion, a new State, a new literature, which will be as vigorous as the new Europe which came out of the smelting pot of the Dark Ages, or that which earlier emerged from the Pelasgic & Etruscan barbarians. *La Nature aime les croisements*.[105]

However, it was neither Crèvecoeur nor Emerson who popularized the melting-pot concept, but the English Jew Israel Zangwill. On October 5, 1908, his drama *The Melting Pot* was first performed at the Columbia Theatre in Washington, and it instantly became a nationwide success.

The hero of the play, which brings together immigrants from different ethnic groups and in different stages of 'Americanization,' is the poor Jewish immigrant and musical genius David Quixano. He has fled Russia after his family was slaughtered in the infamous Kishineff pogrom, and now lives in New York. He is passionately in love with Vera Revendal, the emigrant daughter of a Russian baron, disowned by her conservative father for her liberal views. When, however, David learns that Vera is the daughter of the very anti-Semite who was responsible for the slaughtering of his family, he cannot live up to his ideal of a new and unprejudiced beginning in America and realizes to his dismay that the sins of the past cannot be simply left behind. But finally, on a Fourth of July and on a rooftop overlooking the city of New York and the Statue of Liberty, David and Vera confess their love to each other, and - in a sort of international variation on the Capulet-Montague-motif - the young lovers assert that the hatred dividing the different nations of Europe can be burnt away in the crucible of the new continent, and the protagonist, who not accidentally bears the name which Don Quixote adopted after his conversion, avows that he will compose his American Symphony. Zangwill's play, which triumphantly announces the coming of "the real American, [...] the fusion of all races, perhaps the coming superman,"[106] has hardly

---

105 *The Journals and Miscellaneous Notebooks of Ralph Waldo Emerson*, ed. by William H. Gilman et al. (Cambridge, Mass.: The Belknap Press of Harvard University Press, 1960-1982), vol. IX, *1843 - 1847*, ed. by Ralph H. Orth and Alfred R. Ferguson (1971), pp. 299f.
106 *The Works of Israel Zangwill* (New York: AMS Press, 1969; reprint of the edition London: Globe Publishing Company, 1925), vol. XII, p. 34. - Central passages from *The*

ever been taken seriously as literature, but the final scene of this carefully constructed piece of propaganda deserves to be quoted in full:

> DAVID
> It will make me forget. Kiss me.
> *[There is a pause of hesitation, filled up by the Cathedral music from "Faust" surging up softly from below.]*
> VERA *[Slowly]*
> I will kiss you as we Russians kiss at Easter - the three kisses of peace.
> *[She kisses him three times on the mouth as in ritual solemnity.]*
> DAVID *[Very calmly]*
> Easter was the date of the massacre - see! I am at peace.
> VERA
> God grant it endure!
> *[They stand quietly hand in hand.]*
> Look! How beautiful the sunset is after the storm!
> *[DAVID turns. The sunset which has begun to grow beautiful just after VERA's entrance, has now reached its most magnificent moment; below there are narrow lines of saffron and pale gold, but above the whole sky is one glory of burning flame.]*
> DAVID *[Prophetically exalted by the spectacle]*
> It is the fires of God round his Crucible.
> *[He drops her hand and points downward.]*
> There she lies, the great Melting Pot - listen! Can't you hear the roaring and the bubbling? There gapes her mouth
> *[He points east]*
> - the harbour where a thousand mammoth feeders come from the ends of the world to pour in their human freight. Ah, what a stirring and a seething! Celt and Latin, Slav and Teuton, Greek and Syrian, - black and yellow -
> VERA *[Softly, nestling to him]*
> Jew and Gentile -
> DAVID
> Yes, East and West, and North and South, the palm and the pine, the pole and the equator, the crescent and the cross - how the great Alchemist melts and fuses them with his purging flame! Here shall they all unite to build the Republic of Man and the Kingdom of God. Ah, Vera, what is the glory of Rome and Jerusalem where all nations and races come to worship and look back, compared with the glory of America, where all races and nations come to labour and look forward!
> *[He raises his hands in benediction over the shining city.]*
> Peace, peace, to all the unborn millions, fated to fill this giant continent - the God of our *children* give you Peace.

Melting Pot are reprinted in *From Melting Pot to Multiculturalism: 'E pluribus unum'?*, pp. 6f., with detailed explanations in the accompanying *Resource Book*.

> [*An instant's solemn pause. The sunset is swiftly fading, and the vast panorama is suffused with a more restful twilight, to which the many-gleaming lights of the town add the tender poetry of the night. Far back, like a lonely, guiding star, twinkles over the darkening water the torch of the Statue of Liberty. From below comes up the softened sound of voices and instruments joining in "My Country, 'tis of Thee." The curtain falls slowly.*][107]

The fascinating promise of America as a melting pot, which reverberates with associations of rebirth into a new golden age, of redemption into a new life through Christ and the creation of a new species from the alchemist's crucible, has pervaded the ethnic discourse in America. As can be seen from the two famous cartoons by Joseph Keppler, which were published in 1880 and in 1893 respectively, this promise was evoked by the advocates of assimilation to express America's "Welcome to All!" and denied by the spokesmen of Americanization who forgot that they had once been immigrants themselves and now attempted to bar other newcomers from entering. And even such rabid adherents of Anglo-Saxon racialism as Madison Grant and Thomas Dixon or such liberal exponents of "cultural pluralism"[108] as Horace Kallen have found the rhetoric of the melting pot useful for their contradictory purposes.

The persistent power of this rhetoric is confirmed by the very fact that even those ethnic groups that have not been admitted to the crucible and that reject the notion of the melting pot as a blatant lie, cannot resist its fascination. Thus, African Americans and Native Americans and, to use Michael Novak's term, other "unmeltable ethnics" like the PIGS (= Poles, Italians, Greeks, and Slavs)[109] have made use of the concept. In 1925, for example, Alain Locke could conceive of the "New Negro" as bred in the crucible of Harlem and say about the New York

---

107 *Ibid.*, pp. 183-185.
108 Kallen's seminal article "Democracy versus the Melting Pot: A Study of American Nationality" appeared in *The Nation*, 100 (February 25, 1915), 219-220. It was later incorporated in Kallen's Book *Culture and Democracy in the United States: Studies in the Group Psychology of the American People* (New York: Boni and Liveright, 1924). - Relevant excerpts from the article are reprinted in the EFL-reader *America, the Melting Pot: Fact and Fiction*, ed. by Peter Bischoff (Paderborn: Schöningh, 1978), pp. 37-39.
109 See Michael Novak, *The Rise of the Unmeltable Ethnics: Politics and Culture in the Seventies* (New York: Macmillan, 1972).

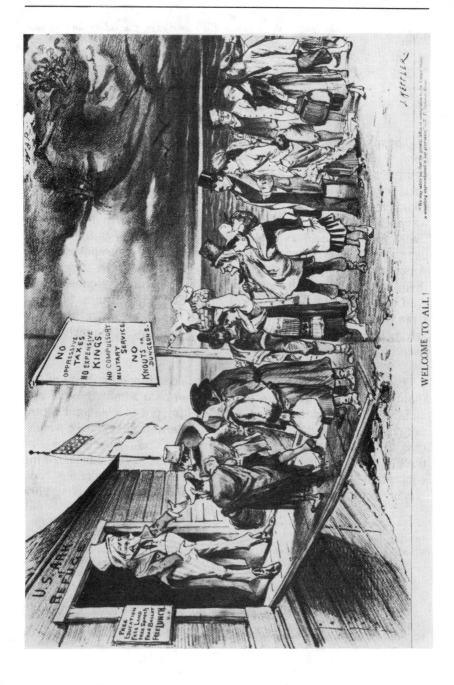

Dream and Nightmare

Black ghetto: "So what began in terms of segregation becomes more and more, as its elements mix and react, the laboratory of a great race-welding."[110] And in 1980, to give just one more example, Edward H. Spicer in his essay about "American Indians" in the *Harvard Encyclo*

110 The essay appeared originally in *The New Negro: An Interpretation*, ed. by Alain Locke (New York: Alfred and Charles Boni, 1925). - The quotation is from the title essay, as reprinted in *Black Voices: An Anthology of Afro-American Literature*, ed. by Abraham Chapman (New York: Mentor Books, 1968), pp. 512-523; here p. 516.

pedia of American Ethnic Groups, could talk about "the crucible of Oklahoma."[111]

But the ubiquitous image of the melting pot, which a representative cartoon from *Puck* (June 26, 1889) depicts as being stirred by an allegorical America with the big ladle of "Equal Rights" and with only a rebellious Irishman refusing to be melted, could not stand the test of everyday reality. In 1963, Nathan Glazer and Daniel Patrick Moynihan investigated the lives of African Americans, Puerto Ricans, Jews, Italians, and Irish in New York and laconically concluded that "the point about the melting pot [...] is that it did not happen,"[112] and a little later the historian Carl N. Degler[113] suggested that the notion of the melting pot be replaced by the supposedly more correct image of a "salad bowl." The adherents of the so-called 'New Ethnicity' flatly rejected the myth of 'melting' as a blatant lie and denounced Americanization as a mere euphemism for 'WASPification,' and meanwhile the unfulfilled promise of the melting pot has been replaced by the notions of a multicultural mosaic or quilt. The controversial melting pot concept, the complex history of which cannot be delineated in this survey,[114] implies the genuinely American promise of a new beginning unfettered by the sins and by the strife of the past, and it translates, in a manner of speaking, the early Puritans' millennial hope for a spiritual birth into Christ's kingdom upon earth into the secularized and more palpable promise of a rebirth as a citizen of a free and democratic nation. It is undoubtedly another central element of the 'American Dream,' but it is a hope which was put in jeopardy at the very beginning of American history because, as Henry Miller critically observes:

---

[111] Edward H. Spicer, "American Indians," in *Harvard Encyclopedia of American Ethnic Groups*, ed. by Stephan Thernstrom (Cambridge, Mass., and London: The Belknap Press of Harvard University Press, 1980), pp. 58-114; here p. 82.

[112] Nathan Glazer and Daniel Patrick Moynihan, *Beyond the Melting Pot: The Negroes, Puerto Ricans, Jews, Italians, and Irish of New York* (Cambridge, Mass.: M.I.T. Press, 1963), p. v.

[113] See chapter X, 4, "Melting Pot or Salad Bowl?" in Carl N. Degler, *Out of Our Past: The Forces that Shaped Modern America* (New York: Harper and Row, rev. ed., 1970), pp. 289-296.

[114] Further details are discussed in chapter 3, the development of the concept is traced in my EFL-reader *From Melting Pot to Multiculturalism: 'E pluribus unum'?*, and an excellent general introduction is provided by Werner Sollors, *op. cit.*

> One of the curious things about these progenitors of ours is that though avowedly searching for peace and happiness, for political and religious freedom, they began by robbing, poisoning, murdering, almost exterminating the race to whom this vast continent belonged.[115]

And it is a hope which has been abandoned in our time, as becomes painfully evident not only from the literature written by so-called minority authors but also from the texts of numerous contemporary pop songs. Thus, Frank Zappa could sing in "Hungry Freaks, Daddy":

> Mister America
> Walk on by
> Your supermarket dream
> Mister America
> Walk on by
> Your liquor store supreme [...]

and call attention to the outsiders and dropouts who

> [...] won't go for no more
> Great mid-western hardware store
>   philosophy
> That turns away from those
> Who aren't afraid to say what's on their minds - -
> The left behinds
> Of the Great Society.[116]

Thus, Jackson Browne, in his song "Downtown," has a stanza that reads:

> Eight blocks off the City Hall
> The rats run free and the winos crawl.
> Darkness falls on the fast machine,
> Where the future stops the American Dream,[117]

---

115 Henry Miller, *op. cit.*, p. 22.
116 From the album *Freak Out*; here quoted from Frank Zappa, *Plastic People: Songbuch* (Frankfurt: Zweitausendeins, 1977), pp. 8 and 10. - It is no accident that Frank Zappa's autobiography, which he wrote together with Peter Occhiogrosso, is ironically entitled *Frank Zappa: I am the American Dream*.
117 Transcribed from Jackson Browne's Electra/Asylum Record Album *Lawyers in Love*, 1983.

and in "Across the Lines," which movingly deals with the obvious inevitability and the terrible human waste of race riots, Tracy Chapman sings:

> Choose sides
> Or run for your life
> Tonight the riots begin
> On back streets of America
> They kill the dream of America.[118]

The Other Side of the Coin: The 'Nightmare'

> [Lee Mellon would have] a fantasy that he would never find another cigarette butt, that he would walk all the way to Seattle without finding one on the highway, and he would turn east and walk all the way to New York, looking carefully month after month along the highway for a cigarette butt without ever finding one. Not a damn one, and the end of an American dream.
> Richard Brautigan, *A Confederate General from Big Sur*[119]

The twin promises of societal progress and individual success, the inspiring challenge of ever new frontiers to man's power and ingenuity, the belief in America's manifest destiny derived from her role in civilization's westward movement, her function as the home of God's

---

[118] Transcribed from Tracy Chapman's Electra/Asylum Record Album *Across the Lines*, 1988. - The depiction and evaluation of the 'American Dream' in popular music certainly deserves a study of its own. The best book on pop music is still Greil Marcus, *Mystery Train: Images of America in Rock 'n' Roll Music* (New York: E. P. Dutton, 1975). Lewis H. Carlson and James M. Ferreira, *Beyond the Red, White, and Blue: A Student's Introduction to American Studies* (Dubuque, Iowa: Kendall / Hunt, 1993), who rightly observe that "no other democratic art form has been so consistently blamed for corrupting the morals of the country [and thereby subverting the promise of the Dream] as has American popular music," provide an intriguing chapter on "The Struggle over Popular Music," in which they assemble central documents of the debate.

[119] Richard Brautigan, *A Confederate General from Big Sur* (London: Pan Books, 1973), p. 73.

chosen people and her unrivalled form of democratic government granting liberty and equality to all her citizens, and the myth of the melting pot with its fascinating promise of a new beginning - these are certainly the most important elements which make up that great and fascinating vision which is called the 'American Dream.' But one need only consider the price paid for the 'Dream' and point out the discrepancies between its gorgeous promises and the glaring shortcomings of the reality to arrive at the other side of the coin, namely, the 'American Nightmare.' As far as the price is concerned, Norman Cousins had this to say in 1970:

> For more than two hundred years, the sense of a Promised Land has imparted a glow to the whole of American history and served as a charmed magnet for the rest of the world. Despite all its ordeals, errors, and flaws, the United States has never lost this enchantment, nor have the world's peoples ever ceased to regard us with wonder and envy. For America is a country that has readily lent itself to dreams. It has offered the promise of growth, space, mobility, confidence, recognizable paths to glory, and liberation from ancestral rigidities.
> In country after country, the pursuit of a workable national design has had its inspiration in the American dream. [...]
> But the dream is dated. For nothing would be more dangerous to the human future than if the American standard were to be achieved in country after country. Consider what would happen if the present level of American industrialization, electrification, transportation, and consumption were extended to the rest of the world. A tidal wave of prosperity would sweep across the globe, but within a very few years the Earth would become uninhabitable. For it is not just affluence but the things that go with it that must be taken into account. If the American way of life were to be universalized, the world's atmosphere would have to sustain 200 times more sulphur dioxide and sulphur trioxide than it does now, 750 times more carbon monoxide, carbon dioxide, and benzopyrene, 10,000 times more asbestos. The streams, lakes, and oceans would be burdened with 175 times more chemical poisons. The Earth's forest areas would be reduced by two-thirds. Thirty million acres would be taken out of cultivation each year to make way for spreading cities and highways.
> [...]
> For years many Americans had no hesitation in prescribing their way of life as a comprehensive remedy for the ills of mankind. Terms such as 'the American Century' or 'the American Mission' reflected their conviction that we had created a design for living within the reach of all men who were ready to accept our institutions, and who were bold

and ingenious enough to apply them. But now we must confront the stark fact that this design is contrary to the human interest.
[...]
[...] the American dream no longer fits the generality of men.[120]

As far as the discrepancies between the promises of the 'Dream' and the reality of everyday life are concerned, American authors have time and again pointed them out. Edward Albee, for example, in his short play *The American Dream* (1960), delivers what he himself calls "an attack on the substitution of artificial for real values in our society, a condemnation of complacency, cruelty, emasculation and vacuity," when in scenes reminiscent of Ionesco he embodies the American dream in a "clean-cut, midwest farm boy type, almost insultingly good-looking in a typically American way,"[121] and makes his young man the harbinger of death and an emotional cripple. And Norman Mailer, in his novel *An American Dream* (1965), which would much more appropriately be called 'An American Nightmare,' lets his hero sojourn through the horrors of a sick society and strive for rebirth through a descent into primordial savagery. All the promises of the 'Dream,' then, have frequently been exposed as unfulfilled or, worse, as distorted into their very opposites. Thus, the promise of progress is disproved by the bitter insight that scientific inventions and technological advancements have led to the poisoning of lakes and rivers, the death of forests by acid rain, the defacement of once beautiful landscapes, the pollution of the air and the disturbance of earth's ecological balance. Hundreds of American authors have raised their warning voices against the after- and the side-effects of unbridled technological progress from James Fenimore Cooper, whose Leatherstocking appeals to Judge Marmaduke Temple in *The Pioneers* (1823) to end the wasteful exploitation of a still plentiful nature - "Put an ind, Judge, to your clearings. An't the woods his [God's] work as well as the pigeons? Use, but don't waste"[122] - to Lawrence Ferlinghetti, who in *A*

---

[120] Norman Cousins, "Needed: A New Dream," *Saturday Review*, June 20, 1970; quoted from the reprint in *Sunshine and Smoke: American Writers and the American Environment*, ed. by David D. Anderson (Philadelphia: J. B. Lippincott, 1971), pp. 496f.
[121] Edward Albee, *The American Dream* (New York: Coward-McCann, 1961), pp. 8 and 70.
[122] James Fenimore Cooper, *The Pioneers; or, The Sources of the Susquehanna: A Descriptive Tale* (New York: James G. Gregory, 1863), p. 272.

Coney Island of the Mind (1958) describes America as a soulless and ruined country

> with its ghost towns and empty Ellis Islands
> and its surrealist landscape of
>   mindless prairies
>   supermarket suburbs
>   steamheated cemeteries
>   cinerama holy days
>   and protesting cathedrals
> a kissproof world of plastic toiletseats tampax and taxis
>   drugged store cowboys and las vegas virgins
>   disowned indians and cinemad matrons
>   unroman senators and conscientious non-objectors
> and all the other fatal shorn-up fragments
> of the immigrant's dream come too true
> and mislaid
>   among the sunbathers[123]

The promise of westward expansion and the challenge of ever new frontiers is equally rejected as a hope that can no longer be sustained. Thus, Walt Whitman's hymnic praise of "the Western movement beat"[124] in his famous "Pioneers! O Pioneers!" is exposed as a pious illusion long disproved by a nightmarish reality in Allen Ginsberg's "A Supermarket in California" (1955), a poem in which the enthusiastic bard of mankind's progress in the wake of the sun has metamorphosed into a "childless, lonely old grubber, / poking among the meats in the refrigerator and eyeing the grocery boys" and the nineteenth-century vision of a great future is ironically replaced by the twentieth-century nostalgia for "the lost America of love."[125] Henry David Thoreau's passionate avowal in his essay "Walking" (1862) that "every sunset which I witness inspires me with the desire to go to a West as distant and as fair as that into which the sun goes down. He appears to migrate westward daily, and tempt us to follow him. He is the Great Western Pioneer whom the nations follow,"[126] finds its con-

---

[123] Lawrence Ferlinghetti, *A Coney Island of the Mind* (New York: New Directions, 1958), p. 13.
[124] *The Complete Writings of Walt Whitman*, vol. I, p. 283.
[125] Allen Ginsberg, *Howl and Other Poems* (San Francisco: City Lights Books, rpt. 1980), pp. 23 and 24.
[126] Henry David Thoreau, "Walking," first in the *Atlantic Monthly*, June 1862; here quoted from *The Writings of Henry David Thoreau*, vol. V, *Excursions and Poems*

temporary counterpart in Thomas Pynchon's *Gravity's Rainbow* (1973) where it is said that "19th-century sunset[s]" no longer exist because "Empire took its way westward, what other way was there but into those virgin sunsets to penetrate and to foul?"[127] The hope which Thoreau set into the westward movement when he stated that "we go eastward to realize history and study the works of art and literature, retracing the steps of the race; we go westward as into the future, with a spirit of enterprise and adventure,"[128] has evaporated, and Oedipa Maas' quest through the California of the 1960's in Thomas Pynchon's *The Crying of Lot 49* (1966) takes place in a neon-lit wasteland of congested freeways, which is totally devoid of "the secret richness and concealed density of dream" and no longer provides any viable "alternative to the exitlessness, to the absence of surprise to life, that harrows the head of everybody American you know."[129]

Walt Whitman, "Facing West from California's Shore," could still speculate about "the circle almost circled" and hopefully look out for "what is yet unfound,"[130] and even Oedipa Maas could cherish, almost in spite of her better knowledge, a belief in "some principle of the sea as redemption for Southern California."[131] But Clay, the drug-addicted drifter in Bret Easton Ellis' *Less Than Zero* (1985), can only lie listlessly on the Californian beach and stare "out at the expanse of sand that meets the water, where the land ends. Disappear here,"[132] and when one relates the young man's empty stare into nothingness to one of the novel's mottoes, a line from Led Zeppelin's "Stairway to Heaven" that reads "There's a feeling I get when I look to the West ...," one realizes that the 'Dream' has finally become a 'Nightmare.' The promise of the West is gone; Larry McMurtry's novels time and again depict the death of the frontier and the impact of this loss on contemporary

---

(Boston and New York: Houghton Mifflin, no date [1893 and 1906]), pp. 205-248; here p. 219.
127 Thomas Pynchon, *Gravity's Rainbow* (New York: Bantam Books, 1974), pp. 249f.
128 Henry David Thoreau, *op. cit.*, p. 218.
129 Thomas Pynchon, *The Crying of Lot 49* (New York: Bantam Books, 1967), p. 128.
130 *The Complete Writings of Walt Whitman*, vol. I, p. 135.
131 Thomas Pynchon, *The Crying of Lot 49*, p. 37.
132 Bret Easton Ellis, *Less Than Zero* (Harmondsworth: Penguin Books, 1986), p. 73. - For details see Peter Freese, "Bret Easton Ellis, *Less Than Zero*: Entropy in the 'MTV Novel'?" in *Modes of Narrative: Approaches to American, Canadian and British Fiction Presented to Helmut Bonheim*, ed. by Reingard M. Nischik and Barbara Korte (Würzburg: Königshausen & Neumann, 1990), pp. 68-87.

Texas; and Sam Shepard's drama *True West* (1981), in which a character declares "There's no such thing as the West anymore! It's a dead issue! It's dried up [...],"[133] demonstrates that the 'true West' has become a desolate region of rootlessness and despair. Thus, it is small wonder that even the western has problems honouring the traditional recipe and that it has found one of its critical counterparts in the more recent 'eco-western,' of which Edward Abbey's *The Monkey Wrench Gang* (1975) is an outstanding example. But since, in Kurt Vonnegut's pithy phrase, scientists have lost their innocence by unleashing the destructive power of the atomic bomb,[134] Richard Brautigan's ecological complaint that nowadays trout streams can be bought in the Cleveland Wrecking Yard[135] becomes negligible in comparison to the ubiquitous threat of mankind's self-annihilation in the apocalyptic blast of nuclear warfare. Donald Barthelme's two soldiers in "Game," for instance, demonstrate - like Goethe's *Zauberlehrling* - that science has created powers which it cannot control any longer and that the erstwhile promise of progress has turned into a deadly menace.[136]

Parallel doubts are raised with regard to the promise of material success. Does not Chris Keller in Arthur Miller's *All My Sons* (1947) desperately denounce America as "the land of the great big dogs, you don't love a man here, you eat him! That's the principle; the only one we live by -"?[137] And does not, as Miller so memorably shows in *Death of a Salesman* (1949), the 'rat race' for financial gain and social status exact the price of abandoning one's personality and neglecting one's family? Does it not lead to alienation and even reification? And are not Happy's final words about his dead father that "he had a good dream. It's the only dream you can have - to come out number-one man,"[138] an indication of the human waste created by the pursuit of

---

[133] Sam Shepard, *True West*, in his *Seven Plays* (London and Boston: Faber and Faber, 1985), p. 35.
[134] See Kurt Vonnegut, "Address to the American Physical Society," in his *Wampeters, Foma & Granfalloons (Opinions)* (New York: Delta Books, 1974), pp. 91-102.
[135] See Richard Brautigan, *Trout Fishing in America* (New York: Dell Books, 1972), pp. 102-107.
[136] See Donald Barthelme, "Game," in his *Unspeakable Practices, Unnatural Acts* (New York: Bantam Books, 1969), pp. 103-111.
[137] Arthur Miller, *All My Sons*; here quoted from Arthur Miller, *Collected Plays* (Lonodn: Secker & Warburg, rpt. 1978), p. 124.
[138] Arthur Miller, *Death of a Salesman*; here quoted from Arthur Miller, *Collected Plays*, , p. 222.

success? From Abraham Cahan's self-made immigrant millionaire David Levinsky, who sums up his spiritual failure at the height of his career in the observation that "there are cases when success is a tragedy,"[139] to Bernard Malamud's *The Assistant* (1957), where financial failure is depicted as a prerequisite for human fulfilment and spiritual rebirth, America's serious writers have time and again denounced the 'bitch-goddess' success. And from Thoreau's experiment at Walden Pond to the dropouts of modern counter-culture who burnt - as Allen Ginsberg says in *Howl* (1956) - their money in wastebaskets,[140] there is a strong anti-materialistic tradition in American literature in which the ideal of outward success is rejected as the golden calf of a dangerous and finally inhumane doctrine.

As for manifest destiny, the American sense of mission can also be called into question, and many critics have argued that it has often been abused as a mere justification for power-politics and economic gain. Europeans have learnt the hard way that the mixing of religion and politics can bring disastrous results, and the unwarranted feelings of superiority which the proselytes of the American way of life sometimes display are cuttingly pinpointed by Ambassador Minton in Kurt Vonnegut's influential novel *Cat's Cradle* (1963), when he observes: "The highest possible form of treason [in America] is to say that Americans aren't loved wherever they go, whatever they do."[141]

That the central values of liberty and equality which Senator Beveridge wanted to export to the rest of the world could do with a bit of promotion in his own country became glaringly obvious as late as August 28, 1963, when - at the Lincoln Memorial in Washington - Martin Luther King articulated his version of the 'American Dream' and said:

> I have a dream that one day this nation will rise up and live out the true meaning of its creed: "We hold these truths to be self-evident; that all men are created equal."

---

139 Abraham Cahan, *The Rise of David Levinsky* (New York: Harper & Row, rpt. 1981), p. 529.
140 See Allen Ginsberg, *Howl and Other Poems*, p. 9.
141 Kurt Vonnegut, *Cat's Cradle* (New York: Dell Books, rpt. 1970), pp. 71f.

> I have a dream that one day on the red hills of Georgia the sons of former slaves and the sons of former slaveowners will be able to sit down together at the table of brotherhood.
> I have a dream that one day even the state of Mississippi, a desert state sweltering with the heat of injustice and oppression, will be transformed into an oasis of freedom and justice.
> I have a dream that my four little children will one day live in a nation where they will not be judged by the color of their skin but by the content of their character.
> I have a dream today.[142]

One could easily add the voice of a Red Indian deprived of his land and his liberty; the voice of a Chinese 'coolie' good enough to work on the transcontinental railroad but then rejected by the Chinese Exclusion Act; the voice of a Japanese from California remembering the bitter experience of the relocation camps after Pearl Harbor, or the voice of a Chicano farm worker describing the squalor of his barrio. Rodolfo Gonzales' germinal Chicano poem *I Am Joaquín* (1972) succinctly expresses the feelings of the many who are excluded from the 'Dream' when he lets his protagonist exclaim:

> I am Joaquín,
> lost in a world of confusion,
> caught up in the whirl of a
>   gringo society,
> confused by the rules,
> scorned by attitudes,
> suppressed by manipulation,
> and destroyed by modern society.
> My fathers
> have lost the economic battle
> and won
>   the struggle for cultural survival.
>
> And now!
> I must choose
>   between
>   the paradox of

---

[142] Martin Luther King, Jr., "I Have a Dream," in *The Annals of America*, vol. XVIII, *1961 - 1968: The Burdens of World Power* (Chicago and London: Encyclopaedia Britannica, 1967), pp. 156-159; here pp. 158f. - Excerpts from this speech are available in the EFL-reader *Language & Politics: Political Speeches in the U.S.A.*, ed. by Michaela Ulich, Wolf Stenger, and Dietrich Büscher (München: Langenscheidt-Longman, 1983), pp. 41-43.

> victory of the spirit,
> despite physical hunger,
>   or
> to exist in the grasp
> of American social neurosis,
> sterilization of the soul
> and a full stomach.
>
> Yes,
> I have come a long way to nowhere,
> unwillingly dragged by that
> monstrous, technical,
> industrial giant called
>   Progress
> and Anglo success. ...[143]

Such voices, too, would offer testimony against the myth of the melting pot. Dudley Randall, in his sarcastic poem "The Melting Pot" (1968), looks at the unfulfilled promise of melting and fusing from the point of view of the Black American:

> There is a magic melting pot
> where any girl or man
> can step in Czech or Greek or Scot,
> step out American.
>
> *Johann* and *Jan* and *Jean* and *Juan*,
> *Giovanni* and *Ivan*
> step in and then step out again
> all freshly christened *John*.
>
> Sam, watching, said, "Why, I was here
> even before they came,"
> and stepped in too, but was tossed out
> before he passed the brim.
>
> And every time Sam tried that pot
> they threw him out again.
> "Keep out. This is our private pot.
> We don't want your black stain."

---

[143] Rodolfo Gonzales, *I Am Joaquín/Yo Soy Joaquín* (New York: Bantam Books, 1972), pp. 8ff.

> At last, thrown out a thousand times,
> Sam said, "I don't give a damn.
> Shove your old pot. You can like it or not,
> but I'll be just what I am."[144]

Finally, too, the idea of the frontier as - in Turner's phrase - "the line of most rapid and effective Americanization" and the breeding place of "individualism, democracy, and nationalism"[145] - is a questionable concept, and the *machismo* of the cowboy myth has been rejected by numerous critics. In the value system of the western there is an adolescent rejection of women, and it is rather revealing that as early as in *The Virginian* the cowboys reject the building of the first schoolhouse as an ominous sign of the impending end of fun and freedom:

> [...] the schoolhouse, roofed and ready for the first native Wyoming crop, [...] symbolized the dawn of a neighborhood, and it brought a change into the wilderness air. The feel of it struck cold upon the free spirits of the cow-punchers, and they told each other that, what with women and children and wire fences, this country would not long be a country for men.[146]

Four years before *The Virginian* allegedly established the genre of the western, Stephen Crane exposed this trait in "The Bride Comes to Yellow Sky" (1898). In this brilliant story the unruly oldtimer Scratchy Wilson confronts sheriff Jack Potter for one of their habitual shootouts only to learn to his dismay that Potter has just married and brought his wife to Yellow Sky on the California Express. When Scratchy asks the sheriff to draw, a dialogue ensues which reveals in a very funny way that the responsibility implied by marriage puts an end to the adolescent fun of the 'Wild West':

> "I ain't got a gun because I've just come from San Anton' with my wife. I'm married," said Potter. [...]
> "Married!" said Scratchy, not at all comprehending.
> "Yes, married. I'm married," said Potter distinctly.

---

144 Dudley Randall, *Cities Burning* (Detroit: Broadside Press, 1968), pp. 322f. - The poem is reprinted in *From Melting Pot to Multiculturalism: 'E pluribus unum'?*, p. 13, and analyzed in the accompanying *Resource Book*.
145 Frederick Jackson Turner, *op. cit.*, pp. 545 and 565.
146 Owen Wister, *The Virginian: A Horseman of the Plains* (New York: Harper & Row, 1965), p. 64.

"Married?" said Scratchy. Seemingly for the first time he saw the drooping drowning woman at the other man's side. "No!" he said. He was like a creature allowed a glimpse of another world. He moved a pace backward, and his arm with a revolver dropped to his side. "Is this - is this the lady?" he asked.
"Yes, this is the lady," answered Potter.
There was another period of silence.
"Well," said Wilson at last, slowly, "I s'pose it's all off now."
[...]
"Well, I'low it's off, Jack," said Wilson. He was looking at the ground. "Married!" He was not a student of chivalry; it was merely that in the presence of this foreign condition he was a simple child of the earlier plains. He picked up his starboard revolver, and placing both weapons in their holsters, he went away. His feet made funnel-shaped tracks in the heavy sand.[147]

But it is not only the adolescent *machismo* of the traditional western that is rightly rejected by many critics.[148] It must also be pointed out that the world view of the traditional western is not at all democratic but, on the contrary, indicative of a racist rejection of all races except the Anglo-Saxon. After all, it was Owen Wister who decreed in "The Evolution of the Cow-Puncher":

> No rood of modern ground is more debased and mongrel [than America] with its hordes of encroaching alien vermin, that turn our cities to Babels and our citizenship to a hybrid farce, who degrade our commonwealth from a nation into something half pawn-shop, half broker's office. But to survive in the clean cattle country requires spirit of adventure, courage, and self-sufficiency; you will not find many Poles or Huns or Russian Jews in that district; but the Anglo-Saxon is still forever homesick for out-of-doors.[149]

---

[147] Stephen Crane, "The Bride Comes to Yellow Sky," in *The Works of Stephen Crane*, ed. by Fredson Bowers, vol. V, *Tales of Adventure* (Charlottesville: University Press of Virginia, 1970), pp. 109-121; here pp. 119f. - The story is reprinted in the EFL-reader *The Frontier and the American West*, pp. 49-58.
[148] The long neglected contribution of women to the mythology of the west is brilliantly explored in Annette Kolodny, *The Land Before Her: Fantasy and Experience of the American Frontiers, 1630-1860* (Chapel Hill: University of North Carolina Press, 1984). - See also *Women and Western American Literature*, ed. by Helen Winter Stauffer and Susan J. Rosowski (Troy, N.Y., The Whitston Publishing Company, 1982).
[149] *The Writings of Owen Wister*, vol. VI, pp. xxiiif.

And it was the narrator of Wister's germinal novel *The Virginian* who said that "all America is divided into two classes, - the quality and the equality."[150]

Moreover, it has been convincingly argued that the western code of manliness and the accompanying cult of the six-shooter, that adolescent phallic surrogate, have bred violence and a dangerous inclination towards self-justice. And one might well reject it as a representative proof of the western's immature glorification of the lonely and asocial misfit when the young narrator of Jack Schaefer's *Shane* (1949) says about the novel's god-like hero:

> He was tall and terrible there in the road, looming up gigantic in the mystic half-light. He was the man I saw that first day, a stranger, dark and forbidding, forging his lone way out of an unknown past in the utter loneliness of his own immovable and instinctive defiance. He was the symbol of all the dim, formless imaginings of danger and terror in the untested realm of human potentialities beyond my understanding.[151]

In recent years, of course, there has been a whole spate of revisionist westerns which have changed the traditional image of the Indian as in *A Man Called Horse*, *Soldier Blue*, *Little Big Man*, and, most recently and most successfully, in Kevin Costner's *Dances with Wolves*;[152] which have openly presented the amoral hero engaging in sadistic acts of violence as in Sergio Leone's so-called spaghetti westerns; and which have either tried to rediscover the Black cowboy as in *The Legend of Nigger Charlie*, *Buck and the Preacher* or *Soul Soldier*, or have brought a kind of Jewish mentality to the west and portrayed, in films like *Butch Cassidy and the Sundance Kid* or *McCabe and Mrs. Miller*, "six-gun schlemiels and existentialists in cowboy boots."[153]

---

150 *The Virginian: A Horseman of the Plains*, p. 97.
151 Jack Schaefer, *Shane* (London: Corgi Books, rpt. 1979), p. 105.
152 The book on which the prize-winning film is based is now easily available in a pocketbook edition: Michael Blake, *Dances with Wolves* (Harmondsworth: Penguin Books, 1991).
153 John G. Cawelti, *Adventure, Mystery, and Romance: Formula Stories as Art and Popular Culture* (Chicago and London: University of Chicago Press, 1976), p. 258.

THE VICTOR'S PRIZE

The Future of the 'Dream'

What happens to a dream deferred?

Does it dry up
like a raisin in the sun?
Or fester like a sore -
And then run?
Does it stink like rotten meat?
Or crust and sugar over
like a syrupy sweet?

Maybe it just sags
like a heavy load.

Or does it explode?

Langston Hughes, "Harlem"[154]

Depending on the respective accentuation, the elements of the 'American Dream' can be praised as fascinating promises or condemned as dangerous temptations. If judged by its effect, the 'Dream' can either be lauded as what William Faulkner called "a sanctuary on the earth for individual man,"[155] or it can be rejected as what Kurt Vonnegut exposes as an excuse for greed and crime in his novel *God Bless You, Mr. Rosewater* (1965):

> When the United States of America, which was meant to be a Utopia for all, was less than a century old, Noah Rosewater and a few men like him demonstrated the folly of the Founding Fathers in one respect: those sadly recent ancestors had not made it the law of the Utopia that the wealth of each citizen should be limited. [...] Thus did a handful of rapacious citizens come to control all that was worth controlling in America. Thus was the savage and stupid and entirely inappropriate and unnecessary and humorless American class system created. [...] Thus the American dream turned belly up, turned green, bobbed to the

---

[154] Langston Hughes, "Harlem," first in *The Panther and the Lash: Poems of Our Time* (New York: Alfred Knopf, 1967); here quoted from *The Poetry of the Negro 1746 - 1970: An Anthology*, ed. by Langston Hughes and Arna Bontemps (Garden City, New York: Doubleday, rev. ed. 1970), p. 199.
[155] William Faulkner, "On Privacy: The American Dream - What Happened to It," *Harper's Magazine*, 211 (1955), 33-38; here p. 33.

scummy surface of cupidity unlimited, filled with gas, went *bang* in the noonday sun.[156]

One's overall judgment of the 'Dream' and its consequences will necessarily depend on one's philosophical position and political convictions. But in spite of growing criticism at home and abroad, the 'American Dream' is as alive as ever. The introductory quotations from acceptance and inauguration speeches demonstrate that from Nixon's warning "The American dream does not come to those who fall asleep" and Carter's promise "The American dream endures" to Reagan's proclamation of "a dream of an America that would be 'a shining city on a hill'" and presidential candidate Michael Dukakis' promise to make every American "a full shareholder in our dream" all recent American presidents have conjured up the vision of the 'Dream.' However, it is not only in political rhetoric that the notion of the 'Dream' flourishes. It is also alive in the Cuban refugees and the Vietnamese Boat People, in the thousands of 'wetbacks' that cross the Rio Grande into the promised land of America, and in the countless immigrants from all over the world who come to the United States with the hope of improving their lives and finding a chance for self-fulfillment. For all of them, the 'Dream' consists of what Lee Iacocca's father taught his children in a "single lesson," namely that "America was the land of freedom - the freedom to become anything you wanted to be, if you wanted it bad enough and were willing to work for it."[157]

In 1925, F. Scott Fitzgerald published *The Great Gatsby*, which is yet the most cogent literary comment on the 'Dream.' In this complex novel, a self-made young man tries to make his idealistic dreams come true by materialistic means, to buy back the love of a woman, and to repeat and thereby correct the past. Young Gatsby, however, that enigmatic mixture of idealistic dreamer with "an extraordinary gift for hope, a romantic readiness,"[158] and a materialistic money-mak-

---

156 Kurt Vonnegut, *God Bless You, Mr. Rosewater or Pearls Before Swine* (London: Panther Books, rpt. 1972), pp. 15f.
157 Lee Iacocca, *op. cit.*, p. 3.
158 F. Scott Fitzgerald, *The Great Gatsby*, in *The Bodley Head Scott Fitzgerald* (London: Bodley Head, rpt. 1977), vol. I, p. 20. - All further page numbers in brackets in the text. - An EFL-edition of the novel is available as *The Great Gatsby*, ed. by Richard

er with underworld connections, fails pathetically. If this man, who "sprang from his Platonic conception of himself" (96), but who, at the same time, "ravenously and unscrupulously" (136) pursues his goals and answers his acquaintance's admonition "You can't repeat the past" with an incredulous "Why of course you can!" (106), is understood as a representative of America, then the novel insists that the 'Dream' was ruined because the idealistic promise was tainted by materialism. The great promise of the pioneers' venture, Fitzgerald insinuates, was betrayed by egotism and greediness: Dan Cody, young Gatsby's mentor, whose name is a meaningful compound of *Dan*iel Boone, the positive hero of the West, and Buffalo Bill *Cody*, the negative slayer of the buffaloes, is a "pioneer debauchee, who [...] brought back to the Eastern seaboard the savage violence of the frontier brothel and saloon" (98), and a personification of the betrayal of the promise of the open frontier as it is repeated, in a debased form, in the open frontier of money-making opportunities. This tension between ideal and reality is evoked in one of the most memorable passages of American literature, in which Nick Carraway thinks of the first sailors approaching the new continent and experiencing

> [...] the last and greatest of all human dreams; for a transitory enchanted moment man must have held his breath in the presence of this continent, compelled into an aesthetic contemplation he neither understood nor desired, face to face for the last time in history with something commensurate to his capacity for wonder (162f.).

The unique chance to begin anew on a new continent, unfettered by the chains of history and free to undo the accumulated mistakes of the European past, will certainly not come again, but the 'Dream' still lingers on. Some believe that it can be reclaimed, but Robert B. Reich's programme for economic renewal, which was based on the premise that "adaptation is America's challenge. It is America's next frontier,"[159] has had little impact upon short-sighted politicians; Charles A. Reich's vision, in his bestselling *The Greening of America* (1970), that the new age dawning beyond the industrial era would be "not a repudia-

---

Martin and Dagmar Pohlenz (Paderborn: Schöningh, 1984), with an accompanying *Teacher's Book* (1986).
159 Robert B. Reich, *The Next American Frontier* (Harmondsworth: Penguin Books, 1984), p. 21.

tion of, but a fulfillment of, the American dream,"[160] has proved to be an abortive hope; and Robert J. Ringer's recipe for *Restoring the American Dream* (1979) by "*minimizing* government and government functions," phasing out taxes as swiftly as is practical, eliminating government services and government employees, allowing "the laws of supply and demand [...] to operate freely," and going back to a brutal 'survival of the fittest' mentality cannot be the sought-for solution.[161]

Other critics urgently call for the 'Dream' to be abandoned: Mike Davis, for example, who predicts that in the next twenty years America will acquire twenty to thirty millions of "workers without citizen rights or access to the political system at all: an American West Bank of terrorized illegal laborers [...] a poor Latin American society thrust into the domestic economy," ends his enraged study with the scathing observation that "we are all, finally, prisoners of the same malign 'American dream.'"[162] And *Newsweek* recently concluded that California, that last stronghold of the 'Dream,' is breaking down under its vast array of problems from smog to gang violence and has finally reached "The End of the Dream."[163] More and more critics, then, are raising their warning voices to point out that "our generation faces a rare moment in human history,"[164] and that it will be up to us to rectify the growing injustice and inequality of social structures, to stop the squandering of earth's finite amount of non-renewable resources, and to make the difficult transition to a new energy environment.

Thus, it might well be our age in which the 'Dream' will either find its ultimate end in the chaos and inertia of maximum thermodynamic and informational entropy or under the mushroom cloud of a nuclear Armaggedon[165] or in which it will be revived and finally implemented

---

160 Charles A. Reich, *The Greening of America* (London: Allen Lane, 1971), p. 261.
161 Robert J. Ringer, *Restoring the American Dream* (San Francisco: QED, 1979), pp. 290 and 294.
162 Mike Davis, *Prisoners of the American Dream: Politics and Economy in the History of the US Working Class* (London: Verso, 1986), pp. 305 and 314.
163 Michael Reese and Jennifer Foote, "The End of the Dream," *Newsweek*, July 31, 1989, pp. 27-33.
164 Jeremy Rifkin with Ted Howard, *Entropy: A New World View* (London: Paladin Books, 1985), p. 271.
165 See Peter Freese, *Surviving the End: Beyond Apocalypse and Entropy in American Literature* (Claremont, Cal.: Claremont McKenna College Center for Humanistic Studies, 1988).

by a sobered mankind conscious of its mistakes and its limited possibilities. If it is to be revived, however, it will certainly have to be redefined because "now that there are no more frontiers or undiscovered continents for rugged individuals to be conquered, we need a different dream."[166]

The new 'Dream,' therefore, can no longer centre on reckless self-fulfillment or the amassing of wealth at the expense of others, it can no longer be built on the belief in an increasingly questionable technological progress, it has to abandon the concept of a chosen nation's manifest destiny, and it must no longer be based on the mythic notion of a melting pot in which a new race of supermen is bred out of diverse ethnic ingredients. In order to become a viable ideal, the 'Dream' of the future must be less grandiose and more mature, a communal rather than an individual aspiration, and it must put ecological considerations before economic gain, multi-cultural coexistence before missionary zeal, and spiritual satisfaction before material affluence. The worried question, then, which Archibald MacLeish asked in a poem of 1939,

> America was always promises.
> From the first voyage and the first ship there were promises -
> [...]
> America was promises - to whom?[167]

is still, and ever more urgently, calling for an answer. And it seems increasingly evident that an acceptable answer has to be provided by the beginning of the new millennium, if mankind wants to have a fair chance of survival.

---

[166] Celeste MacLeod, *Horatio Alger, Farewell: The End of the American Dream* (New York: Seaview Books, 1980), p. 281.
[167] Archibald MacLeish, "America Was Promises," in *The Collected Poems of Archibald MacLeish*, pp. 360f.

3: *E pluribus unum?* Growing up in a Multicultural Society as Depicted in the American Short Story

> Here individuals of all nations are melted into a new race of men, whose labours and posterity will one day cause great changes in the world.
> J. Hector St. John de Crèvecoeur, *Letters from an American Farmer*

> [...] America is God's Crucible, the great Melting-Pot where all the races of Europe are melting and re-forming!
> Israel Zangwill, *The Melting Pot*

> Contrary to the conception implied by the figure of the melting pot, American civilization has not been homogeneous and uniform; even today it is diverse and pluralistic. The evidence is all around us.
> Carl N. Degler, *Out of Our Past: The Forces that Shaped Modern America*

> The point about the melting pot [...] is that it did not happen.
> Nathan Glazer and Daniel Patrick Moynihan, *Beyond the Melting Pot*[1]

---

1 The mottoes are taken from J. Hector St. John de Crèvecoeur, *Letters from an American Farmer and Sketches of 18th-Century America*, ed. by Albert E. Stone (Harmondsworth: Penguin Books, 1981), p. 70; Israel Zangwill, *The Melting Pot*, in *The Works of Israel Zangwill* (New York: AMS Press, 1969; reprint of the edition London: Globe Publishing Company, 1925), vol. XII, p. 33; Carl N. Degler, *Out of Our Past: The Forces That Shaped Modern America* (New York: Harper and Row, rev. ed.,

If a German ponders the topical question of the Federal Republic as a multicultural society and thinks about the manifold problems of how to integrate and acculturate the growing number of foreign guest-workers and political refugees, he or she will have to conclude that the only level on which this formidable task has been achieved so far without any friction is that of food, of ethnic cuisines. And it is intriguing to note that there are quite a number of Germans who are xenophobic or even convinced racists but who love to frequent Italian pizzerias, Yugoslav *Balkan-Stuben*, Chinese restaurants or Greek diners and who do not seem to realize that if their fervent wish of *Ausländer raus* were fulfilled, they would have to go back to *Wiener Schnitzel* and *Deutsches Beefsteak*.

Since it is always one's own daily experience which serves as the indispensable point of reference for any attempt at coming to terms with a 'foreign' problem like that of American multi-ethnicity, the culinary aspect offers a welcome point of comparison. Consequently, two photographs might serve as a motivating and appropriately non-verbal *Einstieg* into the problem when it is tackled in the EFL-classroom. The first picture shows a neon sign photographed in New York in 1975, and it advertises a restaurant in which exotic food (*Chinese*) and genuinely American drinks (*cocktails*) are promised within a *Rathskeller*-atmosphere conjuring up German *Gemütlichkeit*. Such an unlikely combination suggest the important insight that an all too hasty 'fusion' of different ethnic elements can result in a superficial and rather ridiculous mixture. The second picture is a photograph I took in 1981 in the National Museum of History in Washington, and it shows the introductory exhibit of the impressive *A Nation of Nations* exhibition prepared as a contribution to the Bicentennial.[2] The exhibit is a

---

1970), p. 296; and Nathan Glazer and Daniel Patrick Moynihan, *Beyond the Melting Pot: The Negroes, Puerto Ricans, Jews, Italians, and Irish of New York* (Cambridge, Mass.: M.I.T. Press, 1963), p. 5.

2 The first picture is taken from *A Nation of Nations: The People Who Came to America as Seen Through Objects and Documents Exhibited at the Smithsonian Institution*, ed. by Peter C. Marzio (New York: Harper & Row, 1976), p. 589. - This richly illustrated book is a veritable treasure trove for any teacher who wants to deal with American ethnicity in the classroom. The same exhibition is also documented by a series of eighty slides with an accompanying leaflet: *A Nation of Nations: A Visual Presentation from the National Museum of History and Technology*, ed. by Ellen Roney Hughes and Lucinda J. Herrick (Washington: Smithsonian Institution Photographic Services, no date), which is an even more helpful teaching tool.

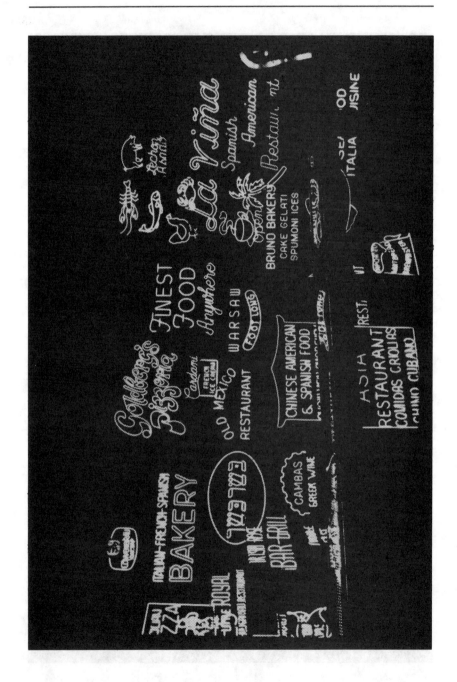

collage of original neon signs used by restaurants and stores in New York, Cleveland, Washington, D.C., and other cities between 1937 and 1971, and it represents nineteen nationalities (not all of which can be seen in the photo). These signs indicate rather forcefully that the 'American' diet is a mixture of ethnic cuisines, and they constitute an interesting comment on the essential question of whether America is something like a 'melting pot' or whether, on the contrary, it is a mosaic or, to use the most recent image, a quilt of coexisting and ultimately 'unmeltable' ethnic elements.

The two pictures might be appropriately complemented by the following excerpt from Jeremy Leven's hilarious novel *Creator* (1980), in which the hero, the mad scientist Dr. Harry Wolper, explains why he loves to eat potato salad on Independence Day:

> Potato salad has always seemed to me to be a particularly apt dish for 4 July, representing an ingenious conglomeration of unlikely elements to make something fairly tasty. That these vegetables are able to get along all in one dish is a miracle to me akin to the ostensible melting pot we have all come together today to make a lot of noise about.
> This is, of course, a myth. There is no more a melting pot here in America than a dish without lettuce and tomatoes is a salad. No matter, the distinction is unimportant. The streets were not, in fact paved with gold, and religious tolerance is neither better nor worse here than anywhere else. Jews and Catholics maintain their distance, blacks and whites fortify themselves and prepare for battle. Young and old starve alike and view each other with little friendliness or regard. We are an armed camp, entrenched to protect what little territory we have left, and brotherly love be damned. We are not cooperators who built this country, and this is not a democracy. We national engineers were competitors and enslavers, and we built us here a republic, to foster competition, protect the interests of the aristocratic founding fathers, and assure that a class system could sustain itself just like in Mother England, in spite of our having no history, a remarkable achievement at the very least.
> It is a country put together with tape and pins, and its longevity is a testimony not to the constitutional design, but to the real wisdom of the founders in taking into account the true adhesive that would bind us together: greed. What is self-evident to me is that it is *my* life, *my* liberty, and *my* pursuit of happiness, not yours. Yours is your problem.
> [...]
> I wonder whether there is any hope for us descendants of those with the stamina and guts to withstand the vast sea and leave everything

they held dear to them behind, everything they knew. Is there any way that this nation of rugged individualists, iconoclasts, self-made men, entrepreneurs, and liberated freethinkers can ever relate, one to the other? Now that would be an event for which to light fire-crackers.
Until then I will console myself that American relationships are not impossible in a country that can combine onions, celery, eggs, and gobs of mayonnaise with subterranean tubers and end up with something as palatable as potato salad.[3]

Leven's sarcastic criticism of the 'melting pot' concept and his playful suggestion of replacing it with the more appropriate image of a bowl of potato salad might then be related to the following excerpt from the well-known historian Carl N. Degler's study *Out of Our Past: The Forces That Shaped Modern America*. In a chapter entitled "Melting Pot or Salad Bowl?" Degler refers to Israel Zangwill's influential play *The Melting Pot* (1908), in which the poor Jewish immigrant David Quixano enthusiastically exclaims "that America is God's Crucible, the great Melting-Pot where all the races of Europe are melting and re-forming!" and speculates that "the real American has not yet arrived. He is only in the Crucible, I tell you - he will be the fusion of all races, perhaps the coming superman."[4] Questioning the feasibility of such optimistic expectations, Degler sceptically asks:

> [...] is this really what happens to the immigrant in America? Do the various national traits "melt and fuse" to form a new American culture when it is clear that many of them remain untouched and persistent? Some traits, to be sure, do disappear after a while. After one or two generations most of the sharply deviant contours are worn down to the common pattern, the brassy earrings, the large mustachios, the gar-licked breath, and the atrociously accented English being replaced by appropriate American substitutes. But true as that may be, it does not make a melting pot, for the dropping of old habits for new is not fusion or melting.
> [...] In view of such failure to melt and fuse, the metaphor of the melting pot is unfortunate and misleading. A more accurate analogy would be a salad bowl, for, though the salad is an entity, the lettuce can still be distinguished from the chicory, the tomatoes from the cabbage.

---

3   Jeremy Leven, *Creator* (Harmondsworth: Penguin Books, 1981), pp. 309 and 310.
4   *The Works of Israel Zangwill*, vol. XII, pp. 33 and 34. - See also the extended quotation from *The Melting Pot* on pp. 154f.

> Contrary to the conception implied by the figure of the melting pot, American civilization has not been homogeneous and uniform; even today it is diverse and pluralistic. The evidence is all around us: [...][5]

The two photographs and the two short texts, one fictional and one expository, are apt to raise central questions concerning the concept of the 'melting pot' and thus constitute a short teaching unit which serves as a highly suitable introduction to any EFL-course on American multiculturalism.[6] And they signal my major criticism of the traditional classroom approach to the question of the American 'melting pot,' which usually concentrates on the provision of relevant facts and data and generally combines statistics (the size of the different 'minority populations' in terms of percentages of the total population, etc.), information about historical developments (phases of immigration, distribution of ethnic groups, etc.), statements about legal and political aspects (immigration laws, fight for equality, political representation, etc.) and material on outstanding contemporary issues. Such an approach can undoubtedly be very informative, but it has one serious drawback, which consists of its limitation to expository texts and, consequently, to the cognitive domain. Expository texts presuppose, in order to be understood, some factual knowledge of the world with which they deal. Therefore, a study of such texts remains necessarily abstract and hardly caters to the learners' need for empathy and identification. The attitude of 'there but for the grace of God go I' is rarely awakened, and thus the acquisition of relevant information remains a mainly theoretical enterprise because the facts and data encountered are not related to the learners' private existence.

---

5   Carl N. Degler, *Out of Our Past: The Forces That Shaped Modern America*, pp. 295f. - Annotated versions of the passage from Leven's novel, of central scenes from Zangwill's *The Melting Pot*, of the quotation from Degler, and of thematically related texts are available in the EFL-reader *From Melting Pot to Multiculturalism: 'E pluribus unum'?*, ed. by Peter Freese (München: Langenscheidt-Longman, 1994), with detailed interpretations in the accompanying *Resource Book*.
6   The teacher who wants to elaborate on the 'food' aspect might make use of Jann Huizenga, *Looking at American Food: A Pictorial Introduction to American Language and Culture* (Bielefeld: Cornelsen-Velhagen & Klasing, 1983), esp. pp. 18f., "Ethnic Eating;" of the relevant material in the *Resource Book* for my EFL-reader *From Melting Pot to Multiculturalism: 'E pluribus unum'?*; and of the theoretical considerations in the critical anthology *Ethnic and Regional Foodways in the United States: The Performance of Group Identity*, ed. by Linda Keller and Kay Mussell (Knoxville: University of Tennessee Press, 1984).

Since the very topic of multiculturalism offers the welcome chance to combine factual and social learning and thus to effect attitudinal and perhaps even behavioural changes in the learners (what, one might ask, is the good of a course on the plight of African Americans if it does not affect German EFL-learners' attitudes towards the political refugees and guest-workers in their own country?), it seems appropriate that the issue of the 'melting pot' myth be approached through literary texts which, by translating general problems into individual experience, appeal not only to the cognitive but to the affective domain as well. Because literary texts build up their own self-sustained world, they can usually be understood without additional information. Therefore, fictional (and, for that matter, semi-fictional, i.e., autobiographical) texts on the multifarious aspects of life in a 'nation of nations' are the most rewarding texts for any attempt at understanding a foreign culture, and they can substantially contribute to the learners' development of tolerance and what is now fashionably called 'intercultural' understanding.

The notion of American multiculturalism is so complex that, to make it teachable within the given limits of the EFL-classroom, it must be reduced to some exemplary aspects, and these aspects must be related to the students' interests and motivations. Quite obviously, then, the most suitable aspects of the target culture are those which young people can immediately understand and imaginatively recreate on the basis of their personal experience and with which they can empathize or even identify. And what could be more interesting to adolescents and young adults than the very problems they have to cope with in their own daily lives, namely, the manifold difficulties of growing up and achieving majority.[7] Luckily, texts dealing with the problems of 'growing up ethnic' are available in great numbers because no other national literature has devoted such loving attention to the pangs and promises of growing up as the American. There is even a genuinely American genre which is entirely devoted to this subject, namely, the coming-of-age novel and story or the novel and story of initiation.[8]

---

[7] A more detailed explanation of this position is offered in Peter Freese, *Growing up Black in America: Stories and Studies of Socialization - Interpretations and Suggestions for Teaching* (Paderborn: Schöningh, 2nd ed., 1979), pp. 1-16.

[8] As far as the novel is concerned, see Peter Freese, *Die Initiationsreise: Studien zum jugendlichen Helden im modernen amerikanischen Roman* (Neumünster: Wachholtz, 1971),

And, with the more prominence of proudly ethnic literatures in the United States and the concomitant rediscovery of older and hitherto unduly neglected texts outside the so-called mainstream or 'malestream,' almost every aspect of growing up ethnic has been awarded its literary treatment, and in recent years numerous anthologies of pertinent stories have been published.[9] The colourful spectrum includes such diverse facets as

---

and Arno Heller, *Odyssee zum Selbst: Zur Gestaltung jugendlicher Identitätssuche im neueren amerikanischen Roman* (Innsbruck: Institut für Sprachwissenschaft, 1973); for the specific field of the African American novel see Heinz Christian Lüffe, *Zur Textkonstitution afro-amerikanischer Initiationsliteratur* (Frankfurt and Bern: Peter Lang, 1982), and for the long neglected tales about female initiation see Gabriele Wittke, *Female Initiation in the American Novel* (Frankfurt: Peter Lang, 1991). As far as the short story is concerned, see Peter Freese, "'Rising in the World' and 'Wanting to Know Why': The Socialization Process as Theme of the American Short Story," *Archiv für das Studium der Neueren Sprachen und Literaturen*, 218 (1981), 286-302; and Peter Freese, "Über die Schwierigkeiten des Erwachsenwerdens: Amerikanische stories of initiation von Nathaniel Hawthorne bis Joyce Carol Oates," in *Die Short Story im Englischunterricht der Sekundarstufe II: Theorie und Praxis*, ed. by Peter Freese and Liesel Hermes (Paderborn: Schöningh, 2nd ed., 1983), pp. 206-254. Annotated texts of ten initiation stories from Hawthorne to Joyce Carol Oates are available in the EFL-reader *The American Short Story I: Initiation*, ed. by Peter Freese (Paderborn: Schöningh, 2nd ed., 1989), which is accompanied by a detailed Teacher's Book, Peter Freese, *The American Short Story I: Initiation - Interpretations and Suggestions for Teaching* (Paderborn: Schöningh, 3rd ed., 1991).

9   See, e.g., the older collections *Growing up Black*, ed. by Jay David (New York: William Morrow, 1968), and *Growing up Black in America: Stories and Studies of Socialization*, ed. by Peter Freese (Paderborn: Schöningh, 6th enl. ed., 1987); and such recent anthologies as *Growing up in the South: An Anthology of Modern Southern Literature*, ed. by Suzanne W. Jones (New York: Mentor Books, 1991); *Growing up Native American: An Anthology*, ed. by Patricia Riley (New York: William Morrow, 1993); *Growing up Latino: Memoirs and Stories*, ed. by Harold Augenbraum and Ilan Stavans (Boston and New York: Houghton Mifflin, 1993); and *Infinite Divisions: An Anthology of Chicana Literature*, ed. by Tey Diana Rebolledo and Eliana S. Rivero (Tuscon and London: The University of Arizona Press, 1993), with a lengthy section on "Growing-up." - Among the numerous multicultural anthologies, the voluminous collection *New Worlds of Literature: Writings from America's Many Cultures*, ed. by Jerome Beaty and J. Paul Hunter (New York and London: W. W. Norton, 2nd ed., 1994), contains a broad spectrum of thematically arranged texts and is accompanied by a helpful *Instructor's Guide* by Carolina Hospital and Carlos Medina (New York and London: W.W. Norton, 1994); the two complementary volumes *Imagining America: Stories from the Promised Land* and *Visions of America: Personal Narratives from the Promised Land*, both ed. by Wesley Brown and Amy Ling (New York: Persea Books, 1991 and 1993), contain 37 short stories from 1900 to the present and personal essays and autobiographical texts by 36 writers of diverse racial and cultural backgrounds respectively; and *Stories from the American Mosaic*, ed. by Scott Walker (Saint Paul: Graywolf Press, 1990), collects 15 stories by contemporary 'ethnic' writers. - An EFL-collection with stories by Jewish-American, African American, Native

- the ritual *bar-mitzvah* of a thirteen-year-old Jewish boy from Newark,
- the humiliation of a Chicano youth by the *gringos* met in the promised land of Texas,
- the culture clash experienced by a Native American adolescent torn between the ancient traditions of his tribe and the puzzling behaviour of white people,
- the devastating "colour shock"[10] undergone by a Black child in a racist school in the South,
- the fumbling experiments with drugs and prostitution engaged in by a bored daughter of an affluent suburban WASP family in Detroit,
- the unbearable cultural tension felt by the bewildered daughter of a Chinese laundryman in San Francisco,
- the inter-cultural conflicts between the Issei and the Nisei in a Japanese immigrant family in America,

and an almost endless number of further variations.[11] The richness of such fictional or autobiographical texts or the fact that such texts are more immediately interesting and more motivating to adolescent learners than expository texts, however, are not yet sufficient to allow a convincing curricular deduction. In addition to what has been said so far, it must be substantiated that an examination of typical patterns of growing up in a multicultural society provides a representative and rewarding approach to a study of the United States as a 'nation of nations,' an ethnic 'salad bowl,' or a multicultural 'quilt.' In other words, the learner-centred argument has to be complemented by subject-orientated considerations.

American, Asian American and Chicano writers is *Growing up in a Multicultural Society: Nine Recent American Stories*, ed. and ann. by Peter Freese (München: Langenscheidt-Longman, 1994).

10 The term was coined by Martin Luther King, *Where Do We Go From Here: Chaos or Community?* (New York: Bantam Books, 1968), p. 130. - The relevant passage is reprinted in *Growing up Black in America: Stories and Studies of Socialization*, ed. by Peter Freese, pp. 8f.

11 As to the enormous amount of ethnic diversity in the U.S.A., consult the *Harvard Encyclopedia of American Ethnic Groups*, ed. by Stephan Thernstrom (Cambridge, Mass., and London: The Belknap Press of Harvard University Press, 1980), which deals with 126 ethnic groups from the Acadians to the Zoroastrians.

The Relevance of Socialization Patterns in a Multicultural Society

> Being an American is not something to be inherited so much as something to be achieved.
> Perry Miller[12]

The strategies which a society develops and the institutions which it sets up to pass on its traditions, its values and its way of life from one generation to the next are, as Eisenstadt says in his influential study *From Generation to Generation*, essential "mechanisms of continuity of the social system."[13] Therefore, it is no accident that a large part of the knowledge accumulated by ethnological research about primitive societies derives from a close study of their initiation rituals, ceremonies through which primitive cultures confer full membership and adult status upon their adolescents. In its attempt to explain the inner mechanism of complex industrial societies, recent sociological research has concentrated on the study of what is now called 'socialization,' that is, "the process by which someone learns the ways of a given society or social group so that he can function within it."[14] Consequently, when one wants to gain insight into the functioning of a given society, a study of the processes of growing up in that society provides highly relevant information.

If the society under consideration consists, as the United States do, of immigrants from numerous countries, such an approach proves even more appropriate. Manifold problems of acculturation will be most obvious in the maturation of the immigrants' children, for here occurs the struggle which results either in further conflict between or

---

12 Quoted from Werner Sollors, *Beyond Ethnicity: Consent and Descent in American Culture* (New York and Oxford: Oxford University Press, 1986), p. 3.
13 S. N. Eisenstadt, *From Generation to Generation: Age Groups and Social Structure* (New York: Free Press, 1966), pp. 35f.
14 Frederick Elkin, *The Child and Society: The Process of Socialization* (New York: Random House, 1968), p. 4. - Short and inexpensive introductions to socialization research are provided by Kurt Danziger, *Socialization* (Harmondsworth: Penguin Books, 1971), and by Wilfried Gottschalch, Marina Neumann-Schönwetter, and Gunther Soukop, *Sozialisationsforschung: Materialien, Probleme, Kritik* (Frankfurt: Fischer, 1971). A students' guide is provided by Dietmar Kamper, ed., *Sozialisationstheorie* (Freiburg: Herder, 1974).

in the fusion of two cultures: the indigenous one handed down from the parents to their children and that of the host country imparted to the children in everyday life and in their state-provided school education. America, who thinks of herself as the 'new world' set off against the 'old world' of Europe, is not only a nation of immigrants and an ethnic 'salad bowl,' but also a country in which youth is accorded the highest esteem. Thus Geoffrey Gorer could say about the U.S.A. that there the years from twelve to twenty-five are looked on as "the chief *raison d'être* of living,"[15] and Ihab Hassan could even diagnose an American "neurosis of innocence."[16] Grace and Fred M. Hechinger found, in their book of the same title, a *Teen-Age Tyranny* established in the United States, and many a critic has varied the derisive quip that America is the only country in the world where one can pass from adolescence to senescence without ever reaching maturity. One reason for such a glorification of youth can be found in the predicament of immigration, for often ignorant immigrant parents feel forced to abdicate their authority to their more 'Americanized' children. Another reason, however, belongs to the history of ideas, for America is a country where parents try to be the pals or even the peers of their children, where the daily behaviour of politicians and other public figures testifies to the pervasive influence of the myth of the boy-man and the girl-woman and where the slogan 'Don't trust anybody over thirty' was coined.

Americans have always connected the dream of beginning anew in the Edenic virgin wilderness of a continent free of the fetters of history with the developmental phase of adolescence, which is why the promise of youth has become inextricably linked with the national vision known, since James Truslow Adams, as the 'American Dream.'[17] Ontogenesis and phylogenesis are looked upon as reflections of the same process, which explains why one of the founding fathers of American psychology, Stanley Hall, could state in his seminal study *Adolescence*

---

15 Geoffrey Gorer, *The American People: A Study in National Character* (New York: W.W. Norton, 1948), p. 121.
16 Ihab Hassan, *Radical Innocence: Studies in the Contemporary American Novel* (New York: Harper & Row, 1966), p. 40.
17 See page 93.

that "the child and the race" are "each keys to the other."[18] Such an analogy pervades American literature, and the developmental stage of adolescence in its precarious borderline existence between the innocence of childhood not yet lost and the experience of adulthood not yet won comes to serve as a paradigm of the complex tension between the contradictory ideals of an innocent Eden on the one hand and of a hard-won Utopia on the other or, in R.W.B. Lewis' terms, borrowed from Emerson, between the Party of Hope and the Party of Memory.[19] Consequently, the basic contrast between 'innocence' and 'experience' is one of the central constituents of American intellectual history and inadvertently bestows a certain symbolic significance upon every youth. Such considerations warrant the thesis that

- the general importance of the socialization process as every society's essential instrument of ensuring its survival,
- the specific importance of this process in an immigrant society as a basic means of fusing contributing cultures into a new and at least partly shared culture, and
- the additional significance of this process in a society which rates youth as the most glorious phase of life

are sufficient reasons for approaching the study of the American 'melting pot' through an exploration of how American children grow up within their different ethnic contexts.

If it is granted that the topic of multi-ethnicity and/or multiculturalism in the U.S.A. can be profitably approached through fictional instead of expository texts, that among the numerous thematically relevant texts those which focus on the process of 'growing up in a multicultural society' are most suitable for the EFL-classroom, and that a study of such texts provides an appropriate means for acquiring a better understanding of the manifold problems of a multi-ethnic society, the approach suggested here turns out to be equally feasible with regard to the need of the students and the subject matter to be

---

18 Stanley Hall, *Adolescence: Its Psychology and Its Relation to Physiology, Anthropology, Sociology, Sex, Crime, Religion and Education* (New York: Appleton, 1924), vol. I, p. viii.
19 See R.W.B. Lewis, *The American Adam: Innocence, Tragedy and Tradition in the Nineteenth Century* (Chicago and London: University of Chicago Press, 1955).

studied. But before individual stories can be discussed, another aspect needs to be considered.

In the context of what is revealingly called *problemorientierter Unterricht*, we tend to contextualize literary texts by means of sociological and psychological concepts, an approach which provides the categories thought necessary for classification and generalization. The notion of *racism*, the contrast between *ingroup* and *outgroup orientation*, the implications of *majority* and *minority status*, the different behavioural manifestations of *prejudice* from mere *antilocution* via *discrimination* to *extermination* provide useful frames of reference for the comprehension of individual and communal actions as depicted in literature and, moreover, they have a high and educationally important transfer value.[20] An acquaintance with Martin Luther King's concept of "colour shock"[21] will be a useful intellectual key to many a Black initiation story, from Ralph Ellison's "Flying Home" to John Hendrik Clark's "The Boy Who Painted Christ Black" and William Melvin Kelley's "The Only Man on Liberty Street." In addition, Grier and Cobbs's provocative study *Black Rage* will certainly help to understand the psychological predicament of many a young protagonist in Richard Wright's stories and novels.[22] An investigation of the religious foundation of the Jewish desire for education, the high social mobility resulting from that education, and the anti-Semitism bred from envy of that very mobility will provide an enlightening context for many a Jewish-American narrative.[23] Some elementary knowledge of the basic discrepancy between the Native American's rejection of the notion of

---

20 For details see the relevant units in Peter Freese, *Growing up Black* (Teacher's Book), e.g., the section "Getting the Course Started," pp. 28-37.
21 See note 10.
22 William Melvin Kelley's "The Only Man on Liberty Street" is available in *Stories from the Black Experience*, ed. by J.B. Stone and Luther K. Masket (Stuttgart: Klett, 1981), pp. 9-16; John Hendrik Clarke's "The Boy Who Painted Christ Black" can be found in *Growing up Black*, pp. 43-50; Ellison's brilliant but difficult story is not yet available in an EFL-edition, but Bernhard Ostendorf, "Ralph Ellison, 'Flying Home' (1944)," in *Die amerikanische Short Story der Gegenwart: Interpretationen*, ed. by Peter Freese (Berlin: Schmidt, 1976), pp. 64-76, provides a helpful analysis and, in footnote 10, information about the anthologies in which the story is included. - William H. Grier and Price M. Cobbs, *Black Rage* (1968), is available as a pocket book (New York: Bantam Books, 1969).
23 See the relevant chapters in Peter Freese, *Bernard Malamud, "The Assistant" - Interpretations and Suggestions for Teaching* (Paderborn: Schöningh, 1983).

private property and his untenable position within a white culture based on that very notion will be one of the prerequisites for an understanding of modern Native American literature. And a psychological inquiry into the consequences of surviving in a culture whose language, religion, and gender-based role ascriptions one does not share will help to grasp some of the recurring motifs of Chicano and Chicana literature.

Helpful as these and many related concepts are, I have learned from my teaching experience that they have two serious limitations. First, they are all too easily misused as a means of domesticating irritating problems by labelling them - the joy of being able to offer a scholarly diagnosis, as it were, makes one forget the necessity to provide a therapy. And secondly, all these concepts are systematic and synchronic and, therefore, sadly devoid of any historical dimension. Such an ahistoricity of conceptual patterns is especially detrimental if one deals with the multicultural aspects of life in the U.S.A. It should be obvious that the slow and often painful growth of a new nation out of the most diverse groups of immigrants needs to be looked at as a historical phenomenon. Of the utmost importance in this context is James Baldwin's variation upon a pervasive American idea, the insight that "the past is all that makes the present coherent,"[24] which lately was so memorably exemplified by Alex Hailey's *Roots* (1976) and the history of its reception. Nobody can presume to understand what is going on in contemporary America without trying to reconstruct to what extent the present situation is the inevitable outcome of past events. This means that the systematic framework provided by social sciences which we like to use for contextualizing ethnic texts must be complemented by the all too often neglected historical dimension, that is, by some elementary survey of the main phases of America's understanding of her national identity.

Henry James, who searched for a 'usable past,' once said that it was 'a complex fate' to be an American. James Baldwin, as many an expatriate before him, needed to leave the country and live for many years in Paris before he could write his well-known essay on "The

---

24 James Baldwin, "Autobiographical Notes", in his *Notes of a Native Son* (London: Corgi Books, 1969), p. 4.

Discovery of What It Means to Be an American," in which he identifies himself "to [his] astonishment, to be as American as any Texas G.I."[25] Both James's and Baldwin's experiences illustrate an insight offered in 1950 by Erik H. Erikson in his seminal study *Childhood and Society*: "We begin to conceptualize matters of identity at the very time in history when they become a problem. For we do so in a country which attempts to make a super-identity out of all the identities imported by its constituent immigrants."[26]

From Melting Pot to Multiculturalism: Changing Concepts of American Identity

> *Ubi panis ibi patria* is the motto of all emigrants. What, then, is the American, this new man?
> J. Hector St. John de Crèvecoeur, *Letters from an American Farmer and Sketches of Eighteenth-Century America*[27]

Simplifying a very complex issue, one might say that the initial settlers on the new continent hardly gave a thought to what made an 'American.' After the Declaration of Independence, however, the newly created nation began to feel the need for some national consciousness. Around 1790, eight out of ten white Americans were of British extraction. Thus, for obvious reasons, the ethnic aspect of the problem was kept in the background and American national identity was thought of in terms of ideology rather than ethnicity. Whoever was willing to adopt the enlightened belief in personal liberty and democratic government, to be orientated towards a promising future, and to share Thomas Jefferson's vision of an agrarian nation of "those

---

25 James Baldwin, "The Discovery of What It Means to Be an American," in his *Nobody Knows My Name: More Notes of a Native Son* (New York: Dell Books, 1967), p. 17.
26 Erik H. Erikson, *Childhood and Society* (Harmondsworth: Penguin Books, 1965), p. 274.
27 J. Hector St. John de Crèvecoeur, *Letters from an American Farmer and Sketches of Eighteenth-Century America*, p. 69.

who labor in the earth" as "the chosen people of God,"[28] could participate in the great experiment and think of him- or herself as an American. Right from the beginning, however, Native Americans and African Americans were excluded from the great experiment, and thus the seeds of future discord were sown and the ethnic dilemma, although not yet an actual problem, lurked in the background.

This early attitude might be called the position of (almost unconditional) ASSIMILATION, and it has found its most famous expression in Emma Lazarus' sonnet *The New Colossus*, which was written in November 1883 and in 1903 was engraved on a plate and mounted on a wall inside the pedestal of the Statue of Liberty. But almost exactly a century before Lazarus, this assimilationist position was first and famously formulated by J. Hector St. John de Crèvecoeur in the third of his *Letters from an American Farmer* (1782). This often quoted letter not only contains the key concepts of the agrarian ideal, the wilderness, and the frontier, the notions of progress and success, and the ideas of the unfolding of history in "a great circle" and of America as an asylum for the poor people of Europe. It also asks the decisive question: "What, then, is the American, this new man?" and provides this answer:

> He is neither an European nor the descendant of an European; hence that strange mixture of blood, which you will find in no other country [...] *He* is an American, who, leaving behind him all his ancient prejudices and manners, receives new ones from the new mode of life he has embraced, the new government he obeys, and the new rank he holds. He becomes an American by being received in the broad lap of our great Alma Mater. Here individuals of all nations are melted into a new race of men, whose labours and posterity will one day cause great changes in the world.[29]

---

28 Thomas Jefferson, *Notes on the State of Virginia* (1784/1785); here quoted from the reprint in *The Norton Anthology of American Literature*, ed. by Ronald Gottesman et.al. (New York and London: W. W. Norton, 1979), vol. I, pp. 500-512; here p. 512.

29 J. Hector St. John de Crèvecoeur, *Letters from an American Farmer and Sketches of Eighteenth-Century America*, pp. 69f. - The famous passage is reprinted in the EFL-reader *From Melting Pot to Multiculturalism: 'E pluribus unum'?*, pp. 4f., and analyzed in detail in the accompanying *Resource Book*. - Since the present revisionist reading of Crèvecoeur rightly stresses the pessimistic aspects of his position, readers should not confine themselves to the frequently anthologized Third Letter, but also read Letter IX ("Description of Charles Town; Thoughts on Slavery; On Physical Evil; A Melancholy Scene") and Letter XII ("Distresses of a Frontier Man").

The New Colossus

Not like the brazen giant of Greek fame,
With conquering limbs astride from land to land;
Here at our sea-washed, sunset-gates shall stand
A mighty woman with a torch, whose flame
Is the imprisoned lightning, and her name
Mother of Exiles. From her beacon-hand
Glows world-wide welcome, her mild eyes command
The air-bridged harbor that twin-cities frame.

"Keep, ancient lands, your storied pomp!" cries she
With silent lips. "Give me your tired, your poor,
Your huddled masses yearning to breathe free,
The wretched refuse of your teeming shore;
Send these, the homeless, tempest-tost to me,
I lift my lamp beside the golden door!"

Emma Lazarus,
November 2nd, 1883.

A facsimile of Emma Lazarus' sonnet *The New Colossus*

The momentous idea of different nationalities, cultures, and languages being melted into something new found its most influential expression in the enormously successful drama *The Melting Pot* by the English Jew, Israel Zangwill, which was first performed on October 5, 1908, at the Columbia Theatre in Washington. Zangwill's poetic translation of Crèvecoeur's concept of assimilation into the charged metaphor of America as "God's Crucible" and "the great Melting-Pot"[30] greatly helped to popularize one of the constitutive American myths which is either wholeheartedly embraced or furiously rejected and which can be used or abused to represent many conflicting attitudes. And it is an additional irony that Zangwill was a Zionist and thus a representative of an important deterrent to the very 'melting' process he eulogized. The texts with which the original 'melting pot' might best be illustrated in the EFL-classroom are pertinent excerpts from Zangwill's play, Dudley Randall's satirical poem on the uselessness of the pot for Black Americans[31] and, as an interesting variation upon the usual anthology pieces, the following lines by a Mr. Frederick J. Haskin published around 1910 in the Chicago *Daily News*:

THE ALIEN IN THE MELTING POT

I am the immigrant.
Since the dawn of creation my restless feet have beaten new paths across the earth.
My uneasy bark has tossed on all seas.
My wanderlust was born of the craving for more liberty and a better wage for the sweat of my face.
I looked towards the United States with eyes kindled by the fire of ambition and heart quickened with new-born hope.
I approached its gates with great expectation.
I entered in with fine hopes.
I have shouldered my burden as the American man of all work.
I contribute eighty-five per cent of all the labour in the slaughtering and meat-packing industries.
I do seven-tenths of the bituminous coal mining.
I do seventy-eight per cent of all the work in the woollen mills.
I contribute nine-tenths of all the labour in the cotton mills.

---

30 See p. 179 and note 1.
31 Dudley Randall's poem "The Melting Pot" originally appeared in his collection *Cities Burning* (Detroit: Broadside Press, 1968), pp. 322f. - It is reprinted on pp. 169f. of this book, included in *From Melting Pot to Multiculturalism: 'E pluribus unum'?*, p. 13, and analyzed in the accompanying *Resource Book*.

I make nine-twentieths of all the clothing.
I manufacture more than half the shoes.
I build four-fifths of all the furniture.
I make half of the collars, cuffs and shirts.
I turn out four-fifths of all the leather.
I make half the gloves.
I refine nearly nineteen-twentieths of the sugar.
I make half of the tobacco and cigars.
And yet, I am the great American problem.
When I pour out my blood on your altar of labour, and lay down my life as a sacrifice to your god of toil, men make no more comment than at the fall of a sparrow.
But my brawn is woven into the warp and woof of the fabric of your national being.
My children shall be your children and your land shall be my land because my sweat and my blood will cement the foundations of the America of To-Morrow.
If I can be fused into the body politic, the Melting Pot will have stood the supreme test.[32]

Around the middle of the nineteenth century, American nationalism became more pronounced - mirrored, for example, in John L. O.Sullivan's concept of "manifest destiny," coined in 1845 and used as a justification of hegemonic claims,[33] and popularized in the 1872 painting of the same title by John Gast[34] - and, consequently, anti-immigrant feelings began to grow. The enormous influx of Catholics, mainly Irish peasants fleeing from the potato blight in their starving mother country, made Catholicism a serious threat to the Protestants, and the attempts of the Irish to set up parochial schools seemed to endanger the cherished ideal of the public school as the main instrument of Americanizing the immigrants. The Know-Nothing movement and other expressions of what came to be known

---

32 Quoted in *The Works of Israel Zangwill*, vol. XII, pp. 197f. - A helpful article on the 'melting pot' concept is Philip Gleason, "The Melting Pot: Symbol of Fusion or Confusion?" *American Quarterly*, 16 (1964), 20-46.
33 See the documents collected in *Manifest Destiny*, ed. by Norman Graebner (Indianapolis: Bobbs-Merrill, 1968); and the scholarly treatment by Albert K. Weinberg, *Manifest Destiny: A Study of Nationalistic Expansionism in American History* (Baltimore: Johns Hopkins Press, 1935). Suggestions for teaching this concept in the EFL-classroom are offered by Peter Bischoff, "'Westward the Star of Empire takes its way': Manifest Destiny and American Expansion; Ein Unterrichtsbaustein zum American Dream für den amerikakundlichen Unterricht in der Sekundarstufe II," *Englisch-Amerikanische Studien*, 1 (1979), 364-384.
34 See the reproduction on p. 141.

as Nativism - and what is characteristically expressed in Thomas Bailey Aldrich's poem *Unguarded Gates*[35] - began to flourish,[36] and consequently the concept of assimilation was replaced by a growing

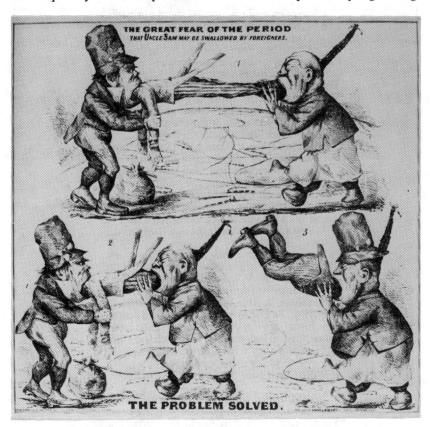

---

35 Both Lazarus' and Aldrich's poems are reprinted in *From Melting Pot to Multiculturalism: 'E pluribus unum'?*, pp. 2f.
36 The most important book to consult in this context is John Higham, *Strangers in the Land: Patterns of American Nativism 1860-1925* (New York: Atheneum, 2nd ed., 1963). - Among the many studies of anti-Catholicism, Ray Allen Billington, *The Protestant Crusade 1800-1860: A Study of the Origins of American Nativism* (New York: Macmillan, 1938), seems particularly helpful. - An aspect of special interest for the EFL-classroom, namely, the expression of anti-Catholicism in contemporary cartoons, is investigated by John and Selma Appel, "The Grand Old Sport of Hating Catholics: American Anti-Catholic Caricature Prints," *The Critic*, November/December 1971, pp. 50-58.

THOMAS BAILEY ALDRICH

Unguarded Gates

Wide open and unguarded stand our gates,
Named of the four winds. North, South, East, and West;
Portals that lead to an enchanted land
Of cities, forests, fields of living gold,
Vast prairies, lordly summits touched with snow,
Majestic rivers sweeping proudly past
The Arab's date-palm and the Norseman's pine -
A realm wherein are fruits of every zone,
Airs of all climes, for lo! throughout the year
The red rose blossoms somewhere - a rich land,
A later Eden planted in the wilds,
With not an inch of earth within its bound
But if a slave's foot press it set him free.
Here, it is written, Toil shall have its wage,
And Honor honor, and the humblest man
Stand level with the highest in the law.
Of such a land have men in dungeons dreamed,
And with the vision brightening in their eyes
Gone smiling to the fagot and the sword.

Wide open and unguarded stand our gates,
And through them presses a wild motley throng -
Men from the Volga and the tartar steppes,
Featureless figures of the Hoang-Ho,
Malayan, Scythian, Teuton, Kelt, and Slav,
Flying the Old World's poverty and scorn;
These bringing with them unknown gods and rites,
Those, tiger passions, here to stretch their claws.
In street and alley what strange tongues are loud,
Accents of menace alien to our air,
Voices that once the Tower of Babel knew.

O Liberty, white Goddess! is it well
To leave the gates unguarded? On thy breast
Fold Sorrow's children, soothe the hurts of fate,
Lift the down-trodden, but with hand of steel
Stay those who to thy sacred portals come
To waste the gift of freedom. Have a care
Lest from thy brow the clustered stars be torn
And trampled in the dust. For so of old
The thronging Goth and Vandal trampled Rome,
And where the temples of the Caesars stood
The lean wolf unmolested made her lair.

The Writings of Thomas Bailey Aldrich (Boston and New York: Houghton Mifflin, 1907), vol. II, pp. 71f.

demand for AMERICANIZATION. In the terms of the melting pot metaphor, which proved useful even for this attitude, A+B+C (the elements to be thrown into the crucible) were no longer supposed to become D (Crèvecoeur's "new race of men" or Zangwill's "coming superman"), but A+B+C were now supposed to become A: newcomers were expected to take over the characteristics of the earlier and now dominant group. Thus, the question of American identity was no longer answered in terms of political conviction and ideological concerns, but under the aspects of ethnic background, religion, and education, and this change in attitude can be well illustrated by four representative cartoons.

"The Great Fear of the Period" is a well-known three-stage depiction of the widespread fear that the Irish and the Chinese would 'swallow' the majority population and that then the Chinese would swallow the Irish. As an American variation upon the myth of the 'Yellow Peril' it is uncomfortably reminiscent of many a German cartoon of the Third Reich about the threat of *Überfremdung*.

Thomas Nast's most powerful anti-Catholic cartoon, which was published in *Harper's Weekly* on September 30, 1871, bears the caption "The American River Ganges: The Priests and the Children" and deals with the hotly debated issue of public support of parochial schools. It shows the U.S. Public School in ruins with the American flag flying upside down as a distress signal. In the background Tammany Hall displays two flags with the Papal Tiara and the Irish Harp. Closer inspection reveals that the heads of the alligators are bishops' miters with Irish faces below. While teachers are led to the gallows, Boss Tweed and his Tammany followers sacrifice the children of the city to the alligators/bishops, and only a lonely teacher with a Protestant Bible tries to interfere.

Whereas "The American River Ganges" is an acid comment on a religious issue, another famous Nast cartoon, which appeared on February 8, 1879, in *Harper's Weekly*, neatly sums up the xenophobia of the times. It bears the caption "Every Dog (No Distinction of Color) Has His Day. Red Gentleman: 'Pale face 'fraid you crowd him out, as he did me.'" It depicts the reversal of the 'Go West' movement with the railway driving the Native American towards the Pacific into a 'Go

Growing up in a Multicultural Society

East' movement with the Chinese 'coolie' beating the drum of 'cheap labor' and driving the white man back to the Atlantic; the Ku Klux Klan slogan 'Down on the Nigger;' the slogan 'The Chinese must go!' of Dennis Kearney of the California Workingmen's Party; a statement on 'The Chinese Problem' and a 'Foreigners Not Wanted' poster; a slur on the German love of beer and the fear of German socialism implicit in the 'Social Fritz;' the rejection of the Irish and the Dutch by an ironically undercut 'Know-Nothingism;' and - as the final touch - the figure of a drowsing Black on the cotton bale in the corner and the ominous warning 'My Day Is Coming.'

NEW CUSTOMERS.

ITINERANT GENTS' FURNISHING GOODS DEALER. — Suspenders! Gollar puttons. Negties!

An anti-Semitic cartoon, which appeared on October 3, 1894, in *Puck*, depicts the unwelcome Jewish immigrant as a stereotyped peddler, and another cartoon, which appeared on January 23, 1892, in *Judge*, expresses a number of interesting aspects of Jewish-American history. The Tzar wielding his whip stands for the pogroms which drove huge masses of Russian Jews to the 'promised land' of America; the renaming of New York as New Jerusalem alludes to both the hopes of the homeless refugees and the fright of the 'natives;' the fact that all the stores and offices are owned by Jews represents the pervasive fear that they will 'take over;' the words "perseverance and industry" on the scroll carried by the dominant figure in the foreground, who shows all the alleged 'Jewish' characteristics and whose dress demonstrates that he has 'made it,' provides a reason - and perhaps some grudging admiration - for the success of the Jews; the figures leaving the city for "the West" define the westward movement as a flight of the 'natives' from the hordes of immigrants; and the ironic detail that their names are exclusively Dutch reminds the reader of the time when New York was still New Amsterdam.

But in spite of the growing hostility to assorted groups of newcomers, an ever increasing stream of immigrants poured into the country; a society conceived of by its founders as a peaceful community of "tillers of the earth"[37] rapidly turned into an industrialized and urban society and, around the turn of the century, a new wave of Americanization led to new immigration laws trying to stem the tide of what were called, in contrast to the 'old immigrants' from northern and western Europe, the 'new immigrants' from southern and eastern Europe. The controversial Literacy Test was finally enacted in 1917, and the quota system was introduced. In this climate, an ethnically restrictive, Anglo-Saxon version of American nationality gained ground: the Daughters of the American Revolution, founded in 1890, campaigned for patriotism; the Ku Klux Klan appropriated and radicalized the concept of Americanism; and the war against Germany led to an almost hysterical denunciation of what came to be called 'hyphenation' and to a movement for a '100 per cent Americanism.' Out of this reaction grew a new form of ethnic pride which found its most militant expression in ANGLO-SAXON RACIALISM. One of the

---

37 J. Hector St. John de Crèvecoeur, *Letters from an American Farmer*, p. 67.

most influential statements of such thinking was Madison Grant's *The Passing of the Great Race* (1916), which combined, as its contemporary European parallels did, romantic notions of national glory with biological hypotheses about the different values of diverse racial stock. In this 'scientific' treatise the concept of the melting pot is rejected as suicidal - "If the Melting Pot is allowed to boil without control, the native American of colonial descent will become as extinct as the Athenian of the age of Pericles and the Viking of the days of Rollo,"[38] - and strong measures against 'undesirables' are demanded. Grant states:

> The transportation lines advertised America as a land flowing with milk and honey and the European governments took the opportunity to unload upon careless, wealthy and hospitable America the sweepings of their jails and asylums. The result was that the new immigration, while it still included many strong elements from the north of Europe, contained a large and increasing number of the weak, the broken and the mentally crippled of all races drawn from the lowest stratum of the Mediterranean basin and the Balkans, together with hordes of the wretched, submerged populations of the Polish Ghettos. Our jails, insane asylums and almshouses are filled with this human flotsam and the whole tone of American life, social, moral and political has been lowered and vulgarized by them.
>
> With a pathetic and fatuous belief in the efficacy of American institutions and environment to reverse or obliterate immemorial hereditary tendencies, these newcomers were welcomed and given a share in our land and prosperity. The American taxed himself to sanitate and educate these poor helots and as soon as they could speak English, encouraged them to enter into the political life, first of municipalities and then of the nation. [...]
>
> These immigrants adopt the language of the native American, they wear his clothes, they steal his name and they are beginning to take his women, but they seldom adopt his religion or understand his ideals and while he is being elbowed out of his own home the American looks calmly abroad and urges on others the suicidal ethics which are exterminating his own race.[39]

---

38 Madison Grant, *The Passing of the Great Race* (New York: Scribner, rev. ed., 1918). - This sentence is quoted by Willi Paul Adams in his informative article "Die Assimilationsfrage in der amerikanischen Einwanderungsdiskussion 1890-1930," *Amerikastudien / American Studies*, 27 (1982), 275-291; here p. 281.

39 Madison Grant, *The Passing of the Great Race*, pp. 89ff. - This passage is reprinted in *From Melting Pot to Multiculturalism: 'E pluribus unum'?*, p. 9, and analyzed in the accompanying *Resource Book*.

UNRESTRICTED IMMIGRATION AND ITS RESULTS — A POSSIBLE CURIOSITY OF THE TWENTIETH CENTURY.
THE LAST YANKEE.

A pictorial anticipation of Grant's thesis of the impending passing of the great race of Anglo-Saxons and its replacement by biologically inferior people, the hordes of uncouth immigrants, can be found in a cartoon with the caption "Unrestricted Immigration and Its Results - A Possible Curiosity of the Twentieth Century: The Last Yankee." This cartoon appeared on September 8, 1882, in *Frank Leslie's Illustrated Newspaper* and shows the last solitary specimen of the allegedly dying species of the tall Yankee surrounded by representatives of diverse groups of immigrants, whose stunted figures and demented faces testify to their inferior racial heritage. In the background on the left one recognizes "Boomelheimer's Delicatessen" with a German with his *Zipfelmütze* looking out of the window, whereas on the right a French *Marianne* observes the spectacle from a window above "Jean Boucois' Americaine Bakery." And a shop-sign that advertises "Yan-kee - Amelican Laundry" conjures up a third ethnic stereotype, namely that of the Chinese laundryman who cannot pronounce an 'r.'

With regard to African Americans, the demeaning racial stereotype of the 'Happy Darky' and the indestructable cliché that Blacks possess 'natural rhythm' were still cruelly and unthinkingly perpetuated. The 'Happy Darky' cliché is best illustrated by the widely disseminated trade cards or 'coon cards' which specialized in the condescending portrayal of childishly grinning and extremely stupid Blacks, such as the two cards from the 1880s that advertise the products of the St. Louis Beef Canning Company with the picture of a grinning Black and the caption "Well fixed!! what more can a Nigger want" or use the picture of an absurdly dressed black man and a piece of garbled 'nigger talk' to canvass for "Nigger Head Tobacco."[40] The cliché of 'natural rhythm,' on the other hand, can be found in numerous nineteenth-century sheet-music covers such as the one about "Whistling Rufus."

Stereotypical views of particular groups of immigrants were now increasingly legitimized by 'scientific' theories about their alleged hereditary characteristics. Thus, for example, a typical example of the common stereotype of the Irishman as an ape-faced man is offered in

---

40 For details see Robert Jay, *The Trade Card in Nineteenth-Century America* (Columbia: University of Missouri Press, 1987).

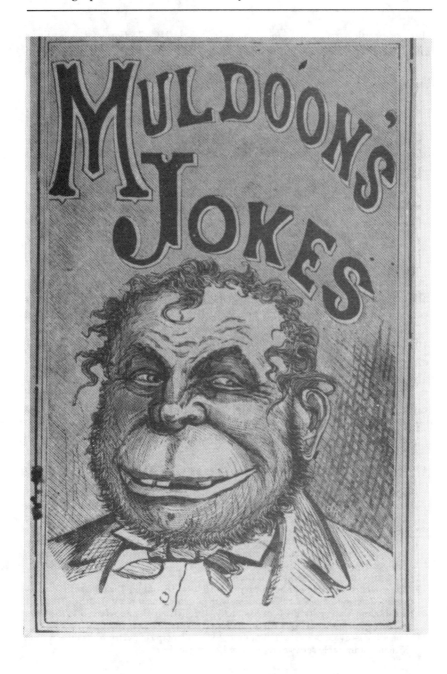

the cover picture of *Muldoon's Jokes: A Select Collection of the Sayings and Doings of Terrance Muldoon*, which was published in New York in 1902[41] and which might be studied in conjunction with the following excerpt from Madison Grant's book:

> Along with other ancient and primitive racial remnants, ferocious gorilla-like living specimens of Paleolithic man are found not infrequently on the west coast of Ireland and are easily recognized by the great upper lip, bridgeless nose, beetling brow with long growing hair and wild and savage aspect. The proportion of the skull which gives rise to this large upper lip, the low forehead and the superorbital ridges are certainly Neanderthal characters. The other traits of this Irish type are common to many primitive races. This is the Irishman of caricature and the type was very frequent in America when the first Irish immigrants came in 1846 and the following years.[42]

A fictional text which expresses the xenophobic attitude and the quasi-scientific hereditary theories of those days with regard to the alleged racial inferiority of Blacks is Thomas W. Dixon's immensely popular novel of 1905, *The Clansman: An Historical Romance of the Ku Klux Klan*, which soon turned into a Broadway hit and was filmed, in 1915, by D. W. Griffith as *The Birth of a Nation*, one of the first great classics of the American cinema. Excerpts from this novel, for example, the revealing dialogue between a sympathetically presented Southerner and a cynical Northern Reconstructionist[43] - combined with a viewing of the film,[44] which James Baldwin called "an elaborate

---

41 For teachers wanting to deal with the wider range of ethnic stereotypes, there is a highly recommendable teaching unit based on the work of John J. Appel and Selma Appel, *The Distorted Image: Stereotype and Caricature in Popular American Graphics 1850-1922* (New York: The Anti Defamation League of B'nai B'rith, no date). This unit consists of a filmstrip containing 60 slides, an accompanying cassette narration and a detailed discussion guide for the teacher, and it is offered as "a penetrating commentary on American attitudes to immigration, the universality of prejudice and stereotyping and, above all, a history of how certain immigrant and ethnic stereotypes originated and developed in our society" (p. 3).
42 Madison Grant, *The Passing of the Great Race*, p. 108.
43 The novel is available in a recent reprint: Thomas Dixon, Jr., *The Clansman: An Historical Romance of the Ku Klux Klan*, with an introduction by Thomas D. Clark (Lexington: University Press of Kentucky, 1970). The passage referred to (Chapter X, "A Night Hawk," of Book III) can be found on pp. 289-294.
44 The film is available as a 158-minute VHS videotape, Spectrum 20.125, in Paul Killiam's admirable series of reproduced silent movies.

justification of mass murder,"[45] graphically illustrate this phase of racist thinking and feeling in the United States.

After 1930, Anglo-Saxon Racialism gradually fell into discredit as the epitome of narrow-minded ethnocentricity. But even while it flourished and found such interesting literary expressions as Tom Buchanan's warning in *The Great Gatsby*, that "if we don't look out the white race will be - will be utterly submerged. It's all scientific stuff; it's been proved,"[46] it met its opposition in a new attitude first formulated in 1915 by Horace Kallen in his essay "Democracy versus the Melting Pot: A Study of American Nationality." This article is rather vague in its metaphorical language, and Kallen talks, for example, about "the symphony of civilization" in which "each ethnic group is the natural instrument."[47] In 1924, Kallen had his earlier article reprinted in his book *Culture and Democracy in the United States*, and here he introduced the term which came to define his anti-assimilationist stance: CULTURAL PLURALISM. According to this view, the melting pot concept in all its contradictory mutations is simply an untenable myth, a position which, in 1963, Glazer and Moynihan would corroborate by flatly stating "The point about the melting pot [...] is that it did not happen."[48] That is, A+B+C can neither be expected to become D as in the position of earlier assimilationism, nor result in A as in the position of Americanization. On the contrary, one will simply have to acknowledge that A+B+C will remain A+B+C. America should, therefore, not aspire to become a homogeneous nation but should realize itself as a political unity made up of different indigenous cultures.

---

45 James Baldwin, *The Devil Finds Work* (London: Corgi Books, 1978), p. 50.
46 F. Scott Fitzgerald, *The Great Gatsby*, in *The Bodley Head Scott Fitzgerald* (London: Bodley Head, rpt. 1977), vol. I, p. 29. - For a detailed discussion of this aspect, which in Tom Buchanan's case is inspired by Lothrop Stoddard's *The Rising Tide of Color against World White Supremacy* (1920), see M. Gidley, "Notes on F. Scott Fitzgerald and the Passing of the Great Race," *Journal of American Studies*, 7 (1973), 171-181; and Peter Gregg Slater, "Ethnicity in *The Great Gatsby*," *Twentieth Century Literature*, 19 (1973), 53-62.
47 Kallen's article appeared first in *The Nation*, 25 February 1915; relevant excerpts are accessible in the EFL-reader *America, the Melting Pot*, pp. 37-39 (the passages quoted are on p. 39, lines 47 and 44). - A helpful article dealing with Kallen's position is John Higham, "Ethnic Pluralism in Modern American Thought," in his *Send These to Me: Jews and Other Immigrants in Urban America* (New York: Atheneum, 1975), pp. 196-230; esp. pp. 203-208.
48 See the fourth motto on p. 179.

Kallen's view is cleverly adopted in several World War I Victory Loan posters aimed at all the different ethnic groups in the U.S.A., appealing to their newly developed patriotism, and asking them to join in the common effort.

It was the position of cultural pluralism which finally led, through several mutations, to the contemporary attitude towards the complex problem of American identity, an attitude which was prepared by such contributing factors as the new interest in cultural expressions outside the 'mainstream;' by the impressive research on immigration done by such eminent historians as John Higham or Oscar Handlin (who began his study *The Uprooted* with the now famous sentence: "Once I thought to write a history of the immigrants in America. Then I discovered that the immigrants *were* American history"[49]); by such influential and controversial insights as the famous 'Hansen's Law' which states that "what the son wants to forget the grandson wishes to remember;"[50] and by the proud self-assertion of formerly docile 'minority populations.' This new attitude was generally referred to as MULTI-ETHNICITY; and Michael Novak's influential book on *The Rise of the Unmeltable Ethnics* (1972) - in which Americanization is rejected as nothing but a euphemism for "WASPification"[51] - has become one of its better known manifestos.

In view of the rather questionable theoretical status of this position, which sometimes appeared to be more an urgent political claim than a well-reasoned social theory, the euphoria it called forth in many minority quarters proved to be a little premature. Novak, for example, details an 'ethnic dream,' passionately argues for 'new ethnic politics' meant to liberate what he calls the 'PIGS' (Poles, Italians, Greeks, and Slavs) and to undo the damage wrought by "The Seven Seals of Americanization."[52] And he defines the differences between

---

49 Oscar Handlin, *The Uprooted: From the Old World to the New* (London: Watts and Co., 1953), p. 3.
50 Marcus Lee Hansen in a speech delivered in 1938 to the Augustana Historical Society, which was later reprinted in an abridged version as "The Third Generation in America," *Commentary*, 14 (November 1952), 492-500; here p. 495.
51 Michael Novak, *The Rise of the Unmeltable Ethnics: Politics and Culture in the Seventies* (New York: Macmillan, 1972), p. 114.
52 According to Novak, these seals include the necessity "to learn loneliness" (p. 91), the giving up of "faith in a beneficent world" (p. 93), the acceptance of the concept

ethnic and mainstream American culture in a rather partisan chain of comparisons, which Stein and Hill systematize in the following table:[53]

ETHNIC	AMERICAN
Natural, Real, Genuine	Artificial
Organic	Anomic
Being	Doing
Nature	History
Heart	Head
Imagination	Rationality
Feeling	Thinking
Rooted	Uprooted
Communality, Inseparability of Self from Group	Privacy, Individuality,
Merge with Earth	Alienation, Separation
Personal, Objective	Impersonal, Subjective
Myth	Science
Visceral	Cerebral
Body, Natural	Machine
Personal Experience	Universal Standards
"Network People" (Novak)	"Atomic People" (Novak)

Stein and Hill, who feel that Novak's insistence on a new ethnicity is just a deplorable symptom of a pervasive crisis cult, come to the conclusion that *The Ethnic Imperative* is nothing but

> [...] a choice of self-condemnation by those who feel condemned and let down. Anthropology, like American culture in general, is woefully misguided if it embraces ethnicity as the wave of the future. The meaning of anthropology, and of America, is ethnic identity and pluralism only if we wish to build the future from our fears, rather than our hopes and aspirations.[54]

---

of "mastery" (p. 94), the adoption of a belief in "the myth of self-help" (p. 96), the belief in "the equation of America with the Kingdom of God" (p. 99), the internalization of "a new system of internal repression" (pp. 101f.), and the adoption of "a new relationship to sexual fears" (p. 107).

53 Howard F. Stein and Robert F. Hill, *The Ethnic Imperative: Examining the New White Ethnic Movement* (University Park and London: Pennsylvania State University Press, 1977), p. 166.

54 Stein and Hill, *op. cit.*, p. 287.

It is beyond the limits of the present simplified survey to discuss in detail the manifold implications of Novak's position, but I think it advisable to heed what Philip Gleason has to say about it in his contribution to the *Harvard Encyclopedia of American Ethnic Groups* (1980), which is itself one of the impressive outcomes of the changed attitude toward 'minority populations':

> These spokesmen [of the new attitude] sometimes stress that the new ethnicity really is *new* and not a carryover from immigrant nationalities of the past, but that is not the impression conveyed by the movement as a whole or by the rhetoric employed by its advocates. In fact, quite the opposite impression is conveyed by the constant reiteration that the melting pot never happened, that assimilation was a myth, that Americanization was a repugnant but futile effort to force everyone into the mold of "Anglo-conformity," that the nation was in the beginning, is now, and ever shall be "unmeltably" ethnic, and that those who called themselves the Americans were only another ethnic group - the WASPs - who lorded it over everyone else for far too long, but who have finally been unmasked.[55]

Meanwhile, two new catchphrases have come to the fore, and a heated controversy is being conducted under the twin battle cries of MULTICULTURALISM and POLITICAL CORRECTNESS. Whereas 'multiculturalism' is a concept for which nobody has yet been able to provide a generally accepted definition[56] and which is used to cover widely different and even incompatible programs, the linguistic and behavioural revolution that goes by the name of 'PC'[57] centres on the

---

55 Philip Gleason, "American Identity and Americanization," in *Harvard Encyclopedia of American Ethnic Groups*, pp. 31-58; here p. 54. - Among the many recent publications on the 'new ethnicity,' *America and the New Ethnicity*, ed. by David R. Colburn and George E. Pozzetta (Port Washington, New York: Kennikat Press, 1979), seems especially useful for the EFL-teacher. This collection of 17 interesting articles deals with the melting-pot re-examined, the emergence of ethnic awareness, the resurgence of ethnicity, and the criticism of the new ethnicity, and it contains a helpful bibliographical essay on "the literature relating to the recent resurgence of ethnic awareness" (p. 227).
56 For a survey of the different meanings see Werner Sollors, "*E pluribus unum*; or, Matthew Arnold Meets George Orwell in the 'Multiculturalism' Debate," Working Paper No. 53 (1992) of the John F. Kennedy-Institut für Nordamerikastudien.
57 See Ruth Perry, "A Short History of the Term *Politically Correct*," *The Women's Review of Books*, February 1992; reprinted in the informative anthology *Beyond P.C.: Toward a Politics of Understanding*, ed. by Patricia Aufderheide (Saint Paul, Minnesota: Graywolf Press, 1992), pp. 71-79. For another collection of relevant essays see the

five deadly sins of racism, sexism, ethnocentrism, ableism, and lookism.[58] Any attempt at disentangling the philosophical-political controversy which is fought under these twin banners would have to start with an analysis of the complex interplay between such crucial developments as

- the process through which the constitutive dream of an eventual integration of all ethnic groups in the American melting pot was revealed as a mere myth in view of the ineluctable heterogeneity of American society with its built-in tragedy of institutionalized racism,
- the sociopolitical inactivity of the Reagan und Bush administrations, which offered no initiatives whatsoever to come to terms with the ever increasing diversity of the American population, and
- the influence which the new philosophy of French deconstructivism has exerted upon the humanities in the U.S. and the degree to which its radical critique of the structural exclusivity of Western culture and its conviction that nothing has intrinsic value because reality cannot be objectively defined have changed the interpretation of the American conundrum.

To understand the considerable impact upon tertiary education which the multiculturalism controversy has had so far, diverse local events as well as the effects of such influential bestsellers as Allan Bloom's *The Closing of the American Mind: How Higher Education Has Failed Democracy and Impoverished the Souls of Today's Students* (1987), Dinesh D'Souza's *Illiberal Education: The Politics of Sex and Race on Campus* (1991), or Arthur M. Schlesinger's *The Disuniting of America: Reflections on a Multicultural Society* (1992) would have to be analyzed, and then the steps through which the different ethnic groups have developed their particular strategies for enforcing their long-denied social recognition would have to be retraced in detail.[59] This cannot be done in the book at hand, but since the fact that America's fast-

---

reader *Debating P.C.: The Controversy Over Political Correctness on College Campuses*, ed. by Paul Berman (New York: Dell, 1992).
58 For definitions and examples see Henry Beard and Christopher Cerf, *The Official Politically Correct Dictionary and Handbook* (New York: Villard Books, 1993).
59 For further details see the relevant chapters in the *Resource Book* that accompanies *From Melting Pot to Multiculturalism: 'E pluribus unum'?*

Growing up in a Multicultural Society

growing 'minority populations' are no longer calling for their long-denied admission to the 'mainstream' - or what feminists ironically refer to as the 'malestream' - but are clamouring for social recognition on their own terms mirrors crucial demographic and cultural changes, some facts about the rapid alteration of the ethnic makeup of the U.S. population are called for.

The 1990 Census counted 248,709,873 Americans and had this to say about their ethnic distribution and their different growth rates:

GROUP	NUMBER	GROWTH SINCE 1980
'whites'	199,686,070	6.0%
African Americans	29,986,060	13.2%
Hispanics	22,354,059	53.0%
Asians	7,273,662	107.8%
Native Americans	1,959,234	37.9%

These figures signal that whereas in 1980 every fifth American was a member of a 'minority population,' by 1990 it was already every fourth, since within a single decade the totality of 'minorities' has grown from 20% to 25% of the overall population. The projection of these demographic figures into the future - it is estimated that by the end of the century Hispanics will have increased by another 21%, Asians by about 22%, African Americans by 12%, and 'whites' by 2% only - has led to a heated discussion of the impending 'browning' or de-Europeanization of America and thus contributed to the nation-wide multiculturalism controversy, which is about nothing less than the redefinition of America's national identity through the fundamental reconstruction of her cultural heritage. This controversy needs to be understood as a major cultural stock-taking and cannot be easily dismissed as a merely 'academic' quarrel between reactionary rightwingers, who want to uphold established traditions and thereby maintain white male prerogatives, and a radical Left of die-hard Marxists, African American activists, and militant feminists, who attack these very traditions in order to abolish the hegemonial claims of what they reject as a logocentric, phallocentric and Eurocentric culture. What the controversy finally amounts to is the choice between pluralism and particularism, which Diane Ravitch convincingly defines as follows:

> The pluralist approach to multiculturalism promotes a broader interpretation of the common American culture and seeks due recognition for the ways that the nation's many racial, ethnic and cultural groups have transformed the national culture. The pluralists say, in effect, "American culture belongs to us, all of us; the U.S. is us, and we remake it in every generation." But particularists have no interest in extending or revising American culture; indeed, they deny that a common culture exists. Particularists reject any accommodation among groups, any interactions that blur the distinct lines between them. The brand of history that they espouse is one in which everyone is either a descendant of victims or oppressors. By doing so, ancient hatreds are fanned and recreated in each new generation. Particularism has its intellectual roots in the ideology of ethnic separatism and in the black nationalist movement. In the particularist analysis, the nation has five cultures: African-American, Asian-American, European-American, Latino/Hispanic, and Native American.[60]

Although it remains to be seen which side will win in the long run, it is already obvious that the new 'race, class, and gender approach' to American history and literature has led to a radical, and in many aspects long overdue, reconstruction of the country's cultural heritage and that the heated debate about 'canonicity' has resulted in a basically changed canon of books thought to represent American culture and wished to be remembered by coming generations.[61]

---

60 Diane Ravitch, "Multiculturalism: E Pluribus Plures," *The American Scholar*, 59, 3 (Summer 1990), 337-354; here pp. 341f.
61 A good general introduction is provided by Jan Gorak, *The Making of the Modern Canon: Genesis and Crisis of a Literary Idea* (London and Atlantic Highlands, New Jersey: Athlone Press, 1991); the complex problems of canon rconstruction are discussed, from a feminist and an African American perspective respectively, by Carey Kaplan and Ellen Cronan Rose, *The Canon and the Common Reader* (Knoxville: University of Tennessee Press, 1990), and by Henry Louis Gates, Jr., *Loose Canons: Notes on the Culture War* (New York: Oxford University Press, 1992). The easiest way to

What this sketchy survey of the history of American identity should have shown is that a certain degree of familiarity with the seven positions of

> ASSIMILATION
>
> "MELTING POT"
>
> AMERICANIZATION
>
> ANGLO-SAXON RACIALISM
>
> CULTURAL PLURALISM
>
> MULTI-ETHNICITY
>
> MULTICULTURALISM

should, and can, be established by means of exemplary texts and pictorial representations. Of course, one needs to be aware of the fact that these positions did not replace each other in a clear-cut chronological succession but often overlapped or even existed side by side. Only if such a reference system is established and the commonly used synchronic concepts are placed within their diachronic dimensions, can the intriguing and presently rather overworked idea of multiculturalism be seen as just one more, and probably not the last, phase in an ongoing discussion. And only if some familiarity with the manifold historical implications of the complex problem of American identity is used to complement such ahistorical concepts as prejudice and discrimination, majority and minority, stereotype and counter-stereo-

---

assess the enormous changes that have taken place is to compare the third edition of *The Norton Anthology of American Literature* (1989), which presents the traditional canon, with its multicultural competitor, *The Heath Anthology of American Literature* (1990). The fourth edition of the *Norton* and the second edition of the *Heath*, which both came out in 1994, show which side has won, since the former now also moves reluctantly in the direction of a multicultural selection, whereas the latter offers an even broader spectrum.

type, can the pervasive myth of the 'melting pot' be adequately assessed and the individual literary depiction of 'growing up ethnic' be understood in its respective historical and ideological context.

It should be obvious by now that I am arguing in favour of a combination of literature and *Landeskunde*.[62] Therefore, I want to point out that, apart from the historical cartoons I have introduced above as important but, unfortunately, unduly neglected teaching tools, there is another type of text which should be used more frequently for cultural analysis, namely, the advertisement. The usefulness of this text type can be most strikingly shown with regard to the Chinese, who went through difficult times in the last two decades of the nineteenth century.

> In 1880 anti-Chinese feelings reached its peak in the Cherry Creek Diggings and bands of white ruffians toured the Chinese section of Denver beating the inhabitants and looting their homes and places of business. One Chinese was saved by white friends who nailed him in a packing case and carried him through the mob. The only white man to defend the Chinese was a gambler and gunman of established local fame who defied the rioters with a gun in each hand, roaring "If you kill Wong, who in hell will do my laundry? Get out, you sons of bitches." Similar riots occurred throughout the Rocky Mountain regions, and in Montana all Celestials were finally expelled from the mines.[63]

Advertisers tried to cash in on the general contempt for the 'Heathen Chinee,' and two striking examples may illustrate this strategy. A late-nineteenth-century advertisement for rat poison called *Rough on Rats* makes use of the anti-Chinese feelings of its time, and it works on the widespread belief among white Americans that the Chinese eat rats. A trade card advertising a new steam washer refers

---

[62] I have established such a position in "Eine Jugend in Harlem: James Baldwins 'Sonny's Blues' als Ausgangstext eines Kurses zur amerikanischen Rassenfrage," in *Literatur und Landeskunde anhand von Texten schwarzer Autoren*, ed. by Peter Freese (*Der fremdsprachliche Unterricht*, No. 42 [May 1977]), 16-26. I have tried to implement such a position, with regard to Black Americans, in *Growing up Black*, and, with regard to Jewish-Americans, in *Bernard Malamud, "The Assistant."* - A similar position is advanced by Lothar Bredella, "Zielsetzungen der Landeskunde im Fremdsprachenunterricht," *anglistik & englischunterricht*, 10 (1980), 9-34.

[63] Lucius Beebe and Charles Clegg, *The American West: The Pictorial Epic of a Continent* (New York: Bonanza Books, 1955), p. 324.

Growing up in a Multicultural Society

to the fact that Chinese laundries were common and uses the new invention as another reason for claiming that "the Chinese must go."

Both advertisements might be complemented with three political cartoons, all of which were published in diverse magazines in the 1880s and 1890s. The first depicts a scene in "Miss Columbia's School" and shows her 'multicultural' class, the malicious members of which can be easily recognized as representatives of diverse ethnic groups including Blacks and Native Americans, in the process of jeering the dreaded 'yellow peril' out of school. Their stereotyped Chinese victim carries a pressing iron and an ironing-board as emblems of his trade and an opium-pipe as sign of his 'oriental perversities.' The class members hold a slate on which is written "Kick out the heathen; he's got no vote," the imposing Miss Columbia as the embodiment of America does not interfere, but a benevolent judge with top hat implores the class to "Be just - even to John Chinaman," and the caption continues: "You allowed that boy to come into your school, it would be inhuman to throw him out now - it will be sufficient in the future

Growing up in a Multicultural Society

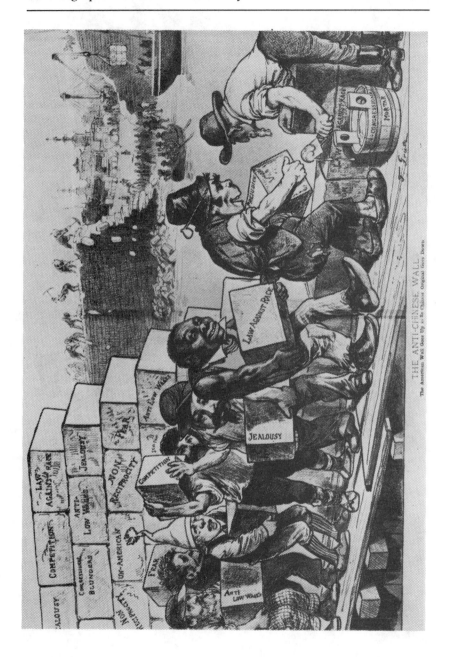

THE ANTI-CHINESE WALL
The American Wall Goes Up as the Chinese Original Goes Down.

THE ARGUMENT OF NATIONALITY.

EXCITED MOB—"*We don't want any cheap-labor foreigners intruding upon us native-born citizens.*"

to keep his brothers out!" The second cartoon shows Uncle Sam applying 'Congressional Mortar,' that is, the legislation resulting in the Chinese Exclusion Act of 1882, to an Anti-Chinese Wall, while representatives of other ethnic groups carry the building blocks to the site. An Irishman brings a block marked 'Prejudice,' a recently emancipated Black brings a block marked 'Law Against Race,' and so on. And the third cartoon drives home the same lesson by showing a Chinese being hanged by immigrants of diverse ethnic stock who call themselves 'Americans.' It is interesting to note that all the ethnic representatives bear the standard characteristics of their groups - see the *Zipfelmütze* of the German and the apish face of the Irishman - and it is highly ironic to realize that here minority members are depicted as gladly helping to exclude another minority.

Whereas the anti-Chinese advertisements are typical examples of the exploitation of inter-ethnic hatred for sales purposes, the stereotype of the German in nineteenth-century America is equally pronounced but less aggressive. A late-nineteenth-century advertisement for what was considered the most characteristic German contribution to American culture, namely, "Lager Bier," as a "healthy, friendly, national, and family drink" shows the obese German brewer with his *Zipfelmütze*; and a lithograph from the same period pokes fun at a German family going for their Sunday walk, well provided with several barrels of beer.[64]

A *Pan Am* advertisement of 1977 represents the very opposite strategy. It demonstrates the latest swing from a narrow insistence on Americanization to an acceptance of pluralism and ethnicity by pro-

---

64 For an investigation of the widespread stereotype of German dipsomania see Peter Freese, "Exercises in Boundary-Making: The German as the 'Other' in American Literature," in *Germany and German Thought in American Literature and Cultural Criticism*, ed. by Peter Freese (Essen: Die Blaue Eule, 1990), pp. 93-132.

Growing up in a Multicultural Society

claiming that "all of us come from someplace else" and therefore wish to visit our place of origin in order to rediscover "the second heritage every American has." Both advertisements, and an endless number of others,[65] can be profitably integrated into a course on ethnicity as interesting examples of historical variations in majority opinion and taste. Here again I would like to insist that only a diachronic arrangement and an inclusion of the historical dimension of these commercial artefacts will make them useful teaching tools.

'Growing up in a Multicultural Society' in Selected American Short Stories

> [...] there were transitions to be made in order to become whole again.
> Leslie Marmon Silko, *Ceremony*[66]

In American literature, the depiction of a young protagonist's coming-of-age, of the disillusioning journey from the innocence of childhood to the experience of adulthood, begins as early as 1799/1800 with Charles Brockden Brown's *Arthur Mervyn; or, Memoirs of the Year 1793*. As far as the presentation of this theme in the field of the short story is concerned, literary historians agree that the first genuine stories of initiation are Nathaniel Hawthorne's masterpieces "My Kinsman, Major Molineux" (1832) and "Young Goodman Brown" (1835). The history of their reception proves that these seminal tales present timeless and archetypal patterns and can be actualized by every new generation of readers within the context of their respective

---

[65] A useful collection of relevant material is provided by Robert Atwan, Donald McQuade, and John W. Wright, *Edsels, Luckies, and Frigidaires: Advertising the American Way* (New York: Delta Books, 1979); and illuminating investigations of the enormous influence of the advertising industry on public taste and opinion are offered by Stuart Ewen, *Captains of Consciousness: Advertising and the Social Roots of the Consumer Culture* (New York: McGraw-Hill, 1976), and Roland Marchand, *Advertising the American Dream: Making Way for Modernity, 1920 - 1940* (Berkeley, Los Angeles, and London: University of California Press, 1985).

[66] Leslie Marmon Silko, *Ceremony* (New York: Viking Penguin, 1986), p. 170.

experience of life.⁶⁷ Consequently, "My Kinsman" suggests itself as the opening story of a thematic sequence.

Hawthorne's story has been variously understood as a political parable on the achievement of American independence, as a re-enactment of the ancient myth of the purificatory deposition of the scapegoat king, as a philosophical exercise on the moral problem of the ubiquity of sin and the theological issue of the fall of man and its consequences, and as a psychoanalytical case study of the rebellious adolescent's rejection of paternal authority. "My Kinsman" can also be seen as an implied criticism of a socio-historical phenomenon of its period of origin. Joseph F. Kett, in his monograph *Rites of Passage: Adolescence in America 1790 to the Present*, describes how the growth of towns after the turn of the century had the effect that, "lured by the new opulence of maritime ports, a steady stream of young men and women from the country descended on the cities." This movement "from plow to countinghouse"⁶⁸ led to a wave of conduct-of-life books meant to provide rural youth with advice as to their behaviour in unknown urban surroundings. Against such a background it seems plausible that, although Hawthorne dates the action of this story around 1730,⁶⁹ young Robin's laborious journey from the pastoral countryside of his childhood to the deeply unsettling experiences in the labyrinthine and mob-thronged streets of nocturnal Boston mirrors an important development of Hawthorne's own times. It was in those times that a transformation began which changed the nation,

---

67 An earlier German EFL-edition of the story, Nathaniel Hawthorne, *Two England Romances*, prefaced and annotated by H. Bernstein (Frankfurt: Hirschgraben, 1962), is no longer in print, but an annotated and illustrated version of the text is now available in *The American Short Story I: Initiation*, pp. 7-29. - For surveys of the story's complex history of reception, see Peter Freese, *The American Short Story I: Initiation - Interpretations and Suggestions for Teaching*, pp. 109-132, and Peter Freese, "Robin und seine vielen Verwandten: Zur Rezeptionsgeschichte von Nathaniel Hawthornes 'My Kinsman, Major Molineux,'" in *Die englische und amerikanische Kurzgeschichte*, ed. by Klaus Lubbers (Darmstadt: Wissenschaftliche Buchgesellschaft, 1990), pp. 12-27.
68 Joseph F. Kett, *Rites of Passage: Adolescence in America 1790 to the Present* (New York: Basic Books, 1977), pp. 94 and 93.
69 Hawthorne wrote the story in 1828/29, and in the introduction he dates the action "not far from a hundred years ago," that is, around 1730. However, it is quite obvious that "the settings and actions are clearly of the immediately pre-Revolutionary period" (Roy Harvey Pearce, "Hawthorne and the Sense of the Past or, The Immortality of Major Molineux," *Journal of English Literary History*, 21 [1954], 327-349; here p. 329).

originally envisaged by Thomas Jefferson as a community of "those who labor in the earth,"[70] into a nation of city-dwellers, and that an agrarian society was being replaced by an industrial one. All these implications make Hawthorne's ambiguous tale, which I have analysed elsewhere under the aspect of its teachability in the EFL-classroom,[71] a highly suitable starting point for the proposed sequence and a tale which will acquaint the students with the recurring thematic issues and structural patterns of the American coming-of-age narrative.

Another important, albeit less well-known, initiation story is Stephen Crane's "An Experiment in Misery" (1894). Here a well-to-do youth masquerades as a bum and spends an unforgettable night in a Bowery flophouse, depicted as a latter-day variation of Dante's hell. This story, whose shaken protagonist confesses at the end that he has "undergone a considerable alteration,"[72] is a fictional comment on the manifold problems arising from urbanization and mass immigration and, more specifically, on the social consequences of the panic of 1893 which resulted in a stock market crash, the failure of 15,000 businesses, and mass unemployment. Crane imaginatively translates into individual terms what Jacob August Riis in his shocking study *How the Other Half Lives* (1890) reveals about the degrading existence of starving children in rat-infested New York tenements, about the filth and sickness and the back-breaking work in sweatshops, about the inhuman way of life of the so-called 'Street Arabs,' and about a type of socialization that inevitably led to either early death or a life of crime and vagrancy.[73] This nighmarish reversal of the 'American Dream,' which takes place in a lodging-house like the one which Riis photographed in Pell Street, makes the often quoted promise of young Ben

---

70 See note 28.
71 See Peter Freese, "Über die Schwierigkeiten des Erwachsenwerdens," pp. 209-218, and *The American Short Story I: Initiation - Interpretations and Suggestions for Teaching*, pp. 89-158.
72 Stephen Crane, "An Experiment in Misery," in *The Works of Stephen Crane*, ed. by Fredson Bowers, vol. XIII, *Tales, Sketches, and Reports* (Charlottesville: University Press of Virginia, 1973), p. 863. - The story is included, together with the opening and conclusion of the original *New York Press* version, in *The American Short Story I: Initiation*, pp. 34-48.
73 An inexpensive paperback reissue of the 1901 republication of the 1890 original of Jacob A. Riis's important book, *How the Other Half Lives: Studies Among the Tenements of New York*, includes 100 photographs from the Jacob A. Riis Collection (New York: Dover Publications, 1971).

Franklin's triumphant entry into Philadelphia[74] look like a pious fraud.

A third well-known coming-of-age story, F. Scott Fitzgerald's "Bernice Bobs Her Hair," was first published in 1920 in *The Saturday Evening Post*. This tale is not only a humorous variation on the traditional device of the pupil excelling the master, here presented as the genuinely American variant of the trickster tricked, but it is also an impressive piece of social history by a man who was rightly called the laureate of the Jazz Age. Moreover, this story is one of the rare earlier stories of initiation in which a girl functions as initiate. This very fact is an interesting comment on the essential change of sexual role ascriptions that took place in the twenties with the advent of the 'flapper.' Fitzgerald tells us about a period when a young woman had to acquire certain graces in order to achieve a promising marriage, which was society's central ambition for her. His story, which is also easily available as a well-made film,[75] "tells us as much about manners and morals, class and caste, in the Midwest after the First World War as a shelf of sociology texts."[76] The appalling innocence and immaturity of a clique of rich adolescents apparently unaffected by the gruesome aftermath of the war becomes all the more obvious when "Bernice" is compared to another, almost contemporaneous story.

Ernest Hemingway's "Soldier's Home" (1924), which is also available in an impressive film version,[77] takes place in the same Midwest, but it movingly describes the total disillusionment of the young war

---

[74] Benjamin Franklin, *The Autobiography and Other Writings*, ed. with an introduction by L. Jesse Lemisch (New York: New American Library, 1961), pp. 38ff. - This famous scene, which can be profitably contrasted with Robin Molineux' arrival in Boston, is included in *The American Short Story I: Initiation*, pp. 30-33.

[75] The story is available in several American and English collections. For a comparison with the film, see *The American Short Story*, ed. by Calvin Skaggs (New York: Dell Books, 1979), which is the most useful edition since it contains not only the text of the story (pp. 151-175), but also the screenplay by Joan Micklin Silver (pp. 176-210), an interview with Joan Micklin Silver (pp. 211-218), and an interpretive article by Matthew J. Bruccoli, "On F. Scott Fitzgerald and 'Bernice Bobs Her Hair'" (pp. 219-223). The film is available as a VHS-or VCR-videocassette (44 minutes) from the *Institut für Film und Bild in Wissenschaft und Unterricht*, Munich, and can either be bought (115 DM) or borrowed from the nearest *Landes-, Kreis- or Stadtbildstelle*.

[76] Matthew J. Bruccoli, "On F. Scott Fitzgerald and 'Bernice Bobs Her Hair,'" p. 221.

[77] The film (37 minutes) costs 115 DM. For details see note 75.

veteran Krebs, who comes home to a world which he can no longer understand. The obtrusive religiosity of his mother and the materialistic ambitions of his father equally nauseate him, the ritualized dating and courting pattern of his peers eludes and bores him, and the provincialism of unchanged daily mores drives him away from a place which he can no longer accept as his 'home.'

A fifth classical initiation story is William Faulkner's brilliant "Barn Burning" (1939), which portrays little Sarty's revolt against his vengeful father and is a dramatic enactment of the ritual parricide each new generation has to commit on the preceding one in order to fulfil itself. At the same time the story is a detailed evocation of the post-bellum South with its crumbling tripartite system of rich plantation owners, poor white share-croppers, and even poorer Negroes and with its pervading tension between an old patriarchal order doomed to ruin and a new success-orientated civilization given to greed and competition.[78]

Apart from being a veritable treasure trove of outstanding American tales of initiation, these five selected stories can serve as stepping stones to an investigation of the growing-up process in various phases of American history. Furthermore, they provide information about diverse cultural regions during different historical periods - pre-revolutionary Boston, the teeming New York of the turn of the century, the South recovering from Civil War and Reconstruction, and the provincial Midwest of the post-World War I era - and with diverse social strata - the poor country parson's son coming to town in order to "rise in the world,"[79] the well-to-do youth going 'slumming' in the Bowery, the rich midwestern leisure class of the Jazz Age, the young middle-class war veteran uprooted from his social background, and the poor white sharecropper's son from rural Mississippi. None of these stories,

---

[78] An annotated and illustrated EFL-version of the story is included in *The American Short Story I: Initiation*, pp. 74-93. The text is also accessible in *The American Short Story*, ed. by Calvin Skaggs (New York: Dell Books, 1980), vol. II, pp. 374-392, together with scenes from Horton Foote's film script (pp. 393-397) and James M. Cox's interpretive essay "On William Faulkner and 'Barn Burning'" (pp. 398-407). The film was not selected for the 'American Short Stories on Film' series by the FWU, but it can be borrowed from the German *Amerikahäuser*.

[79] Nathaniel Hawthorne, "My Kinsman, Major Molineux," in *The American Short Story I: Initiation*, p. 28.

however, seems to have anything to do with 'growing up ethnic,' if that term is understood, as it most often is, to refer to the more visible ethnic groups only. If, as logic would demand, every American is considered an ethnic ("we are a nation of foreigners - a country of immigrants joined together under one flag," Stephanie Bernardo states at the outset of her *Ethnic Almanac*[80]), such an objection proves immaterial. Notwithstanding such terminological niceties, it is important to state that in the classical 'mainstream' literature about growing up in the United States the initiate is white and, with only minor exceptions, male.[81] And it is interesting to note that the more visible ethnics are brought into this literature by means of another, recurring figure, namely, the wise helper, guide, or mentor.

James Fenimore Cooper's immortal Natty Bumppo, in his different rebirths as Deerslayer, Hawkeye, Pathfinder, and Leatherstocking, finds his mentor in the Indian chieftain Chingachgook, whose name, not accidentally, means "'the 'Great Snake.'"[82] Herman Melville's Ishmael, who "account[s] it high time to get to sea as soon as [he] can"[83] whenever he feels the discontents of civilization, finds his fatherly friend and mentor in the Polynesian Queequeg, whose tattooed arm he takes to be a snake. During his painful initiation into the hypocrisies of a slave-holding society, Huckleberry Finn is chaperoned by the wise runaway slave Nigger Jim; Richard Henry Dana is befriended by the Kanaka Hope in *Two Years Before the Mast;* and the nameless protagonist of Sherwood Anderson's "I Want to Know Why" gets help from the Black cook Bildad Johnson. Little Seth in Robert

---

80 Stephanie Bernardo, *The Ethnic Almanac* (Garden City, N. Y.: Doubleday, 1981), p. xiii. - This sometimes rather faddish insistence on a ubiquitous ethnicity is not at all shared by all social historians. John Higham, *Send These to Me: Jews and Other Americans in Urban America,* for example, states: "Contrary to some claims, we are not all ethnics. Everyone has some sense of ancestral belonging, but many Americans, much of the times, feel little ethnic identification." (p. ix).
81 For a possible explanation of the scarcity of female initiates, see Peter Freese, *Die Initiationsreise,* pp. 84ff. - See also the anthology *I'm on My Way Running: Women Speak on Coming of Age,* ed. by Lyn Reese, Jean Wilkinson and Phyllis Sheon Koppelman (New York: Avon Books, 1983), which is meant to complement the many anthologies of male initiation stories with a collection of female examples, but which cannot sustain its claim.
82 See James Fenimore Cooper, *The Pioneers; or, The Sources of the Susquehanna: A Descriptive Tale* (New York: James G. Gregory, 1863), pp. 90 and 170.
83 Herman Melville, *Moby-Dick; or, The Whale,* ed. by Harrison Hayford and Hershel Parker (New York: W. W. Norton, 1967), p. 12.

Penn Warren's "Blackberry Winter" gets advice from the old and wise Negro Jebb; and in "The Bear" William Faulkner's Ike McCaslin is initiated into the mysteries of hunting by Sam Fathers, the son of an Indian chief and a Black slave. The same holds true for the more recent female variations of the pattern: Carson McCullers' motherless Frankie Addams in *The Member of the Wedding* tentatively steps across the threshold of maturity under the loving guidance of the Black cook Berenice Sadie Brown, and Jem and Scout Finch in Harper Lee's *To Kill a Mockingbird* are gently guided by the Black cook Calpurnia, who is, of course - like Berenice Sadie Brown - a literary descendant of William Faulkner's immortal Dilsey in *The Sound and the Fury*. The traditional relationship of that strange pair - a young white neophyte and a fatherly friend and guide of a darker and supposedly more 'primitive' race - is significantly reversed in Ken Kesey's *One Flew Over the Cuckoo's Nest*, where Randle Patrick McMurphy, in his abortive quest for true manhood in a society dominated by castrating female figures represented by Big Nurse, befriends the schizophrenic Indian chieftain 'Broom' Bromden.

It need not be decided here whether the recurring pair of figures, a 'civilized' and a 'natural' man, really is, as Leslie Fiedler would have it, an indication of the fact that American literature is basically a literature about how "to avoid 'civilisation,' which is to say, the confrontation of a man and woman which leads to the fall to sex, marriage, and responsibility"[84] and whether "that sacred-heathen love between White man and coloured man in a world without women" is really the "dearest myth" of American literature.[85] What one has to keep in mind, however, is the fact that the depiction of coming-of-age in classical American literature is, time and again, concerned with growing up white in connection with and under the wise and loving guidance of such 'unmeltable' ethnics as Native Americans and African Americans. This strange constellation began as early as 1809 in Alexander Henry's *Travels and Adventures in Canada and the Indian Ter-*

---

[84] Leslie A. Fiedler, *Love and Death in the American Novel* (New York: Stein and Day, rev. ed., 1966), p. 26.
[85] Leslie A. Fiedler, *The Return of the Vanishing American* (London: Paladin Books, 1972), p. 120.

ritories Between the Years 1760 and 1776[86] with a story of white-Indian blood-brotherhood, which Henry David Thoreau, in *A Week on the Concord and Merrimack Rivers*, then used as an example in his praise of friendship.[87] I would like to suggest that the recurrence of this relationship might be understood as an indication that even earlier American literature tried to redeem Native Americans and African Americans who, in American history, were often rejected as subhuman, and that thus literature attempted to counterbalance the hatred and discrimination that existed in reality by the love and reconciliation that it envisaged as possible.

Of course, even if 'ethnic' is understood in the narrower sense of not being admitted to a dominant 'WASP' mainstream, earlier depictions of growing up ethnic can be found. Books such as James T. Farrell's Studs Lonigan trilogy (1932-35) on the specifically Irish variation of American childhood, youth and young manhood in Chicago's Southside before World War I; Henry Roth's brilliant novel *Call It Sleep* (1934), which depicts the experiences of the immigrant Jewish boy David Schearl between the ages of six and nine in the jungle of New York tenements; or Willa Cather's *My Antonía* (1918), about a Bohemian immigrant girl's life on the Nebraska frontier, come as easily to mind as the first internationally acclaimed Black novel, Richard Wright's *Native Son* (1940), about the hopeless slum existence of Bigger Thomas and its inevitable end in crime and violence.

In the short story of initiation, however, decidedly ethnic variations of growing up are portrayed relatively late. Many an earlier text might yet be unearthed - one thinks, for example, of the recent rediscovery of Abraham Cahan's *Yekl: A Tale of the New York Ghetto* (1896), which gained new popularity when it was filmed as *Hester Street* by Joan Micklin Silver in 1972. To my knowledge, with the possible exception of lesser known tales by Chesnutt and Dunbar, there are no important Black initiation stories before Richard Wright's gruesomely

---

86 The relevant passages are included in *O Brave New World: American Literature from 1600 to 1840*, ed. by Leslie A. Fiedler and Arthur Zeiger (New York: Dell Books, 1968), pp. 27-51.

87 The relevant passages are part of the "Wednesday" section of *A Week on the Concord and Merrimack Rivers*, in *The Writings of Henry David Thoreau* (Boston and New York: Houghton Mifflin, no date [1893 and 1906]), vol. I, pp. 291-293.

effective tales in *Uncle Tom's Children* (1938), and the earliest serious treatment of growing up Chicano is probably John Steinbeck's moving narrative about the *paisano* Pepé Torres, "Flight" (1938), with Jack London's boxing story "The Mexican" (1911) as a possible forerunner. As far as literature by and about Native Americans is concerned, the fact that in most tribal cultures the ceremonious initiation of children into adulthood was a centrally important ritual would make one expect the existence of numerous initiation stories. But until recently this was not the case, and as late as 1974 Kenneth Rosen could state in the introduction to his collection of modern Native American stories, *The Man to Send Rain Clouds*, that in contrast to a growing body of poetry, "contemporary fiction by American Indians is still a rarity."[88] By now, however, this has changed.[89]

Asian-Americans - and especially the Chinese and the Japanese - have had a generally rough time in the United States; from the early anti-Chinese riots throughout the West to the relocation camps for the Japanese in the wake of Pearl Harbor, they often met with discrimination and wholesale rejection.[90] For a long time Charlie Chan, the Chinese detective created in 1925 by the distinctly non-Chinese writer Earl Derr Biggers, served as the ruling stereotype. The editors of the groundbreaking collection *Aiiieeeee! An Anthology of Asian-American Writers*, rightly rejected many earlier books as frauds and put-ons, and according to them, "the first Chinese-American novel set in Chinese America" was Louis Chu's *Eat a Bowl of Tea* (1961).[91] The Japanese are

---

[88] *The Man to Send Rain Clouds: Contemporary Stories by American Indians*, ed. by Kenneth Rosen (New York: Random House, 1975), p. ix. - There is a vast amount of Indian story-telling, as can be seen, for example, in Jeanette Henry, ed., *The American Indian Reader: Literature* (San Francisco: Indian History Press, 1973), but it belongs mostly to an older oral tradition of tribal lore.

[89] Impressive collections of recent stories are *Earth Power Coming: Short Fiction in Native American Literature*, ed. by Simon J. Ortiz (Tsaile, Arizona: Navajo Community College Press, 1983), and *Talking Leaves: Contemporary Native American Short Stories*, ed. by Craig Lesley (New York: Dell, 1991).

[90] The best history of Asian Americans I know of is Ronald Takaki, *Strangers from a Different Shore: A History of Asian Americans* (Boston: Little, Brown, and Company, 1989).

[91] *Aiiieeeee! An Anthology of Asian-American Writers*, ed. by Frank Chin, Jeffery Paul Chan, Lawson Fusao Inada, and Shawn Hsu Wong (Washington, D.C.: Howard University Press, 1974), p. ix. - This anthology was later replaced by a greatly enlarged version, *The Big Aiiieeeee! An Anthology of Chinese American and Japanese American Literature*, ed. by Jeffery Paul Chan, Frank Chin, Lawson Fusao Inada, and

equally under-represented in literature, and the first Japanese-American book which found some resonance was Mine Okubo's *Citizen 13660*, which deals with the relocation camp experience and was published in 1946. Frank Chin and others stated in 1974 that

> in the 140-year history of Asian-America, fewer of ten works of fiction and poetry have been published by American-born Chinese, Japanese and Filipino writers. This fact suggests that in six generations of Asian-Americans there was no impulse to literary or artistic self-expression. The truth is that Asian-Americans have been writing seriously since the nineteenth century, and writing well.[92]

Before such a truth can be generally established, however, many a forgotten text will have to be unearthed and more in-depth research will have to be done. And while older texts might be rediscovered, new ones are published with growing frequency. Thus, an outstanding example like Maxine Hong Kingston's prize-winning *The Woman Warrior: Memoirs of a Girlhood Among Ghosts* (1977) might help to evoke the overwhelming culture conflict endured by a girl who was forced by the circumstances of her childhood to be Chinese and American at the same time, and excerpts from this book - for example, the moving passage about being unable to speak at school[93] - deserve to be part of any sequence on 'growing up ethnic.' Such powerful narratives as Amy Tan's bestselling novels *The Joy Luck Club* (1989), which in a series of interwoven vignettes contrasts the lives of four women in pre-1949 China with the lives of their American-born daughters in California, and *The Kitchen God's Wife* (1991), which is the story of Winnie Louie's life as passed on as a gift to her daughter, deal with mother-daughter relationships and the crucial role which story-telling plays in

---

Shawn Wong (New York: Penguin Books, 1991). - Meanwhile there are also helpful critical surveys such as Elaine H. Kim, *Asian American Literature: An Introduction to the Writings and Their Social Context* (Philadelphia: Temple University Press, 1982), and even specialist investigations such as Amy Ling, *Between Worlds: Women Writers of Chinese Ancestry* (New York: Pergamon Press, 1991).

92 *Aiiieeeee!*, p. xxi.
93 See Maxine Hong Kingston, *The Woman Warrior: Memoirs of a Girlhood Among Ghosts* (London: Pan Books, 1982), pp. 147ff. - Her second book, *China Men* (New York: Ballantine Books, 1981), and her first novel, *Tripmaster Monkey: His Fake Book* (London: Pan Book, 1990), are also highly recommendable. - An impressive and linguistically challenging text for EFL-students would be Milton Murayama's short novel *All I Asking for Is My Body* (San Francisco: Supa Press, rpt. 1981), which has already become an underground classic in Hawaii.

the process of identity-formation, They could be as profitably excerpted for EFL-purposes as Gus Lee's extraordinary narrative *China Boy* (1991),[94] which movingly portrays the perils of growing up between two cultures and might be studied as an exemplary Chinese-American coming-of-age novel.

The overall impression today is that there is a well-established body of Jewish, African American, and Chicano variations on the theme of 'growing up ethnic,' whereas the number of Native American and Asian-American coming-of-age narratives, which until recently was comparatively limited, is growing with astonishing rapidity. This is in accordance with the fact that, in terms of recent literary history, we have experienced the so-called Jewish Renaissance of the fifties, the second Black Renaissance of the sixties and, in the wake of the latter, the steady growth of a literature of Hispanic origin. 'Hispanic' literature is usually divided into a Puerto Rican (or, as it is often called, Nuyorican) branch more concerned with life in the urban ghettos of the Northeast and a Chicano branch mostly concerned with both the rural and the urban experience of the Southwest and attempting to find a shared cultural identity by means of recovering the ancient culture of Aztlán.[95] Piri Thomas' well-known book about childhood in New York's Spanish Harlem during the Depression, *Down These Mean Streets* (1967), is an outstanding example of the first branch, Richard Vasquez' moving novel *Chicano* (1970) about the Sandoval family's plight in California could represent the second.[96]

It is important to realize that Chicano literature has developed a genre which deals in great detail with the theme of 'growing up eth-

---

[94] All three books are now available as inexpensive pocketbooks: Amy Tan, *The Joy Luck Club* (New York: Ballantine Books, 1989), and *The Kitchen God's Wife* (New York: Ballantine Books, 1992); and Gus Lee, *China Boy* (New York: Signet Books, 1992).

[95] See the essays collected in *Aztlán: Essays on the Chicano Homeland*, ed. by Rudolfo A. Anaya and Francisco A. Lomelí (Albuquerque: Academia / El Norte, 1989).

[96] Helpful introductions are provided by Wolfgang Binder, "Die Nordwanderung der Puertoricaner und ihre Literatur," and by Dieter Herms, "Die Literatur des Chicano Movement: Identitätssuche, Kulturkonflikt und Protest," both in *Amerikanische Gettoliteratur*, pp. 323-355 and 293-322. - Bibliographical data can be found in the recent *Biographical Dictionary of Hispanic Literature in the United States: The Literature of Puerto Ricans, Cuban Americans, and Other Hispanic Writers*, ed. by Nicolás Kanellos (New York: Greenwood Press, 1989).

nic.' Bruce-Novoa calls this sub-genre of the novel "the *bildungsroman* within the milieu of immigration, [...] exploring Chicano rites of passage in a variety of social settings [and including] writing itself as an essential factor in the process of maturation."[97] Among the outstanding examples of this sub-genre are

- José Antonio Villarreal's seminal novel *Pocho* (1959), the first Chicano novel to be issued by a major U.S. publishing house, in which young Richard Rubio, the "product of two cultures,"[98] is growing up in pre World War II Santa Clara, California, and must come to terms with the fact that the ruling white culture considers him an unwelcome stranger;
- Rudolfo A. Anaya's enormously successful novel *Bless Me, Ultima* (1972), a kind of Chicano 'Portrait of the Artist as a Young Man,' in which Antonio Márez fondly remembers how, as a child in a small town in the New Mexico of the 1940s, he had to cope with family conflicts, ethnic rejection, religious doubts, and four deaths, and how, guided by Ultima, the wise *curandera*, he managed to replace his lost faith in traditional Catholicism by a new and profound spiritual relationship with surrounding nature and to mature to the insight that "sometime in the future [he] would have to build

---

[97] Bruce-Novoa, "Hispanic Literature in the United States," in *American Writing Today*, ed. by Richard Kostelanetz (Washington, D.C.: USICA Forum Series, 1982), vol. II, pp. 251-261; here p. 258. - By now books on Chicano culture and literature are legion. For details concerning individual authors, see the informative collection by Bruce-Novoa, *Chicano Authors: Inquiry by Interview* (Austin and London, University of Texas Press, 1980), and the relevant entries in *Chicano Literature: A Reference Guide*, ed. by Julio A. Martínez and Francisco A. Lomelí (Westport, Conn.: Greenwood Press, 1985). - Carl R. Shirley and Paula W. Shirley, *Understanding Chicano Literature* (Columbia: University of South Carolina Press, 1988) provide a helpful survey of Chicano literature, and Ernestina N. Eger's ground-breaking *Bibliography of Criticism of Contemporary Chicano Literature* (Berkeley, CA: Chicano Studies Library Publications, 1982) lists the relevant books and articles. - The German EFL-teacher who might find it difficult to get hold of these books should consult Horst Tonn, *Zeitgenössische Chicano-Erzählliteratur in englischer Sprache: Autobiographie und Roman* (Frankfurt: Peter Lang, 1988). - As far as specific material for the German EFL-classroom is concerned, there are so far only two slim volumes with mainly expository texts, namely, *Hispanic Americans*, ed. by Korinna Trautmann (Stuttgart: Klett, 1989), and *Hispanic Groups in the USA*, ed. by Horst Tonn (Berlin: Cornelsen, 1992).
[98] José Antonio Villareal, *Pocho* (Garden City, N.Y.: Doubleday Anchor Books, 1970), p. 129.

[his] own dream out of those things that were so much part of [his] childhood;"[99]
- Tomás Rivera's bilingual collection of fourteen pieces held together by the main character of a nameless Chicano child, "... *y no se lo tragó la tierra*" / *And the Earth Did Not Part* (1971),[100] which deals with diverse aspects of the Chicano experience in hostile cultural surroundings and provides a many-faceted image of the plight of an oppressed people; and
- Oscar Zeta Acosta's *The Autobiography of a Brown Buffalo* (1972), in which an adult Chicano, searching for his identity, travels through the Southwest, experiments with alcohol and drugs, and finally begins to take pride in an ethnic heritage which, in his understanding, makes him a "Brown Buffalo":

> We are all citizens by default. They stole our land and made us half-slaves. They destroyed our land and made us bow down to a dead man who's been strung up for 2000 years. [...] Now what we need is, first to give ourselves a new name. We need a new identity. A name and a language all our own. [...] So I propose that we call ourselves [...] the Brown Buffalo people. [...] The buffalo, see? Yes, the animal that everyone slaughtered. Sure, both the cowboys and the Indians are out to get him [...] and, because we do have roots in our Mexican past, our Aztec ancestry, that's were we get the *brown* from.[101]

While the Jews need no longer be clamorous about being accepted in their own right - authors such as Saul Bellow, Bernard Malamud and Philip Roth, Joseph Heller, Norman Mailer and Arthur Miller are among the leading figures of the post-war literary scene in America - Blacks and Chicanos are understandably vociferous about replacing the allegedly exclusive and inherently racist concept of a mainstream literature by separate and equal ethnic literatures. The Black claim for a genuine 'Black Aesthetics' limited to insiders on the one hand and the Chicano recourse to Indian mythology and the Spanish language on the other make several interesting texts inaccessible to the outsider and, even more so, to German EFL-students, thus limiting the realm of

---

99 Rudolfo A. Anaya, *Bless Me, Ultima* (no place: Tonatiuh International Inc., 15th ed., 1983), p. 248.
100 See Tomás Rivera, "... *y no se lo tragó la tierra*" / *And the Earth Did Not Part*, English transl. by Herminio Ríos (Berkeley, CA: Quinto Sol Publications, 1971).
101 Oscar Zeta Acosta, *The Autobiography of a Brown Buffalo* (San Francisco: Straight Arrow Books, 1972), p. 198.

choice for the proposed sequence. It is the committed fight for a new or a renewed identity to be wrested from a long history of stereotype and caricature - in a phrase borrowed from Erik H. Erikson's *Identity: Youth and Crisis*, the revolt against "'inferiority' feelings and [...] morbid self-hate in all minority-groups"[102] - which permeates the factual reminiscences and fictional projections of growing up outside the 'mainstream.' The very predicament which Paul Goodman defined in 1960, in his influential book of the same title, as *Growing up Absurd* and explained by stating that "it is desperately hard these days for an average child to grow up to be a man, for our present organized system of society does not want men. They are not safe,"[103] has found its indigenous expression in numerous post-war American stories about 'growing up ethnic.' Some of these I shall discuss in a little more detail to complement the five classical examples mentioned above.

In 1947, Ralph Ellison published, in a now defunct British magazine, a story entitled "The Invisible Man."[104] Later, with only a few minor alterations, this story became the first chapter of his influential novel *Invisible Man* (1952). In Ellison's own words, this story deals with "a vital part of behavior pattern in the South," namely, "the initiation ritual to which all greenhorns are subjected."[105] It tells us, from the retrospective I-narrator's point of view, about the traumatic experiences of a Black adolescent who has successfully finished school in a small southern town and who is invited to repeat his valedictory speech at a meeting of the town's white 'big shots.' There, together with nine other Black boys hired for entertainment, he is forced to watch - with fascination and fear - the obscene performance of a white belly dancer, to take part in a free-for-all boxing match in which the blindfolded Black contestants are made to have a 'battle royal,' and to join in a humiliating attempt to grab money - which later turns out to be toy money - from an electrified rug. Only then, badly bruised and thoroughly debased, is he allowed to deliver his speech on social responsibility, which turns out to be a variation upon Booker T. Washington's Atlanta Exposition Address.

---

102 Erik H. Erikson, *Identity: Youth and Crisis* (New York: W. W. Norton, 1968), p. 303.
103 Paul Goodman, *Growing up Absurd* (London: Sphere Books, 1970), p. 23.
104 An annotated reprint of the story is available in *Growing up Black*, pp. 90-104.
105 Ralph Ellison, "The Art of Fiction: An Interview," in his *Shadow and Act* (New York: New American Library, 1966), pp. 169-183; here p. 175.

This highly accomplished tale makes ingenious use of such literary motifs as that of the incipient artist's improbable muse (borrowed from James Joyce's *A Portrait of The Artist as a Young Man*), goes back to Ellison's own childhood experiences (that with the electrified Model T Ford coil, for instance),[106] and brilliantly employs the charged metaphor of seeing versus blindness and a pervasive and revealing animal imagery. "The Invisible Man" is a compressed statement about how a white racist society teaches its despised Black minority how to behave with regard to the essential forces of its existence. In the course of only a few hours, the protagonist-narrator is taught about sexuality (the belly dancer), about violence (the battle royal), and about money (the electrified rug) and thus becomes conditioned to take his rightful 'place.' To grow up Black is revealed as a process which includes the manipulation of sexuality: the white woman is used as a bait to simultaneously arouse lust and instil fear in the Black youth faced with the emasculating choice between brute aggression (see Baldwin's image of the Black man as "a kind of walking phallic symbol"[107] or Eldridge Cleaver's famous essay "On Becoming"[108]) and meek acceptance (note the stereotype of the sexless "Uncle Tom").

It also becomes evident that the Social Darwinist notion of 'the survival of the fittest,' imaginatively translated into the all-Black battle royal, is used to set a minority's raw power against itself (think of the old slogan 'Use a nigger to catch a nigger') and to secure the ruling majority's position by means of the strategy of *divide et impera*. And it is demonstrated how the lure of (fake) money is employed to make the minority fall prey to the promise of a materialistic success ideology and sell their birthright for a mess of potage. Altogether, the provision of destructive outgroup orientation and enforced role ascriptions in order to prevent the achievement of true identity are bril-

---

106 See "On Initiation Rites and Power: Ralph Ellison Speaks at West Point", ed. by Robert H. Moore, *Contemporary Literature*, 15 (1974), 165-186; here p. 182. - For a detailed analysis of the story under EFL-aspects, see Peter Freese, *Growing up Black: Stories and Studies of Socialization - Interpretations and Suggestions for Teaching*, pp. 236-256.
107 See James Baldwin, "The Black Boy Looks at the White Boy," in his *Nobody Knows My Name*, pp. 171-190; here p. 172.
108 See Elridge Cleaver, "On Becoming," in his *Soul on Ice: Selected Essays* (London: Jonathan Cape, 1969), pp. 13-28. - See also "The Allegory of the Black Eunuchs," in the same collection, pp. 103-124.

liantly translated into symbolically charged actions. Thus, Ellison's short text, unanimously celebrated as one of the outstanding stories of postwar American literature, turns into an all-inclusive textbook on the predicament of growing up Black.

Two more recent, and widely anthologized, African American stories which are ideal texts for the EFL-classroom, since they allow a contrastive study of 'growing up Black' in the rural South and in the urban North, are Alice Walker's accomplished tale "Everyday Use" and Toni Cade Bambara's sociocritical story "The Lesson." Alice Walker, who grew up as the youngest of eight children of a poor family of sharecroppers in Georgia, scored her breakthrough to international fame with the Pulitzer Prize-winning bestseller *The Color Purple* (1982), and in the seemingly simple story "Everyday Use," which is dedicated to "your grandmama" and which first appeared in 1973 in *Harper's* and was then collected in *In Love and Trouble: Stories of Black Women* (1973),[109] she contrasts, with wry irony and considerable artistry, two way of dealing with a painful past.

The story is told by a strong and down-to-earth Southern Black woman, who self-ironically contrasts her real appearance as "a large, big-boned woman with rough, man-working hands" (35) with her dreamt-of appearance in a TV show and tells us about a decisive event in the lives of her two daughters, who are extremely opposite in character. Maggie, the shy and caring daughter, who was badly scarred in a fire which her sister might have set to destroy the house she hated, has stayed at home, but Dee, who has always scornfully rejected the backward ways of her rural family, has managed to get an education and left home for the wide world. Now she comes back for a visit, having changed her name into Wangero and adopted the customs and values of the Black Muslims. Returning to her Black roots only because they have now become fashionable, she suddenly begins to admire the simple artifacts of her family heritage, such as the rough benches which her father made or the hand-wrought butter churn which she wants to take away as a decorative "centerpiece for the alcove table" (42). But what she covets most are the quilts which her

---

[109] Annotated versions of the story can be found in *Growing up in a Multicultural Society*, pp. 33-50, and in *Stories from the Black Experience*, pp. 68-78.

grandmother, after whom she was named, made from scraps and pieces of cloth all of which speak of particular persons and events in a long and painful family history. When Dee asks whether she can have these quilts to "hang them" (44) in her living room and is told that they are earmarked for Maggie on her marriage, she erupts: "Maggie can't appreciate these quilts! She'd probably be backward enough to put them to everyday use." (43) Selfless Maggie is once more willing to render her portion to her aggressive sister, but with a sudden insight the mother "snatche[s] the quilts out of Miss Wangero's hands and dump[s] them into Maggie's lap" (44), that is, rescues them from her prodigal daughter and gives them to her backward one, because she recognizes that their value lies in use and not in display and that one's heritage must show its worth in "everyday use."

The popular art of quilt making is not only an apt trope for the creative writer's work, but it also offers, since it creates beauty and pattern from discarded 'scraps,' "a *sui generis* context (a weaving together) of experiences and a storied, vernacular representation of lives conducted in the margins, ever beyond an easy and acceptable wholeness."[110] Using the family quilts in a symbolically charged way and perhaps even relating the two patterns of "Lone Star" and "Walk Around the Mountain" (42)[111] to the characters of the two daughters, Alice Walker not only movingly contrasts the trendy 'blackness' which the fashionable Dee cultivates as her new style with the life-giving tradition of the black community which the demure Maggie has inherited through 'everyday use,' but she also imbues her seemingly simple story with a convincing message about how meaning and order can be created, through artistic activity, even from mere scraps.

Toni Cade Bambara, who grew up as Toni Cade in Harlem and Bedford-Stuyvesant and took the name Bambara from a signature on a sketchbook she found in her great-grandmother's trunk and made it her legal name in 1970, is one of those African American writers who, during the sixties, became directly involved in the cultural activities of their urban communities. She is rightly praised for her unique mas-

---

[110] Houston A. Baker, Jr. and Charlotte Pierce-Baker, "Patches: Quilts and Community in Alice Walker's 'Everyday Use,'" *The Southern Review*, 21, 3 (1985), 706-720; here p. 713.

[111] Page numbers refer to *Growing up in a Multicultural Society*.

tery of the nuances of Black speech and her inimitable rendering of street talk, which is often represented by young girl narrators and employed for the delightful exploitation of comic situations. "The Lesson," which might be Bambara's finest story, was originally published as part of her collection *Gorilla, My Love* (1972), and it is an excellent example of her treatment of serious topics in a humorous vein.[112]

The story is told by young Sylvia, the spunky and intelligent leader of a group of ghetto children who live in a world in which "the winos [...] cluttered up our parks and pissed on our handball walls and stank up our hallways and stairs so you couldn't halfway play hide-and-seek without a goddamn gas mask" (53). Into this world comes Miss Moore, an educated black woman with strong political convictions, who sets herself the task of educating the slum children. One day she takes a group of them to F. A. O. Schwartz, the world-famous toy shop on Fifth Avenue, to teach them a 'lesson' about the economic inequality of American society, and the story ends with the puzzled and angry reaction of the children, who are made to realize that they live in a society "in which some people can spend on a toy what it would cost to feed a family of six or seven" (60). But it would be as wrong to read the story as the blunt statement of a sociocritical message as it would be to miss the vulnerability which young Sylvia tries to hide behind her aggressive and emphatically 'dirty' language. Although on the surface Bambara's story deals with the recognition of social injustice as brought about by a particular lesson, on a deeper level it is about whether Miss Moore will manage to reach through to Sylvia and teach her something at all and thus "about the value of lessons themselves, the value of learning and thinking."[113] It is obvious that by the end of the story Sylvia has undergone a painful disillusionment, although she is not yet willing to grant hateful Miss Moore her point. But she is committed to "think this day through" (60), and that means that Miss Moore has managed to introduce her to the realm of knowledge and perception. Consequently, Sylvia might stand a chance that

---

[112] Annotated versions of the story are included in *Growing up in a Multicultural Society*, pp. 53-69, and in *What Did You Learn in School Today? Seven School Stories from America*, ed. by Hans Hunfeld (Paderborn: Schöningh, 1981), pp. 33-41.
[113] Jerome Cartwright, "Bambara's 'The Lesson,'" *Explicator*, 47, 3 (1989), 61-63; here p. 61.

her defiant closing statement "nobody gonna beat me at nuthin" (60)[114] will come true in a way which she cannot yet understand.[115]

In spring 1958, the *Paris Review* carried a short story entitled "The Conversion of the Jews" by an unknown young writer named Philip Roth, and a year later this story was collected, with four others and a novella, in a small volume, *Goodbye Columbus*, which brought its author, at the early age of twenty-six, not only the National Book Award but also turned him into a controversial literary prodigy. "The Conversion of the Jews" is an impressive exploration of growing up Jewish, and it deals with thirteen-year-old Ozzie Freedman's revolt against his Rabbi Binder and the admiration he earns for his daring from his meek friend Itzie Lieberman. The programmatic names reveal that we are faced with a constellation of characters in which the liberal who wants to be 'free' is pitted against the authoritarian who wants to 'bind' him, with the opportunist who just wants to be 'lieb' providing the dramatic audience. Ozzie cannot understand how the Rabbi can claim the Jews are "the Chosen People," since the Declaration of Independence states that all men are created equal, and he cannot accept the attitude of his mother and grandmother who, when the papers report a plane crash, only mourn for the victims with Jew-

---

[114] Page numbers refer to *Growing up in a Multicultural Society*.
[115] Teachers who want to complement "The Invisible Man," "Everyday Use," and "The Lesson" with other African American stories might consult Peter Bruck, "Black Innocent Eyes: William Melvin Kelleys 'The Only Man on Liberty Street' als Ausgangstext für eine Unterrichtssequenz zur afro-amerikanischen Kurzgeschichte," *Arbeiten aus Anglistik und Amerikanistik*, 5 (1980), 255-269, who suggests, with Kelley's "A Good Long Sidewalk" and John A. Williams' "The Figure Eight," two other stories about growing up Black. Other recommendable stories are Jean Wheeler Smith, "Frankie Mae," which first appeared in *Black World* in 1968 and is reprinted in *Black Short Story Anthology*, ed. by Woodie King (New York: New American Library, 1972), pp. 35-46, and in *Black-Eyed Susans: Classic Stories By and About Black Women*, ed. by Mary Helen Washington (Garden City, N. Y.: Doubleday, 1975), pp. 3-18; Richard Wright's "Almost a Man," which appeared as "The Man Who Was Almost a Man" in Wright's collection *Eight Men* (1961) and is reprinted in *The American Short Story*, ed. by Calvin Skaggs, pp. 257-269 (the impressive film was not selected by the FWU, but can be borrowed from the *Amerikahäuser*); and Ernest J. Gaines's exquisite story "The Sky Is Gray," which appeared in his collection *Bloodline* (1968) and is accessible in *The American Short Story*, ed. by Calvin Skaggs, vol. II, pp. 408-436, accompanied by scenes from Charles Fuller's film script, an interview with Gaines, and Jordan Pecile's critical article on the story. The beautiful film (43 minutes) can be bought from the FWU (115 DM) or borrowed through the nearest *Bildstelle*.

ish names. He openly rebels against his spiritual teacher, who tries to 'bind' his 'free' spirit to orthodox dogma; and the result is a direct confrontation when the Rabbi attempts to reduce Christ to a merely 'historical' figure by denying the possibility of Mary conceiving Jesus without intercourse. Asking subversive questions and receiving pedestrian answers, the boy insults the Rabbi and, after having been hit by him, flees to the roof of the synagogue. From up there he can threaten to commit suicide, and thereby he suddenly acquires the power to make the Rabbi and his classmates obey his orders. He forces them all, including his bewildered mother, to kneel in "the Gentile posture of prayer" and to repeat after him that God can do anything and to promise never again to "hit anybody about God."[116]

This humorous tale about a subversive adolescent who calls into question the traditions of his group can be read as a wish-fulfillment of the rebellious Id overcoming the constraining claims of the Super-Ego, for in the end Ozzie is victorious over all the representatives of social authority, the preacher, the teacher, the fireman, and the policeman. But the story takes its ironical title from Andrew Marvell's poem "To His Coy Mistress" in which "you should if you please refuse / Till the Conversion of the Jews"[117] means 'till the end of the world.' Thus, the context of the quotation informs the discerning reader that Ozzie's rebellion will hardly have a lasting effect. Roth's later statement that the story which he wrote when he was twenty-three "reveals at its most innocent stage of development a budding concern with the oppressiveness of family feeling and with the binding ideas of religious exclusiveness which I had experienced first-hand in ordinary American-Jewish life,"[118] confirms an impression which is important in the context at hand. What for Ellison's Black boy was his being caught in a net of social, political, and sexual discrimination forced upon the Black community from without, for the Jewish boy about to be bar-mitzvahed is his imprisonment in an exclusive religious system built up from within the Jewish community. And that

---

[116] The quotations are from the annotated text of the story in *The American Short Story I: Initiation*, pp. 127-142; here pp.141 and 142.
[117] *The Poems of Andrew Marvell*, ed. by Hugh MacDonald (London: Routledge and Kegan Paul, 1960), p. 21.
[118] Philip Roth, "Writing and the Powers That Be," in his *Reading Myself and Others* (New York: Bantam Books, 1977), pp. 3-12; here p. 8.

the last statement is true and that Roth hit home with his pithy little story is corroborated by the fact that the tale was denounced as detrimental to the Jewish cause in many a synagogue throughout the country.[119]

In 1958 Robert Granat published his story "To Endure," which was later selected as one of the *Prize Stories 1960: The O.Henry Awards*. This brief tale, written by a man who is not a Chicano himself, is a moving study of a Chicano childhood overshadowed by the sudden advent of death. Devoid of any propagandistic under- or overtone, the story bears as its motto Rainer Maria Rilke's famous statement "Wer spricht vom Siegen; überstehn ist alles." This quotation not only indicates the author's purpose, but it also anticipates some famous lines from the seminal poem *I Am Joaquín* by Rodolfo Gonzales in which the protagonist states:

> *I am Joaquín.*
> The odds are great
> but my spirit is strong,
> my faith unbreakable,
> my blood is pure.
> I am Aztec prince and Christian Christ.
> I SHALL ENDURE!
> I WILL ENDURE![120]

Granat lets eleven-year-old Abrán tell the pitiful tale of his uncle's death, and the child's limited power of comprehension and his pathetic attempts at coming to grips with the complexities of the adult world give the tale its specific power, derived from what Mark Twain, in *Adventures of Huckleberry Finn*, introduced into American literature as

---

119 For teachers who are looking for other Jewish initiation stories, Delmore Schwartz's frequently anthologized "In Dreams Begin Responsibilities" (1938) might be an appropriate choice, and Bernard Malamud's "The Last Mohican" (1958) and Saul Bellow's "The Gonzaga Manuscripts" (1954) could be combined to demonstrate the (older) Jew's initiation into his disowned heritage during a stay in Europe. Both stories are analysed in *Die amerikanische Short Story der Gegenwart: Interpretationen*, ed. by Peter Freese, pp. 205-214 and 168-174.
120 Rodolfo Gonzales, *I Am Joaquín / Yo Soy Joaquín* (New York: Bantam Books, 1972), p. 100.

the perspective of the "innocent eye."[121] In order to give the dead uncle a decent burial, the men of the family, who have to take along Abrán's little sister Arcelia, drive in their old pickup to the nearest town to buy a coffin. Thus, ironically enough, it is death which provides the reason for Abrán's first exciting outing into the wide world. On the way home, Abrán's fifteen-year-old brother Francesco, whom the two grown-ups treat like a man by allowing him to come along to a bar to drink whisky and to drive the pickup, loses control over the car, and the heavy empty coffin falls upon little Arcelia and kills her. Thus the men come back with an empty coffin for the uncle and with another little coffin with the small child in it. The simple and dignified tale culminates in the distressed mother's reaction: with another infant at her breast, she bewails the sudden loss of her child. Granat's moving narrative is a haunting evocation of a life in dire poverty, a life full of suffering and fatalistic endurance, a life without even the most elementary benefits of the achievements of modern civilization, but a life that goes on because it draws an unquenchable strength from an imperturbable belief in God's providence. Certainly, many younger and militant Chicano authors would scorn such a praise of 'endurance' and deny Granat's story any representative value, but I believe that it is this very aspect of stoic suffering in the sense of Rilke's "überstehn" (which runs through the story from "the picture Mama cut from the calendar where Jesus is pulling open his chest for to show us his beautiful heart" mentioned in the opening lines to the desperate mother's prayer "to the Virgin"[122] in the closing lines) which adds another important facet to the varicoloured picture of growing up in a multicultural America.[123]

---

121 See Albert E. Stone, *The Innocent Eye: Childhood and Mark Twain's Imagination* (New Haven: Yale University Press, 1961), and Tony Tanner, *The Reign of Wonder: Naivety and Reality in American Literature* (Cambridge: University Press, 1965).

122 The story appeared first in the *New Mexico Quarterly* in Spring 1958, and was reprinted in *Prize Stories: The O.Henry Awards 1960*. References are to the reprint in *The Chicano: From Caricature to Self-Portrait*, ed. by Edward Simmen (New York: Mentor Books, 1971), pp. 228-235; here pp. 228 and 235. - Simmen's seminal anthology has meanwhile been superseded by an updated and greatly enlarged collection, *North of the Rio Grande: The Mexican-American Experience in Short Fiction*, ed. by Edward Simmen (New York: Mentor Books, 1992).

123 Another relevant story is Richard Dokey's "Sánchez," which first appeared in 1967 in the *Southwest Quarterly* and was then reprinted in Simmen's earlier anthology. It deals with a conflict between a Mexican father and his Americanized son and is, like Granat's tale, by an author who is an Anglo.

Fifteen years after Granat's story, the *Arizona Quarterly* published a short tale, entitled "The Circuit," by the widely unknown Francisco Jiménez. According to Jiménez, this touching little story, which deals with a young *bracero's* unfulfilled desire for stability and education and is at the same time a moving illustration of the problems of bilingualism, is an "autobiographical story based on [its author's] childhood experiences."[124] Jiménez was born in 1943 in San Pedro Tlaquepaque in the state of Jalisco, Mexico, and when he was three, his parents moved to Santa Maria, California, as migrant workers or *braceros*. At the age of six, young Francisco joined them on the seasonal circuit, picking strawberries in Santa Maria during the summer, grapes around Fresno in the early autumn, cotton in Corcoran during the winter, and then returning to Santa Maria to harvest carrots and lettuce. Constantly moving along the annually repeated 'circuit,' working long and arduous hours, and unable to speak English, Jiménez predictably failed the first grade, but he persevered and soon mastered his second language. When he had just made it to Junior High School, he was deported to Mexico as an illegal alien. But he returned, became an American citizen, received a scholarship, and entered university. Having earned his M.A. and Ph.D. in Spanish and Latin American Literature, he became a distinguished scholar and teacher, the author of several textbooks, and the co-founder of *Bilingual Review*.

The short and easily accessible story is told by Panchito, one of the children of a poor family of migrant farm workers. Although he is only about twelve years old, he has to work "twelve hours a day, every day, seven days a week, week after week" (70) in order to help support his little brothers and sisters. Only when the season for grape picking comes to an end in November and the family switches to cotton-picking, for which Panchito is still too young, is he allowed to go to school, where, being only able to speak a few English words, he is bound to be a lonely and frightened outsider. But this time the little boy, who wants to learn and works very hard, has the good luck of being assisted by Mr. Lema, a friendly and understanding teacher. Panchito makes great progress, and one day he is even offered the chance to be taught how to play the trumpet. When he comes home to tell his family about the good news, he sees that "everything we

---

[124] Quoted from *Growing up in a Multicultural Society*, p. 69.

owned was neatly packed in cardboard boxes" (75).[125] Once more the family will have to move, and the boy cannot escape 'the circuit' that deprives him of any chance of bettering his fate and of achieving the longed-for stability.

Whereas "The Circuit" deals with the plight of those rural Chicanos that earn their livelihood as migratory farm workers, Danny Santiago's accomplished story "The Somebody" introduces the reader to the world of the urban *barrio*, and the unique genesis and reception of this story teaches an exemplary lesson with regard to the heated opposition between particularism and pluralism in the ongoing multiculturalism debate. "The Somebody" appeared first in 1970 in *Redbook* and was then selected for *The Best American Short Stories of 1971*. In that prestigious collection it was reprinted with a brief note that read:

> Danny Santiago supplies no vital statistics. He has said of himself, 'When it comes to biography, I am muy burro as we say in Spanish which means worse than mulish.' 'The Somebody' is his only published work, but several other stories of his have been mimeographed and are currently floating around in East Los Angeles.[126]

Since readers had no reason to doubt this information, they thought of Santiago as a young and struggling ethnic writer. Thus, when in 1983 his apprentice novel, *Famous All Over Town*[127] was published, it was not only praised as a classic novel of initiation but also given the Rosenthal Award for having added

> luster to the enlarging literary genre of immigrant experience, of social cultural and psychological threshold. [...] The durable young narrator spins across a multi-colored scene of crime, racial violence and extremes of dislocation, seeking and perhaps finding his own space. The exuberant mixes with the nerve-wracking; and throughout sly

---

125 Page numbers refer to *Growing up in a Multicultural Society*.
126 Quoted from *Growing up in a Multicultural Society*, p. 81.
127 This novel, which looks at the world through the eyes of a fourteen-year-old Mexican-American I-narrator and would make excellent reading for the advanced EFL-classroom, is available as a paperback (New York: Penguin Books, 1984). Another novel which is immensely suitable for the EFL-classroom is Sandra Cisneros' acclaimed *The House on Mango Street* (1989; available as a paperback, London: Bloomsbury, 1992), which, in a series of 44 lyrical vignettes, chronicles a young girl's growing up in one of the Hispanic quarters of Chicago.

slippages of language enact a comedy on the theme of communication.[128]

When the shy young author did not turn up at the prize-giving ceremony to pick up his $5,000 cheque, his absence, like his refusal to be interviewed or the fact that no photograph of him was available, was understood as just another sign of his reclusiveness. But then an article in *The New York Review of Books* revealed that the young Chicano writer was neither young nor a Chicano. He was a septuagenarian Anglo named Daniel James (which, of course, is Danny Santiago in Spanish), who had graduated from Andover and Yale and was a prize-winning playwright and the co-author of the successful Broadway musical *Bloomer Girl*. As a Hollywood screen writer he had joined the Communist Party in the thirties, and although he had resigned later, in 1951 the House Committee on Un-American Activities had blacklisted him. Deprived of all job possibilities, he and his wife had quietly withdrawn into the Mexican *barrios* of East Los Angeles, and there he had got to know his Mexican-American neighbours so well that he could write about their experiences as if he were one of them.

"The Somebody" is a story that is both funny and pathetic, and like "The Circuit" it makes use of the intrinsic sociocritical potential of the 'innocent eye' strategy, which it combines with the immediacy of the 'direct address.' Young Chato, who "want[s] no part" (83) of his father and feels estranged from his mother, lives in a barrio in "the Eastside in old L.A." (83) in a street in which all houses, except that of his family, have been torn down to make way for a new railroad track. His only community, the "de Shamrock" (83) street gang, has dissolved since the families of the other gang members had to move away, "except Gorilla is in jail and Blackie joined the Navy because he liked swimming" (83). Thus, Chato is lonely, helpless, and easy prey for the rival gang that persecutes him and makes it impossible for him to go to school. In order to assert himself and to make the world realize that he is a "somebody," he steals "two boxes of crayons and some chalk" (85) and wanders through the city, leaving a trail of artistically executed signatures on buildings and fences. He comments on

---

128 Quoted from *North of the Rio Grande. The Mexican-American Experience in Short Fiction*, p. 212.

his obsessive need to write his name by remarking that the marks he leaves make him "famous" (85) and by cleverly observing that "you put your name on something and that proves it belongs to you" (85). Although he is in dire need of company, he rejects a girl's offer to "go writing together" (88), because he has "[his] reputation to think of" (88),[129] and in the end he stands at a street corner, lost and lonely, and helplessly dreams of becoming a famous graffiti artist.

Simon J. Ortiz is a Native American from Acoma Pueblo who says that for him "language is a way of life. I do not wish to regard language merely as a mechanically functional tool, but as a way of life which is a path, a trail which I follow in order to be aware as much as possible of what is around me and what part I am in that life."[130] His story "Kaiser and the War," published in 1969, is about a Native American youth with the uncommon name of Kaiser who does not want to join the army and therefore ends up in the state penitentiary. On the surface, this tale seems to be only marginally concerned with growing up, but as it is told by a narrator who "was in the fourth grade [when] Kaiser got out of the state pen" (143), the clash of two cultures, the conflict between Native American and white norms is mirrored in a young consciousness. The story thus demonstrates through youthful eyes the impossible predicament of a people estranged from their heritage and unable to come to terms with the behavioural code of the whites; consequently, they are caught in the no-man's land between two widely different cultures. When Kaiser - who does in prison what he was supposed to do in the army, namely, kill a man - is finally released, he comes back to the reservation in a much ridiculed gray suit. The fact that he now wears the outward emblem of a successful resocialization seems to indicate that he has been finally converted to white norms. But, in a final gesture of defiance, he stipulates that when he dies, the torn and tattered suit is to be sent back to the government.

In a world in which it seems the Indian can be turned into an 'American' only by joining the army or by going to prison, the hateful token of assimilation can be rejected in death alone. The narrator of

---

129 Page numbers refer to *Growing up in a Multicultural Society*.
130 In "Notes by the Contributors" in *The Man to Send Rain Clouds*, p. 174.

this ambiguous tale carefully abstains from taking sides and ironically criticizes both "the olden times" (145) of Native American existence and the alleged values of the whites - "that stuff about patriotism, duty, honor" (143)[131] -, mixing humor and pathos. The story not only adds another aspect to the theme of ethnic socialization in the United States, but it also demonstrates, from a Native American viewpoint, the basic problem of the ethnic writer who wants to address both his own ingroup and the larger outgroup, a problem which the Black author James Weldon Johnson defined as early as 1928 when he spoke about "the problem of the double audience" and specified: "It is more than a double audience; it is a divided audience, an audience made up of two elements with differing and often opposite and antagonistic points of view."[132]

By now several nineteenth-century tales about growing up Native American have been rediscovered and numerous new ones have been written,[133] and among the more recent ones Louise Erdrich's "The Bingo Van" is certainly one of the most accomplished. Erdrich, who was born in Little Falls, Minnesota, in 1954, is of German-American and Chippewa descent and a member of the Turtle Mountain Band of Chippewa. Her thematically interrelated novels *Love Medicine* (1984), *The Beet Queen* (1986), *Tracks* (1988), and *The Bingo Palace* (1993) have made her one of the most critically acclaimed among contemporary American writers, but she has also published numerous short stories, for which she has won such prestigious awards as the National Magazine Fiction Award, the Pushcart Prize or the First Prize O.Henry Award. In "The Bingo Van," which first appeared in *The New Yorker* on 19 February 1990 and was then incorporated, in a considerably

---

131 The story appeared first in the *New Mexico Quarterly* in 1969, was then reprinted in both *The Man to Send Rain Clouds* and *The Portable North American Indian Reader*, ed. by Frederick W. Turner III (Harmondsworth: Penguin Books, 1977), pp. 615-625, and is now available in *Growing up in a Multicultural Society*. Page numbers refer to this edition. - The only criticism of this story I know of is by Holger Möllenberg, *Die Rhetorik amerikanischer Literatur: Gedankliche Voraussetzungen moderner Literatur der Indianer Nordamerikas und ihre rhetorische Verwendung zur Beeinflussung einer differenzierten Leserschaft* (Frankfurt: R.G. Fischer, 1982), pp. 100-109.
132 James Weldon Johnson, "The Dilemma of the Negro Author," *American Mercury*, 15 (1928), 477-481; here p. 477.
133 See the thematic anthology *Growing Up Native American* mentioned in note 9.

changed version, into *The Bingo Palace*, she deals with the pains and promises of growing up in a world defined by culture conflict.

The story is about crucial events in the life of young Lipsha Nanapush, "trying to catch [his] bearings in the world" (163). Lipsha is caught between two cultures, since he is familiar with the customs and values of white America by having successfully finished high school, but also possesses a genuinely 'Indian' ability, namely "a healing power I get passed down through the Pillager branch of my background" (164). Having won both a coveted van at bingo and the love of a beautiful girl, he has to lose both through his own carelessness before he can discover the value of his heritage and his true vocation, and Erdrich traces this process by masterfully interweaving Native American oral traditions - Lipsha's very name refers to Manabózho or Nánapush, the trickster hero of the Native Americans of the Great Lakes region - with the narrative strategies of the contemporary short story to convey a moving portrait of a young man who has "to get stupid first, then wise" (163).[134]

Frank Chin is a Chinese-American who was born in Berkeley, California, in 1940, attended several universities, worked at many different jobs, and became known as the author of two plays, *The Chickencoop Chinaman* (1972) and *The Year of the Dragon* (1974), and as the co-editor of the groundbreaking anthology *Aiiieeeee!* (1974) and its sequel *The Big Aiiieeeee!* (1991). He has also written several short stories, eight of which are collected in *The Chinaman Pacific & Frisco R.R. Co.* (1988), but the one which I would suggest for the advanced EFL-classroom is an earlier story entitled "Food for All His Dead," which was first published in *Contact*.[135] Chin is certainly the most outspoken and controversial among contemporary Chinese-American writers, and he describes his position as follows:

> America is illiterate in, hostile to, deadset against the Chinese-American sensibility. I don't like that. Nothing but racist polemics have been written about us, from the 19th century missionaries to Tom Wolfe.

---

[134] Page numbers refer to *Growing up in a Multicultural Society*.
[135] The story was then reprinted in *Asian-American Authors*, ed. by Kai-yu Hsu and Helen Palubinskas (Boston: Houghton Mifflin, 1972), pp. 48-61, and it is now available in *Growing up in a Multicultural Society*, pp. 121-142.

> Nothing but lies that have, through long acceptance, become the sick racist truths of America's collective unconscious coocoo. I don't like that. [...] And all my writing [...] is Chinaman backtalk.[136]

Chin once said that what he most wishes his audience to perceive through his writings is "the kind of sensibility that is neither Chinese of China nor white-American. The sensibility derived from the peculiar experience of a Chinese born in this country [...], with all the stigmas attached to his race, but felt by himself alone as an individual human being."[137] This sensibility is expressed in his moving story "Food for All his Dead," the title of which refers to the Chinese custom of providing food for the dead on anniversaries and other special occasions. The story deals with a Chinese-American college boy who finds himself painfully lost in the no-man's land between two widely different cultures. Johnny, whose tradition-bound family lives in San Francisco's Chinatown but who has managed to make his way out of the ethnic cage by "moving across the bay to school" (133), accompanies his dying father to Chinatown's great celebration of the forty-fifth anniversary of the founding of the Republic of China. But the lion and the dragon dances and the sounding speeches of Chinese dignitaries about "alla us Chinee-'mellican [being] pwowd!" (121) strike him as being ludicrously unrelated to the real world, and he realizes that "nobody shoulda let [him] grow up and go to any school outside of Chinatown" (131). He has left his ethnic heritage behind, but whereas he feels no longer at home in what strikes him as the outdated and artificial world of Chinatown he is still a helpless stranger in the outer world:

> "Here, in Chinatown, I'm undoubtedly the most enlightened, the smartest fortune cookie ever baked to a golden brown, but out there ... God!" He pointed down to the end of Grant Avenue, past ornamented lamps of Chinatown to the tall buildings of San Francisco. "Here, I'm fine - and bored stiff. Out there - Oh, hell, [...]" (131)[138]

---

136 Quoted from *Growing up in a Multicultural Society*, p. 119. For a detailed statement of Chin's position see his essay "Come All Ye Asian American Writers of the Real and the Fake," in *The Big Aiiieeeee!*, pp. 1-92.
137 This declaration of intention is quoted from the introduction to the story in *Asian-American Authors*, p. 47.
138 Page numbers refer to *Growing up in a Multicultural Society*.

It is not only Johnny's faulty belief that he alone knows about his father's fatal illness which heightens the generational conflict between his wish to leave and his ethnically proud father's expectation that he stay and find his place in the Chinatown community, but also the highly ironic fact that this conflict reaches its climax on the very day of the Chinese festivities. The story proper with its allusive animal imagery climaxes with Johnny's excommunication from his family, but it has a laconic coda which deals with his father's burial and briefly mentions that the 'lost son' would always carry a photograph of his dead father in his wallet. Chin's accomplished tale impressively dramatizes the price to be paid for crossing ethnic boundaries and thus documents once more the mendacity of the melting pot myth with regard to a long neglected ethnic group which, due to its enormous success, is presently receiving much attention.[139]

Whereas Chin's "Food for All His Dead" will allow the students a first glimpse of Chinese-American customs and values, Japanese-American culture is best represented by some of the widely dispersed stories which the long neglected Hisaye Yamamoto wrote during her forty-five year career. Born in 1921 in Redondo Beach, California, as the daughter of Japanese immigrants, Yamamoto began to write as a teenager, but had to wait till she was twenty-seven before a magazine accepted her first story. After Pearl Harbor, she was interned for three years in a relocation camp in Poston, Arizona, where she worked as reporter for the camp newspaper. After the war she worked for the *Los Angeles Tribune*, a black weekly, spent two years as a volunteer in a Catholic Worker rehabilitation farm on Staten Island, and then married and returned to Los Angeles, where, since 1961, her duties as a wife and a mother of five children have kept her from writing any

---

[139] The EFL-teacher in search of easily available material might profitably use the following articles from *Time*: The cover story on "Los Angeles: America's Uneasy New Melting Pot," entitled "The New Ellis Island," *Time*, June 13, 1983, pp. 10-17; the article entitled "Asians: To America with Skills" from the special issue on "Immigrants: The Changing Face of America," *Time*, July 8, 1985, pp. 32-34; the cover story on "Strangers in Paradise: Asians try to find their place on North America's West Coast," *Time*, March 5, 1990, pp. 34-41; the article "Beyond the Melting Pot," *Time*, April 9, 1990; pp. 34-37; the article "Kicking the Nerd Syndrome: A new cohort of the best and brightest Asian-American students is rejecting the science stereotype and the ethic behind it," *Time*, March 25, 1991, p. 59; and the article "Excellence in Ethnic Diversity: At Berkeley, Chang-lin Tien becomes the first Asian American to head a leading U.S. university," *Time*, April 1, 1991, p. 63.

new fiction.[140] Yamamoto's subtle and subdued stories grow out of the personal and historical circumstances of Issei (first-generation Japanese-Americans) and Nisei (second-generation Japanese-Americans) in the United States and deal with such issues as growing up with foreign-born parents, mixing with different ethnic groups, and coming to terms with a dual personality. The publication of these stories in diverse magazines made Yamamoto one of the first Japanese-American writers to gain national recognition in the U.S., but although her stories constitute the only literary portrait of pre-war rural Japanese America in existence, it was not before 1988 that fifteen of them were collected as *"Seventeen Syllables" and Other Stories* and thus made available to a larger audience.

One of Yamamoto's most impressive stories is "Yoneko's Earthquake," which first appeared in 1951 in *Furioso*, was chosen as one of Martha Foley's *Best American Short Stories: 1952*, and then collected in *Seventeen Syllables*. This accomplished tale is an excellent example of Yamamoto's 'double-telling,'[141] that is, of her narrative technique of conveying two stories in the guise of one by presenting the surface action through the 'innocent eye' of a naive young girl, whereas the covert story is concerned with the dramas of the adult world which the girl does not yet understand. Thus, the story is seemingly about a young Nisei girl's passing infatuation with the Filipino farmhand Marpo and her short-lived faith in the Christian God, but on a deeper level it deals with the marital problems of her Issei parents, her mother's unhappy love affair with Marpo and her hushed-up abortion, and Yamamoto's consummately executed technique of indirection is a culture-bound indicator of the crucial role which indirect speech and non-verbal communication play in traditional Japanese-American families. The story is told from a third-person limited point of view that looks at the world through ten-year-old Yoneko Hosoume's eyes, and the effaced narrator uses the digressive manner of her childish perceptions to drop telling hints about what goes on in the adult world.

---

140 See Hisaye Yamamoto, "Writing," *American Journal*, 3 (1976), 126-133.
141 See King-Kok Cheung, "Double-Telling: Intertextual Silence in Hisaye Yamamoto's Fiction," *American Literary History*, 3 (1991), 277-293.

The surface story tells about how Yoneko falls in love with the Christian God and how, after a frightening earthquake, which her fervent praying cannot avert and in which her father is wounded and - without her realizing it - made impotent, she becomes a disillusioned "free-thinker" (98), whereas her mother, after the death of Yoneko's little brother Seigo, turns into a devout Christian. One day Marpo is gone "without even saying good-bye" (106), and the Hosoumes break with their well-established routine and drive to the city on a weekday afternoon. On this trip a silent Mr. Hosoume

> [...] drove very fast and about halfway to the city struck a beautiful collie which had dashed out barking from someone's yard. The car jerked with the impact, but Mr. Hosoume drove right on and Yoneko, wanting suddenly to vomit, looked back and saw the collie lying very still at the side of the road. (107)

It turns out that it is the object of the trip to take Yoneko's mother to the hospital, and when she comes out of the building after a long wait, she is obviously in pain and tells her daughter that she has received "some necessarily astringent treatment" (107), whereupon the father admonishes Yoneko and her little brother to keep the trip a secret. On the way home they pass the spot where they had hit the dog, and "Yoneko looked up and down the stretch of road but the dog was nowhere to be seen" (107). The perceptive reader recognizes that Marpo had to leave because he had an affair with Mrs. Hosoume, that she went to the hospital to have an abortion, and that the irate father's unblinking killing of the dog, which then disappears without a trace, is the surface story's equivalent of his insistence that Marpo's unborn child be disposed of in the hospital. It is in this double way that the moving story unfolds, and when at the end, after the death of little Seigo, the disconsolate mother admonishes her daughter, "Never kill a person, Yoneko, because if you do, God will take from you someone you love" (109), and an incomprehending Yoneko answers "Oh, that, I don't believe in that, I don't believe in God" (109),[142] the reader understands that the mother experiences the death of her son as God's punishment for having aborted Marpo's child. By ingeniously employing the 'pregnant' silence of the unspoken word, Yamamoto conveys such essential aspects of Japanese-American life as the patri-

---

[142] Page numbers refer to *Growing up in a Multicultural Society*.

archal family structure, the culture-bound misunderstandings between first-generation mothers and second-generation daughters, the distanced role of immigrant fathers bent upon ensuring their families' material survival, and the problems of religious conversion. But she does even more, because Yoneko who throughout the story has been fascinated by songs, accidental rhymes and word games, has discovered a new power - "whenever the thought of Seigo crossed her mind, she instantly began composing a new song, and this worked very well" -, and thus on another level the story is also a subtle 'Portrait of the Artist as a Young Japanese-American Girl.'

Since elementary logic would demand that every American be considered an ethnic, it seems appropriate to end this sketchy survey with a few remarks on an outstanding coming-of-age story by a so-called 'mainstream' writer. In spring 1969, Joyce Carol Oates, one of the leading figures of the contemporary literary scene, published her brilliant experimental tale "How I Contemplated the World from the Detroit House of Correction and Began My Life Over Again" in *Tri-Quarterly*. A year later, the story was selected for *Prize Stories: The O.Henry Awards 1970*, and then Oates included it in her short-story collection *The Wheel of Love* (1972) and again in her thematic anthology *Where Are You Going, Where Have You Been? Stories of Young America* (1974). This accomplished narrative consists of the disorganized notes of the puzzled protagonist, and the seemingly incongruous text is the structural equivalent of the state of mind of its guilt-ridden and deeply bewildered narrator searching for some hidden meaning behind the chaotic fragments of her crumbling world. The protagonist, a fifteen-year-old girl, leaves the sterile air of an affluent suburb for the turbulent emotions of the inner-city ghetto, goes through traumatic encounters with drugs and prostitution, and is brought home thoroughly bruised by her experiences, so totally different from what she had expected.

"How I Contemplated" unfolds against the background of the anti-Vietnam War demonstrations, the violent ghetto-riots and - in Marcuse's famous phrase - the 'Great Refusal' of a thoroughly dissatisfied and disillusioned youth rising in protest against the materialism and success-orientation of their parents. By her skilful evocation of the spirit of the times, Oates manages to invest the protagonist with representative status. Simon, the poetry-writing dropout who becomes the girl's first lover and turns her out on to the streets as prostitute to earn him the money for his drug habit, defines his development by saying "Once I was Huckleberry Finn, but now I am Roderick Usher,"[143] thereby using classical texts of American literature to contrast two socialization patterns. Oates's difficult but immensely rewarding tale is a very impressive evocation of a painful female initiation in a culture of violent contradictions, generational and ethnic strife, and a desperate search for new values.[144] Read at the end of the sequence of the stories suggested here, it might be used to sum up almost all the themes of a sub-genre of the American short story which deals with the historical mutations and the ethnic variations of growing up in a multicultural society.

When one looks back upon the brief sketch of the changing concepts of American identity and the survey of selected short stories about growing up in a multicultural American, one might draw some tentative conclusions. In every story of initiation, as became evident in the tales of Hawthorne, Crane, Fitzgerald, Hemingway and Faulkner, there is a generational conflict between young and old, innocence and experience, youthful idealism and the disillusioning compromises of reality. If, as in the ethnic coming-of-age story, this generational conflict is superimposed on a cultural conflict, the general world view conveyed by the story will only rarely be an optimistic one. This is not only due to the specific premises on which initiation stories are based, but serious literature on the whole never provides a balanced portrayal of the average, and the ethnically conscious African American, Jewish, Chicano, Native American or Asian American 'minority' author naturally is more interested in pointing out what still needs to

---

[143] The frequently anthologized story is available in an annotated EFL-version in *The American Short Story I: Initiation*, pp. 144 -163; the quotation is from p. 149.

[144] Two articles might help to come to terms with the difficult story: Paul Goetsch, "Joyce Carol Oates, 'How I Contemplated the World from the Detroit House of Correction and Began My Life Over Again' (1969)," in *Die amerikanische Short Story der Gegenwart: Interpretationen*, ed. by Peter Freese, pp. 301-313; and Sue Simpson Park, "A Study in Counterpoint: Joyce Carol Oates's 'How I Contemplated the World from the Detroit House of Correction and Began My Life Ober Again,'" *Modern Fiction Studies*, 22 (1976), 213-224. - A detailed interpretation and suggestions for teaching can be found in Peter Freese, *The American Short Story I: Initiation - Interpretations and Suggestions for Teaching*, pp. 367-408.

be done than in celebrating what has been achieved. Werner Sollors is certainly correct when he observes that "the cultural conflict with the dominant society in America is the most important theme in ethnic writing,"[145] and Michael Novak draws attention to an important aspect when he states that good writing is "characteristically a result of refusing the image of oneself imposed by others" and that, consequently, "good writing in America is inherently subversive of the 'melting pot.'"[146] Thus, it is small wonder that the stories of Ellison, Walker and Bambara, of Roth, of Granat, Jiménez and Santiago, of Ortiz and Erdrich, of Chin and Yamamoto, and, from a different angle, of Oates implicitly or explicitly reject the notion of assimilation on the majority's terms and that a general cultural conflict looms behind the individual humiliation of Ellison's "invisible man," the Johnsons' attitudes to their painful past, and the ghetto children's confrontation with white affluence, behind the religious revolt of Ozzie Freedman, behind the traumatic adventure of Abrán, the deep disappointment of Jiménez' autobiographical protagonist, and the pathetic attempt of Santiago's youth at being recognized, behind the ambiguous life story of Kaiser and the shattering experience of Lipsha Morrissey, behind the shocking experience of Johnny and the disillusionment of Yoneko, and behind Oates's bored protagonist's rebellion against suburban affluence.

Reading a whole sequence of such stories and approaching American multi-ethnicity through the medium of ethnic American fiction, one will hardly gain the impression that Emma Lazarus' high hopes in "The New Colossus"[147] have come true. On the contrary, one will be left with the depressing image of a bleak world of individual failure and social inadequacy. Therefore, it is the task of the teacher to see to it that the imaginatively heightened projections of literature will not be misunderstood as direct social evidence, but that the individual story will be contextualized with relevant expository texts. Only thus can it be ensured that the students' immediate affective reaction -

---

145 Werner Sollors, "Literature and Ethnicity," in *Harvard Encyclopedia of American Ethnic Groups*, pp. 647-665; here p. 659.
146 Michael Novak, *The Rise of the Unmeltable Ethnics*, p. 170.
147 See Emma Lazarus, "The New Colossus." This poem, dedicated to the Statue of Liberty and engraved on a plaque fastened to its pedestal, is reprinted in the EFL-reader *From Melting Pot to Multiculturalism*, p. 2, and on p. 196 of this book.

which nothing can effect as well as literature - will be combined with a more distanced cognitive penetration of the problem at hand, for which detailed historical, sociological, and political information is necessary. It is such a combination of imaginative literature and informative *Landeskunde* which, I think, might stand a fair chance of making the advanced EFL-classroom a place not only of linguistic but also of inter-cultural learning and of an increase in individual and social maturity as well.

This late-nineteenth-century cartoon from *Puck* bears the caption "Castle Garden Emigrant-Catchers," and it shows how "Boarding House Runners," "Money Changers," "Baggage Swindlers," "Temptresses," "Confidence-Men," and "Friends from the Old Country" are waiting for the newly arrived immigrants, whom they will try to fleece.

4: Worshippers of the 'Bitch-Goddess' of Success: Businessmen in American Literature

> [...] the Way to Wealth, if you desire it, is as plain as the Way to Market. It depends chiefly on two Words, INDUSTRY and FRUGALITY: i.e. Waste neither Time nor Money, but make the best Use of both. He that gets all he can honestly, and saves all he gets (necessary Expenses excepted) will certainly become RICH: If that Being who governs the World, to whom all should look for a Blessing on their honest Endeavors, doth not in his wise Providence otherwise determine.
>
> Benjamin Franklin, "Advice to a Young Tradesman"

> I fear the popular notion of success stands in direct opposition in all points to the real and wholesome success. One adores public opinion, the other private opinion; one fame, the other desert; one feats, the other humility; one lucre, the other love; one monopoly, and the other hospitality of mind.
>
> Ralph Waldo Emerson, "Success"

> The exclusive worship of the bitch-goddess SUCCESS [...] is our national disease.
>
> William James in a letter to H. G. Wells[1]

---

1. The mottoes are taken from Benjamin Franklin, *The Autobiography and Other Writings*, ed. with an introduction by L. Jesse Lemisch (New York: New American Library, 1961), p. 187; *The Complete Works of Ralph Waldo Emerson* (New York: AMS Press, 2nd ed., 1979; reprint of the Centenary Edition, Boston: Houghton Mifflin, 1903-04), vol. VII, p. 308; *The Letters of William James*, ed. by his son Henry James (New York: Kraus Reprint Co., 1969; reprint of the edition Boston: Little, Brown & Co., 1926), vol. II, p. 260.

During the 1988 presidential campaign, the Democratic candidate Governor Michael Dukakis frequently told his audiences that, as the son of a Greek immigrant, he fervently believed in the promise of America, and he coined a revealing slogan when he assured them that as president he would strive to make all of them 'shareholders in the American Dream.'[2] This telling phrase combines something as intangible and immaterial as the 'Dream' of human self-fulfilment with the financial concept of 'shareholding,' and it somehow insinuates that happiness and self-realization can be attained by every American citizen in the same way in which bonds can be bought at the stock exchange. Dukakis' formulation is just one of many instances of that persistent American habit of yoking together elements which to a European observer seem to belong to quite different levels. And it raises the intriguing questions as to which role the acquisition of wealth and the social status it confers upon its owner play within the 'American Dream' and as to how the unholy alliance of material success and personal self-fulfilment is depicted in American literature.

In contrast to German literature, in which it is rather difficult to find novels or stories that deal primarily with business and money matters, American fiction boasts of a relevant subdivision, namely, the flourishing genre of the 'business novel.' This will hardly surprise the German observer, who very probably has grown up with the popular image of the United States as a 'land of opportunity,' a country of unlimited possibilities and unbridled capitalism, where dishwashers turn into millionaires or, in an up-to-date variation, students of cybernetics become owners of prosperous computer firms. What surprises him or her, however, is the unexpected fact that the entrepreneurial protagonists of most American business novels are not at all portrayed as positive models worthy of emulation but, on the contrary, as evil and unscrupulous speculators stopping at nothing, as obsessed fortune-hunters neglecting their families, and as bigoted philistines without a sense of higher values. Thus, the two American 'businessmen' best known throughout the world, namely, J. R. Ewing, the villain of the television series *Dallas*, and Donald Duck's uncle, the miserly millionaire Scrooge of the famous comic strip, turn out to re-

---

2   See, for example, the excerpts from his nomination acceptance speech as quoted on pp. 90f.

present, albeit with the exaggeration of caricature, the very variants of the businessman which occur most frequently in serious American literature.

In 1964, Henry Nash Smith concluded his "Search for a Capitalist Hero" in American literature with the following unexpected insight:

> Serious novelists of our day have not even attempted to consider the possibly heroic traits and accomplishments of the businessman. Virtually all of them create protagonists who are antiheroes - outcasts, pariahs, varying only in the manner and degree of their repudiation of a society portrayed as being coterminous with the business system. The search for a capitalist hero has thus led to no viable results, and there is little indication that it will be more successful in the future. For the stereotypes used by the popular novelists cannot sustain a character of real imaginative substance, and serious writers seem unable to take an interest in a system of values based on economic assumptions.[3]

Such a result, which is as valid today as when Smith formulated it, indeed reveals a surprising contradiction. In a country which traditionally thinks of herself as the guardian of free enterprise and in which an endless stream of popular success-literature from Horatio Alger's 'from rags to riches'-novels to the 'how to'-bestsellers of a Dale Carnegie and a Robert Schuller amply illustrates that people have understood the 'American Dream' of unhampered self-realization primarily in terms of business success leading to personal affluence,[4] there

---

3 Henry Nash Smith, "The Search for a Capitalist Hero: Businessmen in American Fiction," in *The Business Establishment*, ed. by Earl F. Cheit (New York: Wiley and Sons, 1964), pp. 77-112; here p. 112. - John Chamberlain, "The Businessman in Fiction," *Fortune*, November 1948, pp. 134-148, had previously reached a similar result. - Other relevant studies are Walter Fuller Taylor, *The Economic Novel in America* (Chapel Hill: University of North Carolina Press, 1952); Walter B. Rideout, *The Radical Novel in the United States, 1900 - 1954: Some Interrelations of Literature and Society* (Cambridge, Mass.: Harvard University Press, 1956); and - as the most recent contribution - Emily Stipes Watts, *The Businessman in American Literature* (Athens: University of Georgia Press, 1982). - A thematic anthology is *Business in Literature*, ed. by Charles Burden, Elke Burden, Sterling Eisiminger, and Lynn Ganim (New York: David McKay, 1977).
4 Critical literature on the success-myth is legion. Basic studies are Irvin G. Wyllie, *The Self-Made Man in America: The Myth of Rags to Riches* (New Brunswick, N.J.: Rutgers University Press, 1954); Kenneth S. Lynn, *The Dream of Success: A Study of the Modern American Imagination* (Boston: Little, Brown and Co., 1955); John G. Cawelti, *Apostles of the Self-Made Man* (Chicago and London: University of Chicago Press, 1965); Richard Weiss, *The American Myth of Success: From Horatio Alger to Norman*

exists a comprehensive and demanding literature which denounces the very myth of success as mendacious, cynical and destructive. This contradiction calls for an explanation, and I will try to provide a necessarily tentative one by considering some pertinent aspects of American intellectual history and by discussing a few representative novels.

Calvinism, Social Darwinism, and Capitalism

> [...] die religiöse Wertung der rastlosen, stetigen, systematischen, weltlichen Berufsarbeit als schlechthin höchsten asketischen Mittels und zugleich sicherster und sichtbarster Bewährung des wiedergeborenen Menschen und seiner Glaubensechtheit mußte ja der denkbar mächtigste Hebel der Expansion jener Lebensauffassung sein, die wir hier als "Geist" des Kapitalismus bezeichnet haben.
> Max Weber, "Die protestantische Ethik und der Geist des Kapitalismus"[5]

Whoever attempts to understand the historical roots of the American brand of capitalism and the 'spirit' behind it, cannot afford to neglect one of the most influential studies ever written about the American understanding of worldly success. I mean Max Weber's essay "The Protestant Ethic and the Spirit of Capitalism,"[6] in which Weber pos-

---

Vincent Peale (New York: Basic Books, 1969); Richard M. Huber, *The American Idea of Success* (New York: McGraw-Hill, 1971); and Lawrence Chenoweth, *The American Dream of Success: The Search for the Self in the Twentieth Century* (North Scituate, Mass.: Duxbury Press, 1974).

5 Max Weber, *Die protestantische Ethik I: Eine Aufsatzsammlung*, ed. by Johannes Winckelmann (München und Hamburg: Siebenstern Taschenbücher, 2nd rev. ed., 1969), p. 180.

6 Apart from the pocketbook edition quoted in note 5, there is another paperback edition, namely, Max Weber, *Gesammelte Aufsätze zur Religionssoziologie I* (Tübingen: J. C. B. Mohr, 9th ed., 1988; UTB 1488). - The English quotations are taken from Max Weber, *The Protestant Ethic and the Spirit of Capitalism*, transl. by Talcott Parsons (London: Unwin Paperbacks, 1985). - A complementary volume, Max Weber, *Die protestantische Ethik II: Kritiken und Antikritiken*, ed. by Johannes Winckelmann (München and Hamburg: Siebenstern Taschenbücher, 1968), documents the critical

tulates an intricate connection between the *Wirtschaftsgesinnung*, that is, the 'economic way of thinking' of bourgeois capitalism with its efficient organization of free labour on the one hand and the rational ethics of ascetic protestantism on the other. Weber finds in Calvinism, whose Puritan variation he sees as the driving force behind the newly emerging American society, a peculiar mixture of masterly business acumen and all-pervasive piety, and he explains this mixture as the result of the Protestant concept of vocation or 'calling' derived not from the Bible but from the new Bible translations.

According to Weber, the Protestant holds in high esteem "the valuation of the fulfilment of duty in worldly affairs as the highest form which the moral activity of the individual could assume" (80). Consequently, for the Protestant, tireless and successful work in his 'calling' as in the field to which he has been 'called' by God becomes a religious duty, and since his work is done for the greater glory of God and not of God's creatures, it assumes "a peculiarly objective and impersonal character, that of service in the interest of the rational organization of our social environment" (109). If one adds to this the extreme isolation of the individual Calvinist which results from the lack of institutionalized sacramental redemption caused by the doctrine of predestination; if one considers that a divine order urges the Calvinist to be successful in his worldly calling but forbids him to enjoy the fruits of his labour in leisure because he is bound to an inner-worldly asceticism; and if one takes into account that the Calvinist, who continuously pines for his *certitudo salutis*, can infer his belonging to the *electi* only from his success in his worldly calling, one arrives at a complex conundrum, which Weber sums up as follows:

> [...] the religious valuation of restless, continuous, systematic work in a worldly calling, as the highest means to asceticism, and at the same time the surest and most evident proof of rebirth and genuine faith, must have been the most powerful conceivable lever for the expansion of that attitude toward life which we have here called the spirit of capitalism. (172)

---

reception of Weber's thesis and his own replies up to Reinhard Bendix's essay of 1966. For more recent statements see notes 7 and 12.

The logical consequence of this attitude is, again in Weber's words, "*Kapitalbildung* durch *asketischen Sparzwang*" (180), that is, the accumulation of capital through an ascetic compulsion to save money. According to Weber, then, the incredible rise which rapidly turned a handful of dissenting communities in the forests of an unexplored continent on the border of the inhabited world into an economic superpower, is finally due to a religious-ethical urge. This urge, however, soon becomes secularized, so that the genuinely American business acumen, originally released by a particular religious conviction, can unfold itself all the more freely.

Whereas Weber used Benjamin Franklin (1706-1790), the largely secularized deist, as his main witness and, as recent research has shown, interpreted Franklin's statements in a rather biased way,[7] two decades later Vernon Louis Parrington chose the Boston merchant Samuel Sewall (1652-1730) as his source for the same thesis, attested to him "the trademan's conception of religion - one has only to understand the profitableness of salvation to be led to invest in it," and characterized him as "the progenitor of a practical race that was to spread the gospel of economic individualism across the continent."[8] At the same time, the British historian of economics Richard Henry Tawney modified the Weber-thesis, with which he principally agreed, described the Puritan as "tempered by self-examination, self-discipline, self-control" and as "the practical ascetic, whose victories are won not in the cloister, but on the battlefield, in the counting-house, and in the market," and concluded that for the Puritan "money-making, if not free from spiritual dangers, was not a danger and nothing else, but that it could be, and ought to be, carried on for the greater glory of God."[9] And the English novelist D. H. Lawrence stated with his characteristic spitefulness:

---

7 See Manfred Pütz's articles "Max Webers und Ferdinand Kürnbergers Auseinandersetzung mit Benjamin Franklin: Zum Verständnis von Quellenverfälschung und Fehlinterpretation," *Amerikastudien / American Studies*, 29, 3 (1984), 297-310; and "Max Webers These vom 'Geist des Kapitalismus' und der Fall Benjamin Franklin," *Jahrbuch der Universität Augsburg*, 1988, pp. 193-207.

8 Vernon Louis Parrington, *Main Currents in American Thought*, vol. I, *1620 - 1800: The Colonial Mind* (New York: Harvest Books, no date), pp. 94 and 98.

9 Richard Henry Tawney, *Religion and the Rise of Capitalism: A Historical Study* (Harmondsworth: Penguin Books, rpt. 1964), pp. 230 and 238.

The 'Bitch-Goddess' of Success

> Now if Mr. Andrew Carnegie, or any other millionaire, had wished to invent a God to suit his ends, he could not have done better. Benjamin [Franklin] did it for him in the eighteenth century. God is the supreme servant of men who want to get on, to *produce*. Providence. The provider. The heavenly storekeeper. The ever-lasting Wanamaker.[10]

These and many other influential studies established an interpretive context within which the successful American businessman necessarily becomes a bigoted, egotistical materialist driven by his lust for money, devoid of social responsibility, and exclusively bent upon the systematic increase of his capital. In this context, Benjamin Franklin with his system of virtues described in the *Autobiography* and with his immensely influential *Poor Richard's Almanack* (1733-1758),

---

10 D. H. Lawrence, *Studies in Classic American Literature* (New York: Viking Press, rpt. 1969), p. 10. - John Wanamaker (1838-1922), a Philadelphia merchant, was the founder of one of the first department stores, served as U.S. postmaster-general, and was a noted leader of the Young Men's Christian Association. Daniel J. Boorstin reprints his speech on "The Evolution of Mercantile Business" (1900) in his *An American Primer* (New York: New American Library, 1985), pp. 654-664.

the proverbs and adages of which have become part of American folk wisdom and been endlessly repeated, as in the preceding nineteenth-century engraving, is made the chief witness of a trite utilitarianism which is divested of its erstwhile religious foundations and for which it is no longer important to develop virtues but to get credit by pretending to own them. As late as 1963, Richard Hofstadter, in his prize-winning book about *Anti-Intellectualism in American Life*, could pinpoint the businessman's lust for profit as the main reason for American anti-intellectualism and trace the widespread "fear of mind and the disdain for culture" in the name of practicability back to these two roots: "first, a widely shared contempt for the past; and second, an ethos of self-help and personal advancement in which even religious faith becomes merely an agency of practicality."[11]

Many more examples could be adduced to demonstrate that the long dominant idea of the 'Puritan work ethic' is undoubtedly one of the main sources for the wholeheartedly negative depiction of the businessman in American literature. Now, more recent research on Puritanism has shown that it was "hardly an ideology that encouraged continuous or unrestrained accumulation"[12] and that the premises of Weber and his successors are not only questionable in the context of intellectual but also in that of 'real' history. The *Mayflower* pilgrims, for example, started their colony by prohibiting private property and only gave up that ideal, which stands in glaring opposition to the Weber-thesis, under the pressure of circumstances. But the notion that it was a Christian's God-given duty to become a successful businessman outlived its allegedly Calvinist origins, and whereas in 1836 the Methodist minister Thomas P. Hunt could write a book with the revealing title *The Book of Wealth; in Which It is Proved from the Bible that It is the Duty of Every Man to Become Rich*, in 1890 Russell H. Conwell, a

---

[11] Richard Hofstadter, *Anti-Intellectualism in American Life* (New York: Alfred A. Knopf, 1963), p. 238.

[12] Michael Walzer, "Puritanism as a Revolutionary Ideology," in *Essays in Colonial American History*, ed. by Paul Goodman (New York: Holt, Rinhart and Winston, 1967), pp. 33-48; here p. 31. - See also the more recent contributions to the Max Weber-thesis mentioned by Manfred Pütz, *op. cit.*, p. 298, note 3; and the general survey of literature about the relationship between business and religion by William T. Doherty, Jr., "The Interaction of American Business and American Religion in the 19th and Early 20th Centuries: A Sampling of Scholarly and Popular Interpretations," *North Dakota Quarterly*, 50, 1 (1982), 91-97.

Baptist minister from Philadelphia, began to acquire fame through his sermon *Acres of Diamonds*, which he delivered several thousand times and in which he admonished his listeners that it was their "Christian and godly duty" to become rich:

> I say that you ought to get rich, and it is your duty to get rich. How many of my pious brethren say to me, "Do you, a Christian minister, spend your time going up and down the country advising young people to get rich, to get money?" "Yes, of course I do." They say, "Isn't that awful! Why don't you pray the gospel instead of preaching about man's making money?" "Because to make money honestly is to preach the gospel." That is the reason. The men who get rich may be the most honest men you find in the community. [...] Money is power, and you ought to be reasonably ambitious to have it. You ought because you can do more good with it than you could without it. Money printed your Bible, money builds your churches, money sends your missionaries, and money pays your preachers, [...][13]

In 1925, Bruce Barton, who introduced himself as "an advertising man" (125),[14] took up the same argument in a different intellectual context, when he published *The Man Nobody Knows: A Discovery of the Real Jesus*. In this idiosyncratic reinterpretation of the life and teachings of Christ, which instantly turned into an outstanding bestseller, Barton advanced the argument that Jesus was an exemplary salesman. (Mis)understanding his question "Wist ye not that I must be about my father's *business*?" (162), Barton portrayed Christ as "The Founder of Modern Business" (chapter VI), read his 'success' in spreading the gospel as "the grandest achievement story of all!" (9), praised the way in which he assembled his disciples as "a startling example of executive success" (23), and extolled his faith in others as "that great principle of executive management" (28). Stating that "every one of the 'principles of modern salesmanship' on which businessmen so much pride themselves, are brilliantly exemplified in Jesus' talk and work" (104), Barton argued that therefore "every one of his conversations, every contact between his mind and others, is worthy of the attentive study of any sales manager" (106). Having

---

13 Russell H. Conwell, *Acres of Diamonds* (1890); here quoted from the reprint in *A Documentary History of Religion in America since 1865*, ed. by Edwin S. Gaustad (Grand Rapids, Michigan: William B. Eerdmans, 1983), pp. 251f.; here p. 252.
14 All page references in brackets in the text refer to Bruce Barton, *The Man Nobody Knows: A Discovery of the Real Jesus* (Indianapolis: Bobbs-Merrill, 1925).

established this picture, Barton could even conclude that Jesus' parables are "the most powerful advertisements of all time" (107) and that Christ "would be a national advertiser today, I am sure, as he was the great advertiser of his own day" (140). Since Barton wrote his book at a time when business was generally understood as 'service,' he could sum up Jesus' "business philosophy" (177) in this way: "1. Whoever will be great must render great service. 2. Whosoever will find himself at the top must be willing to lose himself at the bottom. 3. The big rewards come to those who travel the second, undemanded mile." (177) And he could sum up his teachings by stating:

> Great progress will be made in the world when we rid ourselves of the idea that there is a difference between *work* and *religious work*. [...] Thus *all* business is his Father's business. All work is worship; all useful service prayer. And whoever works wholeheartedly at any worthy calling is a co-worker with the Almighty in the great enterprise which He has initiated but which He can never finish without the help of men. (179; 180)

By now, Barton's book is forgotten. But the various new recipes for successful 'Christian' living which grew out of the New Thought movement, which gained additional momentum in Norman Vincent Peale's *The Power of Positive Thinking* (1952), and which are widely disseminated today in the immensely successful sermons of Robert Schuller and in such bestsellers of his as *Tough Times Never Last, But Tough People Do!* (1983), still have a pervasive influence. All of these doctrines see Christianity less as a moral obligation than as a business opportunity, and behind all of them lies "the idea that the drama of economic salvation parallel[s] that of spiritual salvation in every particular."[15] As a kind of antidote to these popular doctrines, however, mainstream American literature has kept alive the very opposite notion of the incompatibility of open-mindedness, social responsibility and artistic sensitivity on the one hand and what Andrew Carnegie, in an influential study of that title, called *The Gospel of Wealth* (1889) on the other. Time and again, outstanding economic success and an acceptable cultural standard are understood as mutually exclusive, and thus in 1977 the British novelist Tom Sharpe provided only one of

---

15   Irvin G. Wyllie, *The Self-Made Man in America: The Myth of Rags to Riches* (New York: The Free Press, 1966), p. 54.

many pertinent examples when he painted the ironic portrait of an American publisher who owes his economic success to the very fact that he is "the most illiterate publisher in the world [...] he never read the books he bought and [...] the only words he could read were those on cheques and dollar bills. [He] was immensely successful."[16]

The second source for the negative image of the businessman in American literature is unquestionably the theory of Social Darwinism. When the British philosopher Herbert Spencer applied Darwin's theory of biological evolution to man's social behaviour, his thesis of the "survival of the fittest"[17] nowhere gained as many enthusiastic supporters as in the America of the 'Gilded Age.'[18] The reasons for this are obvious: after the Civil War, the necessity for economic reconstruction in a time of rapidly increasing industrialization and the availability of both inexhaustible deposits of raw materials and a defenceless and easily exploitable labour force, constantly replenished by waves of immigrants, resulted in an unheard-of economic boom. In the unscrupulous competition of this period of promoterism, which is rightly called the 'Age of the Robber Barons'[19] or, even more revealingly, 'The Great Barbecue,' the Standard Oil imperium of the Rockefellers and the railroad and shipping company of the Vanderbilts, the U.S. Steel Corporation of Andrew Carnegie and the immense fortunes of a Leland Stanford or a Jay Gould, a J. P. Morgan or a Thomas Mellon, a George Pullman or a Collis P. Huntington came into being. The tycoons of an age which was not 'golden' but, in Mark Twain's apt phrase, 'gilded' and which was characterized by stock-market scandals and illegal speculation on a breathtaking scale, found in the

---

16 Tom Sharpe, *The Great Pursuit* (London: Pan Books, 1979), p. 26.
17 This phrase, which is often wrongly ascribed to Charles Darwin, was coined by Spencer seven years before the appearance of *The Origin of Species* (1859) in his article "A Theory of Population Deduced from the General Law of Animal Fertility," *Westminster Review*, 57 (1852), 468-501.
18 This term, which implies that the earlier dream of a 'Golden Age' on the new continent had turned into the reality of a 'gilded age,' was coined by Mark Twain and Charles Dudley Warner in their novel *The Gilded Age: A Tale of Today* (Hartford: American Publishing Company, 1873), which attacks the unscrupulous business mores of post-bellum America.
19 The term was coined by an embittered group of Kansas farmers who, in an antimonopoly pamphlet of 1880, denounced the railroad magnates as 'robber barons,' because the exorbitant railroad rates threatened the farmers' existence. - See Matthew Josephson, *The Robber Barons 1861 - 1901* (New York: Harcourt Brace, 1962), p. vi.

teachings of Social Darwinism an all too welcome alibi for their unscrupulous transactions.

When Herbert Spencer predicted that free enterprise, which only allowed the fittest to survive, would lead to a process of elimination by which society would constantly purify itself of its worthless members, and that this process would ultimately result "in the establishment of the greatest perfection and the most complete happiness,"[20] those in power loved such a message because it condoned their status and perfectly justified whatever they had done to reach it. And when Spencer's American adherent William Graham Sumner postulated that Americans had only "this alternative: liberty, inequality, survival of the fittest; non-liberty, equality, survival of the unfittest. The former carries society forward and favors all of its best members; the latter carries society downwards and favors all its worst members,"[21] it was easily predictable that the tycoons would choose the first possibility. John D. Rockefeller's pious pronouncement in one of his Sunday School orations that "the growth of a large business is merely a survival of the fittest,"[22] provides a revealing example of the attitude bred by Social Darwinist teachings.

It was Theodore Dreiser who in his trilogy *The Financier* (1912), *The Titan* (1914) and *The Stoic* (1947) painted not only the most comprehensive portrait of one of the industrial magnates of this time but also what might be "the most impressive portrait of a big businessman in American literature."[23] Frank Algernon Cowperwood, the 'hero' of Dreiser's *Trilogy of Desire*, owes many traits to the Chicago operator Charles Tyson Yerkes, and since Dreiser provides him with certain characteristics derived at second hand from Nietzsche, Cowperwood is a kind of amoral superman who is beyond good and evil and stops at nothing: without any consciousness of what is generally regarded as sin, he bribes politicians, cheats shareholders, treats women as purchaseable objects, and collects art for purposes of capital invest-

---

20 Herbert Spencer, *First Principles* (New York: D. Appleton and Company, 1864), p. 530; here quoted from Richard Hofstadter, *Social Darwinism in American Thought* (New York: George Braziller, rev. ed., 1959), p. 37.
21 Quoted from *ibid.*, p. 51.
22 Quoted from *ibid.*, p. 45.
23 Henry Nash Smith, "The Search for a Capitalist Hero," p. 99.

ment. Dreiser illustrates the mentality which enables Cowperwood to pursue his 'career' in a famous scene, in which the inhumanity of the pursuit of financial success at any price is convincingly symbolized. On his way to school, little Frank, "even at ten, [...] a natural-born leader," daily passes an aquarium with a lobster and a squid. Day after day he observes how the aggressive lobster bites off another part of the hapless squid, and one day he sees that the squid has been completely eaten. This experience defines his later philosophy of life:

> The incident made a great impression on him. It answered in a rough way that riddle which had been annoying him so much in the past. "How is life organized?" Things lived on each other - that was it. Lobsters lived on squids and other things. What lived on lobsters? Men, of course! Sure, that was it! And what lived on men? he asked himself. Was it other men? [...] That was it! Sure, men lived on men. Look at the slaves. They were men. That's what all this excitement was about these days.[24]

The expressive parable illustrates the Social-Darwinist theory of the "survival of the fittest," which Jack London so aptly called "the law of club and fang,"[25] and which is defined as follows by Captain Larsen in London's novel *The Sea Wolf* (1904):

> I believe that life is a mess, [...] It is like yeast, a ferment, a thing that moves and may move for a minute, an hour, a year, or a hundred years, but that in the end will cease to move. The big eat the little that they may continue to move, the strong eat the weak that they may retain their strength. The lucky eat the most and move the longest, that is all.[26]

These quotations amply show why a literature that pleads for human values cannot but concur with the narrator of Saul Bellow's novel *More Die of Heartbreak* (1987) in considering "Darwinian self-preservation to be a vulgar ideology" because "its leading exponents are sadists who are always telling you that for the good of the species and in conformity with the law of Nature, they have to do in the gentle spirits

---

24 Theodore Dreiser, *The Financier* (London: Constable, 1927), p. 11.
25 Jack London, *The Call of the Wild and White Fang* (New York: Washington Square Press, rpt. 1964), p. 13.
26 Jack London, *The Sea Wolf* (New York: Bantam Books, 1963), p. 35.

they encounter on life's way,"[27] and why therefore, from a humanistic point of view, any businessman bound to this law must be rejected as a monstrous aberration.

The thesis of the 'Puritan work ethic,' then, still influential in spite of its faultiness, and the historical excrescences of Social Darwinism are doubtlessly the major sources for the negative depiction of the businessman in American literature. A more detailed analysis would have to add at least two more sources, namely, the folk traditions of the Yankee peddler and the confidence-man, that is, of the travelling businessman from New England who can talk his gullible customers into buying anything, and of the tricky and often satanic impostor whose impositions nobody can resist. Thomas Chandler Haliburton's *The Clockmaker, or Sayings and Doings of Samuel Slick* (1837) would be a prominent example of the first, Herman Melville's *The Confidence-Man: His Masquerade* (1857) is the most accomplished example of the second type.[28] Moreover, one needs to realize that the dynamism of success and failure is a theme central to American literature at large and greatly transcends the limited realm of the business novel[29] and that, as the history of the reception of the Weber-thesis so forcefully demonstrates, no intellectual movement can be reduced to mono-causal explanations.

---

27 Saul Bellow, *More Die of Heartbreak* (Harmondsworth: Penguin Books, 1988), p. 139.
28 See the chapter "The Yankee Peddler and the Con Man" in Emily Stipes Watts, *op. cit.*, pp. 33-44.
29 See, for example, Martha Banta, *Failure and Success in America: A Literary Debate* (Princeton: Princeton University Press, 1978).

The Commercial Fall as a Prerequisite for the Moral Rise: William Dean Howells, *The Rise of Silas Lapham*

> Sewell was intensely interested in the moral spectacle which Lapham presented under his changed conditions.
> William Dean Howells, *The Rise of Silas Lapham*[30]

In November 1884, William Dean Howells' novel *The Rise of Silas Lapham* began to appear in instalments in the *Century Magazine*, and a year later it was published as a book. The reviewer of *The Dial* greeted it by observing that it was "almost a new species of work [...] the business man's novel,"[31] and even today literary historians unanimously classify it as the first American business novel proper.[32]

The novel combines a love plot with a business plot that ends in bankruptcy, and its central figure is Silas Lapham, a man in his mid-fifties and "a fine type of the successful American" (6).[33] Lapham has all the characteristics which will soon become the standard features of the literary businessman. He grows up in a large family on his parents' farm in Vermont, he comes to know poverty and hardship at an early age, he is taught by a loving mother "the simple virtues of the Old Testament and *Poor Richard's Almanac*" (7),[34] he is offered no formalized school education, he has a look around the country before he settles down, and he marries the village schoolteacher who is intellectually far above him, before he opens his own business. A strong youth grown up in healthy country air, capable of hard work, endowed with the rudiments of Biblical morality, inspired with the will

---

30 William Deam Howells, *The Rise of Silas Lapham* (New York: New American Library, 1963), p. 335.
31 William Payne, "Recent Fiction," *The Dial*, 6 (1885), 122.
32 See Emily Stipes Watts, *op. cit.*, p. 1: "[...] a question familiar to literary Ph.D. candidates in contemporary academia. Question: 'What was the first American business novel?' Answer: *The Rise of Silas Lapham*."
33 All page numbers in brackets in the text refer to the edition given in note 30.
34 The most important aphorisms from *Poor Richard's Almanack* which refer to business life were collected by Franklin in Father Abraham's speech in "The Way to Wealth" (1758). Among them are "God helps them that help themselves," and several variations upon the insight which in Franklin's "Advice to a Young Tradesman" (1748) is formulated as "Time is Money."

The "Ladder of Fortune" in an 1875 lithograph

to succeed, and loved and guided by an educated wife - that is, according to the countless career-guides, precisely the wood from which to carve the successful self-made man in the land of unlimited opportunities. But another ingredient has to be added: one day hardworking Lapham has the luck which even the competent man needs, and he discovers on his father's farm a mineral-paint mine and immediately realizes that it can be turned into a gold mine. True to the insight from *Poor Richard's Almanac* that "God helps those who help themselves," Lapham sells everything he owns and invests all his possessions in a paint factory. The lucky break on the one hand and the uninhibited willingness to take a risk on the other - that again is exactly the mixture propagated by all 'from-rags-to-riches' manuals. No wonder, then, that Lapham succeeds and becomes rich. But in America it is not enough to be rich since success has "to be recognized by other people."[35] Thus, Lapham moves into the proper surroundings, the better parts of Boston, where he has a huge house built as a visible sign of his new status and where the *nouveau riche*, who believes that his money can buy everything,[36] sets out to introduce his daughters into the snobbish society of the Boston Brahmins.

Up to here Howells, the realist intent on a precise reproduction of everyday life, has translated the standard traits of the American success-myth into a prototypical story, but now he performs the decisive test and poses the crucial question concerning the relation between business acumen and morals. Mr. Rogers, a former partner of Lapham, whom the latter had prevailed upon to leave the business when it began to flourish, appears and asks for a substantial loan. In order to overcome his own guilty feeling and to placate his wife, who charges him with having cheated Mr. Rogers, Lapham gives him a large part of the money which he had planned to invest in the new house. But Lapham had treated Rogers correctly and had given him, when he left, more money than he had invested in the business. He simply had - and according to today's business ethics this is a totally

---

35 See Richard M. Huber, *The American Idea of Success*, pp. 1-9, where one reads, for example, "Success could never be precisely measured, [...] However, it did have to be recognized by other people."

36 See, for example, Lapham's statement "Why don't you get them [the girls] into society? There's money enough!" (30); or the observation of his wife, "He thinks his money can do everything" (137).

'normal' occurrence - bought out a hesitant partner by whom he did not want to be hampered during the envisaged period of expansion. In Howells' eyes, however, this was morally reprehensible, and he makes his narrator comment:

> But Lapham had not created [all the advantages he was looking forward to]. He had been dependent at one time on his partner's capital. It was a moment of terrible trial. Happy is the man forever after who can choose the ideal, the unselfish part, in such an exigency! Lapham could not rise to it. He did what he could maintain to be perfectly fair. (47)

The business ethics of a successful fictional entrepreneur, who in comparison to the actual robber barons of his time is a veritable paragon of virtue, proves deficient before the humanistic claims of the novelist. To be 'fair' is not enough, and Howells drives home that point in no uncertain terms.

Since the reappearance of Rogers, Lapham is going downhill. To regain the money he has lent his former partner he speculates on the stock exchange where he incurs heavy losses; his attempts to be admitted to polite Boston society end in embarrassing fiascos; the affairs of his daughters turn into painful failures; and finally bankruptcy threatens. Lapham's only rescue would be the selling of worthless manufacturing plants to a corrupt syndicate willing to buy them, but he comes to a moral decision, turns down the questionable offer, and goes "unscathed and unstained" (323) into bankruptcy. Here again the rescue of his firm would not have been illegal but 'only' immoral, but Howells' message becomes obvious when the narrator says about Lapham, who returns penniless to the simplicity of the parental farm:

> Adversity had so far been his friend that it had taken from him all hope of the social success for which people crawl and truckle, and restored him, through failure and doubt and heartache, the manhood which his prosperity had so nearly stolen from him. (330f.)

Lapham's commercial fall, then, becomes the prerequisite for his moral rise, and thus Howells' novel turns into a critical contrafactum of the reality of his time. In a period of radical decline of traditional values, during which the robber barons of the Gilded Age daily offended against humanity and decency and violated every existing law in order to amass their unbelievable fortunes, and in which the misery of an exploited labour force exploded in the Chicago Haymarket Riots, Howells portrays a fictional businessman whose life story contains every standard trait of the American entrepreneur but whose rise and fall also demonstrates the incompatibilty of commercial success and moral integrity. In *The Rise of Silas Lapham*, late nineteenth-century business ethics, which were based on a rabid Social Darwinism and in which every means was considered acceptable that served the desired end,[37] are radically called into question. And when Howells makes educated Tom Carey say "there's no doubt but money is to the fore now. It is the romance, the poetry, of our age" (60), and lets Tom's father observe that "all civilization comes through literature now, especially in our country. [...] we must read or we must barbarize" (110), then it becomes evident that he saw a deep abyss between the behaviour of the new entrepreneurs rising out of nothing and the moral standards of the old-established and refined families of New England, that is, between 'business' and 'culture.' Howells tried to bridge this abyss by the very means of literature, and whereas he certainly achieved nothing within the actual world of American business, he introduced an important motif into American literature, namely that of commercial failure as prerequisite for moral growth. This motif is still alive today, and Bernard Malamud's moving novel *The Assistant* (1959) provides an outstanding recent example.[38]

Howells conceived of the individual as being endowed with free will, and consequently he was convinced that wealth would not irretrievably corrupt its possessor and that it would never be too late for a fresh start, as Lapham's moral victory shows. Later critics are much less hopeful than Howells, and when Henry Miller returned to his mother-country from his long exile in Paris, he described America in

---

[37] Patrick Dooley, "Nineteenth Century Business Ethics and *The Rise of Silas Lapham*," *American Studies*, 21, 2 (1980), 79-93; here p. 85, proves from contemporary reviews that "*Silas Lapham* was misread for although Howells saw business and ethics as connected, very many of his contemporaries did not." - Therefore Robie Macauley, "Let Me Tell You About the Rich ...," *Kenyon Review*, 27 (1965), 645-671; here p. 658, is wrong when he says: "Already beginning to have some doubts about the ethics of great fortune-building, Americans wanted an example of the businessman who let conscience triumph over greed - and Howells gave them a gentle portrait of one."
[38] See Peter Freese, "Ökonomisches Scheitern und moralischer Erfolg: Bernard Malamuds *The Assistant* als Kritik am Amerikanischen Traum," in *Die USA in Unterricht und Forschung*, ed. by Lothar Bredella (Bochum: Kamp, 1984), pp. 190-201.

his travelogue as *The Air-Conditioned Nightmare* (1947), that is, as a country in which people believed in a wrong, a "stinking" myth of success, and in which the value of an individual could only be measured in dollars:

> There is one thing America has to give, [...]: MONEY. [...] There's no real life for an artist in America - only a living death. [...] we shall see whether the ability to make money and the ability to survive are one and the same. Then we shall see the meaning of true wealth.[39]

In Sinclair Lewis' novel *Babbitt* (1922), the vulgar and hypocritical protagonist had triumphantly proclaimed that "in other countries, art and literature are left to a lot of shabby bums living in attics and feeding on booze and spaghetti, but in America the successful writer or picture painter is indistinguishable from any other decent business man,"[40] and it was this very attitude which Henry Miller attacked when he denounced the detrimental influence of the American business mentality upon the arts and charged that in America they were deprived of all possibilities by their hateful commercialization.

With Miller, the rift which Howells saw developing during his lifetime and which he tried to solve by making Lapham's conscience triumph over his business acumen has turned into a deep abyss, and the rebellious twentieth-century bohemian can feel nothing but deep contempt for a shirt-sleeved society intent upon competition and success, in which art is at best estimated as a means of investment. The by now indissoluble contrast between 'business' and 'culture,' as it articulates itself, for example, in such terms as *Broadway* and *off-Broadway*, could be illustrated by dozens of relevant examples which would substantiate Epstein's diagnosis that American authors

> - through the nineteenth century, from Cooper's distrust of the self-made man to James's deliciously sneering reference to his countrymen's "grope for wealth" - viewed success in America in terms ranging from equivocation to condemnation. In the twentieth century, the terms have been closer to those of unrelieved contempt. Antisuccess

---

39 Henry Miller, *The Air-Conditioned Nightmare* (London: Panther Books, rpt. 1973), pp. 35, 36, and 37.
40 Sinclair Lewis, *Babbitt* (London: The Albatross, 1947), p. 160.

has perhaps been the strongest strain in American literature of the past half century.[41]

To mention just one pertinent example, let me briefly point to the so-called 'Hollywood novel,' which depicts "Hollywood as a microcosm, not just of America but of the American dream"[42] and attacks the commercialization of art, the artificiality of existence, and the failure of sexuality in the Californian dream factory from Raoul Whitfield's *Death in a Bowl* (1930), Nathanael West's *The Day of the Locust* (1939) and F. Scott Fitzgerald's *The Last Tycoon* (1941) to Budd Schulberg's *What Makes Sammy Run?* (1941), Raymond Chandler's *The Little Sister* (1949), and Norman Mailer's *The Deer Park* (1955). In Schulberg's novel, for instance, a poor copy-boy becomes a powerful Hollywood producer by conducting his life as a "blitzkrieg against his fellow men" (221),[43] but he pays for his success with isolation, anxiety and despair. The incompatibility of a rapid entrepreneurial career with moral integrity is poignantly expressed when the author makes his self-made man say: "Going through life with a conscience is like driving your car with the brakes on." (56)

---

41 Joseph Epstein, *Ambition: The Secret Passion* (Harmondsworth: Penguin Books, 1982), p. 75.
42 Carolyn See, "The Hollywood Novel: The American Dream Cheat," in *Tough Guy Writers of the Thirties*, ed. by David Madden (Carbondale and Edwardsville: Southern Illinois University Press, 1968), pp. 199-217; here p. 200.
43 All page numbers in brackets refer to Budd Schulberg, *What Makes Sammy Run?* (London: Corgi Books, rpt. 1967).

Financial Success as a Sign of Spiritual Failure: Abraham Cahan, *The Rise of David Levinsky*

> This was that vast incredible land, the land of freedom, of immense opportunity, that Golden Land.
> Henry Roth, *Call It Sleep*[44]

> America is so rich and fat, because it has eaten the tragedy of millions of immigrants.
> Michael Gold, *Jews Without Money*[45]

It is the outstanding feature of the American success-myth that it promises success not only to those who already live in the United States but also to the countless immigrants streaming into the country of unlimited possibilities; and at present we observe the ironical fact that the so-called 'Puritan work ethic' is most successfully acted out by Asian immigrants.[46] With the exception of the native Indians, the reverse side of the coin has been most painfully experienced by Black Americans, for the great majority of whom the promise of entrepreneurial self-fulfilment has remained a chimera. And Dick Gregory, the well-known Black entertainer and 1968 presidential candidate, offers an apt comment on the discrepancy between dream and reality when he observes laconically that unfortunately he could not follow the traditional advice to 'pull himself up by his own bootstraps' because he never owned boots.[47]

Another ethnic group, however, namely that of the Jews, has been particularly successful in acting out the American Dream. Even if countless Jewish immigrants came to grief in the merciless rat race of free enterprise, as Michael Gold's socio-critical novel *Jews Without Money* (1930) impressively illustrates, statistics show that an above-average number managed to build up important enterprises. Names

---

44 Henry Roth, *Call It Sleep* (New York: Avon Books, 1964), p. 16.
45 Michael Gold, *Jews Without Money* (New York: Avon Books, 1965), p. 26.
46 See, for example, "Asians: To America with Skills," in *Time*, July 8, 1985, pp. 32-34.
47 See Dick Gregory, *No More Lies: The Myth and the Reality of American History* (New York: Perennial Library, 1972), p. 253; see also the chapter "The Myth of Free Enterprise," pp. 208-218.

like Guggenheim and Seligman, Loeb and Straus exemplify this observation; the story of the poor Jewish tailor Levi Strauss who used rivets when he ran out of thread and thus inadvertently created the most American piece of clothing, namely jeans, has turned into a popular legend; and the association of Samuel Goldfish, Louis B. Mayer and Marcus Loew into Metro-Goldwyn-Mayer signals the leading role of Jewish businessmen in Hollywood - a variant of the success-myth, by the way, which E. L. Doctorow has recently illustrated in all its ambiguity of gain and loss by the metamorphosis of Tateh, the Hester Street pushcart peddler, into Baron Askenazy, the powerful producer of silent movies, in his bestselling novel *Ragtime* (1975).

The business novel which depicts the rise of a Jewish immigrant to wealth and power in greatest detail is undoubtedly Abraham Cahan's *The Rise of David Levinsky* (1917), in which the complex interplay of enculturation and social advancement is presented in a fascinating way and which literary historians have recently rediscovered as "the first full-fledged immigrant novel in English"[48] and as "possibly the best presentation of the Americanization process we have."[49] Cahan, a Lithuanian Jew who arrived in New York in 1882 with no knowledge of the English language, soon became an influential author and labour organizer, edited for almost half a century the largest Yiddish newspaper in the world, the *Jewish Daily Forward*, and was looked up to as a leading figure by the Jewish immigrant masses. His partly autobiographical novel about David Levinsky, which appeared in the very year in which the controversial Literacy Test was introduced as a means of barring unwanted immigrants from entering the country, certainly is no outstanding aesthetic or stylistic achievement - a defect it shares with many business novels and which obviously has to do with the sujet - but it is both an authentic document of American economic history between 1885 and the beginning of World War I and a scathing comment on the myth of success.

In *The Rise of Silas Lapham*, Howells had resolved the tension between the striving for financial success and the shrinking back from its

---

[48] John Higham, "Introduction," to Abraham Cahan, *The Rise of David Levinsky* (New York: Harper and Row, 1960), p. ix.
[49] Jules Zanger, "David Levinsky: Master of Pilpul," *Papers on Language and Literature*, 3 (1977), 283-294; here p. 283.

moral dubiousness by preferring the ethical to the prudential decision and thus celebrating the financial ruin of his self-made hero as the very token of his spiritual regeneration. When he praised Cahan's book as "a pretty good autobiographical novel," although he predictably found it "too sensual in its facts,"[50] he obviously did not recognize that Cahan makes a different and more convincing point: Lapham's bankruptcy, due to his inability to deceive his partners, turns out to be a spiritual success; Levinsky's financial success, however, proves to be a spiritual failure. The Jewish immigrant, who has no pastoral farm to which he can retire for a chastened new beginning, finds himself not so much in a moral but in a historical predicament, and that becomes obvious in the programmatic opening and closing paragraphs of the novel. Levinsky, who retrospectively makes out the balance-sheet of his life, begins his report with the following statement:

> Sometimes, when I think of my past in a superficial, casual way, the metamorphosis I have gone through strikes me as nothing short of a miracle. I was born and reared in the lowest depths of poverty and I arrived in America - in 1885 - with four cents in my pocket. I am now worth more than two million dollars and recognized as one of the two or three leading men in the cloak-and-suit trade in the United States. And yet when I take a look at my inner identity it impresses me as being precisely the same it was thirty or forty years ago. My present station, power, the amount of worldly happiness at my command, and the rest of it, seems to be devoid of significance. (3)[51]

More than five-hundred pages later he concludes his confession with this observation:

> I can never forget the days of my misery. I cannot escape from my old self. My past and my present do not comport well. David, the poor lad swinging over a Talmud volume at the Preacher's Synagogue, seems to have more in common with my inner identity than David Levinsky, the well-known cloak-manufacturer. (530)

These statements show that the tension between the poverty-stricken orphan and unworldly Talmud-scholar in the pogrom-threatened

---

50 In a letter of September 20, 1917 to Francis A. Duneka; here quoted from *Life in Letters*, ed. by Mildred Howells (New York: Doubleday, Doran, 1928), vol. II, p. 375.
51 All page numbers in brackets refer to the edition of the novel given in note 48.

shtetl of Antomir and the completely Americanized, wealthy cloak-manufacturer in the hectic melting pot of New York cannot be resolved. The key for an understanding of Levinsky's discontent is the painful rift between his European past and his American present, which "do not comport well," and this discrepancy provides a representative comment on every immigrant's attempt at beginning anew and starting a 'new life' in America, the promised land "of milk and honey" and "of marvelous transformations" (612).

Since his father died when David was three (4), he grows up, in the Russian town of Antomir, as the only child of a devoted mother. In spite of her dire poverty, the only aim of David's pious mother is her son's religious education, and she manages to send her bright boy to "a school for religious instruction or *cheder*" (16). From there he progresses to a "Talmudic seminary, or *yeshiva*" (27) where he spends "seven years" (28). When his mother is killed in a heroic attempt to take to task some Christian Jew-baiters who have beaten up her son, the orphaned adolescent has no choice but to spend his whole time at the synagogue and in religious schools. Barred by the strict laws of his belief from all contact with the outside world, he is the product of a close culture as yet unaffected by the immense historical changes of the times. His worldly knowledge is next to nothing and his two transcendent values are his reverence for religious learning and his experience of protective family love. Insulated from historical reality by his dedication to the Talmud and by the surrounding community of hostile Christians who keep the Jews confined to their *shtetl*, David grows up, in spite of his poverty, in the security of an ancient tradition. And the young man's world view and priorities are defined by his teacher's statement: "Study the words of God [...] What is wealth? A dream of fools. What is this world? A mere curl of smoke for the wind to scatter. Only the other world has substance and reality; only good deeds and holy learning have tangible worth." (31)

But this security is soon shattered. Sexual longings disturb David, a former fellow Talmudist turned apostate shocks him with the statement that belief in God "is all bosh" (55), his contact with a Russified Jewish family, in which orthodox traditions are abandoned, acquaints him with an unknown way of life, a tempting young woman accuses him that "it's a crime for a young man like you to throw himself away on that idiotic Talmud of yours" (72), and reports about the pogroms and the resulting "great New Exodus" (61) of oppressed Jews from the Russian Pale of Settlement to America fill him with longings to leave Antomir.[52] Thus history invades the timelessness of tradition, worldly aspirations begin to vie with otherworldly devotion, and David, by now an incipient unbeliever, sets out for the promised land. "Centuries of difference" had lain between young Matilda of the "enlightened" family and David (69). How much more must he be the victim of culture shock when he arrives penniless in the teeming city of New York. The clash he has to sustain is one between two ways of life so totally different that the task to be achieved by David seems simply unrealizable: that of a transition from the closed *shtetl* to the open city, from pious learning to manual labour, from protective tradition to vulnerable openness, from the socially sanctioned Talmudist's dedication to the pursuit of otherworldly knowledge to the Lower East Side's relentless competition for worldly success. It is this very predicament of the immigrant which Cahan's novel details in a brilliant case study. At the core of David's spiritual failure, in spite of his impressive financial success, lies the inability to make the two halves of his life "comport well," that is, his inability to forge a new unified identity out of his European and his American existence. When this is recognized, it becomes obvious that the novel is representative of a general issue and sheds light on an aspect of the 'American Dream' which is glossed over by such catch phrases as 'melting pot' or 'Americanization.'

Upon arriving in New York, young David is intent upon assimilating as quickly as possible. Unable to understand what James Baldwin much later formulates in his admonition that "the past is all that makes the present coherent,"[53] he turns into a living example of what D. H. Lawrence said about America: "She starts old, old, wrinkled and writhing in an old skin. And there is a gradual sloughing of the old skin, towards a new youth."[54] But any attempt to forget one's past is,

---

52 For a detailed investigation of this exodus see Irving Howe, *World of Our Fathers* (New York and London: Harcourt Brace Jovanovich, 1976).
53 James Baldwin, "Autobiographical Notes," in his *Notes of a Native Son* (London: Corgi Books, 1969), pp. 1-6; here p. 4.
54 D. H. Lawrence, *Studies in Classic American Literature*, p. 54.

as Nietzsche so prophetically said in "Vom Nutzen und Nachteil der Historie für das Leben,"

> [...] ein gefährlicher, nämlich für das Leben selbst gefährlicher Prozeß: und Menschen oder Zeiten, die auf diese Weise dem Leben dienen, daß sie eine Vergangenheit richten oder vernichten, sind immer gefährliche und gefährdete Menschen und Zeiten. Denn da wir nun einmal die Resultate früherer Geschlechter sind, sind wir auch die Resultate ihrer Verirrungen, Leidenschaften und Irrtümer, ja Verbrechen; es ist nicht möglich, sich ganz von dieser Kette zu lösen.[55]

What Nietzsche calls the impossibility of breaking the chain, is revealed by the very language Levinsky uses to convey the impressions of his first days in New York. Describing the effects of arriving in America, he reverts to the traditional metaphor of "a second birth" (93) and compares himself to "a new-born babe" (86). At the end of the novel, he takes up this image when he states that "the day of an immigrant's arrival in his new home is like a birthday to him" (513), and in the middle of his narrative he extends it to his plans for marriage, thinking of his impending wedding "as a new birth, like my coming to America" (399). This central initiatory symbol of rebirth serves as the focus of a series of outward alterations which include a total change of clothes and the cutting off of the young man's side-locks[56] - both achieved under the tutelage of a Mr. Even, who serves as a friendly mentor to the bewildered neophyte (100ff.) - and the shaving off of David's "sprouting beard" (110). But, while the immigrant's outward appearance is 'Americanized' with the express purpose of freeing him from the taint of "greenhorn" (93), David experiences the silhouette of the great city "in a trance [...] like a divine revelation" (87), ample evidence that inwardly he still feels and thinks in traditional categories.

Levinsky soon sheds his already shattered faith because his "contact with life" deals his "former ideas of the world blow after blow" (110) and because he learns that "America is not Russia. A man

---

55 Friedrich Nietzsche, "Vom Nutzen und Nachteil der Historie für das Leben," in *Werke in drei Bänden*, ed. by Karl Schlechta (München: Karl Hanser Verlag, no date [1965]), vol. I, pp. 209-285; here pp. 229f.
56 In Jewish-American literature, the cutting off of side-locks and beards for men and the discarding of wigs for women is a recurring outward sign of the immigrants' acceptance of the American way of life. See, for example, Gitl's uneasy parting with her wig in Cahan's *Yekl: A Tale of the New York Ghetto* (1896).

must make a living here" (97). And he concentrates on the most important - and most difficult to achieve - badge of Americanization, the mastery of language. Attending "public evening school" (129) "with religious devotion" (133) - again a revealing choice of words - he works hard at attaining the right accent. Later he will state that "people who were born to speak English were superior beings" (176) and will even go as far as to say: "That I was not born in America was something like a physical defect that asserted itself in many disagreeable ways - a physical defect which, alas! no surgeon in the world was capable of removing." (291)

Levinsky adjusts to the new and strange tempo of life - "An American day seemed to be far richer in substance than an Antomir year. I was in an everlasting flutter" (131) - tries his best "to dress like a genteel American" (260), and soon begins to "feel at home in [...] the American streets" (175) in which in the beginning he had felt "like one abandoned in the midst of a jungle" (90). Constantly on the alert to suppress everything that might remind others of his origins, he memorizes Americanisms and parades his idiomatic English (364); he is concerned about his "Talmudic gesticulations" - "a habit that worried me like a physical defect. It was so distressingly un-American" (327) - and painfully conscious of the fact that "my Russian name was against me" (332). He imbibes the keywords of success - "Dil-i-gence, perr-severance, tenacity!" (135) - discovers and learns to use such genuinely American traits as "the unsmiling smile" (130), and soon feels "American enough" (210) to talk contentedly about "my Americanized self" (214).

Outward success, then, is achieved by complete assimilation at the cost of crippling self-abnegation, total immersion in a new cultural surrounding with the express intention of remaking himself at the cost of rejecting his Jewish identity, his European experience, and his religious roots: soon the erstwhile Talmud scholar will be able to say "that an American school-boy should read Talmud seemed a joke to me" (397). Levinsky, it seems, really experiences a 'rebirth' and is remade into a successful American, but the past cannot be totally suppressed. Crèvecoeur's hymnic statement - "*He* is an American, who, leaving behind him all his ancient prejudices and manners, receives new ones from the new mode of life he has embraced, the new government he obeys, and the new rank he holds"[57] - proves to be nothing but a pious hope. Young David's early statement about his new clothes - "When I took a look at the mirror I was bewildered. I scarcely recognized myself." (101) - turns out to be prophetic, and he is continually haunted by a sense of the wrongness and futility of his endeavours. His initial "sense of loneliness and dread of the new world" (89) never leaves him, and statements like "I was excruciatingly homesick" (103) or "I was forever homesick" (325) punctuate the novel like an insistent refrain.

In spite of having become a millionaire, Levinsky remains a dissatisfied man who is continually haunted by "loneliness and desolation" (526). Disturbing "thoughts of the past" fill him "with mixed joy and sadness" (513), and more than once he is possessed by memories which turn his "present life into a dream and [his] Russian past into reality" (389). The man who has exchanged his sense-making and community-building belief in the God of Judaism for the relentless philosophy of Darwin and Spencer and who likes to think of himself as "one of the fittest" (283) - he states: "the only thing I believed in was the cold, drab theory of the struggle for existence and survival of the fittest" (380), again giving himself away by his choice of words - is continually beset by a gnawing and painful discontent. His suppressed past, as it were, comes back with a vengeance, his frantic attempts at total Americanization prove to be impossible, and his very efforts to deny the past make it an everlasting nemesis in his present. Whenever he thinks he has finally "made it" and becomes "too self-confident" (290), he is - on a superficial level - overtaken by his foreign birth in so far as he is faced with a new situation in which he is again "a poor novice" (259; see 515); and whenever he becomes conceited and thinks himself "infallible" (347), he is forced to realize that, in the "great, daring game of life" (189), there are times when, in spite of all his progress, he is nothing but "a novice at the game" (332). On a deeper level, however, it is not the mere knowledge of his limitations which bothers him, but the much more disturbing recognition of his betrayal of self, of his fundamental inauthenticity.

---

57 J. Hector St. John de Crèvecoeur, *Letters from an American Farmer and Sketches of Eighteenth-Century America*, ed. by Albert E. Stone (Harmondsworth: Penguin Books, 1981), p. 70.

This inauthenticity is mainly due to two basic mistakes: Levinsky's abandonment of an intellectual in favour of an entrepreneurial career and his inability to acquire a wife, a home, and an heir. And, of course, in the context of the dichotomy between past and present, these two mistakes are nothing but his failure to continue what he has begun in *cheder* and *yeshiva* and his failure to regain the feeling of belonging and security which he had with his loving mother, or, more abstractly, his lack of attaining the two genuinely Jewish ideals of learning as spiritual fulfilment and of the family as the haven of love and safety.

At the beginning of his American existence, David dreams of an intellectual career, looks upon his money-making attempts as nothing but "a stepping-stone to a life of intellectual interests" (150), and is filled with an insatiable "clamor for knowledge" (156). College becomes for him "the synagogue of my new life" (168), and the mere word seems magic. Evidently, the replacement of religious by secular learning would have been his only chance to fulfil his mother's hopes and to remain true to his former life, to dedicate himself to "the better man in me, to what was purest in my thoughts and most sacred in my emotions" (169). But Levinsky squanders his chance when the means for the attainment of such an ideal - namely the earning of money through manual work in the garment industry - becomes an end in itself. This happens, according to his version, because of a fateful "accident" (187). One day he spills milk on some expensive coats, and his boss, the German Jew Mannheimer, scolds and humiliates him in front of the other employees. Enraged, Levinsky decides to show Mannheimer what he can do, to steal the designer who has made the firm's fortune, and to beat Mannheimer at his own game.

This accident, to which Levinsky refers several times throughout his narrative - "The destruction of my American Temple [college] was caused by a bottle of milk" (215); "The day when that accident turned my mind from college to business seems to be the most unfortunate day in my life" (529) - is, of course, nothing but a realization of his own weakness, and Cahan skilfully disproves any naturalistic interpretation of the event when, several hundred pages later and in one of the few verbal puns of the novel, he makes another character say to Levinsky: "There's at least one saying that has come true. I mean the saying, 'There's no use crying over spilled milk.' Mr. Levinsky, you certainly have no reason to cry over the milk spilled at Manheimer's, have you?" (466) Here the protagonist-narrator, who memorizes English idioms to demonstrate his Americanness, is ironically unmasked as being untrue to himself, for his continual 'crying over spilled milk' and his blaming fate for his change from an intellectual to a business career are only rationalizations of his own inconsistency as brought about by an unresolved tension between two cultures.[58]

The same is true with regard to the second crucial aspect of Levinsky's life, his relationship with women. Reared by a loving mother in a world in which "women were intended for two purposes only: for the continuation of the human species and to serve as an instrument in the hands of Satan for tempting the stronger sex to sin" (42f.), Levinsky is thrown into another and incomparably freer world, and he never manages to adjust to it, to reconcile his affective needs with his sexual cravings. Throughout his adult life, he suffers from a "repressed sexual conflict induced by a complex fear, erotic desire, and Oedipal longing,"[59] and his long and painful history of infatuations, brothel visits, attempted seductions, and broken engagements testifies to the fact that he has a thoroughly disturbed attitude to the opposite sex. Always looking for both a replica of his mother and for an object for the release of his lust, he is simultaneously attracted and repulsed by women, and because his desires are not only contradictory but also unrealistic, they can never be fulfilled.

When, after his fortieth birthday, his desire for a wife and for progeny becomes more prominent than his need for the satisfaction of his sexual urges, Levinsky says:

> The wish to "settle down" then grew into a passion with me. The vague portrait of a woman in the abstract seemed never to be absent from my mind. Coupled with that portrait was a similarly vague image of a window and a table set for dinner. That, somehow, was my symbol of

---

[58] See David Engel, "The 'Discrepancies' of the Modern: Towards a Revaluation of Abraham Cahan's *The Rise of David Levinsky*," Studies in Jewish American Literature, 2 (1982), 36-60; here p. 48.

[59] Sanford E. Marovitz, "The Secular Trinity of a Lonely Millionaire: Language, Sex, and Power in *The Rise of David Levinsky*," Studies in Jewish American Literature, 2 (1982), 20-35; here p. 21.

home. Home and a woman were one, a complex charm joining them into an inseparable force. (376f.)

Here he implicitly admits that he is aware of his problems and that his ideal is of such a composite nature that reality is bound to fall short of it. And here it becomes obvious that his idea of fulfilment is shaped by his recollections of his childhood, that what the middle-aged millionaire dreams of as a perfect future is nothing but a projection of his past, namely, the "security and perpetuity" (377) provided by the closely knit Jewish family which Irving Howe rightly calls "the one bulwark against the chaos of the world."[60] Such a reading is later confirmed by Levinsky's reflection: "My business life had fostered the conviction in me that, outside of the family, the human world was as brutally selfish as the jungle" (380), by his admission that "dreams of family life became my religion" (380), and by his continual brooding over the question, "Who are you living for?" (447).

These two essential failures, then, the failure to pursue an intellectual career and the failure to establish a family and foster an heir, a *kaddish*, to his business imperium, define the price which Levinsky has to pay for his outward "success" (324; 348; 445; 525), and they explain why at the end of his story he sits all alone in his expensive house and recognizes: "There are cases when success is a tragedy." (529) Levinsky's 'tragedy' consists of the fact that despite or, better, because of his money he is a loveless and unloved man whose outwardly successful present is haunted by the unfulfilled dreams of his past. Thus, his empty existence painfully confirms Gavin Stevens' insight in Faulkner's *Requiem for a Nun* that "the past is never dead. It's not even past."[61] Although Cahan makes his protagonist an individual with specific personal problems and with a character which is somehow deficient before he comes to America,[62] the fragmented, inau-

---

60 Irving Howe, "Introduction" to *Jewish-American Stories*, ed. by him (New York: New American Library, 1977), p. 8.
61 William Faulkner, *Requiem for a Nun* (Harmondsworth: Penguin Books, rpt. 1977), p. 81.
62 Several critics agree on the necessity of stressing that David's estrangement from Jewish orthodoxy occurs well before his arrival in America. Thus, David Singer, "David Levinsky's Fall: A Note on the Liebman Thesis," *American Quarterly*, 19 (1967), 696-706; here p. 703, argues that David's sexual awakening, the murder of his mother, the apostasy of his fellow Talmudist Naphtali and his encounter with the Minsker family are responsible for the fact that "Levinsky's estrangement from

thentic and alienated Levinsky is also the quintessential immigrant lost between two conflicting cultures, and his financial success cum spiritual failure turns into a telling comment on the American predicament.

The Rise of David Levinsky, then, disproves the popular myth of success and turns out to be, in Isaac Rosenfeld's apt phrase, "an exemplary treatment of one of the dominant myths of American capitalism, that the millionaire finds nothing but emptiness at the top of the heap."[63] Levinsky's laconic observation that success can become a tragedy, however, not only turns the popular success-myth upside down and expresses both the rather banal insight that money is not everything and the more important recognition that the achievement of success brings an end to the challenge of succeeding. It also refers to a crucial problem which is related to an American foundation myth. Since Crèvecoeur's definition of the 'American' as a new man, the belief in the possibility of a new beginning in the American melting pot has been a central ingredient of popular ideology. And it is this very belief that one can leave one's past behind and embark upon a new and 'successful' future in the New World which is impressively disproved by David Levinsky's story.

In F. Scott Fitzgerald's *The Great Gatsby* (1925), the best-known obituary on the 'American Dream,' Gatsby, the self-made man who follows Benjamin Franklin's prescriptions but earns his money through fraud and corruption, answers Nick Carraway's remonstrance that one cannot repeat the past by saying incredulously "Can't

---

the traditional pattern of East European life [...] was virtually complete before David sailed for the United States." And Sanford E. Marovitz, "The Lonely New Americans of Abraham Cahan," *American Quarterly*, 20 (1968), 196-210; here p. 205, takes up this point when he says that "it is not America, then, that turns Levinsky from Judaism, but the adverse circumstances of his situation in Russia." - Historically speaking, it is only logical that the breaking up of orthodoxy was not so much a result of as a reason for the mass exodus of Russian Jews. But, since Cahan's novel deals with many other aspects besides the loss of religion, a reading of *The Rise of David Levinsky* in terms of a dichotomy of past and present, shtetl and city, Europe and America, is not at all invalidated.

63 Isaac Rosenfeld, "The Jew as American Millionaire," in *Jewish-American Literature: An Anthology*, ed. by Abraham Chapman (New York: Mentor Books, 1974), pp. 618-625; here p. 619.

repeat the past? Why of course you can!"⁶⁴ And it is this naive misjudgment which makes him fail. In Howells' *The Rise of Silas Lapham*, the hero, morally chastened by his commercial failure, returns to the paternal farm "to begin life anew" (325), and the hopeful author implies that this is possible in the pastoral country far removed from urban corruption. For David Levinsky, the day on which he enters the seething metropolis of New York is "a second birth" (93), but this 'rebirth' marks not only the beginning of his entrepreneurial career but also, still unknown to him, the onset of his self-betrayal, not only the start of his success but also the end of his identity. Consequently, Levinsky's 'success' story not only represents the immigrant's predicament but also illustrates a deeper reason for the predominantly negative depiction of the fast-rising self-made man in American literature, namely, his rootlessness, his loss of history, and his abandonment of an organically grown identity, a price for material success which almost all business novels consider far too high.⁶⁵ Cahan was a man who, in the perceptive words of William Dean Howells, "sees things with American eyes, and [...] brings in aid of his vision the far and rich perception of his Hebraic race; while he is strictly of the great and true Russian principles in literary art."⁶⁶ Participating in the traditions of three different cultures, he could treat the genuinely American theme of 'regretful success' from a unique vantage point and thus create a novel which Chametzky rightly calls "a haunting, suggestive, and [...] finally prophetic book"⁶⁷ on the rootless immigrant's spiritual malaise within the world of American affluence.

---

64 F. Scott Fitzgerald, *The Great Gatsby*, in *The Bodley Head Scott Fitzgerald* (London: Bodley Head, rpt. 1977), vol. I, p. 106.
65 One of the most recent and most outspoken examples of this motif can be found in E. L. Doctorow's novel *Loon Lake* (Toronto: Bantam Books, 1981), p. 281, in which the genesis of the self-made man is symbolized as an 'industrial' process and in which the inhuman result of such an 'auto-creation' is formulated in the insight that the accumulation of capital expresses nothing but "the desire for isolation" and that for the millionaire the "godliness [of his wealth] is in its isolation."
66 This observation occurs in Howells' review of *Yekl: A Tale of the New York Ghetto* and is reprinted in an appendix to Rudolf and Clara M. Kirk, "Abraham Cahan and William Dean Howells: The Story of a Friendship," *American Jewish Historical Quarterly*, 52 (1962), 25-27.
67 Jules Chametzky, *From the Ghetto: The Fiction of Abraham Cahan* (Amherst: University of Massachusetts Press, 1977), p. 143.

From Condemnation to Contempt: The Attitude of Anti-Success from F. Scott Fitzgerald to Kurt Vonnegut

> It's misleading for people to read about great successes, since even for middle-class and upper-class white people, in my experience, failure is the norm.
>
> Kurt Vonnegut, *Hocus Pocus*[68]

Whereas earlier American writers had been deeply suspicious of the 'self-made' entrepreneurs of the gilded age because of their lack of culture, their moral unscrupulousness and their denial of history, they still believed in the possibility of improvement - Howells' Lapham converts to an ethical rigorism, and Cahan's Levinsky recognizes that the human price he has paid for his financial success is far too high. In the 1920s, however, the business novel began to abandon the great industrial magnates and founders of the period of industrialization and instead started to concern itself with middle-class businessmen and with the genuinely American figure of the travelling salesman. This change was not only due to World War I and the general disillusionment it brought about, but it was also a reflection of fundamental social changes. In 1920, for example, Amory Blaine, the romantic hero of F. Scott Fitzgerald's novel *This Side of Paradise*, famously summed up this change when he mused:

> As an endless dream it went on; the spirit of the past brooding over a new generation, the chosen youth from the muddled, unchastened world, still fed romantically on the mistakes and half-forgotten dreams of dead statesmen and poets. Here was a new generation, shouting the old cries, learning the old creeds, through a reverie of long days and nights; destined finally to go out into that dirty grey turmoil to follow love and pride; a new generation dedicated more than the last to the fear of poverty and the worship of success; grown up to find all Gods dead, all wars fought, all faiths in man shaken ....[69]

Blaine's disillusioned reverie shows not only that around 1920 "the worship of success" was as strong as ever, but it also implies that "the

---

68 Kurt Vonnegut, *Hocus Pocus* (New York: G. P. Putnam's Sons, 1990), p. 41.
69 F. Scott Fitzgerald, *This Side of Paradise*, in *The Bodley Head Scott Fitzgerald* (London: The Bodley Head, rpt. 1971), vol. III, p. 270.

old creeds" about how to attain this success were no longer valid for "a new generation." The breathtaking success stories of the years of rapid industrial expansion, which were greatly admired and held up as models to emulate, could not be repeated, and by now it had become highly improbable if not outrightly impossible to fulfil the central prescription of the Horatio Alger concept of success, namely, to prove one's worth by outdoing one's parents.

The era of the 'robber barons' was finally over, and it is quite significant that, in *Babbitt*, Sinclair Lewis depicted William Washington Eathorne, one "of those Victorian financiers who ruled the generation between the pioneers and the brisk 'sales-engineers'" (185),[70] as the last survivor of a bygone era. In the twenties, more and more formerly independent businessmen turned into dependent employees, because the business world was increasingly dominated by rapidly expanding corporations with a growing need for so-called 'white collar' workers. This meant that agility became more important than ability, and the erstwhile aim of 'getting ahead' in an open market was replaced by the necessity of 'getting along' within ever more complex corporate structures.[71] And this also meant that the notion of success lost its traditional meaning because the new developments

> [...] indicated the beginning of a process whereby the public was attempting to preserve the success ethic as a philosophy of life while industrial leaders were transforming the dream of success into a corporate ideology designed to justify their power. The effect of this confluence was that Americans, in assuming that they were striving for success, were being acculturated to serve the goals of corporate society rather than their own self interests.[72]

It was in response to these changes that the doubts of earlier writers turned into the unmitigated contempt of contemporary authors. Robert Herrick passionately denounced the 'second generation' of success-orientated businessmen in novel after novel; Thorstein Veblen, Herrick's colleague at the newly opened University of Chicago, scathingly exposed the materialism of the moneyed classes in

---

70 All page numbers in brackets refer to the edition given in note 40.
60 See C. Wright Mills, *White Collar* (New York: Oxford University Press, 1951).
72 Lawrence Chenoweth, *The American Dream of Success: The Search for the Self in the Twentieth Century*, pp. 36f.

his famous study *The Theory of the Leisure Class*; and H. L. Mencken contemptuously considered the Rotarian and his 'Rotary Ann' as representatives of the *Boobus Americanus*, the American imbecile. In 1922, Sinclair Lewis published his bestselling novel *Babbitt*, which would make its pitiful protagonist, the well-off real estate agent George Folansbee Babbitt from Zenith, *the* representative of the average American businessman.

Babbitt, whose god is "the God of Progress" (11), whose maxim is to "get on the job and produce - produce - produce!" (18), who believes that "competition - brings out the best - survival of the fittest" (59), and who thinks of himself as someone who "makes the wheels of progress go round" (159; see 208), is the ultimate conformist. He lives on borrowed ideas and other men's half-digested opinions, and he is the epitome of what David Riesman will later define as an 'other-directed' person.[73]

> Just as he was an Elk, a Booster, and a member of the Chamber of Commerce, just as the priests of the Presbyterian Church determined his every religious belief and the senators who controlled the Republican Party decided in little smoky rooms in Washington what he should think about disarmament, tariff, and Germany, so did the large national advertisers fix the surface of his life, fix what he believed to be his individuality. These standard advertised wares - tooth-pastes, socks, tyres, cameras, instantaneous hot-water heaters - were his symbols and proofs of excellence; at first the signs, then the substitutes, for joy and passion and wisdom. (85)

Like his business associates, Babbitt is the "Standardized American Citizen" (161) spawned by the new religion of business that pays homage to the god of 'turnover,' and for him and his likes, whose interchangeable lives are dedicated to "that clean fighting determination to win Success" (162),

> [...] the Romantic Hero was no longer the knight, the wandering poet, the cowpuncher, the aviator, nor the brave young district attorney, but the great sales-manager, who had an Analysis of Merchandising Problems on his glass-topped desk, whose title of nobility was "Gogetter,"

---

[73] See David Riesman, Nathan Glazer and Reuel Denney, *The Lonely Crowd: A Study of the Changing American Character* (New Haven and London: Yale University Press, 1950).

and who devoted himself and all his young samurai to the cosmic purpose of Selling - not of selling anything in particular, for or to anybody in particular, but pure Selling. (127)

During his half-hearted revolt against the limitations of his other-directed existence, Babbitt painfully perceives that his life is "incredibly mechanical. Mechanical business - a brisk selling of badly built houses. Mechanical religion - a dry, hard church, [...], inhumanly respectable as a top-hat. Mechanical golf and dinner-parties and bridge and conversation" (203). But although he finally realizes that "practically, I've never done a single thing I've wanted to in my whole life!" (340), he cannot give up his meaningless existence because he is too weak to survive without the cat's cradle of business connections which defines his social identity. Babbitt has become so famous that his name and the behavioural pattern named after him, *babbittry*, have entered the English language in which they denote even today the attitude of thoughtless conformity with the bigoted morals of bourgeois materialism. Babbit, then, has become the incarnation of the philistine, who has no viewpoint of his own, who is all too willing to change his convictions for a business deal and who, in his meaningless triviality, is both contemptuous and pathetic. And it is certainly no accident that Lewis invented this character at the very time at which the 30th President of the United States, Calvin Coolidge, impressed a convention of newspaper editors with the notorious statement "The business of America is business."[74]

Three years after Lewis' satirical novel, Theodore Dreiser, that inveterate explorer of the role of money and sex in American life, published his psychogram of young Clyde Griffith, who leaves his miserable family and hopefully sets out into the world to "make more money. A lot of it to spend on himself" (53).[75] He wants "to do something in the world ... [and] to be successful" (162), and quite significantly he does not attempt to achieve the desired money and status by means of daring business transactions but by marrying a rich woman. Since he lacks every ability requisite for carrying out his plans, his abortive career ends in failure and disaster. Sentenced to die in the

---

74 Quoted from Richard Hofstadter, *Anti-Intellectualism in American Life*, p. 237.
75 All page numbers in brackets refer to Theodore Dreiser, *An American Tragedy* (New York: New American Library, 1964).

electric chair for an accidental death which translates into reality a murder he has contemplated and prepared for but does not have the strength to commit, Clyde ends in a death cell where he is left to contemplate "the end of all that wonderful dream!" (790). In his case, then, the 'American Dream' turns into *An American Tragedy*.

In 1949, Lewis' Babbitt found an equally pathetic successor in Willy Loman, the well-meaning and weak anti-hero of Arthur Miller's *Death of a Salesman*. Loman is totally addicted to the idea of success, and his pipe dreams destroy not only himself but also corrupt the lives of his sons.[76] And when in a later play by Miller, *The Price* (1968), two brothers whose greediness and craving for success has made them bitter enemies, meet again and one says to the other "Were we really brought up to believe in one another? We were brought up to succeed, weren't we?"[77] then this insight is representative of modern American literature at large. In numerous novels, plays and short stories the materialistic success ethic is condemned and made responsible for a money-orientated consumer-society, in which decency and humanity have been lost, in which cultural achievements are disregarded, and in which a person's value is measured only in dollars.

Now we encounter not only the successful entrepreneur as victimizer, as, for example, Pierce Inverarity in Thomas Pynchon's *The Crying of Lot 49* (1966), whose "need to possess, to alter the land, to bring new skylines, personal antagonisms, growth rates into being"[78] is held responsible for having turned the Californian dream into a nightmare, but we increasingly meet the small businessman as the

---

[76] Miller's play is not only one of the best-known comments on the untenability of the personality ethic and the end of the American Dream, but also - especially with regard to Willy's pathetic attempt to put seeds in the ground in his cramped little garden, to Biff's vision of a pastoral existence in the West, and to Uncle Ben's ruthless entrepreneurial career - a story about the loss of an open frontier. - For this aspect see Ina Rae Hark, "A Frontier Closes in Brooklyn: *Death of a Salesman* and the Turner Thesis," *Postscript*, 3 (1986), 1-6; for Miller's criticism of the Dream see, e.g., William Heyen, "Arthur Miller's *Death of a Salesman* and the American Dream," in *Amerikanisches Drama und Theater im 20. Jahrhundert*, ed. by Alfred Weber and Siegfried Neuweiler (Göttingen: Vandenhoeck & Ruprecht, 1975), pp. 190-203; and Alfred R. Ferguson, "The Tragedy of the American Dream in *Death of a Salesman*," *Thought*, 53 (1978), 83-98.

[77] Arthur Miller, *The Price*, in his *Collected Plays*, vol. II (London: Secker & Warburg, 1981), p. 368.

[78] Thomas Pynchon, *The Crying of Lot 49* (New York: Bantam Books, 1967), p. 134.

victim of an ever more anonymous and inhuman system of stress and pressure. In *Death of a Salesman*, for example, the central figure is no longer Howard Wagner, the heartless and unfeeling boss, who denies his employee after thirty-four years of hard work on the road the desired change to office work and sends him away with the platitude "business is business,"[79] but the burnt-out little salesman who can no longer find his way in an increasingly impersonal system. That not only the little but also the leading employees are by now victimized by a system which they have helped to create, is demonstrated in Joseph Heller's controversial novel *Something Happened* (1974), in which the outwardly successful middle manager Bob Slocum suffers from the meaninglessness, anxiety and aimlessness of his other-directed existence and offers a revealing commentary on his working life when he says:

> In the office in which I work there are five people of whom I am afraid. Each of these five people is afraid of four people (excluding overlaps), for a total of twenty, and each of these twenty people is afraid of six people, making a total of one hundred and twenty people who are feared by at least one person. Each of these one hundred and twenty people is afraid of the other one hundred and nineteen, and all of the one hundred and forty-five people are afraid of the twelve men at the top who helped found and build the company and now own and direct it.[80]

Whereas in the fifties there had been a widespread belief in John Kenneth Galbraith's thesis that America was turning into an example of *The Affluent Society* and that, with a few marginal exceptions, the problem of poverty had been conquered,[81] the sixties were shocked by Michael Harrington's discovery that about a third of the citizens of the United States were still living in poverty and thus forming *The Other America*.[82] Since then there have always been major problems with inflation and unemployment, and in view of the fact that a hostile reality seemed to make the dream of 'getting rich quick' ever more im-

---

79 Arthur Miller, *Death of a Salesman* in his *Collected Plays* (London: Secker & Warburg, rpt. 1978), p. 180.
80 Joseph Heller, *Something Happened* (London: Corgi Books, 1975), p. 19.
81 See John Kenneth Galbraith, *The Affluent Society* (New York: New American Library, 1958).
82 See Michael Harrington, *The Other America: Poverty in the United States* (New York: Macmillan, 1962).

probable, it hardly came as a surprise when at the end of the seventies Christopher Lasch observed in *The Culture of Narcissism* that Horatio Alger as the model of personal success had been replaced by "the happy hooker" and that in an era, in which the issue had shifted from financial success to psychological survival, the prostitute selling herself had become more representative than the salesman selling his goods.[83]

Lasch was certainly right in so far as such hallowed props of the Alger myth as hard work and clean living were now wholeheartedly abandoned, but he was definitely wrong in playing down the importance of financial success. In the late seventies and early eighties the newly rising und completely unbridled materialism of a yuppie-culture orientated towards private possessions and impressive status symbols[84] was accompanied by a greater amount of handbooks and articles, seminars and lectures on how to get rich quickly than ever before since the Gilded Age, and in all these 'how to'-recipes the Christian foundations of the way to success were radically abolished and "the ideals of Horatio Alger [were] discarded in favor of those of Niccolò Machiavelli, the Renaissance statesman whose name has come to symbolize unscrupulous, deceitful behavior in pursuit of one's goal."[85] In 1977, for example, Robert J. Ringer quite unabashedly argued in his *Looking Out for Number One*, which immediately turned into a bestseller, that a concern for anybody but oneself was nothing but a sign of immaturity and that the reckless pursuit of unbridled self-interest was the only way towards financial success. "Unless someone is poor because you robbed him, no downtrodden individual is your responsibility and shouldn't be a mental blockage in your happiness."[86] Rin-

---

[83] See Christopher Lasch, *The Culture of Narcissism: American Life in an Age of Diminishing Expectations* (New York: Warner Books, 1980), p. 53. - Lasch's allusion to "the happy hooker" refers to Xaviera Hollander's bestseller *The Happy Hooker* (New York: Bell Publ. Co., 1972) and to the countless 'soft-porn' novels with which 'New York's best-known callgirl' has been immensely successful.

[84] See Marissa Piesman and Marilee Hartley, *The Yuppie Handbook: The State-of-the-Art Manual for Young Urban Professionals* (New York: Pocket Books, 1985).

[85] Celeste MacLeod, *Horatio Alger, Farewell: The End of the American Dream* (New York: Seaview Books, 1980), p. 196.

[86] Robert J. Ringer, *Looking Out for Number One* (New York: Funk & Wagnalls, 1977), p. 117. - It is interesting to note that the same author had earlier written a national bestseller revealingly entitled *Winning Through Intimidation* (Los Angeles: Los An-

ger's ethic, if that is what it can be called, consists of nothing but the welcome reassurance that anybody can play the money-game without the least consideration for others, and Bob Greene correctly sums it up by saying "that if you are selfish, greedy, avaricious, cutthroat, and without morals, you will find true happiness."[87] A similar message was propagated in the same year in another bestseller, Michael Korda's *Success! How Every Man and Woman Can Achieve It*, where it is cynically argued that "Greed Is Good for You," and where one reads:

> If you're going to work at all, and most of us have to, you might just as well become rich, famous and successful in the process [...] The people who succeed do not as a rule work all that much harder than the people who fail, and in some cases very much less hard - they have simply mastered the rules of success.
> [...]
> It's O.K. to be greedy.
> It's O.K. to be ambitious.
> It's O.K. to look out for Number One.
> It's O.K. to have a good time.
> It's O.K. to be Machiavellian (if you can get away with it).
> It's O.K. to recognize that honesty is not always the best policy (provided you don't go around saying so).
> It's O.K. to be a winner. And it's *always* O.K. to be rich.[88]

In view of these and other manuals and the inhumane attitude they stand for, it is hardly surprising that in American postwar literature the earlier doubts about whether the human cost of material success might not be too high have gradually deepened into an outraged condemnation of an increasingly cynical success ideology. Nowhere is this more outspokenly expressed than in the novels of Kurt Vonnegut. *God Bless You, Mr. Rosewater* (1965), for example, opens with the sarcastic sentence "A sum of money is a leading character in this tale about people, just as a sum of honey might properly

---

geles Book Publishing Company, 1974), and that he would later write a book entitled *The Restoration of the American Dream* (San Francisco: QED, 1979).

87 Bob Greene, "Let Us Now Praise Greedy Men," *San Francisco Sunday Examiner and Chronicle*, September 25, 1977; here quoted from Celeste MacLeod, *Horatio Alger, Farewell*, p. 196.

88 Michael Korda, *Success! How Every Man and Woman Can Achieve It* (New York: Random House, 1977), p. 4.

be a leading character in a tale about bees" (9).[89] This highly critical and enormously funny novel reveals the genesis of a great family fortune as a history of meanness and fraud, of exploitation and criminal manipulation. Here the 'American Dream' has long become an American nightmare, and the narrator can observe:

> *E pluribus unum* is surely an ironic motto to inscribe on the currency of this Utopia gone bust, for every grotesquely rich American represents property, privileges, and pleasures that have been denied to the many. An even more instructive motto, [...], might be: *Grab much too much, or you'll get nothing at all.* (16)

In *The Sirens of Titan* (1959), the relationship between 'business' and 'culture' is tellingly illustrated when a rich entrepreneur, in "the free-enterprise way of handling beauty" (56),[90] uses the Mona Lisa for an advertising campaign for his purgative suppositories and thus explains the age-old mystery of her smile as an expression of relief caused by his laxative. This novel also delivers the wittiest parody of the Max Weber-thesis, when the "Yankee traveling salesman" (71) Noel Constant builds up his industrial empire Magnum Opus out of nothing by using a Gideon Bible found in a hotel room, by dividing the words of the opening sentence of Genesis into pairs of letters, and by successively buying shares in corporations with these initials. Using, in a literal sense, the Bible as "his investment counselor" (73), he becomes a millionaire with the help of God. And when in *Breakfast of Champions* (1973), a novel whose title is the brandname of a cereal and which deals with the destruction of the globe in the name of a blind belief in progress, the narrator resignedly remarks that "almost all the messages which were sent and received in his country, [...], had to do with buying or selling some damn thing,"[91] then such an observation sums up the attitude which dominates American postwar literature.

---

89 All page numbers in brackets refer to Kurt Vonnegut, *God Bless You, Mr. Rosewater, or Pearls Before Swine* (London: Panther Books, rpt. 1972).
90 All page numbers in brackets refer to Kurt Vonnegut, *The Sirens of Titan* (New York: Dell Books, rpt. 1972).
91 Kurt Vonnegut, *Breakfast of Champions, or Goodbye Blue Monday!* (New York: Dell Books, 1974), pp. 54f.

In his book *Die amerikanische Zumutung* (1990), Rolf Winter sketches the lives of outstanding American entrepreneurs and concludes that they were all scoundrels and criminals. Arguing that the lives of such generally admired founding fathers as Johann Jacob Astor, Cornelius Vanderbilt, Jim Fiske, John Pierpoint Morgan, and John D. Rockefeller provide ample proof for the thesis that capitalism is by nature criminal, Winter observes:

> Das Federal Bureau of Investigation, das FBI, die Bundespolizei der Vereinigten Staaten, schätzt, daß 1990 jeder amerikanische Bürger, der einen Einkauf tätigt, mit 15 Prozent des von ihm verlangten Preises "White collar crimes", also Wirtschaftsverbrechen, finanziert. Den Jahr für Jahr entstehenden wirtschaftlichen Schaden, der durch die kriminelle Vereinigung gegenwärtig tätiger Unternehmen angerichtet wird, beziffert das FBI auf rund 200 Milliarden Dollar - das ist noch mehr, als in der seit Jahrzehnten auf Höchstkonjunktur laufenden Branche des ordinär-kriminellen Raubes.
> Nicht, daß von "Petty crimes" die Rede wäre, begangen von obskuren Unternehmungen, die in einem Holzschuppen am Stadtrand hausen und zum Betrug als dem letzten Mittel zum Überleben greifen. Die Kriminalität ist vielmehr im Herzen des Kapitalismus zu Hause, im Establishment, in der staatstragenden Großindustrie, in den großen Häusern mit den "Blue chips" und dem globalen Einfluß. Von den Giganten, die in der "Fortune 500"-Liste aufgeführt werden, von den Marktführern aller möglichen Branchen also, sind zwei Drittel zwischen 1975 und 1985 wegen schwerer Verbrechen rechtskräftig verurteilt worden.[92]

It is small wonder, then, that an economic system bent upon fast profit, which unscrupulously does business with destructive weaponry as well as with environmental poisons and which has led to an ever increasing gulf between the immeasurable wealth of a few and the unbearable poverty of the many in a country which is fast "dividing into two societies - the affluent and the nonaffluent,"[93] is unanimously rejected as indefensible and inhumane. Countless manuals about how to become successful, popular success stories,

---

92 Rolf Winter, *Die amerikanische Zumutung: Plädoyers gegen das Land des real existierenden Kapitalismus* (München: Wilhelm Heyne, 1990), pp. 98f.
93 Celeste MacLeod, *Horatio Alger, Farewell*, p. 141. - MacLeod's study about jobless young people and migration in search of employment as the two most glaring indications of "the end of the American dream" (p. 4) might be profitably read in conjunction with Lewis H. Lapham's scathing dissection of *Money and Class in America: Notes and Observations on the Civil Religion* (London: Pan Books, 1989).

bestselling autobiographies such as that of Lee Iacocca,[94] television soap operas and the devotional rhetoric of politics still tout the American myth of success for everybody, but from the very beginning almost all major American writers have depicted the very figure which embodies this myth, namely, the successful businessman, with scepticism and then with growing resentment, contempt and pity. More recently, this attitude can even be found in the short-lived bestsellers of popular fiction in which, according to Elizabeth Long, "success is a recurring concern and a matter of almost obsessional importance," but which, in the period between 1945 and 1975, "chronicle the disappearance of the entrepreneurial reality and ethos"[95] and thus document the gradual disappearance of the belief in the availability of material success for everybody.

Since Nathaniel Hawthorne published his short story "My Kinsman, Major Molineux" in 1832 and with it offered a pessimistic contrafactum upon the famous scene in Franklin's *Autobiography*, in which seventeen-year-old Ben arrives friendless and penniless in the streets of Philadelphia to embark upon his career as businessman, statesman, author and inventor,[96] serious American writers have accompanied the development of their country's business morals with ever increasing criticism. It certainly cannot be denied that many of these authors have become rich by denouncing the gospel of wealth, that several of them, after having 'made it,' have shown the very behaviour they attacked in their novels, and that "nowadays one road to personal literary success in America has come to be through attacking the idea of success itself."[97] In spite of such puzzling contradictions, the fact remains that American authors have been, and still are, highly critical of the myth of material success. And because they are used to deducing their criteria of evaluation neither from the balance-sheets nor from the social prestige of the businessmen they portray, but from their own notions of decency, responsibility and quality of life, their fictional entrepreneurs are usually highly negative characters who

---

94 See Lee Iacocca, *Iacocca: An Autobiography* (Toronto: Bantam Books, 1984).
95 Elizabeth Long, *The American Dream and the Popular Novel* (Boston and London: Routledge & Kegan Paul, 1985), pp. 7 and 11.
96 See Peter Freese, *The American Short Story I: Initiation - Interpretations and Suggestions for Teaching* (Paderborn: Schöningh, 3rd ed., 1991), pp. 125-127.
97 Joseph Epstein, *Ambition: The Secret Passion*, p. 86.

range from unscrupulous villains and bigoted babbitts to the pitiful victims of anonymous corporations and faulty value systems.

Right from the beginning, then, the myth of material success, which is still so central to popular American culture, has been almost unanimously rejected as a moral aberration by accomplished American writers. Therefore, it is one thing when Celeste MacLeod observes that "it is time to say 'Horatio Alger, farewell.' The hallowed dream of millions for everyone who works hard enough is obsolete,"[98] and when numerous other critics assert that the 'Dream' of success for everybody has been finally disproved and thus is no longer feasible in view of a given reality.[99] But it is quite another thing to realize that serious American literature has always insisted that such a 'Dream,' totally independent of its feasibility, is not at all desirable. Serious American literature, then, amply demonstrates that in the United States literature and lucre, 'culture' and 'business' have always existed in a highly strained relationship. Ambrose Bierce's entry under "Mammon" in *The Devil's Dictionary* - "The god of the world's leading religion. His chief temple is in the holy city of New York."[100] - might

---

98 Celeste MacLeod, *Horatio Alger, Farewell*, p. 279.
99 The sociological literature on this question is legion. Influential earlier studies such as David Riesman, Nathan Glazer and Reuel Denney, *The Lonely Crowd: A Study of the Changing American Character* (New Haven and London: Yale University Press, 1950); C. Wright Mills, *White Collar* (New York: Oxford University Press, 1951); and William H. Whyte, Jr., *The Organization Man* (New York: Simon & Schuster, 1956) concentrated mainly on the revolutionary changes brought about by the development of large-scale bureaucratic organizations and on the negative effect which the concomitant specialization and concentration had on mobility, social stratification and individual aspirations; and they deplored the fact that a nation of independent entrepreneurs had been changed into one of dependent employees. Writing after the turbulent sixties in which the predicted increase of conformity had been emphatically disproved, later critics developed a different perspective. Thus, Daniel Bell, in *The Cultural Contradictions of Capitalism* (New York: Basic Books, 1976); Richard Sennett, in *The Fall of Public Man: On the Social Psychology of Capitalism* (Cambridge: Cambridge University Press, 1977); and Christopher Lasch, in *The Culture of Narcissism: American Life in an Age of Diminishing Expectations* (New York and London: W. W. Norton, 1978), saw American society, quite on the contrary, as highly disjunctive, as a war of all against all, and Sennett even turned around Riesman's argument by asserting that people were moving from other-direction to inner-direction. These critics also developed a strikingly different view of the role of the 'Protestant Ethic' which they saw not so much in terms of independence and self-reliant competitiveness but as having provided the necessary restraint so deplorably lost in a hedonistic age of joyless self-gratification.

serve as an ironic motto for most literary treatments of the business world; and a character's observation in John Dos Passos' *Manhattan Transfer* - "Why the hell does everybody want to succeed? I'd like to meet somebody who wanted to fail. That's the only sublime thing."[101] - could define the major direction of the criticism levelled against that world. In the very language of business, the relationship between culture and commerce can be characterized as one in which literature critically accompanies an economic system obsessed with its financial 'credit' with the express purpose of continuously reminding it of its moral 'debit.'

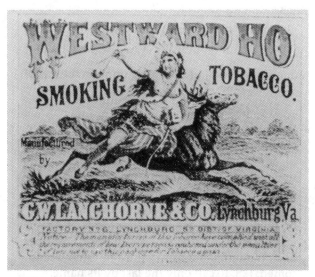

This is an example of mid-nineteenth century advertising. An allegorical figure, which is a combination of Miss Liberty and a Native American, is used to promote "Westward Ho" tobacco by conjuring up the lure of the West.

---

100 Ambrose Bierce, *The Enlarged Devil's Dictionary*, ed. by Ernest Jerome Hopkins (Harmondsworth: Penguin Books, rpt. 1983), s.v. "Mammon."
101 John Dos Passos, *Manhattan Transfer* (New York: Bantam Books, 1959), p. 139.

5: "America Is West": A Popular Myth and Its Revisionist Interpretations

American social development has been continually beginning over again on the frontier. This perennial rebirth, this fluidity of American life, this expansion westward with its new opportunities, its continuous touch with the simplicity of primitive society, furnish the forces dominating American character. The true point of view in the history of this nation is not the Atlantic coast, it is the Great West.

> Frederick Jackson Turner, "The Significance of the Frontier in American History"

America is West [...] A shining thing in the mind.

> Archibald MacLeish, "American Letter"

From the earliest times, American writers have tended to define their own country - and much of our literature has, consequently, tended to define itself - topologically, as it were, in terms of the four cardinal directions: a mythicized North, South, East, and West. Correspondingly, there have always been four kinds of American books: Northerns, Southerns, Easterns, and Westerns, though we have been accustomed, [...], to call only the last by its name.

> Leslie A. Fiedler, *The Return of the Vanishing American*[1]

---

1   The mottoes are taken from Frederick Jackson Turner, "The Significance of the Frontier in American History," in *An American Primer*, ed. by Daniel J. Boorstin (New York: New American Library, 1985), p. 545; Archibald MacLeish, "American Letter," in his *Collected Poems 1917 - 1952* (Boston: Houghton Mifflin, 1952), p. 63; and Leslie A. Fiedler, *The Return of the Vanishing Adolescent* (London: Paladin Books, 1972), p. 14.

When one looks for the origins of that most ubiquitous of all popular American genres, the 'western,' Charles Brockden's Brown's complaint, in his preface to *Edgar Huntly; or, Memoirs of a Sleepwalker* (1799), about the scarcity of indigenously American themes in the new nation's fledgling literature provides an appropriate starting point. It was Brown who admonished his fellow-writers that "the incidents of Indian hostility, and the perils of the western wilderness" would be suitable topics for aspiring novelists and that "for a native of America to overlook these, would admit of no apology."[2] About three decades later, James Fenimore Cooper, the 'American Scott,' heeded Brown's advice and established, with immense success, the first version of what was to become the enormously influential formula of the western. It was Cooper's lasting achievement to have combined the ancient pattern of the adventure story with the specifically American material of western settlement and to have created the immortal Nathaniel Bumppo alias Leatherstocking, who "became the prototype for the western hero and thus the progenitor of countless stories, novels, films, and television programs that use the formula Cooper first articulated."[3]

The early instances of the new genre such as Cooper's five *Leatherstocking Tales* or, in a different vein, William Gilmore Simms's *The Yemassee* (1835) and Montgomery Bird's *Nick of the Woods* (1837) owed only a small part of their success to the rather questionable authenticity which they derived from using among their sources the biographies of 'real' western heroes such as Daniel Boone. More important than their factual 'correctness,' later so scathingly denied by Mark

---

2 Charles Brockden Brown, *Edgar Huntly; or, Memoirs of a Sleepwalker* (New York: AMS Press, 1976; reprint of the edition Philadelphia: H. Maxwell, 1799), p. 4.
3 John G. Cawelti, *Adventure, Mystery, and Romance: Formula Stories as Art and Popular Culture* (Chicago and London: University of Chicago Press, 1976), p. 194. - In his research report on "The Western," in *Handbook of American Popular Culture*, ed. by M. Thomas Inge (Westport, Conn.: Greenwood Press, 1978), vol. I, pp. 355-376, Richard W. Etulain differentiates between two critical schools. According to him, one school argues "that the Western is strongly tied to several nineteenth-century sources: the *Leatherstocking Tales* of James Fenimore Cooper, dime novels, and western local color writing." The other school maintains that "the Western is primarily the product of the dynamic climate of opinion surrounding 1900" (355). It seems to me that these two perspectives need not be mutually exclusive and that Cawelti's stress on Cooper's importance is justified.

Twain in "James Fenimore Cooper's Literary Offences,"[4] was the fact that they gave literary expression to an essential American concern by placing their heroes between the contending forces of civilization and wilderness and by making them experience their hair-raising adventures in that frontier environment which Frederick Jackson Turner would succinctly define as "the meeting point between savagery and civilization."[5] This borderline position, however, implied an ideological tension which finally turned out to be unresolvable.

Daniel Boone

---

4   See Mark Twain, "James Fenimore Cooper's Literary Offences," in *The Writings of Mark Twain* (St. Clair Shores: Scholarly Press, 1976; reprint of the edition New York and London: Harper & Brothers, 1897-1899), vol. XXII, *How to Tell a Story and Other Essays*, pp. 78-97.
5   Frederick Jackson Turner, "The Significance of the Frontier in American History," p. 545.

Henry Nash Smith has shown that the different biographies of Daniel Boone from John Filson's *Discovery, Settlement, and Present State of Kentucke* (1784) to Timothy Flint's *The Life and Adventures of Daniel Boone, the First Settler of Kentucky* (1833) remain finally undecided as to whether Boone should be portrayed as "the standard-bearer of civilization and refinement or the child of nature who fled into the wilderness before the advance of settlement,"[6] and thus it is small wonder that it remained Cooper's greatest problem, throughout the almost twenty years he was occupied with his Leatherstocking Saga, to reconcile within his composite hero's character the contradictory allegiances he harbours to a free and unfettered life in the unspoilt wilderness on the one hand and to the orderly ways of advancing civilization on the other.

The strangely reversed genesis of the five Leatherstocking novels begins with *The Pioneers* (1823), in which Natty is an old man in danger of being made obsolete by a rapidly spreading 'civilization' and in which his aged Indian friend Chingachgook is reduced to a miserable alcoholic. And it ends with *The Deerslayer* (1841), in which young Natty and his heroic red companion enjoy a glorious existence in the as yet unspoilt wilderness around Lake Glimmerglass. This curious sequence made D. H. Lawrence observe that Cooper's books "go backwards, from old age to golden youth" and that this is "the true myth of America. She starts old, old, wrinkled and writhing in an old skin. And there is a gradual sloughing of the old skin, towards a new youth."[7] And the same sequence led John G. Cawelti to comment that "Cooper's transformation of his western narrative from a story of the re-establishment of the gentry in the new West, to a tale of the isolated hero whose very virtues make him flee the oncoming civilization, summarizes the evolution of the western itself from the epic of the pioneers in the nineteenth century to the ambiguous myth of the gunfighter in the 1950s."[8]

---

6 Henry Nash Smith, *Virgin Land: The American West as Symbol and Myth* (Cambridge, Mass.: Harvard University Press, rpt. 1982), p. 55.
7 D. H. Lawrence, *Studies in Classic American Literature* (New York: Viking Press, rpt. 1969), p. 54.
8 John G. Cawelti, *Adventure, Mystery, and Romance*, p. 195.

Cooper, who in spite of all his shortcomings is far too often wrongly underrated as a mere writer of 'romances,' managed to achieve the rare feat of combining the ancient European pastoral tradition with the actual violence of American frontier life. And it was this very mixture, together with the precarious balance between the two contradictory value systems of nature and civilization, which established the dialectic structure that would become constitutive for the western formula and which allowed John G. Cawelti to observe: "By creating a setting and a group of plot patterns through which the irreconcilable conflicts of society and individual freedom, of peaceful civilization and uncontrolled violence, could be resolved in action, Cooper brought the western into existence."[9]

Soon after Cooper, the strong appeal of the new formula to a rapidly growing reading public incited adventurous publishers to attempts at providing cheap variations of western adventures for a mass audience. Thus, in 1858, Erastus Beadle began his weekly series of so-called 'Dime Novels' about such heroes as Buffalo Bill and the James Brothers, Deadwood Dick, Seth Jones, and Calamity Jane, and by 1865 his thriving firm had sold almost five million copies. The authors of these decidedly subliterary mass productions, however, did not care about the ideological tension between solitary self-fulfilment and societal norms and concentrated instead on the elevation of outlaws into noble heroes according to certain recipes which catered for a widespread need for adolescent escapism. And they "gave the country an utterly false picture of the West, much of which remained fixed in the public mind forever after. By 1890 the stereotypes of Western fiction were so strong that it seemed doubtful they could ever be changed [...]."[10]

When the endless variations of the lonely hunter, who by now had been transferred from the woods to the prairies, began to reach "the point of absurdity,"[11] Western fiction found the sought-for variation of the traditional hero in the cowboy. Several related facts were responsible for this momentous development. On the one hand, the enor-

---

9   *Ibid.*, p. 209.
10 Russel Nye, *The Unembarrassed Muse: The Popular Arts in America* (New York: Dial Press, 1970), p. 287.
11 *Ibid.*, p. 287.

mously popular Wild West Shows of Buffalo Bill Cody featured authentic cowboys and thus introduced the new hero to large audiences. On the other hand, prolific hack writers like Ned Buntline and Prentiss Ingraham brought out hundreds of books about both Buffalo Bill and Buck Taylor, one of Cody's outstanding cowboy stars. And all of this happened during an epoch in American history in which the old West was rapidly disappearing and an everyday reality characterized by increasing industrialization and mass immigration had bred a climate of growing nostalgia for a vanishing era. Thus, the cowboy's victorious emergence as the new Western hero was much more than a mere literary fashion, and his elevation into a mythic figure at the very moment of his historical demise - at the end of the thirty years of the range cattle industry between the Civil War and the completion of the major railroad lines - forcefully indicates that there was a widespread need for the preservation, and the elevation through story-telling, of a vanishing way of life whose impending disappearance was experienced as a major loss.

The man who fulfilled this need was a young Harvard graduate in music and a fellow-student and friend of Theodore Roosevelt. His name was Owen Wister, and in 1902 he published a seminal novel with the title *The Virginian: A Horseman of the Plains*, which he dedicated to President Roosevelt. With this novel, which became an instant success and turned the cowboy into the genuinely American successor to the medieval knight-errant and the noble heroes of Scott and Cooper, the 'cowboy novel' proper was born, Cooper's dialectic between civilization and wilderness as the opposition between man and nature was replaced by a new dialectic between the West and the East as the opposition between two divergent cultural systems, and the fictional propagation of an indigenously American, and rather dangerous, political stance came into being.

Owen Wister's *The Virginian,* or the Dubious Politics of the Western

> "There can be no doubt of this:- All America is divided into two classes,- the quality and the equality. The latter will always recognize the former when mistaken for it."
> Owen Wister, *The Virginian*[12]

The formulaic western, which conceited intellectuals tend to look down upon as a mass-produced vehicle of evasive entertainment for an undemanding mass audience, is not only the most indigenous genre of U.S. literature but also an eloquent expression of basic 'American' values. This is why its admirers can praise the western as "an allegory of freedom, a memory and a vision of the deepest meaning of America"[13] and even celebrate its countless variations as "a never-ending course in citizenship and the American way of life."[14] But this is also why a less enthusiastic observer can ironically state that *High Noon*, one of the highlights of the genre, is "the most honest explanation of American foreign policy."[15] In the countless B-westerns of later days the political implications are often easily overlooked, but in Owen Wister's *The Virginian: A Horseman of the Plains* (1902) they are too obvious to be missed. When one reads this unembarrassedly propagandistic novel, which "created our mythical West, the heroic West, with its gunfighters, its grim code of honor, its ritualized violence,"[16] one soon realizes that its author's aim is not just to entertain his audience with a thrilling story but to address those among his fellow Americans who share his patriotic need for a clarification of basic national values in a difficult time. Such an intention is clearly announced in Wister's "Rededication and Preface" of 1911, in which he defines his

---

12 Owen Wister, *The Virginian: A Horseman of the Plains* (New York: Harper & Row Perennial Classics, 1965), p. 97. All further page references are to this edition.
13 Anonymous, "Westerns: The Six-Gun Galahad," *Time*, 30 March 1959, p. 43.
14 Marshall W. Fishwick, "The Cowboy: America's Contribution to the World's Mythology," *Western Folklore*, 11 (April 1952), p. 92.
15 Harry Schein, "The Olympian Cowboy" [transl. from the Swedish by Oda M. Alcock], *The American Scholar*, 24 (1955), p. 316.
16 David Mogen, "Owen Wister's Cowboy Heroes," in *The Western: A Collection of Critical Essays*, ed. by James K. Folsom (Englewood Cliffs, N.J.: Prentice-Hall, 1979), p. 66. - This assessment is undisputed; see, e.g., John G. Cawelti, *Adventure, Mystery, and Romance*, p. 215; and Richard W. Etulain, "The Western," p. 358.

novel as "an expression of American faith" (xv) and claims its pertinence to "the severest test of political man," namely, "the test of Democracy" (xv).

Ironically enough, *The Virginian* owes its existence to its author's nervous breakdown. It was in 1885 that Wister's doctor suggested to the sophisticated Harvard graduate in music and student of composition in Paris, the grandson of the famous British actress Fanny Kemble and protégé of Henry James that he might best recuperate in the healthful air of a Wyoming cattle ranch. Consequently, Wister undertook his first trip to the Far West, and there the eastern greenhorn found the 'real America' which would then come to figure prominently in his political vision. When he later settled down in Philadelphia to practice law, he frequently took time off to travel to diverse regions of the West and to translate his extensive travel notes[17] into sundry 'western' tales.

In 1895, two years after Frederick Jackson Turner's seminal lecture on "The Significance of the Frontier in American History," Wister published his programmatic treatise on "The Evolution of the Cow-Puncher," in which he expressed his belief in the central role of the cowboy in "our Wild West" (E xxv).[18] In this essay he gave a new twist to that explosive mixture of *translatio imperii* and *manifest destiny* which had caused Lyman Beecher to observe as early as 1832 "that the religious and political destiny of our nation is to be decided in the West"[19] and allowed Josiah Strong to state in 1885 that "the West is today an infant, but shall one day be a giant, in each of whose limbs shall unite the strength of many nations."[20] Wister combined such praise of the West with a strong dose of that rabid Anglo-Saxon ra-

---

[17] See *Owen Wister Out West: His Journals and Letters*, ed. by Fanny Kemble Wister (Chicago: University of Chicago Press, 1958).

[18] All page numbers preceded by an E in brackets in the text refer to Owen Wister, "The Evolution of the Cow-Puncher," in *The Writings of Owen Wister* (New York: Macmillan, 1928), vol. VI.

[19] Lyman Beecher, *A Plea for the West* (Cincinnati: Truman and Smith, 2nd ed., 1835); here quoted from the partial reprint in *God's New Israel: Interpretations of American Destiny*, ed. by Conrad Cherry (Englewood Cliffs, N.J.: Prentice-Hall, 1971), pp. 120f.

[20] Josiah Strong, *Our Country: Its Possible Future and Its Present Crisis*, ed. by Jurgen Herbst (Cambridge, Mass.: The Belknap Press of Harvard University Press, 1963), p. 39.

cism which five years later Senator Albert J. Beveridge of Indiana would express most succinctly by declaring that "God has [made] the English-speaking and Teutonic peoples [...] master-organizers of the world to establish system where chaos reigns. [...] He has marked the American people as His chosen nation to finally lead in the redemption of the world."[21]

It was within this tradition that Wister contrasted the admirably heroic and racially pure West of the recent past with the insufferable degeneration of his contemporary East and stated:

> No rood of modern ground is more debased and mongrel with its hordes of encroaching alien vermin, that turn our cities to Babels and our citizenship to a hybrid farce, who degrade our commonwealth from a nation into something half pawn-shop, half broker's office. But to survive in the clean cattle country requires spirit of adventure, courage, and self-sufficiency; you will not find many Poles or Huns or Russian Jews in that district; but the Anglo-Saxon is still forever homesick for out-of-doors. (E xxiiif.)

And he not only postulated that it was "the cardinal surviving fittest instinct that ma[de] the Saxon through the centuries conqueror, invader, navigator, buccaneer, explorer, colonist, tiger-shooter" (E xxvf.), but also argued that the "unpolished fellow of the cattle trail" (E xxvii) was the last precious remnant of untainted Anglo-Saxon stock in an increasingly 'mongrelized' America. Consequently, he could elevate the western cowboy into a latter-day reincarnation of the medieval knight-errant:

> [...] in personal daring and in skill as to the horse, the knight and the cowboy are nothing but the same Saxon of different environments, [...] and no hoof in Sir Thomas Malory shakes the crumbling plains with quadruped sound more valiant than the galloping that has echoed from the Rio Grande to the Big Horn Mountains. But we have no Sir Thomas Malory! (E xxvii)

Seven years after this essay and prepared by numerous western stories for the arduous task of doing for the cowboy what Sir Thomas Malory had done for the knight-errant, Wister published *The Virgin-*

---

21 Quoted in Ernest Lee Tuveson, *Redeemer Nation: The Idea of America's Millennial Role* (Chicago and London: University of Chicago Press, 1978), p. vii.

ian. In the light of the earlier essay, this seminal novel must be understood as his tribute to that very "American descendant of Saxon ancestors, who for thirty years flourished upon our part of the earth, and, because he was not compatible with Progress, is now departed, never to return" (E li). But the disgruntled Anglo-Saxon conservative was not at all content with a nostalgic evocation of the mythical Far West of twenty-five years ago, he also wanted the heroes of that admirable American past to serve as exemplary models for the inhabitants of what he loathed as his effete and increasingly 'un-American' present. Thus, it is small wonder that he dedicated *The Virginian* to the leading politician of his times, President Theodore Roosevelt, his former classmate at Harvard and a fellow admirer of the West,[22] and that he claimed additional dignity for his tale by defining it in a prefatory address "To the Reader" as a "historical" (xvii) novel harking back to the Territory of Wyoming "between 1874 and 1890" (xvii). In those bygone years, Wister argued, Wyoming was "a colony as wild as was Virginia one hundred years earlier" (xvii), and it was inhabited by people who still owned the constitutive 'American' virtues which he saw in danger of getting lost in his own days of mass immigration, urbanization and the growth of industrial corporations. Consequently, Wister's approach to the West resulted in a narrative point of view which combines retrospective nostalgia with hortatory didacticism.

Since the Philadelphia lawyer told his story at a time when "the West [was] growing old" (97f.), he made his narrator look longingly back upon an earlier, and better, period of U.S. history in which the "vanished world" (xvii) of Wyoming was still "the newest part of a new world" (146) and provided in its endless "virgin wilderness" (301; 318) a "great playground of young men" drawn there from all over the country by "the romance of American adventure" (45). In those days the outstanding inhabitants of the vanished West were the admirable "cowpuncher[s]," whom Wister set out to celebrate as "the last romantic figure[s] on our soil" (xviii). By the time of his writing, these "bachelors of the saddle" (65) had become extinct, and Wister felt that their contribution to the opening up of the continent was not sufficiently appreciated. Therefore he anticipated that his fictional embodiment of these legendary figures, the eponymous Virginian, would be

---

22 See the four volumes of Theodore Roosevelt, *The Winning of the West* (1889-1896).

slighted as anachronistic by "Wall Street," the hateful epitome of corporate capital in an industrialized world, and disapproved of as old-fashioned by "Newport" (xviii), the effete meeting-place of fashionable eastern society.

Wister urgently wanted to correct such undeserved disregard of the defunct cowpuncher, and consequently his novel became the historico-political testament of a man who saw his beloved country going through a precarious state of "transition" (xviii) and who tried to call his lax contemporaries to order by presenting them with his vision of a freer and simpler society, in which good and bad could still be easily distinguished, in which Anglo-Saxons of pure stock and personal daring roamed across a glorious American landscape, and in which everyone could fulfil his personal destiny as "a man who was a man" (289). Setting himself the double task of alerting his readers to the imminent danger of squandering their truly American heritage and of convincing them that the western cowboy was the model to emulate, Wister was sufficiently aware of the literary customs of his day to realize that his vision of a better America would never convince his genteel audience if its fictional projection did not conform to their expectations. Consequently, he payed homage to the ruling taste by giving a "romantic" (xviii) touch to his allegedly realistic subject, and he cleverly devised a narrative perspective which not only enabled him to leave his autobiographical material largely unchanged but which at the same time invited the empathy or even identification of his intended audience.

Like Howells in his business novel *The Rise of Silas Lapham* (1885), he complied with genteel expectations by integrating into his western story an extended 'Love Plot,' in the convoluted course of which the noble hero "radiate[s] romance" (86) and the steadfast heroine fights with her resolution never to marry "below her station" (209). And while he cleverly made this conventionally Victorian strand of action to serve his political intentions, Wister solved the problem of finding a suitable narrative perspective by adopting a strategy which before him Mark Twain had successfully employed in *Roughing It* (1872). Choosing as his I-narrator an eastern 'greenhorn' or 'tenderfoot' who ventures forth into the strange world of the West, Wister managed to make the clash between eastern 'civilization' and western 'wilderness' the structural principle of his narrative and thus turned his narrator into the very embodiment of his genteel audience's expectations and preconceptions.

Predictably, the 'machine' by means of which Wister transports his eastern tenderfoot into the 'garden' of the West[23] is a transcontinental train, a "Pullman" (3), and when the I-narrator arrives in the little settlement of Medicine Bow and discovers to his dismay that his baggage has been lost, he finds himself over "two thousand miles" away from home in "the great cattle land," with his last ties to eastern civilization cruelly severed. With a shock he realizes that he is now "a stranger," a "deserted" and "forlorn" (4) waif at the mercy of his host, Judge Henry of Sunk Creek ranch, who has promised to meet him at the station. But there is no Judge Henry, and when the train leaves "to the far shores of civilization" and slowly disappears "in the unending gulf of space," the easterner is gripped by loneliness and fear. Feeling "marooned in a foreign ocean" (7) and thus, in a metaphor familiar since Melville's days, experiencing the endless prairie as if it were the hostile sea, he attempts to check his growing nervousness by admiring a cowboy who adeptly ropes a rebellious pony with movements as smooth and easy as those of "a tiger" and as quick as those of "a sudden snake" (4) and by then overhearing this cowboy's humorous dialogue with an elderly gentleman intent upon marrying, whom the cowboy mockingly asks "What's the use o' being married?" (6). Predictably, this cowboy, who is "a slim young giant, more beautiful than pictures," who deeply impresses the Easterner with "the splendor that radiated from his youth and strength" (5), and who to the reader's surprise is a Southerner, turns out to be the very man whom the Judge has dispatched to look after his guest. Thus, by the end of a cleverly constructed first chapter, the East-West dichotomy is personified in the constellation of tutor and tiro, a strong and knowledgeable but uncouth Westerner on the one hand and an educated but inexperienced and effete Easterner on the other; the still rather improbable theme of marriage which is later to become so central is introduced in a yet inconspicuous aside; and the unexpected personification of western manhood by a cowboy from the South, who will henceforth go by

---

23 See Leo Marx, *The Machine in the Garden: Technology and the Pastoral Ideal in America* (London and New York: Oxford University Press, 1964).

the generic name of 'the Virginian,' creates additional wonder and interest in the reader.

Since the Easterner and his guide must wait for the next train, which will hopefully bring the lost baggage, they have to spend a night in Medicine Bow, and that provides Wister with the possibility of acquainting his ignorant narrator - and through him his eastern readers - with some more details of life in the West and of staging the first encounter of the 'good' western hero with his 'bad' antagonist and thereby introducing the second and genuinely western strand of the action. In the course of the novel this 'Confrontation Plot' will frequently intersect with the 'Love Plot,' and both will eventually coalesce in a final dramatic 'showdown.' Wister knows that his prejudiced eastern audience has still to be convinced of the 'democratic' reality underlying the savage appearance of western life, and thus he selects the easily accessible level of linguistic usage for a first treatment of the discrepancy between being and seeming. His narrator opens the second chapter with the platitude that "we cannot see ourselves as others see us" (8), and when his ill-considered attempt at condescending familiarity is calmly rebuffed by the Virginian, he realizes with surprise and with the ready self-criticism in which his retrospective point of view enables him to indulge that "this handsome, ungrammatical son of the soil," by rejecting his educated guest's patronizing attitude, has "come off the better gentleman of the two." The narrator's heavily didactic comment that "the creature we call a gentleman lies deep in the hearts of thousands that are born without chance to master the outward graces of the type" (10) shows once more that Wister's tenderfoot not only has a story to tell but also a message to convey, and this message is cleverly illustrated by the following action.

The narrator enthusiastically evokes the pristine surroundings in which the "shapeless pattern" of the dilapidated town with its "twenty-nine buildings" and its carelessly strewn "garbage" is nothing but a disturbing enchroachment of human ineptitude upon an "immaculate and wonderful" nature serenely "bathing in the air of creation's first morning" (10), and thus he once more subtly reverses the traditional connotations of 'civilization' and 'wilderness.' In this environment the eastern greenhorn becomes the proverbial "outsider"

(11) in "a world new to me indeed." In scenes which betray Wister's pronounced Anglo-Saxon racism, his narrator observes with his "tender-foot innocence" how the cowboys play fun of some Jewish 'drummers,' and he wonderingly observes how his mentor is affectionately called "a son-of-a -" (12; see also 18) by his friend Steve. "I had expected that the man would be struck down. He had used to the Virginian a term of heaviest insult. [But] used thus, this language was plainly complimentary." (12) A little later, however, he watches a poker game between the Virginian and a dealer named Trampas, whose words and countenance the narrator finds characterized by "ugliness" (20) and who is here introduced as the hero's villainous antagonist. When Trampas says to the Virginian "Your bet, you son-of-a -" (21), one of the most famous scenes in all western literature ensues:

> The Virginian's pistol came out, and his hand lay on the table, holding it unaimed. And with a voice as gentle as ever, the voice that sounded almost like a caress, but drawling a very little more than usual, so that there was almost a space between each word, he issued his orders to the man Trampas: -
> "When you call me that, *smile!*" And he looked at Trampas across the table.
> Yes, the voice was gentle. But in my ears it seemed as if somewhere the bell of death were ringing; and silence, like a stroke, fell on the large room. All men present, as if by some magnetic current, had become aware of this crisis. In my ignorance, and the total stoppage of my thoughts, I stood stock-still and noticed various people crouching, or shifting their positions.
> "Sit quiet," said the dealer, scornfully to the man near me. "Can't you see he don't want to push trouble? He had handed Trampas the choice to back down or draw his steel." (21)

This scene not only initiates the 'Confrontation Plot' that will end in a final and deadly showdown because "a public back-down is an unfinished thing," but it also provides the narrator with a linguistic insight which is yet another variation upon the theme of appearance versus reality or nurture versus nature. The Easterner who has grown up in a world of appearances, in which nurture is superimposed upon nature, realizes "the old truth, that the letter means nothing until the spirit gives it life" (22). In the same way, then, in which a 'gentleman' is not defined by the clothes he wears but by his innate nobility, it does not matter what one says but how one says it, and consequently

Wister's eastern narrator - and the genteel audience he represents - are made to realize that their customary rejection of the allegedly uncultivated cowboy with his seemingly uncivilized speech is based on a faulty premise.

By the end of the first three chapters, then, Wister has achieved a number of important goals. He has established his narrator as the personification of his audience's preconceptions and, through that narrator, has begun with the education of his readers as to the admirable reality which is hidden behind the uncouth appearance of the West. He has introduced his eponymous hero as a man who is more than he seems to be, namely, a rough diamond whose outward appearance hides a born gentleman. He has created the necessary narrative suspense by planting the clue for an inevitable and final confrontation between the protagonist and the antagonist, the nameless Virginian and Trampas, that is, between good and evil, law and lawlessness or, in Turner's famous terms, civilization and savagery. And he has provided a first sense of the glory and grandeur of western nature as "a world of crystal light," in which close neighbours live hundreds of miles apart from each other in "a land without end" that covers "a space across which Noah and Adam might come straight from Genesis" (11).

But Wister is not content with these achievements, and he cleverly uses his opening chapters about life in the little frontier settlement of Medicine Bow to score some more points. Through the 'innocent eye'[24] of his narrator he conveys an impression of the simple fun the cowboys have when they 'come to town' after months of backbreaking work, and he introduces their custom of telling "tall stories" (149) as a way of verbal combat which will become centrally important in the following action. And when he lets us know that the noisy carousing and the practical jokes of the boisterous cowboys immediately end when they hear of a sick woman needing her rest, he makes us realize that these rough people possess the natural courtesy which many Easterners lack. The "lusty horsemen," then, in "this Rocky Mountains place" are much more 'civilized' than the depraved frequenters of "city

---

24 For this concept see Albert E. Stone, Jr., *The Innocent Eye: Childhood in Mark Twain's Imagination* (New Haven: Yale University Press, 1961).

saloons" (23). And the enchanted narrator, who because of his English clothes is now dubbed "The Prince of Wales" (25), once more drives home his point when he engages in this celebratory patriotic reflection:

> Daring, laughter, endurance - these were what I saw upon the countenances of the cow-boys. And this very first day of my knowledge of them marks a date with me. For something about them, and the idea of them, smote my American heart, and I have never forgotten it, nor ever shall, as long as I live. In their flesh our natural passions ran tumultuous; but often in their spirit sat hidden a true nobility, and often beneath its unexpected shining their figures took a heroic stature. (23f.)

Chapter IV opens with the second day of the tenderfoot's experience, and he is once more forced to correct his - and his audience's - ingrained notions when he reflects about the role which portable and ready-made food such as tinned sardines have played in the opening of the West: "The cow-boy is now gone to worlds invisible: the wind has blown away the white ashes of his camp-fires; but the empty sardine box lies rusting over the face of the Western earth." (30) Here the encroachment of eastern civilization upon western nature is again depicted as anything but positive. Before tutor and tiro, the calm and self-assured Virginian and the inexperienced dude, set out upon their five-day journey on horseback towards Judge Henry's ranch, Wister sees to it that the love theme is kept alive in the reader's mind. Not only has Uncle Hughey, the aging man whom in the opening chapter the cowboy had ribbed about his urge to marry, come back as the newly-wed husband of a young woman, but also the otherwise unapproachable landlady of the village inn has fallen prey to the masculine charm of the Virginian.

Riding through a "quiet, open, splendid wilderness," in which "every breath [...] was pure as water and strong as wine" (37) and in which they pass no human beings but encounter all sorts of animals, the taciturn cowboy and the awe-struck tenderfoot exchange only a few words, but the retrospectively omniscient narrator informs his readers that his companion

> had set out for a 'look at the country' at the age of fourteen; and that by his present age of twenty-four he had seen Arkansas, Texas, New

Mexico, Arizona, California, Oregon, Idaho, Montana, and Wyoming. Everywhere he had taken care of himself and survived; nor had his strong heart yet waked up to any hunger for a home. (36)

The Virginian, then, is one of those strong nomadic men who have followed Horace Greeley's famous injunction "Go West, Young Man"[25] and helped to open up the continent.

Somewhere on their way, the western knight-errant and his eastern charge happen to meet a married neighbour named Taylor, and Wister uses this encounter to reinforce the still muted 'Love Plot' in a subtly disguised way. Taylor, who has already heard of the Trampas incident and through his references to it keeps the 'Confrontation Plot' alive, informs the Virginian about plans for erecting a schoolhouse. This, of course, would signal the end of the all-male world of the West, and the Virginian's retort "Well, if this hyeh Territory is goin' to get full o' fam'ly men and empty o' game, I believe I'll -" (40) foreshadows the shocked reaction which his fellow cowboys will later show in front of the newly built schoolhouse:

> [The schoolhouse] symbolized the dawn of a neighborhood, and it brought a change into the wilderness air. The feel of it struck cold upon the free spirits of the cow-punchers, and they told each other that, what with women and children and wire fences, this country would not long be a country for men. (64)

The cowboys' frightened reaction to the two worst threats - 'good' women and school - which civilization holds in store will soon become a standard ingredient of the western, and one need only think of Stephen Crane's brilliant story "The Bride Comes to Yellow Sky" (1898), in which the marriage of marshal Jack Potter brings "another world" into his frontier settlement and makes the shocked oldtimer

---

25 This is the abbreviated version in which that famous admonition is usually quoted. In occurs in an article on "The Preemption System" which Horace Greeley published in his weekly news journal *The New Yorker* on 25 August 1838 and reads: "If any young man is about to commence the world, with little in his circumstances to prepossess him in favor of one section more than another, we say to him, publicly and privately, Go to the West; there your capacities are sure to be appreciated, and your industry and energy rewarded."

Scratchy Wilson comment "I s'pose it's all off now."[26] If one builds a schoolhouse, one also needs a teacher, and so the Virginian asks Taylor "Got your eye on a schoolmarm?" (41) This question is rendered prominent by occurring at the chapter's end, and only later does the reader realize that it functions as a signal of things to come, for it is the very schoolmarm to be hired for the planned school on whom the Virginian will 'get his eye.' The question of how to acquire a teacher for the wilderness settlement serves as clue for the omniscient narrator, and in the next chapter he switches his attention quite abruptly from the Southern-born cowboy in the Far West to a young woman in the Northeast who is preparing herself for a job as 'schoolmarm' in Wyoming.

Chapter I, "Enter the Man," is thus complemented by chapter V, "Enter the Woman," and after the many anticipatory hints at love and marriage, the 'Love Plot' is finally set in motion. The woman who will soon appear on the scene of action is Mary Stark Wood from Bennington, Vermont, and in the further course of action, we learn that she is as exceptional as her lover to be. What makes her so unusual are both "her descent" (60) from an outstanding colonial family and her "character," which is "the result of pride and family pluck battling with family hardship" (61). Mary Stark Wood named Molly can trace her family back to the famous Captain John Wood who on August 16, 1777, so valiantly won the battle of Bennington against John Burgoyne. This young lady, who is luckily "not a New Woman" (67) and thus free of the godless emancipatory notions gaining ground in the East, is courageous enough to set out for the West, thus repeating her ancestors' feats in settling the eastern seashore by becoming a pioneer woman on the western prairie.

It is this exceptional woman whom the heroic cowboy will marry after "three years of faithful battle" (293), and he will do so on "July third" (288), the eve of Independence Day. The delayed and complicated courtship which leads to this symbolically charged union is as crucial to the novel as the 'Confrontation Plot,' and it also contains the

---

26 Stephen Crane, "The Bride Comes to Yellow Sky," in *The Works of Stephen Crane*, ed. by Fredson Bowers, vol. V, *Tales of Adventure* (Charlottesville: University Press of Virginia, 1970), pp. 109-121.

explanation for Wister's strategy of making his archetypal Westerner a Southerner. Of course, this choice could be explained biographically, for Wister completed the final draft of his novel in "Charleston, S.C." (xix), and the romantic pre-Civil War atmosphere of this splendid city proved most conducive to his dreams of a better America. With his usual insistence on Anglo-Saxon exceptionalism, he praised Charleston as "retaining its native identity, its English-thinking, English-feeling, English-believing authenticity holding on tight to George Washington and the true American tradition,"[27] and thus it is small wonder that he wanted to incorporate this "true American tradition" into his picture of a visionary America better und purer than the hateful immigrant-cluttered country of the big modern cities.

But even if we knew nothing about Wister's biography, we could explain his choice of a Virginian as his hero from the novel itself. We would only have to remember that, when Wister wrote, the country was still suffering from the rift between the North and the South which the Civil War had brought about and that the dangers of sectionalism were not yet overcome. Consequently, for somebody who spoke out for the rejuvenation of the lost American values of pioneer days and who found the only true 'America' in the Far West, Wister had almost inevitably to arrive at the solution which his story implies, namely, at a plea for a promising new beginning to be brought about by a 'marriage' of the best traits of the North and the South on the plains of the West. Consequently, he transported heroic Molly Stark as the personification of colonial womanhood and as the standard-bearer of civilization by means of education to the prairies of Wyoming and made her meet and marry the equally heroic Virginian as the personification of Southern (gentle)manhood and as the conquerer of the wilderness by means of strength and daring, thus creating a couple whose offspring would achieve what Wister so urgently desired, namely, in an apposite phrase from Crèvecoeur, "one day cause great changes in the world."[28]

---

27 Quoted from G. Edward White, *The Eastern Establishment and the Western Experience: The West of Frederic Remington, Theodore Roosevelt, and Owen Wister* (New Haven and London: Yale University Press, 1968), p. 138.
28 J. Hector St. John de Crèvecoeur, *Letters from an American Farmer and Sketches of 18th-Century America*, ed. Albert E. Stone (Harmondsworth: Penguin Books, 1981), p. 70.

Whereas the drawn-out courtship and triumphant marriage of the northern woman from a Vermont pioneer family and the southern man "of old stock in Virginia English and one Scotch Irish grandmother" (244), brought about in the transcendent landscape of the Far West, doubtlessly provide the major fictional illustration of Wister's vision of a new American unity to be achieved by a mutually beneficent merging of regional traits, the interplay between the narrator and the hero is at least equally important. On the one hand, the narrator's 'civilizing' influence upon the Virginian functions as a preparation for the latter's courtship of Molly, and on the other, the development of a true friendship between the two initially hostile men serves as yet another demonstration of Wister's belief that the East and the West could each learn and profit from the other. At the beginning, the western mentor is sorely embarrassed by the ineptitude of his eastern charge, and the sophisticated Easterner looks down upon his western guide's lack of education. But during the five years of the novel's action,[29] the two unequal men become close friends. Consequently, it is not the heroic Virginian alone who provides the ideological centre of the novel, but the mutually beneficial interplay between him on the one hand and his eastern friend and his Vermont sweetheart on the other which embodies Wister's belief in a better 'America' resulting from the combination of her incomplete sections.

During the first two thirds of the novel the ignorant and vulnerable tenderfoot learns countless things from the western cowboy. And when he recalls his pathetic "tender-foot innocence" (12) and complete ignorance of western mores, recounting with ironic self-depreciation how in his "notorious helplessness" (46) he becomes an "object of mirth" (45) for Judge Henry's cowboys, one might feel inclined to think that the novel is solely concerned with the initiation of a citified Easterner into "the code" (193) of the West. This, however, would be another serious misjudgment because the process of education be-

---

[29] The time covered by the novel's action can be inferred from several references to the Virginian's age: in chapter I he is "twenty-four" (6), in chapter XI "twenty-seven" (88), in chapter XVIII "nearing thirty" (142), and in chapter XXXV "twenty-nine years old" (300). - That the time scheme is sometimes interrupted and rather blurred might be partly due to the fact that Wister was not completely successful in integrating six of his earlier tales - as, for example, the famous story about "Em'ly" - into the novel, but the major reason is certainly that he needed a longer duration to bring off his narrator's change from tenderfoot to self-sufficient man.

tween the cowboy and the greenhorn is a mutual one, as becomes evident in the last third of the novel when the Virginian, in following his code, has to execute his former friend Steve as a rustler and is severely tortured by his conscience.

At this low point of his career, he is met by the Easterner who by now has completed his western education, who can ride on his own "into the wilderness" (246), and who can proudly reflect: "[...] remembering my Eastern helplessness in the year when we had met first, I enjoyed thinking how I had come to be trusted. [...] The man who could do this was scarce any longer a 'tenderfoot.'" (247) On their ride through an Indian-infested wilderness, the two friends are assailed by fear and superstition, and for once the strong-willed Virginian is overcome by his memories. When he loses his proverbial countenance, it is now the erstwhile neophyte who consoles his former mentor:

> [The Virginian] gave a sob. It was the first I had ever heard from him, and before I knew what I was doing I had reined my horse up to his and put my arm around his shoulders. I had no sooner touched him than he was utterly overcome. "I knew Steve awful well," he said.
> Thus we actually come to change places; [...] (261)

Thus, after five years of mutual influence upon each other, the two men who on their first meeting represented two totally different and quite incompatible worlds have now become capable of 'changing places,' and this once more proves Wister's central thesis. If the eastern tenderfoot, without losing his intellectual sophistication, could acquire the practical faculties which characterize self-sufficient western manhood and if the unpolished western cowboy, guided by both Molly and his eastern friend, could develop an advanced sense of right and wrong and a differentiated emotional life, then this is ample proof of the beneficial influence which a combination of sectional characteristics might exert.

With Molly, however, the Virginian has to undergo a more demanding education which is in many ways the exact opposite of his eastern friend's strenuous initiation. Whereas the Easterner has to acquire the skills which ensure survival in the western wilderness, the Westerner, who heroically saves Molly from the stranded coach and thus becomes "her unrewarded knight" (79), cannot win her by simply "radiat[ing] romance" (86), but must prove worthy of her affections. Promising her that "You're going to love me before we get through" (88), he devotes all his energy to the task of winning Molly's heart, and for that purpose he even courageously decides that he "ain't too old for education" (90). Thus be begins to "watch her ways and learn" (90) and to read books as the major means of catching up on "his education" (91). The "wild man [Molly is] taming" (147) laboriously ploughs through numerous books ranging from Sir Walter Scott to Jane Austen and George Eliot and from Shakespeare to Browning; and here again Wister's preferences as voiced through the Virginian's 'uneducated' but penetrating comments on these writers together with the narrator's explanatory remarks leave no doubt as to the novel's overall message. Thus, the cowboy immediately recognizes the greatness of Shakespeare, but predictably finds that "Romeo is no man" (182). And thus, with regard to Molly's preference for Browning's poetry, which elicits the narrator's revealing comment that "the pale decadence of New England had somewhat watered down her good old Revolutionary blood" (227), the high-flown sentiments of the Victorian poet are cooly destroyed by the Virginian's comments about "masculine courage and modesty" as ideas which "a smarty" (228) like Browning cannot convey correctly.

Wister abhors the levelling effects of egalitarian democracy, and throughout the novel he lets his narrator expostulate on the hateful misconception of human 'equality.' When the Easterner says that "it was through the Declaration of Independence that we Americans acknowledged the *eternal inequality* of man" (97) and then asserts that "true democracy and true aristocrary are one and the same" (97), he states his creator's position in no uncertain terms, and he returns to this issue time and again, as when he observes that being "equal to the occasion [...] is the only kind of equality which I recognize" (133). Consequently, it is no accident that a visiting Puritan preacher is rejected because his doctrine of original sin jars with the cowboys' sense of being masters of their own fates, that the credo of Social Darwinism is evoked several times, and that from the battle of wits in telling tall tales to the battle of guns in lethal showdowns it is "the survival of the fittest" (149) concept which defines the western world view.

"Let the best man win" (97) is the eastern narrator's credo, whereas the Virginian is convinced that "equality is a great big bluff" (95) and that "man helps them that help themselves" (177). The latter revealingly defines the difference between the 'civilized' East and the 'Wild West' by observing that "back East you can be middling and get along. But if you go to try a thing on in this Western country, you've got to do it *well*" (262). It is in the context of such an aristocratic world view, which imbues the 'Wild West' with notions of both romantic chivalry and atavistic power-struggle, that the troublesome western custom of self-justice is justified, a custom which till today has remained a controversial issue in all criticism of the western and of the allegedly negative influence of this genre upon its adherents.

When Molly learns that her suitor has gone out to hunt down rustlers and to execute them on the spot, she is overwrought and cannot forgive him for taking part in what to her is nothing but a criminal and inexcusable 'lynching.' Wister skilfully uses the lovers' quarrel as pretext for a dissertation on the necessity of western self-justice, and he cleverly allots the task of defending this custom to a veritable judge. Judge Henry, who has been established as a character beyond reproach, takes it upon himself to explain to the distraught woman from the East "that which, at first sight, nay, even at second and third sight, must always seem a defiance of the law more injurious than crime itself" (282), and his explanation turns out to be yet another variation of the novel's central theme of appearance versus reality: "the same act may wear as many different hues of right or wrong as the rainbow, according to the atmosphere in which it is done." (283) Judge Henry's explanation centres on the difference between "burning Southern Negroes in public" and "hanging Wyoming cattle-thieves in private" (284), and he argues that "the burning [is] a proof that the South is semi-barbarous, and the hanging [is] a proof that Wyoming is determined to become civilized" (285). Explaining to Molly that Wyoming does not yet have functioning courts and that its citizens have to defend themselves against the threat of anarchy, he advances the argument which by now has become the standard defense of western self-justice:

> [...] in Wyoming the law has been letting our cattle-thieves go for two years. We are in a very bad way, and we are trying to make that way a little better until civilization can reach us. At present we lie beyond its pale. The courts, or rather the juries, into whose hands we have put the law, are not dealing the law. [...] And so when your ordinary citizen sees this, and sees that he has placed justice in a dead hand, he must take justice back into his own hands where it was once at the beginning of all things. Call this primitive, if you will. But so far from being a *defiance* of the law, it is an *assertion* of it - the fundamental assertion of self-governing men, upon whom our whole social fabric is based. (286)

By learning to accept that in the unchartered wilderness of the West "a man that is a man" (170) must sometimes take the law in his own hands and administer judgment to those who threaten the peaceful development of the country, Molly is being prepared for her final lesson. When, on the eve of her wedding, she realizes that things between her husband to-be and Trampas have "come to that point where there was no way out, save only the ancient, eternal way between man and man" (304), she confronts the Virginian with the alternative of either shooting it out with Trampas or receiving her hand in marriage. Predictably, the Virginian who is suffering terribly from being caught between the call of love and the duty of restoring his reputation and who even asks the Bishop of Wyoming for advice, cannot run away from the showdown because "this community knew that a man had implied he was a thief and a murderer; it also knew that he knew it" (305). So he goes out and kills treacherous Trampas, and when he comes back to the hotel, the woman who has just told him that "if you do this, there can be no to-morrow for you and me" (312), thanks God that he is safe and falls into his arms. The romantic code of the knight-errant of the prairie puts manly reputation above everything else, and this is why the sacred world of 'good' women is to be separated from the inevitable cruelty of the world and why in the Virginian's "scheme, good women were to know only a fragment of men's lives" (297).

In *The Virginian*, then, we do not yet encounter the lonely western hero of later days who rides off into the setting sun after he has saved a frontier community from the threat of savagery by means of his own 'illegal' abilities, but an honest pioneer on horseback who, under the influence of eastern sophistication and the civilizing force of woman, gradually turns into a leading exponent of the civilization he helps to establish by daringly wiping out the forces of evil, who wins his beloved woman by polishing his 'uncouth' western ways with some home-made eastern education, and who becomes the father of "many children" (330) who, in their turn, will contribute further towards "making our country" (330). On the surface, then, Wister's bestselling novel might appear to be just another well-made fictionalization of Bishop Berkeley's momentous prediction that "Westward the Course of Empire takes its Way,"[30] but this is not the whole picture. Admittedly, *The Virginian* deserves a place in American literary history because it marks the beginning of an enormously influential genre of American popular literature by introducing most of its stock-in-trade motifs from the cowboys' 'code' of honour through the healing influence of the transcendental western landscape to the dramatic showdown. But it must not be overlooked that Wister's ingeniously Americanized version of medieval knight-errantry carries a very dangerous political message.

This message receives its explosive and detrimental power from the heady mixture of rabid Anglo-Saxon racism, a romanticized version of ruthless Social Darwinism, a questionable defense of self-justice, an atavistic rejection of democratic equality, and a primitive macho notion of God-given gender roles. Consequently, on closer scrutiny the first and trend-setting example of that indigenous American genre which its admirers like to tout as the most democratic art form, carries a message which is the very opposite of egalitarian democracy, and the disgruntled eastern aristocrat who invented the western novel in order to disseminate his belief in Anglo-Saxon exceptionalism, used his cleverly constructed tale to preach the message that "all America is divided into two classes, - the quality and the equality."

As the most popular western ever written, *The Virginian* marks a watershed after which "western writing was never the same."[31] Wister's novel presents the West "not as a set of natural values basically antithetical to civilization, but as a social environment in which

---

30 *The Works of George Berkeley, Bishop of Cloye*, ed. by A. A. Luce and T. E. Jessop. Nendeln: Kraus Reprint, 1979), vol. VII, p. 373.
31 Richard W. Etulain, "The Western," p. 358.

the American dream could be born again,"³² and thus it shows more clearly than most of its countless successors that the western not only caters to adolescent dreams of power in a fantasy world where everyone can be the architect of his own future and where good and bad

---

The Cowboy's "Ten Commandments" as provided by the singing cowboy GENE AUTRY

1: A cowboy never takes unfair advantage, even of an enemy.

2: A cowboy never betrays a trust.

3: A cowboy always tells the truth.

4: A cowboy is kind to small children, old folks, and animals.

5: A cowboy is free of prejudice.

6: A cowboy is always helpful.

7: A cowboy is a good worker.

8: A cowboy is clean in thought, work, and deed.

9: A cowboy respects womanhood, his parents, the laws of his country.

10: A cowboy, above all, is a patriot.

Transcribed from the educational sound filmstrip *The American West: Myth and Reality* (Pleasantvolle, N.Y.: Educational Audio Visual Inc, 1976).

---

can be clearly distinguished,³³ but that it also carries an important ideological message. This is a message which William F. Rickenbacker

---

32 John G. Cawelti, *Adventure, Mystery, and Romance*, p. 225.
33 By now it is a critical commonplace that "the Western expresses the conflict between the adolescent's desire to be an adult and his fear and hesitation about the nature of

formulated in no uncertain terms when, in an essay entitled "60,000,000 Westerners Can't Be Wrong," he spoke out in defense of the "glorious shows" of serialized television westerns and declared:

> [...] they speak a language very close to the heart of the American Dream: the dream of righteousness, the flowering of personal virtue and the power that flows therefrom, the selfless battle against Evil, the simple moral code, the sense of community, the respect for the poor, for the downtrodden, for the tempest-tossed.[34]

And this is a message which in our days an actor named Marion Morrison, who turned himself into the national icon known by the name of John Wayne, perpetuated in dozens of western films, in which he depicted violence and aggression, conquest and dominance as manly and heroic virtues.[35]

During the twentieth century, the ever flourishing western branched out in several directions. Most importantly, it became enormously successful in the growing film and, later, television industry, because its picturesque setting in the wide open spaces and its basic plot of chase and confrontation proved to be especially suitable for visualization. As far as writing was concerned, Zane Grey, a dentist from Ohio, dominated the field between 1910 and 1930 and, in terms

---

adulthood" (John G. Cawelti, *The Six-Gun Mystique* [Bowling Green, Ohio: Bowling Green University Popular Press, no date (1971)], p. 82), and psychoanalytical analyses of the western are legion. See, for example, Warren J. Baker, "The Stereotyped Western Story: Its Latent Meaning and Psychoeconomic Function," *Psychoanalytic Quarterly*, 24 (1955), 270-280, who considers the western as "a heroic myth in which are concealed themes of oedipal and other conflicts" (p. 279); or Kenneth J. Munden, "A Contribution to the Psychological Understanding of the Origin of the Cowboy and His Myth," *American Imago*, 15 (1958), 103-148, who argues that "the cowboy myth in its form of the manifest denial of the female or mother figure, represents the intense childhood desires for her and the fears attending those desires, namely that gratifying these wishes carries with it the implication that she is weak and powerless in the face of father, in a culture with matriarchal tendencies stemming from a freedom-loving son who has fled from patriarchal dominance and tyranny" (p. 145).

34 William F. Rickenbacker, "60,000,000 Westerners Can't Be Wrong," *National Review*, 13 (October 23, 1962), 322-325; here p. 322.
35 For details see James M. Ferreira, "John Wayne: An American Hero," and Walter Kühnel, "'I Tell You This Neither in a Spirit of Self-Revelation Nor as an Exercise in Total Recall': John Wayne, the Man Whom German Intellectuals Love(d) to Hate," both in *Popular Culture in the United States*, ed. by Peter Freese and Michael Porsche (Essen: Die Blaue Eule, 1994), pp. 195-212 and 213-234.

of sales figures, turned out to be the most successful western author ever, whose 54 novels had sold more than twenty million copies by 1969. Frederick Faust, who wrote under seventeen pen names the most popular of which was Max Brand, published more than 500 books and among them over 100 westerns. Between 1930 and 1950, Ernest Haycox attempted to make the formula western more believable by creating less stereotyped characters and using historical incidents for his plot lines. In the 1950s and 1960s Frederick Glidden became widely popular under his pen name Luke Short, and by the early 1970s Louis L'Amour, the favourite writer of President Reagan, took over as the leading author of western novels, stories, and filmscripts. These and countless other writers reworked the standard recipes with minor variations and thereby contributed to the widespread critical attitude towards the western as a standardized subliterary product meant for immediate consumption and not worth sustained critical attention.

During the early 1960s, however, a cultural climate developed which led to both a growing scepticism with regard to traditional values and a general upgrading of the formerly neglected expressions of so-called 'popular culture.' Within this context, the numerous attempts at closing the traditional gap between 'high' and 'popular' art brought about a rediscovery of such hitherto neglected formulaic genres as the western, science fiction and pornography by young writers and academic critics alike. Thus, the formula western was granted serious scrutiny as a projection of communal hopes and dreams, and as a result of that scrutiny it came under attack as a vehicle of ideas about the national past which were no longer acceptable. Consequently, and ironically, the very rediscovery of the genre opened the gates for its radical revision. Leslie A. Fiedler was one of the first to describe this development when he observed that young innovative writers were looking for forms of expression removed as far as possible from art, *avant-garde,* and literary pretension and that they were opting for the genres most closely associated with exploitation by the mass media:

> Most congenial of all is the 'Western,' precisely because it has for many decades now seemed to belong exclusively to pulp magazines, run-of-the-mill TV series and class B movies; which is to say, has been experienced most purely as myth and entertainment rather than as 'literature'

> at all - and its sentimentality has, therefore, come to possess our minds so completely that it can now be mitigated without essential loss by parody, irony - and even critical analysis. In a sense, our mythological innocence has been preserved in the Western, awaiting the day when, no longer believing ourselves innocent in fact, we could decently return to claim it in fantasy.[36]

Fiedler's praise of the 'postmodern' western as a major art form in an Age of Pop might be a little exaggerated, but there is no question that in the sixties, which in the realm of the film witnessed the enormous success of Sergio Leone's 'spaghetti westerns' with their amoral heroes and their sadistic violence, new western novels came into being which radically revised the genre's traditional value system. Turner's thesis that the frontier environment had bred American optimism, idealism, and democracy was increasingly rejected as a pious cliché, the dominant perspective of the triumphant white conqueror was replaced by that of his suffering red victim, the black cowboy who was historically very important but so far had been almost completely absent from the western was finally given his due, the stereotyped distinction of women into either the revered standard-bearers of civilization or the willing objects of sexual gratification was critically reconsidered, and the myth of the redemptive open spaces of the West came under fire.

Parallel to revisionist historians who began to rewrite the history of the Old West by complementing the idealistic hopes and democratic convictions of the settlers with their hitherto neglected ethnic and religious conflicts, class struggles, and economic deprivations, the new 'westerns' painted a radically different picture of the mythical Wild West, and the western formula which had so far been a ready-made means of celebrating the 'American way of life' by touting the concept of self-sufficient manhood, the notion of frail womanhood, and the myth of redemptive violence now turned into a vehicle of scathing social criticism and the pitiless exposure of entrenched ideologies.

---

36 Leslie A. Fiedler, "Cross the Border - Close That Gap: Post-Modernism," in *American Literature Since 1900*, ed. by Marcus Cunliffe (London: Sphere Books, 1975), pp. 344-366; here pp. 351f.

In this context, John Barth's mock-heroic epic *The Sot-Weed Factor* (1960), which ironically reworks the satirical poem of the same title published in 1708 by Ebenezer Cooke, the self-proclaimed poet laureate of the colony of Maryland, deserves to be mentioned as well as Thomas Berger's highly accomplished mock-heroic novel *Little Big Man* (1964) about the mythical American West, which offers a hilarious indictment of the attitudes that led to racism and warfare among Indians and whites and which satirically inverts the traditional version of the nature of life on the western frontier. Other books that belong to this new movement are Ken Kesey's bestselling novel *One Flew Over the Cuckoo's Nest* (1962), which offers a contemporary variation of the self-reliant individual's fight against the antagonistic forces of society and ingeniously varies the traditional theme of white-Indian friendship, and his ambitious second novel *Sometimes a Great Notion* (1964), which again deals with the conflict between a heroic frontier individual and the levelling forces of civilization. And Norman Mailer's scatological *Why Are We in Vietnam?* (1967), which is reminiscent of Faulkner's "The Bear," is yet another book about the 'western' ideal of personal self-fulfilment, because it reworks the conflict between the individual and the corporations and deals with the plight of individual thinking in a world dominated by the surfeit of information provided by the mass media.

These and many other novels relentlessly question the popular concept of the West in highly accomplished texts which go far beyond the established formula. Since their authors recreate the frontier life of the West against the background of their contemporary experience, their portrayals of both the historical and the mythic West are radically different from the entrenched Hollywood version. These writers' awareness of the threat of nuclear annihilation and their haunting memories of cruel warfare in Korea and Vietnam, their knowledge of the McCarthy witch-hunts of the fifties and the race riots of the sixties, and their experience of the youthful counter-culture's revolt against all traditional norms and values make them concentrate on the hitherto hidden side of the historical frontier and bring to light the social and the moral tensions which have so far been almost completely neglected in the historical records of the Old West and the mythic projections of the Wild West alike. Thus, they devise a new and darker image of the West, which replaces the adolescent optimism of the Marlboro man by a more mature world view and which contrasts the ever triumphant heroes of the Hollywood B-western with real protagonists that also know failure and defeat.

One of the first writers who masterfully subverted the conventions of the formula western and used the traditional plot line for a revisionist exploration of the most popular American myth was Edgar Laurence Doctorow with his novel *Welcome to Hard Times* (1960). One year after him, Bernard Malamud, like Doctorow an urban Jew from the East, published his novel *A New Life* (1961), which is not a western but a college novel that approaches the task of re-evaluating the myth of the West from a different angle and within different generic conventions. These two novels are revealing examples of the critical re-evaluation to which one of the constitutive elements of the 'American Dream' was subjected in the sixties.

E. L. Doctorow's *Welcome to Hard Times*, or the Fraudulence of the Popular Western

> All hail, thou western world! by heaven design'd
> Th' example bright, to renovate mankind.
> Soon shall thy sons across the mainland roam;
> And claim, on far Pacific shores, their home;
> Their rule, religion, manners, arts, convey
> And spread their freedom to the Asian sea.
> Timothy Dwight, *Greenfield Hill*[37]

It was in his nomination acceptance speech, delivered on July 15, 1960, in Los Angeles, that the Democratic Presidential Candidate John F. Kennedy extolled the valour of the pioneers who had conquered the West and reminded his listeners that "we stand today on the edge of a new frontier - the frontier of the 1960s, a frontier of unknown oppor-

---

37 Timothy Dwight, *Greenfield Hill: A Poem* (New York: Childs and Swaine, 1974), p. 52.

tunities and perils, a frontier of unfulfilled hopes and threats."[38] In the same year in which the charismatic President-to-be ingeniously redefined the erstwhile geographic frontier of the West and the subsequent social frontier of opportunity as the scientific frontier of space and thereby offered his audience the much desired new challenge, an unknown young Jewish writer named Edgar Laurence Doctorow published his first novel, *Welcome to Hard Times*, and offered a new and surprising version of the 'Wild West' which turned Kennedy's picture inside out and debunked the myth of the formula western in the most savage way. Doctorow's novel was among the first of a steadily growing number of so-called revisionist westerns, and it bears out Cawelti's observation that "since the high water mark of the late 1950's, the cultural significance of the western has perceptibly shifted" and that there is a continuously increasing number of western books and films which "share a disillusioned and pessimistic view of society and an obsession with the place of violence in it."[39]

In his influential study *Frontier: American Literature and the American West*, Edwin Fussell rightly observed "that the American West was neither more nor less interesting than any other place [...] until by interpretation the great American writers - all of whom happened to be Eastern - made it seem so."[40] Consequently, the 'West' which we daily encounter in an endless array of popular western novels, films, and TV serials is essentially a place of the mind, a "symbol and myth."[41] Thus, Richard Etulain is quite correct in stating that the western, as the most indigenously American genre, "remains a valuable source for attempting to understand the American popular mind."[42] This means that allegedly 'sophisticated' literary critics, who snub the western as a trivial concoction of popular dreams and stereotypes, deprive themselves of an excellent possibility of discovering behind its standard-

---

[38] Quoted from *U.S. News & World Report*, July 25, 1960; pp. 100-102; here p. 102. - Excerpts are reprinted in the EFL-reader *American Dreams - American Nightmares*, ed. by Brian Tracy and Erwin Helms (Paderborn: Schöningh, 1981), pp. 100f.
[39] John G. Cawelti, *Adventure, Mystery, and Romance*, pp. 252 and 259.
[40] Edwin Fussell, *Frontier: American Literature and the American West* (Princeton, N.J.: Princeton University Press, 1965), p. 13.
[41] See Henry Nash Smith's seminal study *Virgin Land: The American West as Symbol and Myth*.
[42] Richard W. Etulain, "The Western," p. 363.

ized surface the shared values and beliefs of a large segment of the American population.[43]

More recently, German-EFL-methodologists have finally become aware of the promising possibilities which the western offers for the advanced EFL-classroom,[44] but so far their attention has been focused on the 'classic' western. When a novel is tackled in some detail at all, it is usually Jack Schaefer's *Shane* (1949),[45] which is often studied in combination with George Steven's well-known film version of 1953. Both the book and the film are certainly highly rewarding texts from which one can learn a lot about 'America' and about the emergence and the functions of a national myth, but they offer only one side of the picture. This is why *Shane* should be contrasted with a new, a revisionist western which reformulates the myth of the 'West' from a radically different point of view and thus offers an alternative reading of the national past and a changed understanding of its importance for the present. *Welcome to Hard Times* is especially suited for such an endeavour because, like Thomas Berger's *Little Big Man* (1964), Edward Abbey's 'eco-westerns' such as *The Monkey Wrench Gang* (1975) or the 'serious' westerns by William Eastlake and Larry McMurtry, it is a highly accomplished work of literature and, in contrast to most of the other new westerns, it has the additional methodological advantage of being both short and narrated in easily accessible language. There is also a rather garbled film version of Doctorow's novel entitled

---

43 See John G. Cawelti, *The Six-Gun Mystique*.
44 See, for example, Klaus H. Köhring, "The Western," in *Projects in Literature: Modelle und Materialien zur Textarbeit im Englischunterricht*, ed. by Wilfried Brusch (Heidelberg: Quelle & Meyer, 1977), pp. 57-76; and the EFL-readers *Indians, Outlaws, and Western Heroes*, ed. by Hans-Martin Braun and Karl-Heinz Göller (Frankfurt: Diesterweg, 1979); *The Frontier and the American West*, ed. by Peter Bruck (Paderborn: Schöningh, 1980) with its accompanying *Teacher's Book*; and *Western Stories*, ed. by Peter Bischoff and Peter Noçon (Paderborn: Schöningh, 1984) with its excellent *Teacher's Book* (1986).
45 See Peter Bruck, "Jack Schaefer: Shane (1949)," in *Der Roman im Englischunterricht der Sekundarstufe II: Theorie und Praxis*, ed. by Peter Freese and Liesel Hermes (Paderborn: Schöningh, 2nd rev. and enl. ed., 1981), pp. 269-283. - The very accomplished film, for which A. B. Guthrie Jr. wrote the script, was produced in 1953 by Paramount with George Stevens as director and Alan Ladd as Shane. In Germany, it is available as *Mein großer Freund Shane*, and whereas in Hessen it can be borrowed from the Landesfilmdienst, Kennedy-Allee 105a, 6000 Frankfurt, in all other states it has to be bought from commercial video-stores.

Killer on a Horse, which was produced in 1966 by Metro-Goldwyn-Mayer with Henry Fonda playing the lead.[46]

In 1980, Doctorow, who by then had become the famous author of *Ragtime* (1975), said in an interview with Larry McCaffery:

> I don't imagine I would have written *Welcome to Hard Times*, if I'd not been working at that film company and reading lousy screenplays week after week. I had no affinity for the genre - I'd never been west of Ohio. I thought Ohio *was* the West. Oh, as a kid I'd liked Tom Mix radio programs and maybe I went to see a few movies: but, really, I had no feeling for Westerns. But from reading all these screenplays and being forced to think about the use of Western myth, I developed a kind of contrapunctual idea of what the West must really have been like.[47]

Thus he confirmed that his novel did not grow out of any personal experience of the West, but came into being as a reaction to a cultural tradition, a ubiquitous myth he could not help encountering and wanted to rectify. And when he added, "I liked the idea of using disreputable genre materials and doing something serious with them. I liked invention. I liked myth,"[48] he made it obvious that what he started with were the recurring ingredients of the popular western formula.

The basic and endlessly varied situation of the popular western is a confrontation between law and order on the one hand and lawlessness and savagery on the other. This confrontation has to happen at a point in time at which the latter are still strong enough to pose a serious challenge to a newly established community and at a place on the western frontier, that is, in Turner's famous phrase, at

---

[46] The mediocre film, which drastically changes the message of the novel, was directed by Burt Kennedy, who also wrote the script. The German version is quite inappropriately entitled *Mordbrenner von Arkansas*. - See Joanna Rapf, "'Some Fantasy on Earth': Doctorow's *Welcome to Hard Times* as Novel and Film," *Literature / Film Quarterly*, 13 (1985), 50-55.

[47] Larry McCaffery, "A Spirit of Transgression" [interview with E. L. Doctorow], in *E. L. Doctorow: Essays and Conversations*, ed. by Richard Trenner (Princeton, N.J.: Ontario Review Press, 1983), pp. 31-47; here pp. 33f.

[48] *Ibid*, p. 36.

"the meeting point between savagery and civilization."[49] Of these constitutional elements the locale is the most important. "The Western formula," Cawelti observes in *The Six-Gun Mystique*, "is initially defined by its setting,"[50] and thus it is no accident that the western is the only genre that owes its name to a point of the compass. Consequently, it comes as no surprise that Doctorow could say about the genesis of *Welcome to Hard Times* that it originated from

> [...] just a sense of place which moved me tremendously. It was the landscape. I loved writing about it, imagining it. I had never been West. Halfway through the book, it occurred to me that maybe I ought to make sure it really was a possible terrain. I went to the library and read a geographic book by Walter Prescott Webb - a marvelous book called *The Great Plains*. Webb said what I wanted to hear: no trees out there. Jesus, that was beautiful. I could spin the whole book out of one image. And I did.[51]

The 'place' which Doctorow imagined for his novel is a wretched little settlement fittingly called Hard Times "in the Dakota Territory" (7).[52] A character's later reference to "the badlands" (20), the statement that the town lies within "nothing but miles of flats" (7) to the east, south and west and "hills of rock" with "the lodes" (7) to the north, and passing references to "Silver City" (114, 118) and "Deadwood" (26), the old town famous in the 1870's for the exploits of Wild Bill Hickok and Calamity Jane, make it obvious that, with the eroded Dakota Badlands, Doctorow picked a region charged with associations of Western exploits ranging from the adventures of the gold miners in the Black Hills and the fights against Sitting Bull and his valiant Sioux to the deeds of legendary frontier heroes and the terrible hardships of the settlers who tried to domesticate a forbidding, hostile, and inhospitable landscape proverbially known as 'hell with the fires out.' The eroded lunar landscape of the Badlands and the little town lost in its endless expanse of dusty emptiness are introduced as part of the "Dakota Territory," and that means that the action must take place

---

49 Frederick Jackson Turner, "The Significance of the Frontier in American History," p. 545.
50 John G. Cawelti, *The Six-Gun Mystique*, p. 35.
51 Larry McCaffery, "A Spirit of Transgression," p. 39.
52 All page numbers in brackets refer to the pocketbook edition of *Welcome to Hard Times* (London: Pan Books, 1977).

after 1861, when the Territory was organized, and before 1889, when both Dakotas achieved the statehood which the protagonist-narrator is frequently dreaming about (see 14, 75, 114). When one considers that one of the town's inhabitants, Major Munn, the Civil War "veteran" (20) who talks about having been an able-bodied fighter "at [the siege of] Richmond" (29) in 1864/65, is now "a bent old man" (20), the time of action can be narrowed down to the 1880's, and thus the fundamental prerequisite of the traditional western is fulfilled: The place of action is an endangered outpost of civilization in the still unconquered wilderness, a fragile settlement hovering on the outer frontier of a thinly populated Territory where "nothing fixes" and "people blow around at the whiff of the wind" (104). But there is one decisive difference. Whereas the landscape of the classic western is always both violent and transcendental and provides the redemptive quality of unspoiled God-given nature, the barren flats of *Welcome to Hard Times* are nothing but hostile and deadly and come across as the work not of God but the Devil.

The extreme changes between arctic winters with their notorious "Dakota blizzard[s]" (65), which mercilessly kill every unprotected person and put "a wilderness of snow-crusted flats" between the frozen settlers "and the rest of the world" (79), and the oppressive heat and dust of scorching summers make Hard Times a place where either "the drought" or "the blizzards" will "get you" (26) and which is frequently called a "Hell" (79). The only animals referred to are predatory cats and the ubiquitous carrion-hunting buzzards, scavenging coyotes and marauding wolves ever ready to attack and to devour the corpses of the many settlers who lose their lives and cannot be decently buried in the hard ground. There is no vegetation to speak of. A newcomer from the East states dazedly "I haven't seen a tree in seven days" (60); and when a woman tries to lay out a garden, the narrator comments "that only [an] Indian could raise anything out of this ground" (86; see 124). Water must be laboriously drilled out of the earth - a "gawky windmill" (21) operating an artificial well (see 31) is the one asset of Hard Times. Victuals must be brought in by the irregularly appearing stagecoach that cannot reach the town in winter, and since there are no trees the timber for building houses has to be brought from far away or to be reclaimed from neighbouring ghost towns.

Man's attempt, then, to imprint his mark on this wilderness and to achieve "a root on the land" (77) seems to be utterly futile; towns are as quickly abandoned as they have been erected, and "nothing fixes in this damned country" (104). The narrator sums up the prevailing attitude early in the novel in a symbolically charged statement:

> When I came West with the wagons, I was a young man with expectations of something, I don't know what. I tar painted my name on a big rock by the Missouri trailside. But in time my expectations wore away with the weather, like my name had from that rock, and I learned it was enough to stay alive. (10)

Life is a continuous fight for survival staked upon the short-lived hope of finding gold in the nearby lodes or on the vague expectation that the town will be "going on the map" (97) and that prosperity will come to the general store, the saloon, and the assorted petty entrepreneurs.

Consequently, Doctorow's western, which has no rolling grasslands, no cattle and no cowboys, and not even a real sheriff, does not concentrate on the few dramatically heightened days of a decisive battle between the forces of good and evil, but its action extends over more than two years, following the painful cycle of the seasons and unfolding the everyday lives of a motley group of townspeople all of whom wait for a better future. And the novel does not climax in a triumphant finale, with the victorious hero riding into the setting sun after he has re-established law and order and rescued an incipient civilization from the threat of savagery, but it ends with an orgy of violence and destruction and a dying man's bitter insight into the fraudulence of his western dream and the utter impossibility of beginning anew.

The protagonist-narrator of *Welcome to Hard Times* is Blue, who twenty years ago "put [his] young wife into the ground after the cholera took her" (25), who since has "moved from one side of the West to the other, like a pebble rolling in the pan" (26), and who, a year before the beginning of the action, got stuck in Hard Times. Blue is "forty-nine years old" (9) and has a weakness "for documents and deeds and such like" (74). Therefore he has taken it upon himself "to keep records in case the town got large enough to be listed, or in case statehood came ever about" (14). He writes everything down in some "ledgers" (21) which he has bought from a travelling lawyer on his way to the gold mines, and he is obsessed with the idea "to keep a record [...], to write things down" (91; see 98). This puts him in the position of a town leader, and he becomes a sort of honorary mayor of Hard Times. His efforts to keep "a write on things" (103), that is, to keep a hold on things by putting them down in writing, betray his need to attain some stability in a world of constant flux, to create some tangible roots and a local history to build upon.

But Blue will soon have to recognize himself "for a fool for all the bookkeeping I've done" (135) and to discover that "notations in a ledger" cannot "fix life," that "some marks in a book" cannot "control things" (135). In the end, the dying Blue writes down his tale about the destruction, the rebirth and the final death of Hard Times in the same ledger in which he had kept the town records: "There is only one record to keep and that's the one I'm writing now, across the red lines, over the old marks" (135). Although the novel, then, comes to us as a tale bearing the authenticity of an eye-witness account and the dignity of a dying man's testament, it is shot through with the doubts of a writer who is painfully aware of the provisional nature of his attempts to fix reality by means of language. Thus, *Welcome to Hard Times* is not only a western that turns the western formula upside down, but also, by means of its self-reflexive narrative stance, a western that comments on the genesis of the western myth.

Blue assumes the role of leader not because he can handle a six-gun but because he can wield a pen, and his ledgers contain two layers of text superimposed upon each other, one of legal facts and the other of the tale that grew from them, thus becoming "a palimpsest which symbolizes the process by which fact is transformed into fiction."[53] Doctorow, therefore, not only replaces the traditional western man of action with a man of thought, but he also makes his western an implied epistemological exercise on the possibilities and limits of storifying.[54] Thus Blue muses:

---

53 Paul Levine, *E. L. Doctorow* (London and New York: Methuen, 1985), p. 30.
54 All of Doctorow's novels are not historical novels in the traditional sense but rather novels about how to write historical novels. For an investigation of the fact that they

> I'm trying to put down what happened but the closer I've come in time the less clear I am in my mind. I'm losing my blood to this rag, but more, I have the cold feeling everything I've written doesn't tell how it was, no matter how careful I've been to get it all down it still escapes me: like what happened is far below my understanding beyond my sight. In my limits, taking a day for a day, a night for a night, have I showed the sand shifting under our feet, the terrible arrangement of our lives? (146f.)

His puzzlement is outwardly due to his injury and to the fact that he is a dying man, but on a deeper level it expresses Doctorow's doubt whether allegedly 'objective' history can ever be more than a combination of subjective stories. And when Blue sceptically asks himself: "Does the truth come out in such scrawls, so bound by my limits?" (153), he asks a question which Doctorow forcefully answers in his essay "False Documents." There he concludes that "there is no history except that it is composed" and that "there is no fiction or nonfiction as we commonly understand the distinction: there is only narrative."[55] Blue's account, then, in spite of its author's attempts at veracity and precision, is a mere 'fiction,' an individual's subjective account of events. And this implies that the popular view of the West as expressed in the countless westerns which *Welcome to Hard Times* is meant to rectify is also nothing but fiction, a myth which says less about the actual west than about the needs and limitations of the myth-makers. Therefore, Doctorow's revisionist western not only debunks the facile assumptions of the popular genre, but it also suggests the psychological needs that brought them into existence - and that is what makes the novel such an accomplished 'false document.'

Quite in keeping with the narrator's preoccupation, Blue's account unfolds in three "Ledgers" of four, five and five chapters respectively. Instead of the traditional sequence of beginning, middle and end sug-

---

deal not so much with history but with historiography, that is, not with the recreation of a documented past by fictional means but with a dramatization of the very task of perceiving that past in the context of an experienced present, see Peter Freese, "Doctorow's 'Criminals of Perception,' or What Has Happened to the Historical Novel?" in *Reconstructing American Literary and Historical Studies*, ed. by Günter H. Lenz, Hartmut Keil, and Sabine Bröck-Sallah (Frankfurt and New York: Campus Verlag and St. Martin's Press, 1990), pp. 345-371.

55 E. L. Doctorow, "False Documents," in *E. L. Doctorow: Essays and Conversations*, pp. 24 and 26.

gested by its tripartite structure, however, the novel tells about an end, a new beginning, and another and final end. Thus, the plot line that ranges "from one end to the other" (153) signals that here the linear progression of the popular western is replaced by the circular repetition of a very different tale.

The First Ledger, which covers a single week and unfolds in a series of scenically rendered events, deals with the sudden appearance of a "Bad Man from Bodie" (11) who, in an orgy of sadistic violence, kills five of the townspeople and then sets the town on fire. Nobody dares to face his physical menace, and Blue, who is painfully aware of his own cowardice, muses on the wrongness of the common saying that Sam Colt made all men equal: "Colt gave every man a gun, but you have to squeeze the trigger for yourself." (28) When the Bad Man leaves, maimed corpses are strewn around and the town is a smouldering heap of ashes. The surviving settlers pack up their few belongings and leave, and Blue finds himself alone with Molly, the badly burnt prostitute, with Jimmy, the murdered carpenter's son and "the only child in town" (8), and with John Bear, "the deaf-and-dumb Pawnee who served for our doctor" (9). Haunted by the memory of his cowardice and feeling responsible for the injured woman and the lost child, he makes the unwilling Indian see to Molly's burns and tries to calm the traumatized child. Saddled with a woman who will never forgive him for not helping her against the Bad Man and a boy who will never recover from seeing his father being killed and his corpse being attacked by the buzzards, Blue builds a primitive dug-out that looks like "a grave" but is meant to be "a place to live" (31) and scavenges some tinned food from the ashes. Sitting in a hostile wilderness with the embers of his nightly fire "glowing on the ground like peepholes to Hell" (27), Blue knows that his chances of survival are next to nothing, and it seems as if the powers of savagery and evil have prevailed over the frail forces of an incipient civilization.

But a Russian entrepreneur and his four whores come along in their covered wagon, and Blue can persuade them to stay and to wait for the miners who come to Hard Times every Saturday to spend their money on women and whiskey. Driven by his guilt and feeling that he and Molly "had been wedded by the Bad Man from Bodie" (49), Blue tells the newcomers that Molly is his wife and Jimmy his son.

The weekend business convinces the Russian to stay, he and Blue drive to a neighbouring ghost town to fetch wood for new buildings, and the First Ledger ends with their decision to rebuild the town and officially christen it Hard Times. Thus there is a tentative promise of a new beginning, but the possible future is overshadowed by a gruesome and unforgettable past. Blue knows this, and when he jokingly calls the newly laid out cemetery "the beginnings of a town anyway" (25), he implies that there will be no future unencumbered by a past. Just as the new town they hope for will never be able to hide "the scar of the old street" (101; see 109), so Blue is all too aware that "the only hope we have is that we can pay off on our failures" (30). That hope, however, is futile because neither a community nor an individual can ever "bury the past" (91). So, right at the beginning of Doctorow's novel, the constitutive premise of the popular western, namely, the belief that one can start anew unfettered by the sins of the past, is forcefully unmasked as a delusion. The town will be rebuilt over the graves of its murdered founders. Jimmy and Molly will be forever haunted by their gruesome experiences, and Blue will never be able to forget his failures and will finally come to the bitter conclusion that "we can never start new, we take on all the burden: the only thing that grows is trouble, the disaster gets bigger, that's all" (135). The optimistic belief in linear progress which underlies the formula western is replaced by the pessimistic awareness of generational guilt.

Another crucial change in the popular pattern is also introduced in the First Ledger. While the classic western owes much of its mass appeal to the assumption that the economic exploitation which defines life in the densely settled industrial East is absent from the agrarian West where every individual determines his own free existence, Doctorow depicts the West as a mere extension of the eastern capitalistic market economy, and it is no accident that Hard Times owes its rebirth to the appearance of Zar and his whores. The first business that is opened in the rebuilt town, then, is a makeshift whorehouse, that is, a business which reduces women to chattels and which is conducted by a man who literally owns one of his whores, whom he has bought for $100. In Doctorow's disillusioned view, which is much closer to historical reality than the popular myth, the settling of the West was not the grand epic of roaming cowboys, self-sufficient farmers, and law-enforcing marshals, but the story of petty and unscrupulous entrepreneurs who exported the capitalism of the cities to the prairies. Zar, the indomitable Russian immigrant, offers a pithy summary of this view when he explains to Blue:

> "Frand ... I come West to farm ... but soon I learn, I see ... farmers starve ... only people who sell farmers their land, their fence, their seed, their tools ... only these people are rich. And is that way with everything ... not miners have gold but salesmen of burros and picks and pans ... not cowboys have money but saloons who sell to them their drinks, gamblers who play with them Faro ... not those who look for money but those who supply those to look. These make the money ... So I sell my farm ... and I think ... what need is there I shall fill it ... and I think more than picks and pans, more than seed, more even than whiskey or cards is need for Women. [...] (51)

To Zar, then, "the potential of the West is not for heroic individual action, but for mercantile success."[56] Since almost all the characters of Doctorow's novel share his view, another aspect of the traditional western is notably absent in *Welcome to Hard Times*. The genteel woman, the revered standard-bearer of civilization, has no place in Hard Times. Instead of Owen Wister's good-looking and noble-minded schoolmarm Molly Stark Wood and her countless successors, there are only the matter-of-fact whores who market themselves in a truly capitalistic spirit.

And there is yet another crucial difference because the Anglo-Saxon racialism of the traditional western is replaced by a much more accurate acknowledgment of the ethnic variety of the West. Owen Wister, the father of the classic western, had been appalled by the "hordes of encroaching alien vermin" cluttering the Eastern shores of America, and he had written *The Virginian* on the assumption that the "spirit of adventure, courage, and self-sufficiency" required for survival on the prairies could not be found in "many Poles or Huns or Russian Jews" but only in the heroic "Anglo-Saxon" who is the born "conqueror, invader, navigator, buccaneer, explorer, colonist, tiger-shooter."[57] Consequently, he had relegated the few non-English characters in his novel to the most menial jobs and used them as clownish

---

56 Frank W. Shelton, "E. L. Doctorow's *Welcome to Hard Times*: The Western and the American Dream," *Midwest Quarterly*, 25 (1983), 7-17; here p. 12.
57 Owen Wister, "The Evolution of the Cow-Puncher," in *The Writings of Owen Wister* (New York: Macmillan, 1928), vol. VI, pp. xix-li; here pp. xxiii, xxiv, and xxvi.

objects of derision. His romantic - and racist - notion of the western cowboy as the direct descendant of Sir Thomas Malory's medieval knight-errants set the pace for the popular western, but this is an attitude for which Doctorow provides the necessary correction. In *Welcome to Hard Times* we encounter the ebullient Russian entrepreneur Zar and his nameless Chinese whore, the German craftsman Hausenfield with his bathtub brought all the way from St. Louis, the taciturn Swede Bergenstrohm with his mad wife Helga, the Irish ex-whore Molly Riordan "speaking the brogue" (72), the brothers Ezra and Izaac Maple from Vermont with their Puritan attitudes, the sulking Pawnee Indian John Bear, and a motley assortment of people from different nationalities, who turn Hard Times into a veritable melting pot.

The Second Ledger, which switches from a scenic to a more panoramic presentation and covers a time span of "a full year, and a half again another" (106), tells about the gradual rise of the new town. After a terrible winter, in which Molly and Blue nearly freeze and starve to death and Jimmy only just recovers from a hacking cough, spring brings "a greenness of hopes" (84). The town is put back on the route of the stagecoach, more and more people drift in and decide to stay, new buildings go up, and it looks as if "better times" (77), "good times" (97) or even "big times" (99) are in store for Hard Times. Molly apparently makes her peace with Blue, and for a while even something like love and trust seems to develop between them.

Blue, who has worked on the assumption that it is not "the site but the settling of it that matter[s]" (74) and who has stubbornly fought for the renewal of the town, takes up his record-keeping again and assumes the role of mayor. Although he is haunted by a sense of futility, he convinces himself that this time things will be better. When there is talk that a road will be built to connect the town to the mines and when an official from the Governor of the Territory comes in to survey the place, everybody is certain that they are "going on the map" (97). A first marriage is performed by Blue and taken as a token of a better future, and when Molly voices her ever-present fear that the Bad Man from Bodie will reappear, Blue, ever the believer in civilization's irresistible progress, consoles her by saying: "[...] this time we'll be too good for him" and by arguing that lawless men are unable to harm an established settlement: "When the business is good and the life is working they can't do a thing, they are destroyed." (110) But he has to force himself to believe in his own assertions, and he is constantly aware of Molly's smouldering hatred, Jimmy's growing rebelliousness, and his own "almost forgotten pain" (109).

The Third Ledger begins with "the time of our greatest prosperity" (117), but again Doctorow drives home the point that the "brisk business" (113) enjoyed by the established inhabitants of Hard Times is based on the exploitation of the less fortunate newcomers and that the thriving economy of the little western town is nothing but a small-scale replica of Eastern capitalism. Whereas the steadily growing community appears to prosper, however, Blue's fragile private life is shattered when he discovers that under her complacent exterior Molly still hates him from the depths of her heart and has secretly been training Jimmy into a gunman "for the Bad Man, [...] breaking him into a proper mount for her own ride to Hell" (117). When she even sets the incipient killer on Blue, he realizes in despair that he has failed again, this time in his capacity as father to the orphaned boy. Blue tries to talk to Jimmy and to explain to him that he will never be able to undo one unjustice by committing another, but the boy reacts with pure hatred. So Blue must admit to himself that Jimmy is lost to civilization and that vengeful Molly is a prisoner of her irreversible corruption, must realize that this insight is "the true end of [him]" (123), and he is overwhelmed by "a sudden breathless vision [...] of [his] unending futility" (123).

Soon the breaking up of Blue's private life is followed by the sudden shattering of the town's hopes. To keep the increasing number of squatters waiting for work and living on credit from getting restless and making trouble, Blue pays out all his savings to them and has them perform several useful tasks that keep them in a hopeful mood till the beginning of the expected construction work. But then a letter arrives, and the terrible news spreads like wildfire: not only will no road be built, but the mines will be closed down because what the miners have dug out of the ground "wasn't ore [...] 'Twas only the color" (134). "Like the West, like my life," the terribly disappointed Blue comments: "The color dazzles us, but when it's too late we see what a fraud it is, what a poor pinched-out claim." (134) He has to confess to himself that it had really been clear for a long time that the town's hopes were illusory, and in utter despair he gives up his faith in progress and civilization. The man, then, who had almost single-handedly brought the new town into existence by the sheer force of his convictions has to recognize that "there is no fool like a fool in the West," whom one can "fool [...] so bad he won't even know his possibilities are dead, his hopes only ghosts" (139). So the never-ending cycle of disaster "from one end to the other" (153) is about to enter a new turn, and Blue finally discovers "that we are finished before we ever got started, our end was in the beginning" (135).

Fired miners drift glumly down to the town only to be confronted by furious townspeople, and in the oppressive heat of a scorching summer day the sudden frustration of pent-up hopes leads to a mad explosion of violence. The "lunatic town" (149) erupts into an orgy of rioting and looting, and in the middle of this savagery the Bad Man from Bodie reappears. While the few sane inhabitants leave hastily, Blue's will is paralyzed. In dismay he faces another destruction of his life's work, and in a final confrontation with gleeful Molly he must learn that she has waited all this time for the return of her violator, devoting her whole existence to the moment of revenge. Having earlier received "a kick in the side" (122) from his recalcitrant foster-son, Blue is now wounded by Molly with a stiletto and receives a painful "rent in [his] side" (145). Both injuries conjure up a parallel with the wounded Christ and thus underscore Blue's role as a suffering scapegoat in a world gone mad.[58]

This time, however, Blue will not run away, and so he sets out into the milling chaos, catches the Bad Man in a trap of barbed wire, beats him insensible and, with trance-like determination, carries the maimed gunman to his house. There Molly attacks the unconscious man with her knife in an insane orgy of retribution, and when victim and victimizer are locked in a deadly embrace, the horrified Jimmy kills them both with one shot "booming of birth" (153), thus being reborn as the symbolic son of their union of hate. Having killed his 'parents' and wounded Blue, who vainly attempts to deflect his gun,

---

[58] For a closer investigation of the religious implications of the novel see Marilyn Arnold, "Doctorow's *Hard Times*: A Sermon on the Failure of Faith," *Literature and Belief*, 3 (1983), 87-95.

Jimmy rides off into the flats, "another Bad Man from Bodie" (154). Thus the outlaw is resurrected in his killer, the cycle of suffering and revenge goes on and on, the "regeneration through violence"[59] results in the creation of another murderer. Blue remains in his house, slowly bleeding to death, surveying the corpse-strewn wreckage of his town and writing down what has happened in the hope that his ledger "will be recovered and read" (135), but knowing that his account will achieve nothing except perhaps "add to the memory" (135).

Welcome to Hard Times thus ends in good old western fashion with "a showdown" (147), but here we no longer have the traditional confrontation of the clearly distinguishable 'goodies' and 'baddies' in which the strict code of the face-to-face duel is scrupulously observed and the forces of progress and civilization triumph over savagery and lawlessness. Instead, we are faced with an orgy of hatred, violence, and brutality which ends in death and destruction and makes the "jackals and vultures, flies, bugs, mice" (154) of a merciless universe reclaim the remnants of what for a short time had been an outpost of civilization in the barren wilderness.

After the first attack of the curiously stylized Bad Man from Bodie, who not only refers to a well-established western tradition,[60] but also seems like a *bogeyman*, an archetypal embodiment of the forces of evil, Blue had observed: "Bad Men from Bodie weren't ordinary scoundrels, they came with the land, and you could no more cope with them than you could with dust or hailstones." (10) Later, the Bad Man is identified as Clay Turner (40), and that name could refer to the deaths and the burials, the 'turning of clay' which he leaves behind, and could also be an ironic hint at Frederick Jackson Turner and his famous frontier thesis.[61] When the Bad Man appears again, however,

---

[59] See Richard Slotkin's important study *Regeneration through Violence: The Mythology of the American Frontier, 1600-1860* (Middleton, Conn.: Wesleyan University Press, 1973).

[60] The mining town of Bodie in California's Mono County close to the Nevada border had the reputation of being the wickedest city in the American West, and 'The Bad Man from Bodie' was a proverbial figure to which, among others, Mark Twain referred in his western tales. For details see the chapter "Life Was Cheapest of All in Wicked Bodie" in Lucius Beebe and Charles Clegg, *The American West: The Pictorial Epic of a Continent* (New York: Bonanza Books, 1955), pp. 278-284.

[61] The first connection is hinted at by Arthur Saltzman, "The Stylistic Energy of E. L. Doctorow," in *E. L. Doctorow: Essays and Conversations*, pp. 73-108; here p. 76, when

it becomes obvious that he is not the evil 'other,' but a force that exists within everybody. Blue realizes this when he says: "He never left the town, it was waiting only for the proper light to see him where he's been all the time." (143) The outlaw, then, is not only bred by the land as a quasi natural force which one has to endure - a notion which can be found in many westerns - but he is an embodiment, a projection of the evil urges latent in every man. Thus, when he comes again, he is no intruder from outside but the logical result of the strife and the disintegration of the townspeople. And this view is forcefully driven home when Blue retrospectively observes about the Bad Man's first appearance that "he came that time," too, because "we wanted him" since "the hope was already dead" (110), and when he predicts that the villain's second coming will be an inevitable consequence of the town's repeated disintegration: "I knew it wouldn't be long and we'd all be suffering Turner, feeling his sermon." (137) Turner is "just a man, my God!" (151), and his importance lies not in himself but in his representative and symbolic quality: whenever man's hope is crushed, violence breaks out, "even if the external wilderness can be held off for a moment, the internal wilderness remains."[62]

The message of *Welcome to Hard Times*, then, is that the dream of self-realization in the West is illusory because it is built on the premise that evil is on the outside and can be conquered. This premise, however, proves to be wrong because violence and savagery lie hidden in every man and are bound to break out periodically. The 'goodies' cannot attain perfection by eliminating the 'baddies' because good and bad are inextricably mixed in every individual. Thus progress is a false promise, a new beginning is impossible because the past cannot be exorcized. History cannot be changed but only repeated, and that is as true for the 'civilized' reader in his cozy parlour in New York whom Blue imagines perusing his ledgers as it is for the uncouth pioneer of the West: "Your father's doing is in you, like his father's was in him, and we can never start new." (135) But, although Blue's hard-

---

he calls Clay Turner "a remarkable name for someone with so absolute a capacity for sending folks to their graves." The second connection is suggested by Frank W. Shelton, *op. cit.*, p. 9, who understands 'Turner' "perhaps as an ironic reference to the frontier historian Frederick Jackson Turner."

62 Marilyn Arnold, "History as Fate in E. L. Doctorow's Tale of a Western Town," in *E. L. Doctorow: Essays and Conversations*, pp. 207-216; here p. 215.

earned pessimism and his repeated failures as a man and a pioneer forcefully give the lie to the traditional Western myth, the dying man cannot give up hope, and he ends his account with the confession: "I have to allow, with great shame, I keep thinking someone will come by sometime who will want the wood." (155)

Edgar Laurence Doctorow's *Welcome to Hard Times* is a highly accomplished first novel. It takes up a well-established national myth and neatly turns it upside down. One by one, it disproves the premises of the popular western as wishful thinking by revealing the alleged epic of valiant self-realization in a redemptive landscape to be the tragedy of communal failure in a barren wilderness[63] and by demonstrating that economic exploitation and entrepreneurial greediness were as common in the West as they were in the East, a fact which is subtly underscored by Blue's writing of his tale in 'ledgers.' The novel unmasks the adolescent fantasy of a clear-cut division between the forces of good and the forces of evil and replaces it with the mature concept of man as a composite being with both benign and malevolent urges. It denies the belief in the possibility of new beginnings as self-delusion and convincingly shows that the past cannot be escaped. And it replaces the facile notion of linear progress with the tragic concept of generational guilt and its cyclical resurgence. By making his western hero a man of thought instead of a man of action and by letting him accompany his tragic tale of defeat and destruction with reflections about the power and the limits of storifying, Doctorow not only demythicizes the most popular American myth by showing that the promise of the West is a collective illusion invented to offset the pressures of reality, but he also implicitly provides an explanation of how that myth came into being as a surrogate fantasy of evasion and compensation. But while he mercilessly debunks the 'American Dream' as expressed in the formulaic western, he also acknowledges man's need for hope.[64]

---

63 See J. Bakker, "E. L. Doctorow's *Welcome to Hard Times*: A Reconsideration," *Neophilologus*, 69 (1985), 464-473; here p. 472, who concludes that in Doctorow's novel "for the first time in the history of the Western we meet the Westerner as a tragic figure [...]."

64 That some critics have great difficulty accepting such a revisionist version of the West becomes clear in Stephen L. Tanner's essay "Rage and Order in Doctorow's *Welcome to Hard Times*," *South Dakota Quarterly*, 22 (1984), 79-85; here p. 84. Tanner angrily rejects the claim that the novel is "a more 'valid' or significant treatment of

Blue, the faithful keeper of the records with his give-away name, is painfully aware of the limitations of man and of his own irredeemable failures, but it is his indomitable hope for the ascendancy of civilization that gives him the strength to keep up the good fight and that makes the dying man end his tale with the embarrassed admission that he cannot but think that his efforts, in spite of all their futility, might be of some use to posterity. Blue, then, is a kind of intellectualized American Adam, fallen from grace but unwilling to acknowledge the ubiquity of evil in the very face of it. Like Fitzgerald's Gatsby, he attempts to rebuild the past, to extend the fleeting "moment when we reached what perfection was left to our lives" (102) into the future. And like Gatsby, he is bound to fail because he does not find himself in a pastoral Eden out towards the setting sun, which the popular western evokes time and again, but in a harsh world of economic competition, human greed, and natural adversity. So he has to complete his bitter journey from hope to despair and to realize that man cannot achieve perfection.

It is this message of man's tragic limitation which turns *Welcome to Hard Times* into what might be called a dystopian western and which makes Doctorow's novel an impressive work of art which uses the mythic elements of a popular genre "to teach us the inner truths of [American] national traditions, truths concealed rather than revealed by the traditional Western."[65] And it is Doctorow's forceful revision of a central national myth that makes the novel a challenging and re-

---

the Western," and says: "[the established] myth and legend derive from a certain reality - a certain courage, self-sufficiency, generosity, and hopefulness. Doctorow denies that germ of reality along with the myth and legend. He portrays a West inhabited by sadistic destroyers on the one hand and weak, selfish, death-wishing losers hopelessly trapped in the meaningless cycles of history on the other. Westerns take great liberty with reality, but Doctorow, in allegedly correcting such distortions, takes even greater liberties. Good Westerns, even with their larger-than-life quality, can be useful as well as entertaining, can be inspiring in their way. By arousing rage at the disruption of order and then purging that rage through the reestablishment of order, Westerns can satisfy a significant craving for meaning and purpose on the part of society as well as individuals. When order is a cheat and illusion in the first place, as it is in Doctorow's world, rage to maintain it is purposeless and even destructive. *Welcome to Hard Times* is essentially empty of hope and human affirmation because it fails to acknowledge grounds for justified anger and moral outrage."

65 David S. Gross, "Tales of Obscene Power: Money and Culture, Modernism and History in the Fiction of E. L. Doctorow," *Genre*, 13 (1980), 71-92; here p. 74.

warding text for the EFL-classroom. Comparing almost any popular western with *Welcome to Hard Times*, Doctorow's "contrapunctual idea of what the West must really have been like,"[66] one can easily work out such crucial contrasts as the following:

- a transcendental and redemptive nature versus the violent and inhospitable 'hell' of the Dakota Badlands,
- the hero as a man of action versus Blue as a man of thought,
- the heroine as schoolmarm and flagbearer of civilization versus the prostitute as pawn in money-making enterprises,
- the promise of a new beginning versus the recognition of generational guilt and the knowledge that every present it conditioned by the past,
- the belief in western freedom and self-sufficiency versus a version of the West as a less polished imitation of Eastern capitalism and entrepreneurial greed,
- the clichés of Anglo-Saxon racialism versus the West as a multi-ethnic melting pot,
- the concept of self-justice and revenge versus the insight that one crime cannot blot out another,
- the clear-cut distinction between the goodies and the baddies versus the recognition that all men are composite beings; or, the belief that evil is outside and can be overcome versus the knowledge that evil is inside and must be lived with,
- the concept of history as progress versus the concept of history as repetition.

These and many other differences make the comparison of a traditional western with Doctorow's novel an extremely rewarding enterprise. And the fact that *Welcome to Hard Times* is not only a revisionist western but at the same time an epistemological treatise on the origin of stories and an exploration of the process of mythopoiesis provides an important additional advantage because it invites a general consideration of the genesis and the social functions of narrative formulas. Doctorow's novel, then, is a 'false document' in the sense of a fictional reconstruction of historical reality, which challenges the collective memory kept alive in the traditional western and thereby invites

---

66   See note 47.

us to reconsider critically one of the most durable myths of popular American culture.[67]

Bernard Malamud's *A New Life*, or the Mendacity of the Myth of the West

> Let's admit - wherever Levin had been, someone had been before (no Chingachgook he, even in the primeval forest, even forest of the night).
> Bernard Malamud, *A New Life*[68]

In 1949, a Jewish intellectual from New York named Bernard Malamud accepted a teaching position at Oregon State College in Corvallis and went West with his Italian-born wife and his two-year-old son. Joining in "the most absurd and touching of all the waves of migration that have ever moved across [America] from East to West: the migration of certain upwardly mobile, urban, Eastern young academics, chiefly Jews, into remote smalltown State Universities, Cow Colleges, and Schools of Education,"[69] Malamud duplicated on an individual scale one of the great collective movements of American history, belatedly acted out Horace Greeley's 'Go West, young man,'[70] discovered a new America, and tested, as it were, the feasibility of central themes and motifs in American literature which he knew all too well as a student of English and an incipient writer. Only twelve years later, however, after two novels, a collection of stories, and a National Book Award, did he manage to translate his experience into literary expression when he published his third novel, *A New Life* (1961).

---

[67] Winifred Farrant Bevilacqua's article "The Revision of the Western in E. L. Doctorow's *Welcome to Hard Times*," *American Literature*, 61 (1989), 78-95, which came to my attention only after the completion of the manuscript, mainly corresponds with my own reading.

[68] Bernard Malamud, *A New Life* (New York: Pocket Books, 1973), p. 305.

[69] Leslie Fiedler, "The Many Names of S. Levin: An Essay in Genre Criticism," in *The Fiction of Bernard Malamud*, ed. by Richard Astro and Jackson J. Benson (Corvallis, Oregon: Oregon State University Press, 1977), pp. 149-161; here p. 155.

[70] For Greeley's proverbial injunction, which was first formulated in an editorial for August 25, 1836, in his journal *The New Yorker*, see p. 126.

This novel is both a thinly disguised *roman à clef* about Malamud's own experiences as an Eastern stranger in a closely knit Western community[71] and a knowledgeable comment on the American myth of the West and its role in both classic American literature and post-World War II American politics. Consequently, the novel denies easy classification, for it combines a college novel satirically unveiling the hair-raising short-comings of a disastrously incompetent academic institution, a love story probing both the destructive and the redeeming effects of love outside the moral bounds set by society, a political novel concerned with the troubled American fifties, and what Fiedler rightly calls "a neo- or meta-Western"[72] dealing not only with life in the West but also with the popular formula of the western. This is why critics have found it difficult to come to terms with *A New Life* and why they have commonly complained that its diverse strands are not sufficiently integrated. Such reproaches as Richman's, that the novel is "really two books,"[73] or Mandel's, that "the comic and satiric elements do not function thematically in relation to the novel's serious theme,"[74] have only recently been rejected as unwarranted.[75] The controversial question of the novel's artistic unity, however, will not be my concern. I will deal with *A New Life* as a fictional comment on the function of art and imagination in a world of pragmatism and utilitarian interests and as an emphatic rejection of the myth of the Edenic West as a mere pretext for the evasion of responsibility. For this purpose, I will offer a close reading of the opening chapter, the complexity of which has gone unrecognized in previous criticism, and then attempt to unravel the rich texture of literary allusions which make the book's fumbling protagonist a fallen American Adam in a deceptive Garden of Eden and which testify to the necessity of the 'fortunate fall' as a prerequisite for the achievement of human maturity.

---

71 See Richard Astro, "In the Heart of the Valley: Bernard Malamud's *A New Life*," in *Bernard Malamud: A Collection of Critical Essays*, ed. by Leslie A. Field and Joyce W. Field (Englewood Cliffs, N.J.: Prentice-Hall, 1975), pp. 143-155.
72 Leslie A. Fiedler, "The Many Names of S. Levin: An Essay in Genre Criticism," p. 150.
73 Sidney Richman, *Bernard Malamud* (New York: Twayne Publishers, 1966), p. 82.
74 Ruth B. Mandel, "Bernard Malamud's *The Assistant* and *A New Life*: Ironic Affirmation," *Critique: Studies in Modern Fiction*, 7 (1965), 110-121; here p. 118.
75 See John A. Barsness, "*A New Life*: The Frontier Myth in Perspective," *Western American Literature*, 3 (1969), 297-302; and Iska Alter, *The Good Man's Dilemma: Social Criticism in the Fiction of Bernard Malamud* (New York: AMS Press, 1981).

The novel opens with "S. Levin, formerly a drunkard," arriving "after a long and tiring transcontinental journey" in the little Western town of "Marathon, Cascadia" on the evening "of the last Sunday in August, 1950" (1).[76] He is "bearded, fatigued, lonely" and looks hopefully "around in a strange land for welcome" (1). These very first sentences establish the traditional narrative formula of 'Enter Mysterious Stranger,' which Malamud had so convincingly used in his previous novel, *The Assistant*,[77] and they suggest an analogy between Levin's predicament and that of the weary immigrant looking around for welcome in a strange land after a transatlantic journey. But Bishop Berkeley's westward course of empire and Hector St. John de Crèvecoeur's great circle have reached another stage, and Levin's Ellis Island has mutated into Marathon, Cascadia, the fictional equivalent of Corvallis, Oregon, with Cascadia referring to an actual western mountain range, "the Cascades" (2). Instead of the promised land of America, then, Levin has reached the promised land of the American West, and it is certainly no accident that his destination bears the name of the place at which the 'Western' Athenians beat the 'Eastern' Persians in 490 B.C., thus ringing in one of the greatest flowerings of democracy and the humanities.

Levin is met by a man "with a rich head of red hair" (1) who introduces himself as "Dr. Gilley" (1), thus insinuating that he has received the Ph.D. which Levin still must aquire as "your union card if you want to stay in college teaching" (18), and by Dr. Gilley's wife, a "tall, flat-chested woman in a white linen dress" (1) named Pauline. But the expected 'red-white-and-blue' of this opening 'American' tableau does not come off because what Levin has to add to Gilley's red hair and Pauline's white dress is his "black fedora" (1), a piece of clothing that immediately gives him away as an Eastern stranger in Western surroundings. With Levin's luggage stowed away in the trunk of Gilley's car, the three drive off, and the fact that they are all sitting in front, with Pauline squeezed in between the two men, foreshadows coming developments.

---

76 All page numbers in brackets refer to the pocketbook edition of *A New Life* as given in note 68.
77 See Peter Freese, *Bernard Malamud's 'The Assistant': Interpretations and Suggestions for Teaching* (Paderborn: Schöningh, 1983), p. 191.

Looking out at "a broad farm-filled valley between distant mountain ranges laden with forests, the vast sky piled high with towering masses of golden clouds" (2), the Eastern Jew is overwhelmed by the grandeur and majesty of a landscape reminiscent of Albert Bierstadt's colossal paintings: "My God, the West, Levin thought. He imagined the pioneers in covered wagons entering this valley for the first time, and found it a moving thought." (2) What he knew so far only from literature has miraculously become reality. Like a latter-day Huckleberry Finn, Levin has managed to 'light out for the Territory,' and fleeting images of the pioneers cross his excited mind. His "sense of having done the right thing in leaving New York" (2) is renewed, and when he learns from Pauline that beyond the coastal range there is "the Pacific" (2), all he can say is "marvelous" (2). The urban Jew from the New York ghetto finds himself on the verge of a new birth. He has exchanged the claustrophobic tenements of the Lower East Side for the vast sky of the pastoral Northwest, the East River for the Pacific, and his intention to begin anew seems decidedly feasible. A little later he will say "One always hopes that a new place will inspire change - in one's life" (15), thereby conjuring up the popular myth of a new start in the Edenic landscape of the West.

Gilley asks him "Seymour shortens to Sy - isn't that right?" (3), encourages him to call him Gerald and comments: "People aren't too formal out this way. One of the things you'll notice about the West is its democracy." (3) Here another stereotype is called up, namely, Frederick Jackson Turner's influential notion of "the promotion of democracy in the West,"[78] which Owen Wister made a stock-in-trade ingredient of the western when he wrote *The Virginian* as "an expression of American faith" and as an example of how the United States could stand "the test of Democracy."[79] But in *A New Life* this belief is subtly undercut because Gilley's earlier insistence on being "Dr. Gilley" signals to the attentive reader that myth and reality might not always concur.

Pauline then points out the "huge snow-capped peak" of "Mt. Chief Joseph" (3), and thus Malamud implicitly refers to the chieftain of the

---

78 Frederick Jackson Turner, "The Significance of the Frontier in American History," p. 562.
79 Owen Wister, *The Virginian: A Horseman of the Plains*, p. xv.

Nez Perces who surrendered in 1887. This Indian leader's famous speech in 1879 in Washington - "Treat all men alike. Give them all the same law. Give them all an even chance to live and grow. All men were made by the same Great Spirit Chief"[80] - and the cruel way he and his tribe were driven away from their hunting grounds give the lie to Gilley's boast about Western democracy. The name of Mount Chief Joseph, however, bears another, much more complex meaning which has to do with the ingenious onomasiological games Malamud plays with his characters' names. The epigraph of *A New Life* is taken from Joyce's *Ulysses* and reads: "Lo, levin leaping lightens / in eyeblink Ireland's westward welkin!" This quotation implies not only a reference to Levin's "westward" movement but also establishes as one of the many meanings of the protagonist's name that of the poetic noun 'levin,' that is, '(flash of) lightning.' Levin, as the novel will bear out, functions as the light from the East which illuminates the darkness of ignorance and narrow-mindedness of the Western college, and it is no accident that later on the cracked glass in his office will remind him of "forked lightning" (211). Moreover, Levin is the 'leaven,' the yeast, the spreading and transforming influence which produces fermentation. Malamud confirmed this pun to Tony Tanner and admitted that it was meant to suggest "what the marginal Jew may bring in attitude to the American scene."[81] A third reference, made more probable by Malamud's use of the same analogy in his previous novel *The Assistant*, is that to Tolstoy's Levin from *Anna Karenina*, and a fourth meaning, of course, is that which defines Levin as a Jew by relating him to Israel's priestly tribe of the Levites.

The same complexity can be found in Levin's first name. Introduced as Seymour, he is defined as the one who, like Salinger's Seymour Glass, can 'see more' because he has acquired a degree of maturity bred only by suffering. But soon - "Seymour shortens to Sy - isn't that right?" (3) - he becomes Sy, a version that reminds one of 'sigh' and that foreshadows the new suffering he will have to live through. Later Pauline, by then Levin's mistress, will say "I love you, Lev.

---

[80] Chief Joseph, "Broken Promises," in *Looking Far West: The Search for the American West in History, Myth, and Literature*, ed. by Frank Bergon and Zeese Papanikolas (New York: Mentor Books, 1978), pp. 51-52; here p. 51.
[81] Tony Tanner, *City of Words: American Fiction 1950 - 1970* (London: Jonathan Cape, 1971), p. 330.

That's my name for you. Sy is too much like sigh, Lev is closer to love" (204), thus adding a new variation. And in the end, when he leaves the West with pregnant Pauline as his wife-to-be and her two adopted children on the way to yet another 'new life,' he corrects her when she calls him Lev and says "Sam, they used to call me home" (343). Seymour/Sy/Lev/Sam Levin/leaven/the light-bringing Levite, then, goes through many stages. His protean name signals that he is a tortured and unintegrated man in search of himself, and it indicates his function as the leavening element in a petrified community. It is within this complex pattern of literary allusions that Pauline's reference to Mount Chief Joseph acquires additional significance because later we will learn that her "maiden name was Josephson" and that "Joseph was [her] father's name" (338). Mount Chief Joseph, then, could also be a subtle allusion to the woman who points it out to Levin and who will soon function as a female 'Joseph,' that is, a "fruitful bough"[82] for him.

After a short drive, Levin and the Gilleys reach the little college town in which Levin is to begin his teaching career, and Gilley introduces it as "Easchester" (3). Here, again, the name is programmatic, and Alter rightly points out its many implications when she observes:

> First, the environment is clearly not the EAST, so says the absence of that *t*. Second, such a designation defines a world of EASE, where achievement, success, happiness are meant to come EASY and without pain. Third, the word CHESTER, derived from the latin word *castra* meaning camp or fortress, and the Old English word *ceaster* meaning walled town, describes, in fact, what the town really is, armed against the complexities of the world beyond Cascadia. This symbolic location may indeed be the paradisal garden [...].[83]

Easchester thus turns out to be a latter-day variation of the *hortus conclusus* with Pauline, who looks "like a lily on a long stalk" (1), playing Eve to the newly arrived Adam. Another ironic reason why the western town could not be named Westchester is the fact that God "planted a garden *east*ward in Eden."[84] But there is more to Gilley's short introduction. When he points out the college where Levin is to

---

82 Genesis 49:22.
83 Iska Alter, *op. cit.*, p. 30.
84 Genesis 2:8.

teach, he says: "that tall building just over those trees is Chem Engineering. That one is the new Ag building. You can't see Humanities Hall, where we hang out [...]" (3). Later a shocked Levin will discover "that Cascadia College wasn't a liberal arts college" (22), but "mostly a science and technology college" (22). This is prefigured by the symbolically charged fact that Chemical Engineering is in a "tall" and Agriculture is in a "new" building, whereas the Humanities building cannot be seen.

When they reach the Gilleys' flower-decked house, Levin remembers that he has a recently purchased copy of *Western Birds, Trees and Flowers* in his valise, and this reveals him once more as the Eastern greenhorn or tenderfoot come West to discover the wonders of unspoilt nature. Levin, the former drunkard set upon a new life, declines the proffered welcome drink, and when Gilley toasts "To a successful career for Sy" (5), Malamud ironically refers to a famous line from American literary history. This becomes more obvious a little later when the head of department, Professor Fairchild, says to Levin on his first visit: "I greet you at the beginning of a great career" (48), using the exact wording from Emerson's letter to Walt Whitman following the publication of *Leaves of Grass*.[85]

Levin learns that he will live in the same apartment in which, eighteen years ago, Gilley spent his first week in Easchester, and it will soon become obvious that this is not going to be the only thing the new instructor will take over from his host. While they engage in polite conversation, Levin looks around the room and sees "a black and white print of a hunter shooting at a bird" (5). A little later Pauline will tell him that her husband is "an excellent photographer" and especially "talented at candid shots" (12). The most important of his 'shots,' which will play a crucial role in the further action, is the picture which Gilley, 'hunting' his wife and her lover, secretly took of naked Pauline and Leo Duffy. And, since Pauline soon turns out to be

---

85 See Emerson's letter to Walter Whitman of July 21, 1855: "I find incomparable things said incomparably well [in *Leaves of Grass*], as they must be. I find the courage of treatment, which so delights me, and which large perception only can inspire. I greet you at the beginning of a great career, [...]." Quoted from the reprint in *The Norton Anthology of American Literature*, ed. by Nina Baym et al. (New York and London: W. W. Norton, 3rd rev. ed., 1989), vol. I, p. 1077.

a rather queer 'bird,' the print assumes prophetic significance. The same holds true for Gilley's information that Levin will be the "twenty-first man" (6) in the department because it foreshadows the disruption, the coming-of-age, as it were, which the 'leaven' from the East will bring to the complacent Western college.

Pauline, who has "been talking for years about visiting New York" (6) and who thus demonstrates that she is as keen on going to the city of the East as Levin is on coming to the country of the West, serves a quickly prepared supper, significantly consisting of "tuna fish and mashed potatoes" (7), and accidentally drops a hot gob of it into Levin's lap. This is not only the first of many ludicrous misfortunes of the Jewish *shlemiel* come West but also another pointer towards events to come. Trying to make up for her clumsiness, Pauline literally forces Levin to put on a pair of her husband's pants so she can wash and iron Levin's stained trousers. Thus, Levin takes over Gilley's former apartment and, a few hours after his arrival, he wears Gilley's pants - a certain sign for the astute reader that soon he will also take possession of Gilley's wife.

Gilley, we learn from Pauline, is "a wonderful dry fly fisherman" (12), and now his name too assumes symbolic significance. The man who likes to fish and who later tries to make the bookish Jew join him on a fishing expedition (with Levin answering that he is content with reading Izaak Walton [30], referring to *The Compleat Angler* of 1653), fittingly bears a name that refers to 'gills,' the respiratory organs of fishes. We will learn in due time that Gilley is sterile (178), his two children being adopted. It will then become obvious that, like Pop Fisher in Malamud's first novel, *The Natural* (1952),[86] he is the maimed Fisher King presiding over the spiritual wasteland of an illiberal college and that Levin is cast in the role of the questing knight-errant, bringing the light from the East and searching, "lance at his side" (127), for his personal "grail" (181) which, since he is looking for it in the "Eden" (133) of the West, he can self-ironically define as "my manifest destiny" (101). In this context, Pauline's characterization of her husband as a dry-fly fisherman turns out to be one of Malamud's un-

---

[86] For Malamud's ingenious 'Americanization' of the Grail Quest see Peter Freese, "Parzival als Baseballstar: Bernard Malamuds *The Natural*," *Jahrbuch für Amerikastudien*, 13 (1968), 143-157.

erring puns because the sterile lover of photography is a man with a 'dry fly.'

When the children come in to look at the stranger, little Eric begins to cry, and Gilley caustically comments "Bet it's the beard" (9). Levin, who has grown his beard to signal a new beginning - "It's - er - given me a different view of myself" (20) - must learn that the cherished Western democracy is more myth than reality because in Easchester a bearded man is "an oddball" (20) and the College President's wife is quoted as having observed that "every time she lays eyes on a beard the thought of a radical pops up in her head" (20). But Levin, who cherishes his beard - "I felt a new identity" (188) - and who will only take it off, in true Malamudian fashion,[87] when he enters another 'new life' (229, 310), counters Gilley's illiberal view by suggesting that he might hang up a picture of Abraham Lincoln in his office. The little boy soon calms down, getting used to the strange beard much more easily than the adult 'democrats' of Easchester, and he asks Levin "something that sounded like 'Tory?'" (9). Levin, always "fortune's fool" (246) and a man "who creates his own peril" (54), does not realize that the boy asks for a 'story' but answers "No, I'm a liberal" (9), thus giving himself away as what conservative Westerners will consider a radical. But this is not the end of his embarrassment, for, while Eric is sitting on his lap, he urinates, and Levin has to change his pants another time.

Thus, Levin's "first night in the Northwest" (8), which has brought him "so far out" (8), is filled with a series of hilarious mishaps, and when he can finally sit down, attired in his freshly ironed pants, his eyes come to rest on a bookcase with *"The American*, Henry James" (11). Here Malamud plants another deft clue to the novel's further unfolding. In James's early novel, Christopher Newman, the *new man* from the continent discovered by *Christopher* Columbus, goes to Paris to be confronted with the crucial difference between American and French ways of conduct, and thus, within the different context of the 'international theme,' he goes through an experience similar to that of

---

[87] See Peter Freese, "Bernard Malamud," in *Amerikanische Literatur der Gegenwart in Einzeldarstellungen*, ed. by Martin Christadler (Stuttgart: Kröner, 1973), pp. 105-128; here pp. 111f.

the Eastern Jew confronted with the mores of the West. And when Pauline reacts to Levin's mentioning of the novel by telling him about her husband's earlier scholarly pursuits and presents as proof "a short article on Howells" (11) produced by Gilley at the beginning of his career, the choice of the subject is again symptomatic. Gilley, who has long ago given up all attempts at research and considers scholarly papers "a bore" (12), picked an author whose insistence on a tasteful realism and 'the more smiling aspects of life' concur with his own ideas of proper conduct, and Gilley's present hobby of photography, that is, of the capturing of surface reality, logically continues such an attitude.

Trying to account for her husband's loss of interest in literature, Pauline makes a very revealing statement when she says: "Nature here can be such an esthetic satisfaction that one slights others" (12). This, of course, is another popular assumption behind the myth of the West. But Levin, the refugee from a troubled urban past who is overwhelmed by his new experience of nature and hopes that it will have a healing effect upon him, will soon have to learn that the promise of the West as a redemptive environment is an illusion. Easchester turns out to be a town "without visible or tangible connection with the past. Nature was the town's true history" (69), and that is not enough to provide the necessary context for cultural and individual self-definition. The complacent citizens of Easchester, who refuse to take notice of "the world outside Easchester" (85), attempt to replace the town's non-existent past with the Western myth of its *ex nihilo* creation and thus deprive themselves of a meaningful identity, which cannot be achieved without what Henry James called 'a useable past.' The past-haunted Eastern Jew, who time and again has to realize that his attempt at a new beginning is self-delusory and who knows all too well "how past-drenched present time was" (22), will later confront Gilley with the famous quotation from George Santayana: " [...] if you don't remember the past you were condemned to relive it." (271) Gilley is too stupid to realize that "the past is all that makes the present coherent,"[88] but Pauline seems to be aware of the questionable nature of her statement when she says a little later about Easchester "how sheltered we are, landlocked, and bland" (16), and thus significantly rela-

---

88 James Baldwin, *Notes of a Native Son* (London: Corgi Books, 1969), p. 4.

tivizes the attitude of her husband, who would "swear that Easchester is paradise" (16).

If Easchester is, as the Western myth would have it, a paradise, a garden of Eden that promises a new beginning unfettered by the burdens of the past, then the alleged innocence of its inhabitants is nothing but ignorance. And then Levin, the man who is pursued by the failures of his past and who soon realizes that a new beginning is impossible and undesirable, becomes the bearer of light, or, in Latin, Lucifer, who brings knowledge into Eden and, through both his private and his public actions, forces the Westerners to face moral ambivalence and to give up their "unearned innocence" (13, 255). In this context, it becomes quite significant that Levin wants "to teach literature" (18), to deal with the imaginary projections of the buried life, whereas Gilley, the superficial pragmatist and photographer of surface reality, placidly states that he "prefer[s] teaching comp to lit" because it brings "more satisfaction" (18) and results in measurable improvement.

Many more examples could be adduced to show that Malamud's perfectly structured introductory chapter contains *in nuce* all the themes and motifs of the novel to come. It not only foreshadows both the academic conflict between a service-orientated teacher of composition and an enthusiastic believer in the liberating potential of great literature and the moral entanglements to develop from a triangle of two men and one woman, but it also introduces Malamud's criticism of the mendacity of the myth of the West by thematizing the task of man's self-realization in relation to nature and culture. With regard to the latter theme, the novel makes subtle use of a wide range of classic American literature, which provides Levin's development with representative meaning.

The action of *A New Life* begins in August 1950 and covers about a year, unfolding in accordance with both the seasonal cycle of nature and the sequence of the academic year. Malamud makes it quite clear that 1950 marks a special time in American history when he says:

> The cold war blew on the world like an approaching glacier. The Korean war flamed hot, although less hopelessly for America. The

> country had become, in fear and self-accusation, a nation of spies and communists. Senator McCarthy held in his hairy fist everyman's name. And there were rumors of further frightening intercourse between scientists and atomic things. America was in the best sense of a bad term, un-American. Levin was content to be hidden amid forests and mountains in an unknown town in the Far West. (89)

This and similar references to the nationwide state of affairs make it obvious that the struggle between the self-styled conservatives of Easchester and the romantic liberal Levin in the English department of a Cow College in the allegedly democratic West is but a small-scale reflection of a larger conundrum. These are the days when the whole country is "frightened silly of Alger Hiss and Whittaker Chambers, Communist spies and Congressional committees" (213). American democracy is "defended by cripples who crippled it" (213), the mere wearing of a beard makes one suspected of being "a radical" (20), and people who articulate liberal ideas are denounced as "fellow-traveling radical[s]" (42). Consequently, Levin's single-handed quixotic fight for the liberal arts against service-orientated grammar courses is not only a fictional projection of Malamud's attempt to come to terms with his own outsider position at Corvallis but also a representative comment on central aspects of American history and mythology.

It soon becomes clear to Levin that it is impossible to evade political obligations by hiding "amid forests and mountains in an unknown town in the Far West" (89) and that nature can be no equivalent of culture. Moreover, the fronts are fast established. The same Gilley who had extolled the "democracy" (3) of the West now talks about Cascadia as "a conservative state" (25) and defends his choices by saying that "we have the Russkies to think about" (25). The chairman of the department, an academic bungler appropriately named Fairchild, defines the function of the teaching of English as "to satisfy the needs of the professional schools on the campus with respect to written communication" (36) and argues that foresters, farmers and engineers are much more important than English majors because "you can't fell a tree, run a four-lane highway over a mountain, or build a dam with poetry" (36). The college president Dr. Labhart is of the opinion that "Plato, Shelley, and Emerson have done more harm than good to society" (268), and the department's alleged scholar and self-proclaimed liberal, Dr. Fabrikant, whom the Depression drove from

Harvard to the Far West, has turned into a malevolent coward because Easchester values neither his research nor his questionable liberalism. He is a disillusioned romantic who extolls the achievement of the Western pioneers and discards their contemporay descendants as "pygmies" afraid "that tomorrow will be different from today" (101), without realizing that he himself has become a 'Fabrikant,' a *fabric*ator of mere *cant*.[89] When Malamud depicts this disgruntled loser tending a lonely cow named Lady Macbeth (66) and gallopping across the countryside on horseback, looking like "U.S. Grant" without "his whiskey barrel" (66), the cowboy myth is hilariously debunked and the popular Western cliché of self-sufficient manhood is revealed as a mere 'fabrication.'

Levin, who began his new life as a dedicated student and teacher after a phase as alcoholic bum and dropout, now bases his conviction that only the liberal arts can ensure true humanity on his life-changing vision which taught him "that life is holy" (187). He single-handedly takes on the bunch of complacent anti-intellectuals that make up the staff of the English Department and tries to convince them that ideas must be taught before tools and techniques can be passed on. His function as a voice of romantic idealism crying in the wilderness of superficial utilitarianism is not made easier when he sleeps with one of his students, has an abortive sexual encounter with a spinsterish colleague, and begins a complicated affair with Pauline Gilley. The tragicomic outcome of his battle makes him realize that he cannot run away from his "past-contaminated self" (154) and that "his escape to the West" has "come to nothing" (154). He learns that "space [is] corrupted by time" (154), that is, that the allegedly redemptive landscape of the West cannot blot out the sins of his past in the East. Thus his outward failure but inner victory not only gives the lie to the American myth of starting anew in the West, but also convincingly demonstrates that "the notion of a clean break with history that was the heritage of all American emigrants, had always ignored the hard core of evidence that nature did not automatically provide the good life nor intuitively compel virtue."[90] Through a complex pattern of allusions and references Levin's process of recognition and purgation also offers

---

89 See Iska Alter, *op. cit.*, p. 42.
90 John A. Barsness, *op. cit.*, p. 197.

a running commentary on classic American literature and contrasts the tragic world view of a Jewish-American author writing "in defense of the human"[91] with the idealism of those American writers who extolled the possibilities of the virgin land.

When early in the novel an enthused Levin wanders around in the forest, he enjoys "the mystery of the wood, the presence of unseen life in natural time, and the feeling that few men had been where he presently was" (182), but his elation is ironically debunked when he realizes that he is in an area used for experimenting by the Department of Forestry. Here a twentieth-century New York Jew pretends to be a latter-day Leatherstocking, and at first glance it seems small wonder that Levin "now understood the soul of Natty Bumppo, formerly paper" (182). But this romantic act of empathy, in which an intellectual plays at reliving a pastoral scene he has read about, is subtly undercut when Levin envisages a sign reading "Here, D. Boone CILLED A BAR" (182) and thus compounds James Fenimore Cooper's fictional protagonist and the actual figure of the Kentucky woodsman into a single romantic archetype complete with uneducated spelling. But only a few minutes after his dreams, Levin meets Pauline, and they fall upon the ground and consummate their long-smouldering passion "in the open forest, nothing less, what triumph!" (185).

In contrast to chaste Leatherstocking, whose "sweetheart [is] in the forest"[92] and who withdraws from the civilizing force of woman into the security of male friendship, Levin has his pastoral idyll invaded by illicit sexuality. Thus it becomes ironically evident that Cooper's vision of solitary man's self-realization in the redemptive wilderness of a virgin continent can be no more than a fleeting self-delusion for Levin "from the East" (1), and it is much more appropriate when he later thinks of himself as the protagonist of another and gloomier writer, namely, Nathaniel Hawthorne, whose great novel of adultery also features a decisive scene in the forest: "Levin had sulfurous visions of himself as Arthur Dimmesdale Levin, locked in stocks on a platform in the town square, a red A stapled on his chest" (227). But

---

91 Haskel Frankel, "Bernard Malamud," [Interview] *Saturday Review*, September 10, 1966, pp. 39-40; here p. 40.
92 James Fenimore Cooper, *The Deerslayer; or, The First War-Path: A Tale* (New York: W. A. Townsend and Company, 1861), p. 146.

his carnality is not the only fact that makes Levin incapable of inhabiting the virgin wilderness of Cooper's Lake Glimmerglass; he also has to learn that he can never be the first: "Let's admit - wherever Levin had been, someone had been before (no Chingachgook he, even in the primeval forest, even forest of the night)." (305) For Levin, the myth of a new beginning in the Edenic forest turns out to be nothing but a myth and he has to learn again that every present is necessarily predicated upon a past. The romantic idealist who "gave up the Metropolitan Museum of Art" and got in exchange a Lawrentian "love in a haystack" (75) must recognize that "part of the experience of paradise was when it was no longer paradise" (230), that maturity can only be reached after 'Paradise Lost.'

Another classic American view of redemptive nature is the Thoreauvian vision, and this too proves unattainable to Levin. Early in the novel, he "momentarily thought of himself as a latter-day Thoreau, but gave that up - he had come too late to nature" (52). Later he attempts to console himself that the smallness of Easchester does not really matter: "Had not Concord been for Thoreau a sufficient mininature of the universe?" (70) Gilley, the advocate of direct sensory experience, admonishes Levin to go out to hunt and fish, asking "How will you ever teach Thoreau, once you have your Ph. D., without ever in your life having been to a wild place?" Levin answers "I've been to Walden Pond - " (269). Of course, this is an ironically appropriate answer to a man who thinks one cannot teach Thoreau without having imitated his experience *and* having acquired an academic degree. But the references to Thoreau also remind the reader that Levin's steadfast sticking to his principles bears some close resemblance to the convictions of the author of "Civil Disobedience." And Thoreau's idea that the West was not so much an actual place as a state of the mind[93] points to the very solution which Levin will reach when he overcomes his delusion and discards the popular cliché of the West as a lie. Again, however, the major point which Malamud makes is that a historical experience cannot be repeated and that doing the same thing in a different historical situation is not the same thing. Thus - and here the message is couched in yet another literary analogy - Levin, although he "obsessively seek[s] what was lost - unlived - in the past,"

---

93 See Edwin Fussell, *op. cit.*, pp. 184f.

must learn that he has really "no wish to be [...] Gatsby" (129) because in contrast to Fitzgerald's romantic dreamer he has painfully recognized that "you can't repeat the past."[94]

To Levin, then, the Transcendentalists' elevation of the joys of unspoilt nature over the burden of history and Emerson's injunction that one should not "grope among the dry bones of the past" but instead replace tradition with insight and achieve "an original relation to the universe"[95] cannot be realized. Levin is initially led astray by the Transcendentalist concept of man's immediate relation to nature, but later he learns that his must be the position of Washington Irving who deplored the absence of "storied and poetical association,"[96] that is, the shared memory of human history, in the unrelated greatness of an American landscape referring to nothing but itself.

Levin listens secretly to Fabrikant's "course in liberalism in American literature" (31) and thus hears portions of lectures on "The Noble Savage in James Fenimore Cooper," "Huck Finn's River Journey," and "The American Past" (211). When Fabrikant proceeds from these topics, all of which are subtly related to Levin's life, to "Emerson" (212), Levin hears him recite "Whoever would be a man must be a nonconformist. He who would gather immortal palms must not be hindered by the name of goodness ..." (216). This famous statement from "Self-Reliance"[97] seems to sum up Levin's own position because he is a stubborn non-conformist insisting upon his principles, and his affair with Pauline violates what society considers 'good.' So Levin can rightly sigh "Amen" when Fabrikant goes on with the quotation "Nothing at last is sacred but the integrity of your mind" (216). Later, however, when he gives up Pauline "out of love" (224) and then takes her back "on principle" (326), Levin learns that individualistic nonconformity is not enough, but that consideration for others, the wil-

---

94 F. Scott Fitzgerald, *The Great Gatsby* in *The Bodley Head Scott Fitzgerald* (London: Bodley Head, rpt. 1977), vol. I, p. 106.
95 Ralph Waldo Emerson, "Nature," in his *Essays and Lectures* (New York: The Library of America, 1983), p. 7.
96 Washington Irving, *The Sketch-Book of Geoffrey Crayon, Gent.* (New York and London: G. P. Putnam's Sons, 1894), vol. I, p. 3.
97 Ralph Waldo Emerson, "Self-Reliance," in *The Complete Works of Ralph Waldo Emerson* (New York: AMS Press, 2nd ed., 1979; reprint of the Centenary Edition, Boston: Houghton Mifflin, 1903-1904), vol. II, *Essays: First Series*, p. 50.

lingness to accept responsibility, and 'Pauline' charity are the prerequisites for the "new life" (see, e.g., 154, 156, 181, 189, 303) which he so desperately seeks.

Another classic author repeatedly referred to is Herman Melville. On the one hand, the characteristically Malamudian fish-symbolism that pervades the novel functions within the larger context of the Waste Land analogies, but on the other it refers to *the* 'fish' in American literature, namely, the white whale. Melville is first mentioned when Gilley, at work on a "picture book of American lit[erature]" (28) by cutting suitable photos from *Life*, argues that contemporary students who "can't tell Herman Melville from the Smith Brothers on the cough drop box" (28) should be given a chance "to see what some of our writers looked like" (28). Later, Levin thinks about appropriate subjects for an article he plans to write. He discards "The Forest as Battleground of the Spirit in Some American Novels" and "The Stranger as Fallen Angel in Western Fiction" (248), topics which are so closely related to his own function as a stranger appearing like a fallen angel in the forests of the West that he shies away from them. He then briefly considers "The American Ideal as Self-created Tradition" (248), a theme he cannot live up to because by now he has lost faith in the belief that "the idea of America will always create freedom" (248). And he rejects both "White Whale as Burden of Dark World" and "Moby Dick as Closet Drama" (248), although he likes "the idea of an intellectual task, the whale on his head, relief through balancing the weight on the heart" (248). The dissociation of 'head' and 'heart' alluded to in his reasoning is Captain Ahab's great mistake and thus establishes another subtle parallel between Levin's state of mind and Melville's great novel. Thus it is small wonder that the theme proves so fascinating that later Levin picks it up again and attempts "to work on a paper about a white whale" (302). It might be too far-fetched to point to Melville's many comparisons of the whale with the West,[98] but here another field of cross-references could be implied.

In the same way in which most of the hopes and assumptions of Cooper, Thoreau and Emerson turn out to be unfeasible for the twentieth-century Jewish instructor seeking a 'new life' in a West which

---

98 See Edwin Fussell, *op. cit.*, pp. 273ff.

does not come up to its mythic promise, the proverbial statements of another founding father of American literature are ironically debunked by the very context in which they occur. Professor Fairchild has a "framed tapestried motto" (34) hanging in his office which reads:

> "STRANGERS ARE WELCOME HERE BECAUSE THERE IS ROOM FOR ALL OF THEM, AND THEREFORE THE OLD INHABITANTS ARE NOT JEALOUS OF THEM - ." B. Franklin (34)

But in the light of what Levin has already learned about the illiberalism and the xenophobia of the inhabitants of Easchester, this motto is only a pious hope which is daily disproved by a faulty reality. And when, much later in the novel, Levin secretly accompanies his frightened mistress home to her husband's house at daybreak and quotes "'Tis the rising, not the setting sun" by "B. Franklin" (233), a worried Pauline can only tersely comment "He was wrong" (233). When moody Levin goes once more through a phase of elation and deeply enjoys nature's annual rebirth, he thinks of Walt Whitman's calling the grass "God's handkerchief" (254), but it will soon turn out that the only purpose for which he will need a handkerchief is to dry his tears of renewed anxiety and desperation. The same ironic contradictoriness applies to Thomas Jefferson's well-known statement about the "natural aristocracy among men" (296) which Levin uses in his election platform for the departmental chairmanship and which, in view of his own questionable motives and the narrow-minded bickering among his non-aristocratic colleagues, is as much out of place as the reference to William James's essay on "The Social Value of the College Bred" (65).

There is no space to pursue the many hints at European authors from Plato and Shakespeare to Thomas Hardy, the subject of Malamud's thesis, and Lord Byron. What should have become obvious from the examples discussed, however, is the following: Malamud's protagonist who travels from the metropolis of the East to the wide open spaces of the West in order to begin 'a new life' and to overcome the haunting failures of his oppressive past in the redemptive landscape of a timeless Eden must learn that the Western myth of rebirth is a delusion, that space is always 'contaminated' by time, that there can be no worthwhile present without a useable past. Since he is a well-read intellectual, he cannot but experience the actual West through the 'storied and poetical associations' of classic American literature, but both the actual and the mythic West turn out to be failures. The twentieth-century West he encounters is inhabited by undemocratic and illiberal, intolerant and anti-intellectual people who successfully manage to resist the allegedly regenerative influence of their surroundings. And the mythic West evoked in Cooper's novels and in Emerson's and Thoreau's essays proves to be based on assumptions which Levin discovers to be faulty and immature.

Levin learns the hard way that the paradise man longs for can never be that of the prelapsarian Adam but only the Paradise Lost of fallen man, matured through sin and repentance. And the freedom man craves cannot be the superficial freedom of the roaming cowboy but ultimately only the freedom of the choice to do without it. Thus, Hawthorne's tragic vision of man's 'fortunate fall' and Melville's epistemological scepticism prove to be more acceptable than Cooper's dream of a solitary life in the unspoilt wilderness and Emerson's and Thoreau's optimism with regard to man's immediate relation to nature. Culture as the guiding memory of a shared human past is unrenounceable and cannot be replaced by mere nature, however unspoilt and fascinating it might be. A town of which it is said that "nature was [its] true history" and that it had nothing "to commemorate word or deed or any meaningful past event" (69) may be a 'paradise,' but the 'innocence' of its inhabitants can be nothing but ignorance. This is why literature acquires such central educational importance and why Levin preaches to his uncomprehending students that "the liberal arts, you can't get enough" (256).

The Eastern Jew, who finally comes into his own through a painful process of trial and error and recognizes, with a final touch of self-irony, that he is "chosen" (339) instead of choosing, defines his educational goal as "teaching how to keep civilization from destroying itself" (108). In view of both the general climate of his times, characterized by McCarthy's witch hunts, the Korean War, and frightening new discoveries in atomic weaponry, and the state of affairs in Easchester, characterized by the mendacious myth of instant Western democracy and by the substitution of nature for culture, Levin's position seems all the more necessary. And when he angrily declares with regard to the remedial grammar courses he is forced to teach: "I sometime feel I'm engaged in a great irrelevancy, teaching people how to write who don't know what to write" (107), he pithily sums up his, and Malamud's, liberal humanism which, as *A New Life* so convincingly demonstrates, cannot be replaced by the facile optimism of the mendacious myth of rebirth and regeneration in an Edenic West.

This imaginative conception of the discovery of the New World was published in 1621 in *Novo Typis Transacta Navigatio*.

Conclusion

The first insight which the book at hand should have furnished is this: from the very beginning, our hetero-images of 'America' have oscillated between delight and disgust, loving admiration and disappointed rejection. From Rodríguez de Montalvo's hopeful belief that the "island called California" is "very close to the side of the Terrestrial Paradise" to Lenau's enraged denunciation of all Americans as "himmelanstinkende Krämerseelen," and from Duden's praise of the paradisiacal living conditions in Missouri to Halfeld's revulsion against the American "Dollardiktatur" and its uncultured "Maschinenmenschen," our contradictory German *Amerikabilder* have revealed more about the hopes and fears of the subjects who projected them upon a strange 'other' than about the object they were meant to characterize. The consequence of this insight is obvious: any attempt at understanding the culture and literature of the United States must be preceded by what I would call an imagological stock-taking. We must investigate the experiential background of our individual images of 'America' and try to become aware of the degree to which we are unconsciously conditioned by the culturally transmitted hetero-images of 'America' which are part of our cultural matrix. For EFL-teachers aiming at providing their students with what is now fashionably called 'intercultural' understanding, such a stock-taking is even more important, because without it they will remain unaware of the generational differences between their images of 'America' and those of their students and will thus be bound to talk at cross-purposes.

Only after we have become sufficiently aware of the fact that our view of any foreign culture is ineluctably qualified, if not outrightly distorted, by the hetero-images of this 'other' which are part of our cultural heritage, can we proceed to a tentative investigation of the target-culture's auto-images, which help both to constitute its members' conception of themselves and to condition their way of life. In the case of 'America,' these auto-images coalesce in the complex and contradictory conundrum which is either admired as the 'American Dream' or denounced as the 'American Nightmare.' Any attempt at reconstructing this 'Dream' must concentrate on its constitutive elements, the most important of which I take to be

- the double promise of individual 'success' and societal 'progress,'
- the challenge of an open 'frontier,'
- the belief in a 'manifest destiny,' and
- the hope for either an ethnic and religious merging in a magical 'melting pot' or the friendly coexistence of diverse ethnic groups in a multicultural 'quilt.'

As cultural concepts, these elements, and with them their respective mixtures, are of course subject to historical change. Thus, the original religious motivation behind the striving for success as an indication of positive predestination gave way to utilitarian considerations; the concept of the frontier changed from a geographical into a social challenge to be then revived as the open frontier of space; the initial image of the melting pot was qualified into that of the salad bowl, brought forth the opposite positions of nativism and Anglo-Saxon racialism, and has only recently been replaced by the concept of multiculturalism. Consequently, any attempt at understanding the 'Dream' must combine a systematic and a historical perspective, because it is the continual interplay between the challenge of the foundation myths as kept alive and tested in the timeless works of literature and the limitations of every-day reality as recorded by historiography which constitutes the respective cultural context. As Baldwin said, "the past is all that makes the present coherent," and therefore some familiarity with the elements of the 'Dream' as unfolding and changing in time is a necessary prerequisite for any attempt at understanding 'America.'

Examining in detail the three most important elements of the 'Dream,' namely the myth of the 'Melting Pot' as the magic provider of equality for all, the myth of the attainability of personal 'Success' by means of hard work and frugal living, and the myth of the 'West' as a region of individual fulfilment in harmony with virgin nature, and looking for either confirmations or rejections of these myths in political rhetoric, promotional tracts and popular narratives on the one hand and in outstanding texts of American literature on the other, one finds an all-pervasive tension between hope and despair, fervent belief and cautionary scepticism and one realizes that American auto-images are even more contradictory than our prejudiced *Amerikabilder*. The popular belief in the 'Melting Pot' stands in stark opposition to the lesson of numerous initiation stories which depict 'growing up ethnic' as a painful process ending ever so often in pain and disillusionment; the ubiquitous promise of 'Success' is falsified by countless business novels which reveal that getting rich through shirt-sleeved business transactions is a dubious accomplishment to be paid for by a loss of humanity; and the triumphant visions of popular western tales and films are exposed as mendacious lies which differ greatly from an historical reality which is defined by ethnocide, greed, and moral failure.

This, however, does not at all mean that by now the central elements of the 'American Dream' can be safely rejected as fraudulent because American authors themselves call them into question. Such a deduction would repeat the very mistake under which many know-all *Amerikakritiker* are labouring when they precipitately discard the constitutive 'American' foundation myths as having been disproved by the faulty reality of the United States, and it would ignore the considerable power which these myths still exert. Larry McMurtry, himself an accomplished writer of western novels, has recently commented on this issue with regard to the ongoing rewriting of the history of westward expansion. Observing that revisionist historians are presently bent upon demonstrating that "America's westward expansion was a mosaic of failure, financial and personal, but also, in the largest sense, moral," (34),[1] he concedes that these Revisionists are right in many respects and that the version of the earlier Triumphalists is in need of correction. But he also insists that the issue is not simply one of 'correct' historiography but "that the winning of the West was in large measure an imaginative act" (37) and that "the dream of the West as a place of freedom and opportunity has retained its energy virtually all the way through the 20th century, in defiance of hugely altered conditions, and also of a huge mass of negative fact" (37). This is the decisive point, which can likewise be made with regard to the ideas of 'Success' and the 'Frontier,' of 'Manifest Destiny' and the 'Melting Pot,' and which should make us realize that we cannot understand

---

1   All page numbers refer to Larry McMurtry, "The Winning of the West in Retrospect," *Dialogue*, No. 92 (1991), 34-39. See also the excellent catalogue that accompanied a 1991 revisionist exhibition of Western images, William H. Truettner, ed., *The West as America: Reinterpreting Images of the Frontier, 1820 - 1920* (Washington and London: The Smithsonian Institute Press, 1991).

'America' without learning about its central aspect, namely, the continuous interplay, both painful and creative, between its promises and its achievements, its mythical projections and its factual realities.

It is the very gulf between the enchanting promises of 'America' and the disillusioning reality of the United States which has time and again induced foreign observers to take Americans to task for not having come up to their pretensions. But such criticism has been voiced by Americans themselves from the very beginning, and the lasting opposition between the optimistic promises of political rhetoric and popular fiction on the one hand and the worried scepticism of poetic probing and fictional evocation on the other, an opposition which characterizes American cultural history, testifies to an indigenously 'American' tension bred by a gradually evolving culture beginning with high hopes and finding itself unable to sustain them. In the wake of Kennedy's influential study about the rise and fall of great powers,[2] it has become a fashionable parlour game to speculate about the foreseeable decline of the United States and to draw parallels between the collapse of Soviet communism and the impending end of the 'American Century;' and some defiant Americans have felt called upon to counter such prophesies by proclaiming the possibility of "The Second American Century."[3] In the contributions to this discussion by self-styled European experts on 'America' one not only finds countless simplifications and generalizations, but also many rash diagnoses of the American present and prognoses about the American future which reveal a deplorable ignorance about the American past. It is this very past and the cultural tradition which has evolved from it which we should try to acquaint ourselves with before we precipitately engage in self-righteous condemnations.

---

2 See Paul M. Kennedy, *The Rise and Fall of the Great Powers: Economic Change and Military Conflict from 1500 to 2000* (London: Unwin Hyman, 1988).
3 See Henry Grunwald, "The Second American Century," *Time*, October 8, 1990, pp. 46-51.

Haus- und Taschenbibliothek für Amerika-Auswanderer.
Zweiter Band.

Nützliches Reisebuch für Amerika.

Unentbehrliches Taschenbuch für Auswanderer nach Amerika, das über alle amerikanischen Verhältnisse, Reiserouten, Ansiedlung, Rechtsverhältnisse, Erwerb, Geld, Länderei-Käufe, Anbau, Handel und Gewerbe u. s. w. die genaueste Auskunft und Belehrung gibt.

Nach eigenen Erfahrungen und den besten Quellen bearbeitet von
Hans Rau in New-York.
Vierte verbesserte Auflage.
Mit 1 Karte von Amerika und Abbildungen der amerik. Gold- u. Silbermünzen.

Druck und Verlag der J. Ebner'schen Buchhandlung in Ulm.

Bibliography

ABBEY, Edward. *The Monkey Wrench Gang*. New York: Avon Books, 1976.
ACHILLES, Jochen. "Die Paradiesvorstellung von der Versöhnung des Menschen mit der Natur: Literaturgeschichtliche Betrachtungen zu einem Aspekt des amerikanischen Traumes." *Amerikastudien - American Studies*, 35 (1990), 203-218.
ACOSTA, Oscar Zeta. *The Autobiography of a Brown Buffalo*. San Francisco: Straight Arrow Books, 1972.
ADAMS, James Truslow. *The Epic of America*. Boston: Little, Brown and Company, 25th ed., 1943.
ADAMS, John. *The Works of John Adams, Second President of the United States: with a Life of the Author, Notes and Illustrations*, by His Grandson Charles Francis Adams. Boston: Little, Brown and Company, 1854.
ADAMS, Willi Paul. "Die Assimilationsfrage in der amerikanischen Einwanderungsdiskussion 1890 - 1930." *Amerikastudien - American Studies*, 27 (1982), 275-291.
ALBEE, Edward. *The American Dream*. New York: Coward-McCann, 1961.
ALGER, Horatio. *Ragged Dick and Struggling Upward*, ed. with an introduction by Carl Bode. New York: Viking Penguin, 1985.
ALTER, Iska. *The Good Man's Dilemma: Social Criticism in the Fiction of Bernard Malamud*. New York: AMS Press, 1981.
The American Dream. Fiftieth Anniversary Issue of *Newsweek*. Spring 1983.
AMES, Nathaniel. *The Essays, Humor, and Poems of Nathaniel Ames*, ed. by Samuel Briggs. Cleveland: Short & Forman, 1891.
ANAYA, Rudolfo. *Bless Me, Ultima*. No Place: Tonatiuh International Inc., 15th ed., 1983.
----, and Francisco A. LOMELI, eds. *Aztlán: Essays on the Chicano Homeland*. Albuquerque: Academia / El Norte, 1989.
APPEL, John, and Selma APPEL. "The Grand Old Sport of Hating Catholics: American Anti-Catholic Caricature Prints." *The Critic*, November/December 1971, pp. 50-58.
----. *The Distorted Image: Stereotype and Caricature in Popular American Graphics 1850 - 1922*. New York: The Anti-Defamation League of B'nai B'rith, no date.
ARNOLD, Marilyn. "History as Fate in E. L. Doctorow's Tale of a Western Town." In *E. L. Doctorow: Essays and Conversations*, ed. by Richard Trenner. Princeton, New Jersey: Ontario Review Press, 1983. Pp. 207-216.
----. "Doctorow's *Hard Times*: A Sermon on the Failure of Faith." *Literature and Belief*, 3 (1983), 87-95.
"Asians: To America with Skills." *Time*, July 8, 1985, pp. 32-34.
ASTRO, Richard. "In the Heart of the Valley: Bernard Malamud's *A New Life*." In *Bernard Malamud: A Collection of Critical Essays*, ed. by Leslie A. Field and Joyce W. Field. Englewood Cliffs, New Jersey: Prentice-Hall, 1975. Pp. 143-155.
ATHEARN, Robert G. *The Mythic West in Twentieth-Century America*. Lawrence: University Press of Kansas, 1986.
ATWAN, Robert, Donald McQUADE, and John W. WRIGHT. *Edsels, Luckies, and Frigidaires: Advertising the American Way*. New York: Delta Books, 1979.
AUFDERHEIDE, Patricia, ed. *Beyond P.C.: Toward a Politics of Understanding*. Saint Paul, Minnesota: Graywolf Press, 1992.
AUGENBRAUM, Harold, and Ilan STAVANS, eds. *Growing Up Latino: Memoirs and Stories*. New York: Houghton Mifflin, 1993.
BAKER, Warren J. "The Stereotyped Western Story: Its Latent Meaning and Psychoeconomic Function." *Psychoanalytic Quarterly*, 24 (1955), 270-280.

Bibliography

BAKER, Houston A., Jr., and Charlotte PIERCE-BAKER. "Patches: Quilts and Community in Alice Walker's 'Everyday Use.'" *The Southern Review,* 21, 3 (1985), 706-720.
BAKKER, J. "E. L. Doctorow's *Welcome to Hard Times*: A Reconsideration." *Neophilologus,* 69 (1985), 464-473.
BALDWIN, James. *Notes of a Native Son.* London: Corgi Books, 1969.
----. *Nobody Knows My Name: More Notes of a Native Son.* New York: Dell Books, 1967.
----. *The Devil Finds Work.* London: Corgi Books, 1978.
BAMBARA, Toni Cade. *Gorilla, My Love.* New York: Vintage Books, 1981.
----. "The Lesson." In *Growing up in a Multicultural Society: Nine American Stories,* ed. by Peter Freese. München: Langenscheidt-Longman, 1994. Pp. 51-67.
BANTA, Martha. *Failure and Success in America: A Literary Debate.* Princeton, New Jersey: Princeton University Press, 1978.
BARLOW, Joel. *The Works of Joel Barlow,* intr. by William K. Bottorff and Arthur L. Ford. Gainesville, Florida: Scholars' Facsimiles & Reprints, 1970.
BARSNESS, John A. "A New Life: The Frontier Myth in Perspective." *Western American Literature,* 3 (1969), 297-302.
BARTH, John. *The Sot-Weed Factor.* London: Panther Books, 1965.
BARTHELME, Donald. *Unspeakable Practices, Unnatural Acts.* New York: Bantam Books, 1969.
BARTON, Bruce. *The Man Nobody Knows: A Discovery of the Real Jesus.* Indianapolis: Bobbs-Merrill, 1925.
BASLER, Otto. "Amerikanismus: Geschichte des Schlagwortes." *Deutsche Rundschau,* 56 (August 1930), 142-146.
BAUSCHINGER, Sigrid, Horst DENKLER and Wilfried MALSCH, eds. *Amerika in der deutschen Literatur: Neue Welt - Nordamerika - USA.* Stuttgart: Philipp Reclam, 1975.
BAYM, Nina, et al., eds. *The Norton Anthology of American Literature.* 2 vols. New York and London: W. W. Norton, 3rd rev. ed., 1989; 4th rev. ed., 1994. - Accompanied by: Marjorie PRYSE. *Teaching with the Norton Anthology of American Literature, Fourth Edition: A Guide for Instructors.* New York and London: W. W. Norton, 1994.
BEARD, Henry, and Christopher CERF. *The Official Politically Correct Dictionary and Handbook.* New York: Villard Books, 1993.
BEATY, Jerome, and J. Paul HUNTER, eds. *New Worlds of Literature: Writings from America's Many Cultures.* New York and London: 2nd ed., 1994.
BEEBE, Lucius, and Charles CLEGG. *The American West: The Pictorial Epic of a Continent.* New York: Bonanza Books, 1955.
BEECHER, Lyman. *A Plea for the West.* Cincinnati: Truman and Smith, 2nd rev. ed., 1835.
BEHRMANN, Günter C. "Antiamerikanismus in der Bundesrepublik: 1966 - 1984." *Amerikastudien - American Studies,* 31 (1986), 341-349.
BELL, Daniel. *The Cultural Contradictions of Capitalism.* New York: Basic Books, 1976.
BELLAMY, Edward. *Looking Backward: 2000 - 1887.* New York: New American Library, 1960.
BELLOW, Saul. *The Dean's December.* Harmondsworth: Penguin Books, 1982.
----. *More Die of Heartbreak.* Harmondsworth: Penguin Books, 1988.
BERG, Peter. *Deutschland und Amerika 1918 - 1929: Über das deutsche Amerikabild der zwanziger Jahre.* Lübeck and Hamburg: Matthiesen Verlag, 1963.
BERGER, Thomas. *Little Big Man.* Greenwich, Connecticut: Fawcett Crest Books, no date.
BERGON, Frank, and Zeese PAPANIKOLAS, eds. *Looking Far West: The Search for the American West in History, Myth, and Literature.* New York: Mentor Books, 1978.

BERKELEY, George. *The Works of George Berkeley, Bishop of Cloyne*, ed. by A. A. Luce and T. E. Jessop. Nendeln: Kraus Reprint, 1979. [Reprint of the edition London and New York: Thomas Nelson and Sons, 1951].
BERMAN, Paul, ed. *Debating P.C.: The Controversy Over Political Correctness on College Campuses.* New York: Dell, 1992.
BERNARDO, Stephanie. *The Ethnic Almanac.* Garden City, New York: Doubleday, 1981.
BEVERIDGE, Albert J. *The Meaning of the Times and Other Speeches.* Indianapolis: Bobbs-Merrill, 1908.
----. "The March of the Flag." In *An American Primer*, ed. by Daniel J. Boorstin. New York: New American Library, 1985. Pp. 644-653.
BEVILACQUA, Winifred Farrant. "The Revision of the Western in E. L. Doctorow's *Welcome to Hard Times*." *American Literature*, 61 (1989), 78-95.
"Beyond the Melting Pot." *Time*, April 9, 1990, pp. 34-37.
BIERCE, Ambrose. *The Enlarged Devil's Dictionary*, ed. by Ernest Jerome Hopkins. Harmondsworth: Penguin Books, rpt. 1983.
BILLINGTON, Ray Allen. *The Protestant Crusade 1800 - 1860: A Study of the Origins of American Nativism.* New York: Macmillan, 1938.
----. *Westward Expansion: A History of the American Frontier.* New York: Macmillan, 1949.
----. ed. *The Frontier Thesis: Valid Interpretation of American History?* Huntington, New York: R. E. Krieger, 1977.
BINDER, Wolfgang. "Die Nordwanderung der Puertoricaner und ihre Literatur." In *Amerikanische Gettoliteratur: Zur Literatur ethnischer, marginaler und unterdrückter Gruppen in Amerika*, ed. by Berndt Ostendorf. Darmstadt: Wissenschaftliche Buchgesellschaft, 1983. Pp. 323-355.
BIRD, Robert Montgomery. *Nick of the Woods, or The Jibbenainosay.* Philadelphia: Carey, Lea & Blanchard, 1837.
BISCHOFF, Peter, ed. *America, the Melting Pot: Fact and Fiction.* Paderborn: Ferdinand Schöningh, 1978; and BISCHOFF, Peter. *America the Melting Pot: Fact and Fiction - Interpretations and Suggestions for Teaching.* Paderborn: Ferdinand Schöningh, 1978.
----. "'Westward the Star of Empire takes its way': Manifest Destiny and American Expansion; Ein Unterrichtsbaustein zum American Dream für den amerikakundlichen Unterricht in der Sekundarstufe II." *Englisch-Amerikanische Studien*, 1 (1979), 364-384.
----, and Peter NOCON, eds. *Western Stories.* Paderborn: Ferdinand Schöningh, 1984; and *Western Stories - Teacher's Book.* Paderborn: Ferdinand Schöningh, 1986.
BLAKE, Michael. *Dances with Wolves.* Harmondsworth: Penguin Books, 1991.
BLOOM, Allan. *The Closing of the American Mind: How Higher Education Has Failed Democracy and Impoverished the Souls of Today's Students.* New York: Simon and Schuster, 1987.
BOLD, Christine. *Selling the Wild West: Popular Western Fiction 1860 - 1960.* Bloomington: Indiana University Press, 1987.
BOORSTIN, Daniel J. *The Image or What Happened to the American Dream.* New York: Atheneum, 1961.
BRADFORD, William. *Of Plymouth Plantation.* In *The Norton Anthology of American Literature*, ed. by Ronald Gottesmann et al. New York and London: W. W. Norton, 1979. Vol. I. Pp. 26-40.
BRANT, Sebastian. *Narrenschiff*, ed. by Friedrich Zarncke. Darmstadt: Wissenschaftliche Buchgesellschaft, 1973. [Reprint of the edition Leipzig 1854].
BRAUN, Hans-Martin, and Karl-Heinz GÖLLER, eds. *Indians, Outlaws, and Western Heroes.* Frankfurt: Moritz Diesterweg, 1979.
BRAUTIGAN, Richard. *Trout Fishing in America.* New York: Dell Books, 1972.
----. *A Confederate General from Big Sur.* London: Pan Books, 1973.

BREDELLA, Lothar. "Zielsetzungen der Landeskunde im Fremdsprachenunterricht." *anglistik & englischunterricht*, 10 (1980), 9-34.
BRINKMANN, Carl. *Demokratie und Erziehung in Amerika*. Berlin: S. Fischer, 1927.
Brockhaus Enzyklopädie. Mannheim, 19th, completely rev. ed., 1986.
BROWN, Charles Brockden. *Edgar Huntly; or, Memoirs of a Sleepwalker*. New York: AMS Press, 1976. [Reprint of the edition Philadelphia: H. Maxwell, 1799].
BROWN, Wesley, and Amy LING, eds. *Imagining America: Stories from the Promised Land*. New York: Persea Books, 1991.
----, eds. *Visions of America: Personal Narratives from the Promised Land*. New York: Persea Books, 1993.
BROWN, William R. *Image Maker: Will Rogers and the American Dream*. Columbia, Missouri: University of Missouri Press, 1970.
BROWNE, Jackson. *Lawyers in Love*. Electra/Asylum Record Album, 1983.
BRUCCOLI, Matthew J. "On F. Scott Fitzgerald and 'Bernice Bobs Her Hair.'" In *The American Short Story*, ed. by Calvin Skaggs. New York: Dell Books, 1979. Pp. 219-223.
BRUCE-NOVOA, Juan. *Chicano Authors: Inquiry by Interview*. Austin and London: University of Texas Press, 1980.
----. "Hispanic Literature in the United States." In *American Writing Today*, ed. by Richard Kostelanetz. Washington, D.C.: USICA Forum Series, 1982. Vol. II, pp. 251-261.
BRUCK, Peter, ed. *The Frontier and the American West*. Paderborn: Ferdinand Schöningh, 1980; and BRUCK, Peter. *The Frontier and the American West - Interpretations and Suggestions for Teaching*. Paderborn: Ferdinand Schöningh, 1980.
----. "Black Innocent Eyes: William Melvin Kelleys 'The Only Man on Liberty Street' als Ausgangstext für eine Unterrichtssequenz zur afro-amerikanischen Kurzgeschichte." *Arbeiten aus Anglistik und Amerikanistik*, 5 (1980), 255-269.
----. "Jack Schaefer: *Shane* (1949)." In *Der Roman im Englischunterricht der Sekundarstufe II: Theorie und Praxis*, ed. by Peter Freese and Liesel Hermes. Paderborn: Ferdinand Schöningh, 2nd rev. and enl. ed., 1981. Pp. 269-283.
BURDEN, Charles, Elke BURDEN, Sterling EISIMINGER, and Lynn GANIM, eds. *Business in Literature*. New York: David McKay, 1977.
CAHAN, Abraham. *Yekl and The Imported Bridegroom and Other Stories of the New York Ghetto*, with an introduction by Bernard G. Richards. New York: Dover Publications, 1970.
----. *The Rise of David Levinsky*, with an introduction by John Higham. New York: Harper & Row, rpt. 1981.
CALDER, Jenni. *There Must Be a Lone Ranger: The Myth and Reality of the American Wild West*. London: Sphere Books, 1976.
CARLSON, Lewis H., and James M. FERREIRA. *Beyond the Red, White, and Blue: A Student's Introduction to American Studies*. Dubuque, Iowa: Kendall / Hunt, 1993.
CARNEGIE, Andrew. *The Gospel of Wealth*. London: F. C. Hagen & Co., 1889.
CARPENTER, Frederick I. *American Literature and the Dream*. New York: Philosophical Library, 1955.
CARTWRIGHT, Jerome. "Bambara's 'The Lesson.'" *Explicator*, 47, 3 (1989), 61-63.
CATHER, Willa. *My Antonía*. London: Virago, 1986.
CAWELTI, John G. *Apostles of the Self-Made Man*. Chicago and London: University of Chicago Press, 1965.
----. *The Six-Gun Mystique*. Bowling Green, Ohio: Bowling Green University Popular Press, no date [1971].
----. *Adventure, Mystery, and Romance: Formula Stories as Art and Popular Culture*. Chicago and London: University of Chicago Press, 1976.

CHAMBERLAIN, John. "The Businessman in Fiction." *Fortune*, November 1948, pp. 134-148.
CHAMETZKY, Jules. *From the Ghetto: The Fiction of Abraham Cahan*. Amherst: University of Massachusetts Press, 1977.
CHAN, Jeffery Paul, Frank CHIN, Lawson Fusao INADA, and Shawn WONG, eds. *The Big Aiiieeeee! An Anthology of Chinese American and Japanese American Literature*. New York: Penguin Books, 1991.
CHANDLER, Raymond. *The Little Sister*. Boston: Houghton Mifflin, 1949.
CHAPMAN, Abraham, ed. *Black Voices: An Anthology of Afro-American Literature*. New York: Mentor Books, 1968.
CHAPMAN, Tracy. *Across the Lines*. Electra/Asylum Record Album, 1988.
CHENOWETH, Lawrence. *The American Dream of Success: The Search for the Self in the Twentieth Century*. North Scituate, Massachusetts: Duxbury Press, 1974.
CHERRY, Conrad, ed. *God's New Israel: Religious Interpretations of American Destiny*. Englewood Cliffs, New Jersey: Prentice-Hall, 1971.
CHEUNG, King-Kok. "Double-Telling: Intertextual Silence in Hisaye Yamamoto's Fiction." *American Literary History*, 3 (1991), 277-293.
CHIAPPELLI, Fredi, ed. *First Images of America: The Impact of the New World on the Old*. Berkeley: University of California Press, 1976.
CHIN, Frank. "Food for All His Dead." In *Growing up in a Multicultural Society: Nine American Stories*, ed. by Peter Freese. München: Langenscheidt-Longman, 1994. Pp. 119-140.
----, Jeffery Paul CHAN, Lawson Fusao INADA, and Shawn Hsu WONG, eds. *Aiiieeeee! An Anthology of Asian-American Writers*. Washington, D.C.: Howard University Press, 1974.
CHU, Louis. *Eat a Bowl of Tea*. Seattle and London: University of Washington Press, rpt. 1982.
CISNEROS, Sandra. *The House on Mango Street*. London: Bloomsbury, 1992.
CLARKE, John Hendrik. "The Boy Who Painted Christ Black." In *Growing up Black in America: Stories and Studies of Socialization*, ed. by Peter Freese. Paderborn: Ferdinand Schöningh, 6th enl. ed., 1987. Pp. 43-50.
CLEAVER, Eldridge. *Soul on Ice: Selected Essays*. London: Jonathan Cape, 1969.
COLBURN, David R., and George E. POZZETTA, eds. *America and the New Ethnicity*. Port Washington, New York: Kennikat Press, 1979.
COLUMBUS, Christopher. *The Voyages of Christopher Columbus. Being the Journals of His First and Third, and the Letters Concerning His First and Last Voyages, to Which Is Added the Account of His Second Voyage Written by Andreas Bernaldez*, newly transl. and ed. by Cecil Jane. Amsterdam: N. Israel, and New York: Da Capo Press, 1970. [Reprint of the edition London: Argonaut Press, 1930].
COMPTON, James V. *Hitler und die USA: Die Amerikapolitik des Dritten Reiches und die Ursprünge des Zweiten Weltkrieges*. Oldenburg and Hamburg: Stalling, 1968.
CONWELL, Russell H. *Acres of Diamonds*. In *A Documentary History of Religion in America since 1865*, ed. by Edwin S. Gaustad. Grand Rapids, Michigan: William B. Eerdmans, 1983. Pp. 251-252.
COOPER, James Fenimore. *The Deerslayer; or, The First War-Path: A Tale*. New York: W. A. Townsend and Company, 1861.
----. *The Pioneers; or, The Sources of the Susquehanna: A Descriptive Tale*. New York: James G. Gregory [successor to W. A. Townsend and Company], 1863.
COOVER, Robert. *The Public Burning*. New York: Viking Press, 1977.

COUSINS, Norman. "Needed: A New Dream." In *Sunshine and Smoke: American Writers and the American Environment*, ed. by David D. Anderson. Philadelphia: J. B. Lippincott, 1971. Pp. 496-497.
COX, James M. "On William Faulkner and 'Barn Burning.'" In *The American Short Story*, ed. by Calvin Skaggs. Vol. II. New York: Dell Books, 1980. Pp. 398-407.
CRANE, Stephen. *The Works of Stephen Crane*, ed. by Fredson Bowers. Charlottesville: University Press of Virginia, 1969ff.
CREVECOEUR, J. Hector St. John de. *Letters from an American Farmer and Sketches of Eighteenth-Century America*, ed. with an introduction by Albert E. Stone. New York: Viking Penguin, 1981.
DANA, Richard Henry, Jr. *Two Years Before the Mast: A Personal Narrative*. New York: New American Library, 1964.
DANZIGER, Kurt. *Socialization*. Harmondsworth: Penguin Books, 1971.
DARWIN, Charles. *On the Origin of Species by Means of Natural Selection*, ed. by J. W. Burrow. Harmondsworth: Penguin Books, 1982.
DAVID, Jay, ed. *Growing Up Black*. New York: William Morrow, 1968.
DAVIS, Kenneth S. *The Hero: Charles A. Lindbergh and the American Dream*. Garden City, New York: Doubleday, 1959.
DAVIS, Mike. *Prisoners of the American Dream: Politics and Economy in the History of the US Working Class*. London: Verso, 1986.
DEGLER, Carl N. *Out of Our Past: The Forces that Shaped Modern America*. New York: Harper and Row, rev. ed., 1970.
DeMAUSE, Lloyd. *Reagan's America*. New York and London: Creative Roots, Inc., 1984.
Der Große Herder: Nachschlagewerk für Wissen und Leben. Freiburg: Herder & Co., 1931.
"Deutsch-amerikanische Beziehungen." [Thematic issues of] *Englisch-Amerikanische Studien*, 6, # 1 and # 2 (1984).
"Die U.S.A. und Deutschland: Ursprünge und Funktionen gesellschaftlicher und kultureller Stereotypen." [Thematic issue of] *Amerikastudien - American Studies*, 31, # 3 (1986).
DIXON, Thomas, Jr. *The Clansman: An Historical Romance of the Ku Klux Klan*, with an introduction by Thomas D. Clark. Lexington: University Press of Kentucky, 1970.
DOCTOROW, E. L. *Welcome to Hard Times*. London: Pan Books, 1977.
----. *The Book of Daniel*. Toronto: Bantam Books, 1979.
----. *Ragtime*. London: Pan Books, 1976.
----. *Loon Lake*. Toronto: Bantam Books, 1981.
----. "False Documents." In *E. L. Doctorow: Essays and Conversations*, ed. by Richard Trenner. Princeton, New Jersey: Ontario Review Press, 1983. Pp. 16-27.
DÖNHOFF, Marion Gräfin. *Amerikanische Wechselbäder: Beobachtungen und Kommentare aus 4 Jahrzehnten*. Stuttgart: Deutsche Verlagsanstalt, 1983.
DOHERTY, William T. Jr. "The Interaction of American Business and American Religion in the 19th and Early 20th Centuries: A Sampling of Scholarly and Popular Interpretations." *North Dakota Quarterly*, 50 (1982), 91-97.
DOKEY, Richard. "Sánchez." In *The Chicano: From Caricature to Self-Portrait*, ed. by Edward Simmen. New York: Mentor Books, 1971. Pp. 254-267.
DOOLEY, Patrick. "Nineteenth Century Business Ethics and *The Rise of Silas Lapham*." *American Studies*, 21 (1980), 79-93.
DRAYTON, Michael. *The Poems of Michael Drayton*, ed. with an introduction by John Buxton. London: Routledge and Kegan Paul, 1953.
DREISER, Theodore. *The Financier*. London: Constable, 1927.
----. *An American Tragedy*. New York: New American Library, 1964.

D'SOUZA, Dinesh. *Illiberal Education: The Politics of Sex and Race on Campus.* New York: The Free Press, 1991.
DUDEN, Gottfried. *Bericht über eine Reise nach den westlichen Staaten Nordamerika's und einen mehrjährigen Aufenthalt am Missouri (in den Jahren 1824, 25, 26 und 1827), in Bezug auf Auswanderung und Uebervölkerung, oder: Das Leben im Innern der Vereinigten Staaten und dessen Bedeutung für die häusliche und politische Lage der Europäer, dargestellt a) in einer Sammlung von Briefen, b) in einer besonderen Abhandlung über den politischen Zustand der nordamerikanischen Freistaaten, und c) in einem rathgebenden Nachtrage für auswandernde deutsche Ackerwirthe und Diejenigen, welche auf Handelsunternehmungen denken.* Elberfeld: Sam. Lucas, 1829.
----. *Die nordamerikanische Demokratie und das von Tocqueville'sche Werk darüber, als Zeichen des Zustandes der theoretischen Politik. Nebst einer Aeusserung über Chevalier's Nordamerikanische Briefe, insbesondere hinsichtlich der wahren Ursachen des Bankstreites und der neuesten Unfälle in dem Handelsleben.* [Enthält als Zusatz:] *Duden's Selbst-Anklage wegen seines amerikanischen Reiseberichtes, zur Warnung vor fernerm leichtsinnigen Auswandern.* Bonn. E. Weber, 1837.
DURZAK, Manfred. *Das Amerika-Bild in der deutschen Gegenwartsliteratur: Historische Voraussetzungen und aktuelle Beispiele.* Stutttgart: Kohlhammer, 1979.
DWIGHT, Timothy. *Greenfield Hill: A Poem.* New York: Childs and Swaine, 1974.
DYSERINCK, Hugo. "Komparatistische Imagologie: Zur politischen Tragweite einer europäischen Wissenschaft von der Literatur." In *Europa und das nationale Selbstverständnis: Imagologische Probleme in Literatur, Kunst und Kultur des 19. und 20. Jahrhunderts,* ed. by Hugo Dyserinck and Karl Ulrich Syndram. Bonn: Bouvier, 1988. Pp. 13-37.
EDWARDS, Jonathan. *The Works of Jonathan Edwards,* general editors Perry Miller and John E. Smith. New Haven: Yale University Press, 1957 - 1985.
EGER, Ernestina N. *Bibliography of Criticism of Contemporary Chicano Literature.* Berkeley, CA: Chicano Studies Library Publications, 1982.
EISENSTADT, S. N. *From Generation to Generation: Age Groups and Social Structure.* New York: Free Press, 1966.
EKIRCH, Arthur Alphonse, Jr. *The Idea of Progress in America, 1815 - 1860.* New York: Columbia University Press, 1944.
ELKIN, Frederick. *The Child and Society: The Process of Socialization.* New York: Random House, 1968.
ELLIS, Bret Easton. *Less Than Zero.* Harmondsworth: Penguin Books, 1986.
ELLISON, Ralph. "The Invisible Man." In *Growing up Black: Stories and Studies of Socialization,* ed. by Peter Freese. Paderborn: Ferdinand Schöningh, 6th enl. ed., 1987. Pp. 90-104.
----. *Invisible Man.* New York: New American Library, rpt. 1964.
----. *Shadow and Act.* New York: New American Library, 1966.
----. "On Initiation Rites and Power: Ralph Ellison Speaks at West Point" ed. by Robert H. Moore. *Contemporary Literature,* 15 (1974), 165-186.
EMERSON, Ralph Waldo. *The Complete Works of Ralph Waldo Emerson.* New York: AMS Press, 2nd ed., 1979. [Reprint of the Centenary Edition Boston: Houghton Mifflin, 1903-1904].
----. *The Journals and Miscellaneous Notebooks of Ralph Waldo Emerson,* ed. by William H. Gilman et al. Cambridge, Massachusetts: The Belknap Press of Harvard University Press, 1960 - 1982.
ENGEL, David. "The 'Discrepancies' of the Modern: Towards a Revaluation of Abraham Cahan's *The Rise of David Levinsky.*" *Studies in Jewish American Literature,* 2 (1982), 36-60.
EPSTEIN, Joseph. *Ambition: The Secret Passion.* Harmondsworth: Penguin Books, 1982.

ERDRICH, Louise. "The Bingo Van." In *Growing up in a Multicultural Society: Nine American Stories*, ed. by Peter Freese. München: Langenscheidt-Longman, 1994. Pp. 160-189.
ERIKSON, Erik H. *Childhood and Society*. Harmondsworth: Penguin Books, 1965.
----. *Identity: Youth and Crisis*. New York: W. W. Norton, 1968.
ETULAIN, Richard W. "The Western." In *Handbook of American Popular Culture*, ed. by M. Thomas Inge. Westport, Connecticut: Greenwood Press, 1978. Vol. I, pp. 355-376.
EWEN, Stuart. *Captains of Consciousness: Advertising and the Social Roots of the Consumer Culture*. New York: McGraw-Hill, 1976.
"Excellence in Ethnic Diversity: At Berkeley, Chang-lin Tien becomes the first Asian American to head a leading U.S. university." *Time*, April 1, 1991, p. 63.
FAULKNER, William. "On Privacy: The American Dream - What Happened to It." *Harper's Magazine*, 211 (1955), 33-38.
FAULKNER, William. *Requiem for a Nun*. Harmondsworth: Penguin Books, rpt. 1977.
----. "Barn Burning." In *The American Short Story I: Initiation*, ed. by Peter Freese. Paderborn: Ferdinand Schöningh, 2nd ed., 1989. Pp. 74-93.
----. "The Bear." In *Go Down, Moses*. Harmondsworth: Penguin Books, rpt. 1961.
----. *The Sound and the Fury*. New York: W. W. Norton, 1988.
FERGUSON, Alfred R. "The Tragedy of the American Dream in *Death of a Salesman*." *Thought*, 53 (1978), 83-98.
FERLINGHETTI, Lawrence. *A Coney Island of the Mind*. New York: New Directions, 1958.
FERNAU, Joachim. *Halleluja - Die Geschichte der USA*. München: Herbig, 1977.
FERREIRA, James M. "John Wayne: An American Hero." In *Popular Culture in the United States: Proceedings of the German-American Conference in Paderborn, 14 - 17 September 1993*, ed. by Peter Freese and Michael Porsche. Essen: Die Blaue Eule, 1994. Pp. 195-212.
FIEDLER, Leslie A. *Love and Death in the American Novel*. New York: Stein and Day, rev. ed., 1966.
----, and Arthur ZEIGER, eds. *O Brave New World: American Literature from 1600 to 1840*. New York: Dell Books, 1968.
----. *The Return of the Vanishing American*. London: Paladin Books, 1972.
----. "Cross the Border - Close That Gap: Post-Modernism." In *American Literature Since 1900*, ed. by Marcus Cunliffe. London: Sphere Books, 1975. Pp. 344-366.
----. "The Many Names of S. Levin: An Essay in Genre Criticism." In *The Fiction of Bernard Malamud*, ed. by Richard Astro and Jackson J. Benson. Corvallis, Oregon: Oregon State University Press. Pp. 149-161.
FILSON, John. *The Discovery, Settlement, and Present State of Kentucke*. Wilmington, Del.: John Adams, 1784.
FISCHER, Manfred. *Nationale Images als Gegenstand Vergleichender Literaturgeschichte: Untersuchungen zur Entstehung der komparatistischen Imagologie*. Bonn: Bouvier, 1981.
FISHWICK, Marshall W. "The Cowboy: America's Contribution to the World's Mythology." *Western Folklore*, 11 (April 1952), 77-92.
FISKE, John. "Prophetic Voices About America: A Monograph." *Atlantic Monthly*, 20 (September 1867), 275-306.
FITZGERALD, F. Scott. *The Bodley Head Scott Fitzgerald*. 6 vols. London: Bodley Head, 1963 - 1967 and rpt.
----. *The Great Gatsby*, ed. and annotated by Richard Martin and Dagmar Pohlenz. Paderborn: Ferdinand Schöningh, 1984.
----. "Bernice Bobs Her Hair." In *The American Short Story*, ed. by Calvin Skaggs. New York: Dell Books, 1979. Pp. 151-175.
FLINT, Timothy. *The Life and Adventures of Daniel Boone, the First Settler of Kentucky*. Cincinnati: U. P. James, 1868.

FOLSOM, James K., ed. *The Western: A Collection of Critical Essays*. Englewood Cliffs, New Jersey: Prentice-Hall, 1979.
FOSSUM, Robert H., and Joseph K. ROTH. *The American Dream*. No place: BAAS Pamphlets in American Studies, 1981.
FRANKEL, Haskel. "Bernard Malamud" [Interview]. *Saturday Review*, September 10, 1966, pp. 39-40.
FRANKLIN, Benjamin. *The Writings of Benjamin Franklin*, coll. and ed. with a Life and Introduction by Albert Henry Smyth. New York: Haskell House, 1970. [Reprint of the edition New York and London: Macmillan, 1905-1907].
----. *The Autobiography and Other Writings*, ed. with an introduction by L. Jesse Lemisch. New York: New American Library, 1961.
FRENEAU, Philip. *A Collection of Poems on American Affairs and a Variety of Other Subjects Chiefly Moral and Political*. Delmar, New York: Scholars' Facsimiles & Reprints, 1970. [Reprint of the edition New York: D. Longworth, 1815].
FROST, Robert. *In the Clearing*. New York: Holt, Rinehart and Winston, rpt. 1979.
FREESE, Peter. "Parzival als Baseballstar: Bernard Malamuds *The Natural*." *Jahrbuch für Amerikastudien*, 13 (1968), 143-157.
----. *Die Initiationsreise: Studien zum jugendlichen Helden im modernen amerikanischen Roman*. Neumünster: Wachholtz, 1971.
----. "Bernard Malamud." In *Amerikanische Literatur der Gegenwart in Einzeldarstellungen*, ed. by Martin Christadler. Stuttgart: Alfred Kröner, 1973. Pp. 105-128.
----, ed. *Die amerikanische Short Story der Gegenwart: Interpretationen*. Berlin: Erich Schmidt, 1976.
----. "Eine Jugend in Harlem: James Baldwins 'Sonny's Blues' als Ausgangstext eines Kurses zur amerikanischen Rassenfrage." In *Literatur und Landeskunde anhand von Texten schwarzer Autoren*, ed. by Peter Freese [= *Der fremdsprachliche Unterricht*, No. 42 (May 1977)]. Pp. 16-26.
----, ed. *Growing up Black: Stories and Studies of Socialization*. Paderborn: Ferdinand Schöningh, 6th enl. ed. 1987; and Peter FREESE. *Growing up Black in America: Stories and Studies of Socialization - Interpretations and Suggestions for Teaching*. Paderborn: Ferdinand Schöningh, 2nd ed., 1979.
----. "'Rising in the World' and 'Wanting to Know Why': The Socialization Process as Theme of the American Short Story." *Archiv für das Studium der neueren Sprachen und Literaturen*, 218 (1981), 286-302.
----. "Über die Schwierigkeiten des Erwachsenwerdens: Amerikanische *stories of initiation* von Nathaniel Hawthorne bis Joyce Carol Oates." In *Die Short Story im Englischunterricht der Sekundarstufe II: Theorie und Praxis*, ed. by Peter Freese and Liesel Hermes. Paderborn: Ferdinand Schöningh, 2nd ed., 1983. Pp. 206-254.
----, ed. *Bernard Malamud, "The Assistant."* Paderborn: Ferdinand Schöningh, 3rd ed. 1988; and FREESE, Peter. *Bernard Malamud, "The Assistant" - Interpretations and Suggestions for Teaching*. Paderborn: Ferdinand Schöningh, 1983.
----. "Growing up Ethnic in the American Short Story: An Alternative Approach to the 'Melting Pot' Issue in the Advanced EFL-Classroom." *Englisch-Amerikanische Studien*, 6 (1984), 470-502.
----, ed. *The American Short Story I: Initiation*. Paderborn: Ferdinand Schöningh, 2nd ed., 1989; and FREESE, Peter. *The American Short Story I: Initiation - Interpretations and Suggestions for Teaching*. Paderborn: Ferdinand Schöningh, 3rd ed., 1991.
----. "Ökonomisches Scheitern und moralischer Erfolg: Bernard Malamuds *The Assistant* als Kritik am Amerikanischen Traum." In *Die USA in Unterricht und Forschung*, ed. by Lothar Bredella. Bochum: Ferdinand Kamp, 1984. Pp. 190-201.

----. "The American Dream and the American Nightmare: General Aspects and Literary Examples." *anglistik & englischunterricht*, 25 (1985), 7-37.
----. "From Talmud Scholar to Millionaire, or a Jewish Variant of 'Making It' in America: Abraham Cahan's *The Rise of David Levinsky*." In *Das Verstehenlehren einer paradoxen Epoche in Schule und Hochschule: The American 1920s*, ed. by Lothar Bredella. Bochum: Ferdinand Kamp, 1985. Pp. 114-134.
----. "E. L. Doctorow's *Welcome to Hard Times* and the Mendacity of the Popular Western." *Literatur in Wissenschaft und Unterricht*, 20 (1987), 202-216.
----. "'Teaching People How to Write Who Don't Know What to Write': Bernard Malamud's *A New Life* and the Myth of the West." In *Perspectives on Language in Performance: Studies in Linguistics, Literary Criticism, and Language Teaching and Learning to Honour Werner Hüllen on the Occasion of His Sixtieth Birthday*, ed. by Wolfgang Lörscher and Rainer Schulze. Tübingen: Narr, 1987. Vol I. Pp. 642-657.
----. "'Innocents Abroad' versus 'Coca Cola Conquistadores,' or Contradictory German Images of America." *Lock Haven International Review*, 2 (1988), 101-119.
----. *Surviving the End: Beyond Apocalypse and Entropy in American Literature*. Claremont, California: Claremont McKenna College Center for Humanistic Studies, 1988.
----. "Das Unternehmerbild in der amerikanischen Literatur." In *Wirtschaft und Kultur*, ed. by Horst Brezinski. Frankfurt: Peter Lang, 1989. Pp. 83-106.
----. "Doctorow's 'Criminals of Perception,' or What Has Happened to the Historical Novel." In *Reconstructing American Literary and Historical Studies*, ed. by Günter H. Lenz, Hartmut Keil and Sabine Bröck-Sallah. Frankfurt: Campus Verlag, and New York: St. Martin's Press, 1990. Pp. 345-371.
----. "Kunst versus Kommerz, oder das amerikanische Unternehmerbild als Herausforderung an die Fremdsprachendidaktik." In: *Textdidaktik für den Fremdsprachenunterricht - isoliert oder integrativ?* ed. by Karlheinz Hellwig. Tübingen: Narr, 1990. Pp. 86-107.
----. "Exercises in Boundary-Making: The German as the 'Other' in American Literature." In *Germany and German Thought in American Literature and Cultural Criticism: Proceedings of the German-American Conference in Paderborn, May 16-19, 1990*, ed. by Peter Freese. Essen: Die Blaue Eule, 1990. Pp. 93-132.
----. "Robin und seine vielen Verwandten: Zur Rezeptionsgeschichte von Nathaniel Hawthornes 'My Kinsman, Major Molineux.'" In *Die englische und amerikanische Kurzgeschichte*, ed. by Klaus Lubbers. Darmstadt: Wissenschaftliche Buchgesellschaft, 1990. Pp. 12-27.
----. "Bret Easton Ellis, *Less Than Zero*: Entropy in the 'MTV Novel'?" In *Modes of Narrative: Approaches to American, Canadian and British Fiction Presented to Helmut Bonheim*, ed. by Reingard M. Nischik and Barbara Korte. Würzburg: Königshausen & Neumann, 1990. Pp. 68-87.
----. "Kind Uncle or Hateful Big Brother? Some Reflections on the Spectre of 'Anti-Americanism.'" In *Mediating a Foreign Culture: The United States and Germany - Studies in Intercultural Understanding*, ed. by Lothar Bredella. Tübingen: Narr, 1991. Pp. 62-80.
----. "Über die Anbetung der *Bitch-Goddess Success*, oder Geschäftsleute in der amerikanischen Literatur." *literatur für leser*, # 1 (1992), 66-82.
----. "Owen Wister's *The Virginian*, or the Dubious Politics of the Western." In *Neue Brennpunkte des Englischunterrichts: Festschrift für Helmut Heuer zum 60. Geburtstag*, ed. by Dieter Buttjes, Wolfgang Butzkamm and Friederike Klippel. Frankfurt: Peter Lang, 1992. Pp. 64-77.
----, and Michael Porsche, eds. *Popular Culture in the United States: Proceedings of the German-American Conference in Paderborn, 14 - 17 September 1993*. Essen: Die Blaue Eule, 1994.

----, ed. *From Melting Pot to Multiculturalism: 'E pluribus unum'?* Viewfinder Topics. Accompanied by a *Resource Book*. München: Langenscheidt-Longman, 1994.
----, ed. *Growing up in a Multicultural Society: Nine Recent American Stories.* Viewfinder Literature. München: Langenscheidt-Longman, 1994.
FUSSELL, Edwin. *Frontier: American Literature and the American West.* Princeton, New Jersey: Princeton University Press, 1965.
GAINES, Ernest J. "The Sky Is Gray." In *The American Short Story*, ed. by Calvin Skaggs. Vol. II. New York: Dell Books, 1980. Pp. 408-436.
GALBRAITH, John Kenneth. *The Affluent Society.* New York: New American Library, 1958.
GARDNER, Ralph D. *Horatio Alger, or the American Hero Era.* Mendota, Illinois: Wayside Press, 1964.
GATES, Henry Louis, Jr. *Loose Canons: Notes on the Culture War.* New York: Oxford University Press, 1992.
"German-American Relations: Of Love and Hatred." [Thematic issue of] *Englisch-Amerikanische Studien*, 10, # 2 (1988).
GHOSE, Zulfikar. "Observations from a Correspondence: From Thomas Berger's Letters." *Studies in American Humor*, new series 2 (1983), 5-19.
GIDLEY, M. "Notes on F. Scott Fitzgerald and the Passing of the Great Race." *Journal of American Studies*, 7 (1973), 171-181.
GINSBERG, Allen. *Howl and Other Poems.* San Francisco: City Lights Books, rpt. 1980.
GLANZ, Dawn. *How the West Was Drawn: American Art and the Settling of the Frontier.* Ann Arbor: UMI Research Press, 1982.
GLAZER, Nathan, and Daniel Patrick MOYNIHAN. *Beyond the Melting Pot: The Negroes, Puerto Ricans, Jews, Italians, and Irish of New York.* Cambridge, Massachusetts: M.I.T. Press, 1963.
GLEASON, Philip. "The Melting Pot: Symbol of Fusion or Confusion?" *American Quarterly*, 16 (1964), 20-46.
----. ""American Identity and Americanization." in *Harvard Encyclopedia of American Ethnic Groups*, ed. by Stephan Thernstrom. Cambridge Massachusetts, and London: The Belknap Press of Harvard University Press, 1980. Pp. 31-58.
"Global Beat." Time, April 1, 1991, pp. 20-25.
GOETHE, Johann Wolfgang von. *Goethes Werke* [Weimarer Ausgabe], hg. im Auftrag der Großherzogin Sophie von Sachsen. Weimar: Hermann Böhlau, 1887-1920.
GOETSCH, Paul. "Joyce Carol Oates, 'How I Contemplated the World from the Detroit House of Correction and Began My Life Over Again' (1969)." In *Die amerikanische Short Story der Gegenwart: Interpretationen*, ed. by Peter Freese. Berlin: Erich Schmidt, 1976. Pp. 301-313.
----, and Gerd HURM, eds. *Die Rhetorik amerikanischer Präsidenten seit F. D. Roosevelt.* Tübingen: Gunter Narr, 1993.
GOLD, Michael. *Jews Without Money.* New York: Avon Books, 5th pr., no date.
GONZALES, Rodolfo. *I Am Joaquín / Yo Soy Joaquín.* New York: Bantam Books, 1972.
GOODMAN, Paul. *Growing up Absurd.* London: Sphere Books, 1970.
GORAK, Jan. *The Making of the Modern Canon: Genesis and Crisis of a Literary Idea.* London and Atlantic Highlands, New Jersey: Athlone Press, 1991.
GORER, Geoffrey. *The American People: A Study in National Character.* New York: W. W. Norton, 1948.
GOTTSCHALCH, Wilfried, Marina NEUMANN-SCHÖNWETTER, and Gunther SOUKOP. *Sozialisationsforschung: Materialien, Probleme, Kritik.* Frankfurt: Fischer, 1971.
GRAEBNER, Norman, ed. *Manifest Destiny.* Indianapolis: Bobbs-Merrill, 1968.

GRANAT, Robert. "To Endure." In *The Chicano: From Caricature to Self-Portrait*, ed. by Edward Simmen. New York: Mentor Books, 1971. Pp. 228-235.
GRANT, Madison. *The Passing of the Great Race*. New York: Scribner, rev. ed., 1918.
GREENE, Bob. "Let Us Now Praise Greedy Men." *San Francisco Sunday Examiner and Chronicle*. September 25, 1977.
GREGORY, Dick. *No More Lies: The Myth and the Reality of American History*. New York: Perennial Library, 1972.
GRIER, William H., and Price M. COBBS. *Black Rage*. New York: Bantam Books, 1969.
GROSS, David S. "Tales of Obscene Power: Money and Culture, Modernism and History in the Fiction of E. L. Doctorow." *Genre*, 13 (1980), 71-92.
GRUNWALD, Henry. "The Second American Century." *Time*, October 8, 1990, pp. 46-51.
HALEY, Alex. *Roots*. New York: Doubleday, 1976.
HALFELD, Adolf. *Amerika und der Amerikanismus: Kritische Betrachtungen eines Deutschen und Europäers*. Jena: Eugen Diederichs, 1928.
HALIBURTON, Thomas Chandler. *The Clockmaker, or the Sayings and Doings of Samuel Slick of Slickville*. Toronto: McClelland and Stewart, 1986.
HALL, Stanley. *Adolescence: Its Psychology and Its Relation to Physiology, Anthropology, Sociology, Sex, Crime, Religion and Education*. New York: Appleton, 1924.
HANDLIN, Oscar. *The Uprooted: From the Old World to the New*. London: Watts and Co., 1953.
HANSEN, Marcus Lee. ""The Third Generation in America." *Commentary*, 14 (November 1952), 492-500.
HARK, Ina Rae. "A Frontier Closes in Brooklyn: *Death of a Salesman* and the Turner Thesis." *Postscript*, 3 (1986), 1-6.
HARPPRECHT, Klaus. *Der fremde Freund. Amerika: Eine innere Geschichte*. Stuttgart: Deutsche Verlagsanstalt, 1982.
HARRINGTON, Michael. *The Other America: Poverty in the United States*. New York: Macmillan, 1962.
HARRISON, J. Derek, and Alan B. SHAW, eds. *The American Dream: Vision and Reality*. San Francisco: Canfield Press, 1975.
HASSAN, Ihab. *Radical Innocence: Studies in the Contemporary American Novel*. New York: Harper & Row, 1966.
HAWTHORNE, Nathaniel. "My Kinsman, Major Molineux." In *The American Short Story I: Initiation*, ed. by Peter Freese. Paderborn: Ferdinand Schöningh, 2nd ed., 1989. Pp. 7-29.
----. *Two England Romances*, prefaced and annotated by H. Bernstein. Frankfurt: Hirschgraben, 1962.
----. *The Centenary Edition of the Works of Nathaniel Hawthorne*, gen. eds. William Charvat, Roy Harvey Pearce, and Claude Simpson. 20 vols. Columbus, Ohio: Ohio State University Press, 1963 - 1988 and rpt.
HEARN, Charles. *The American Dream in the Great Depression*. Westport, Connecticut: Greenwood Press, 1977.
HECHINGER, Grace, and Fred M. HECHINGER. *Teen-Age Tyranny*. New York: William Morrow and Company, 1963.
HEGEL, Georg Wilhelm Friedrich. *Sämtliche Werke: Neue kritische Ausgabe*, ed. by Johannes Hoffmeister. Hamburg: Felix Meiner, 5th ed., 1955.
HELLER, Arno. *Odysse zum Selbst: Zur Gestaltung jugendlicher Identitätssuche im neueren amerikanischen Roman*. Innsbruck: Institut für Sprachwissenschaft, 1973.
HELLER, Joseph. *Something Happened*. London: Corgi Books, 1975.

HEMINGWAY, Ernest. "Soldier's Home." In: *The American Short Story*, ed. by Calvin Skaggs. New York: Dell Books, 1979. Pp. 224-231.
HENRY, Jeanette, ed. *The American Indian Reader: Literature*. San Francisco: Indian History Press, 1973.
HERMS, Dieter. "Die Literatur des Chicano Movement: Identitätssuche, Kulturkonflikt und Protest." In *Amerikanische Gettoliteratur: Zur Literatur ethnischer, marginaler und unterdrückter Gruppen in Amerika*, ed. by Berndt Ostendorf. Darmstadt: Wissenschaftliche Buchgesellschaft, 1983. Pp.293-322.
HESKIN, Allan D. *Tenants and the American Dream*. New York: Praeger, 1983.
HEYEN, William. "Arthur Miller's *Death of a Salesman* and the American Dream." In *Amerikanisches Drama und Theater im 20. Jahrhundert*, ed. by Alfred Weber and Siegfried Neuweiler. Göttingen: Vandenhoeck & Ruprecht, 1975. Pp. 190-203.
HIGHAM, John. *Strangers in the Land: Patterns of American Nativism 1860 - 1925*. New York: Atheneum, 2nd ed., 1963.
----. *Send These to Me: Jews and Other Immigrants in Urban America*. New York: Atheneum, 1975.
HINE, Robert V. *The American West: An Interpretive History*. Glenview, Ill., and London: Scott, Foresman and Company, 2nd ed., 1984.
"Historische Amerikastudien: Beiträge zur Geschichte der Vereinigten Staaten und der deutsch-amerikanischen Beziehungen." [Thematic issue of] *Amerikastudien - American Studies*, 33, # 3 (1988).
HOCHHUTH, Rolf. *Guerillas*. Reinbek: Rowohlt, 1970.
----. *Tod eines Jägers*. Reinbek: Rowohlt, 1976.
----. *Judith*. Reinbek: Rowohlt, 1984.
HOFSTADTER, Richard. *Social Darwinism in American Thought*. New York: George Braziller, rev. ed., 1959.
----. *Anti-Intellectualism in American Life*. New York: Alfred A. Knopf, 1963.
HOLITSCHER, Arthur. *Amerika: Heute und morgen - Reiseerlebnisse*. Berlin: S. Fischer, 1912.
HOLLANDER, Xaviera. *The Happy Hooker*. New York: Bell Publ. Co., 1972.
HONOLKA, Harro. *Schwarzrotgrün: Die Bundesrepublik auf der Suche nach ihrer Identität*. München: C. H. Beck, 1987.
HONOUR, Hugh. *The New Golden Land: European Images of America from the Discoveries to the Present Time*. New York: Pantheon Books, 1975.
HOSPITAL, Carolina, and Carlos MEDINA. *Instructor's Guide for 'New Worlds of Literature.'* New York and London: W. W. Norton, 1994.
HOWE, Irving. *World of Our Fathers*. New York and London: Harcourt Brace Jovanovich, 1976.
----, ed. *Jewish-American Stories*. New York: New American Library, 1977.
HOWELLS, Mildred, ed. *Life in Letters*. New York: Doubleday, Doran, 1928.
HOWELLS, William Dean. *The Rise of Silas Lapham*. New York: New American Library, 1963.
HSU, Kai-yu, and Helen PALUBINSKAS, eds. *Asian-American Authors*. Boston: Houghton Mifflin, 1972.
HUBER, Richard M. *The American Idea of Success*. New York: McGraw-Hill, 1971.
HUGHES, Ellen Roney, and Lucinda J. HERRICK, eds. *A Nation of Nations: A Visual Presentation from the National Museum of History and Technology*. Washington: Smithsonian Institution Photographic Services, no date.
HUGHES, Langston. *The Panther and the Lash: Poems of Our Times*. New York: Alfred Knopf, 1967.

----, and Arna BONTEMPS, eds. *The Poetry of the Negro 1746 - 1970: An Anthology*. Garden City, New York: Doubleday, rev. ed., 1970.
HUIZENGA, Jann. *Looking at American Food: A Pictorial Introduction to American Language and Culture*. Bielefeld: Cornelsen-Velhagen & Klasing, 1983.
HUNFELD, Hans, ed. *What Did You Learn in School Today? Seven School Stories from America*. Paderborn: Ferdinand Schöningh, 1981.
----. *Geschichten vom deutschen Amerika*. Bochum: Ferdinand Kamp, 1984.
HUNT, Thomas Poage. *The Book of Wealth; in Which It is Proved from the Bible, that It is the Duty of Every Man, to Become Rich*. New York: E. Collier, 1836.
HUNTER, Evan. *The Blackboard Jungle*. London: New English Library, rpt. 1974.
HUXLEY, Aldous. *Brave New World*. London: Chatto & Windus, 1932.
IACOCCA, Lee. *Iacocca: An Autobiography*. Toronto: Bantam Books, rpt. 1988.
INGE, Thomas M., ed. *A Nineteenth-Century American Reader*. Washington, D.C.: United States Information Agency, 1988.
IRVING, Washington. *Life and Voyages of Christopher Columbus*. New York: G. P. Putnam's Sons, 1892.
----. *The Sketch-Book of Geoffrey Crayon, Gent*. New York: G. P. Putnam's Sons, 1894.
JAMES, William. *The Letters of William James*, ed, by his son Henry James. New York: Kraus Reprint Co., 1969. [Reprint of the edition Boston: Little, Brown and Company, 1926].
JAY, Robert. *The Trade Card in Nineteenth-Century America*. Columbia: University of Missouri Press, 1987.
JEFFERSON, Thomas. *Writings*, ed. by Paul L. Ford. New York and London: Putnam, 1892-1899.
----. *The Political Writings of Thomas Jefferson: Representative Selections*, ed. by Edward Dumbauld. New York: The Liberal Arts Press, 1955.
JIMÉNEZ, Francisco. "The Circuit." In *Growing up in a Multicultural Society: Nine American Stories*, ed. by Peter Freese. München: Langenscheidt-Longman, 1994. Pp. 68-80.
JOHANN, A. E. [i.e. Alfred Wollschläger]. *Das Land ohne Herz: Eine Reise ins unbekannte Amerika*. Berlin: Deutscher Verlag, 1942.
JOHNSON, Edward. *Johnson's Wonder-Working Providence, 1628 - 1651*, ed. by J. Franklin Jameson. New York: Barnes & Noble, rpt. 1959.
JOHNSON, James Weldon. "The Dilemma of the Negro Author." *American Mercury*, 15 (1928), 477-481.
JONES, Ernest. *Das Leben und Werk von Sigmund Freud*. Bern and Stuttgart: Verlag Hans Huber, 1960 - 1962.
JONES, Suzanne W., ed. *Growing Up in the South: An Anthology of Modern Southern Literature*. New York: Mentor Books, 1991.
JONG, Erica. *Any Woman's Blues*. London: Arrow Books, 1990.
JOSEPHSON, Matthew. *The Robber Barons 1861 - 1901*. New York: Harcourt Brace, 1962.
KADE, Gerhard. *Die Amerikaner und wir*. Köln: Pahl-Rugenstein, 1983.
KALLEN, Horace. "Democracy versus the Melting Pot: A Study of American Nationality." *The Nation*, 100 (February 25, 1915), 219-220.
----. *Culture and Democracy in the United States: Studies in the Group Psychology of the American People*. New York: Boni and Liveright, 1924.
KAMPER, Dietmar, ed. *Sozialisationstheorie*. Freiburg: Herder, 1974.
KANELLOS, Nicolás, ed. *Biographical Dictionary of Hispanic Literature in the United States: The Literature of Puerto Ricans, Cuban Americans, and Other Hispanic Writers*. New York: Greenwood Press, 1989.
KAPLAN, Carey, and Ellen Cronan ROSE. *The Canon and the Common Reader*. Knoxville: University of Tennessee Press, 1990.

KEIL, Hartmut. "Die Funktion des 'American Dream' in der amerikanischen Gesellschaft." Phil. Diss., München, 1968.
KELLER, Linda, and Kay MUSSELL, eds. *Ethnic and Regional Foodways in the United States: The Performance of Group Identity.* Knoxville: University of Tennessee Press, 1984.
KELLEY, William Melvin. "The Only Man on Liberty Street." In *Stories from the Black Experience,* ed. by J. B. Stone and Luther K. Masket. Stuttgart: Ernst Klett, 1981. Pp. 9-16.
KENNEDY; John F. "Nomination Acceptance Speech, July 15, 1960." *U.S. News & World Report.* July 25, 1960, pp. 100-102.
KENNEDY, Paul M. *The Rise and Fall of the Great Powers: Economic Change and Military Conflict 1500 to 2000.* London: Unwin Hyman, 1988.
KESEY, Ken. *One Flew Over the Cuckoo's Nest.* New York: New American Library, no date.
----. *Sometimes a Great Notion.* New York: Bantam Books, rpt. 1971.
KETT, Joseph F. *Rites of Passage: Adolescence in America 1790 to the Present.* New York: Basic Books, 1977.
"Kicking the Nerd Syndrome: A new cohort of the best and brightest Asian American students is rejecting the science stereotype and the ethic behind it." *Time,* March 25, 1991, p. 59.
KIM, Elaine H. *Asian American Literature: An Introduction to the Writings and Their Social Context.* Philadelphia: Temple University Press, 1982.
KING, Martin Luther, Jr. "I Have a Dream." In *The Annals of America,* vol. XVIII, *1961 - 1968: The Burdens of World Power.* Chicago and London: Encyclopaedia Britannica, 1967. Pp. 156-159.
----. *Where Do We Go From Here: Chaos or Community?* New York: Bantam Books, 1968.
KINGSTON, Maxine Hong. *China Men.* New York: Ballantine Books, 1981.
----. *The Woman Warrior: Memoirs of a Girlhood Among Ghosts.* London: Pan Books, 1982.
----. *Tripmaster Monkey: His Fake Book.* London: Pan Books, 1990.
KIRK, Rudolf, and Clara M. KIRK. "Abraham Cahan and William Dean Howells: The Story of a Friendship." *American Jewish Historical Quarterly,* 52 (1962), 25-27.
KNAUER, Sebastian. *Lieben wir die USA? Was die Deutschen über die Amerikaner denken.* Hamburg: Stern-Bücher, 1987.
KNODT, Kenneth S., ed. *Pursuing the American Dream.* Englewood Cliffs, New Jersey: Prentice-Hall, 1976.
KOCH-LINDE, Birgitta. *Amerikanische Tagträume: Success und Self-Help Literatur der USA.* Frankfurt and New York: Campus Verlag, 1984.
KÖHRING, Klaus H. "The Western." In *Projects in Literature: Modelle und Materialien zur Textarbeit im Englischunterricht,* ed. by Wilfried Brusch. Heidelberg: Quelle & Meyer, 1977. Pp. 57-76.
KOLODNY, Annette. *The Land Before Her: Fantasy and Experience of the American Frontiers, 1630 - 1860.* Chapel Hill: University of North Carolina Press, 1984.
KORDA, Michael. *Success! How Every Man and Woman Can Achieve It.* New York: Random House, 1977.
KÖTTGEN, Carl. *Das wirtschaftliche Amerika.* Berlin: VDI-Verlag, 1925.
KRAMPIKOWSKI, Frank, ed. *Amerikanisches Deutschlandbild und deutsches Amerikabild in Medien und Erziehung.* Baltmannsweiler: Burgbücherei Schneider, 1990.
KRONZUCKER, Dieter, and Klaus EMMERICH. *Das amerikanische Jahrhundert.* Düsseldorf: Econ, 1989.
KÜHNEL, Walter. "'I Tell You This Neither in a Spirit of Self-Revelation Nor as an Exercise in Total Recall': John Wayne, the Man Whom German Intellectuals Love(d) to Hate." In *Popular Culture in the United States: Proceedings of the German-American Con-*

ference in Paderborn, 14 - 17 September 1993, ed. by Peter Freese and Michael Porsche. Essen: Die Blaue Eule, 1993. Pp. 213-234.
KÜRNBERGER, Ferdinand. *Der Amerikamüde: Amerikanisches Kulturbild.* Wien and Leipzig: R. Löwit, no date.
KUNERT, Günter. "Linke Melancholie." In *Bilder von Amerika: Gespräche mit deutschen Schriftstellern,* ed. by Heinz D. Osterle. Münster: Englisch-Amerikanische Studien, 1987. Pp. 137-155.
LAMAR, Howard R., ed. *The Reader's Encyclopedia of the American West.* New York: Thomas Y. Crowell, 1977.
LASCH, Christopher. *The Culture of Narcissism: American Life in an Age of Diminishing Expectations.* New York: Warner Books, 1980.
LATHROP, Samuel K. *Oration Delivered before the City Authorities of Boston. July 4, 1866.* In *Nationalism and Religion in America: Concepts of American Identity and Mission,* ed. by Winthrop S. Hudson. Gloucester, Massachusetts: Peter Smith, 1978. P. 54.
LAUTER, Paul, et al., eds. *The Heath Anthology of American Literature.* 2 vols. Lexington: D. C. Heath, 1990; 2nd rev. and enl. ed., 1994. - Accompanied by: John ALBERTI, ed. *Instructor's Guide for the Heath Anthology of American Literature, Second Edition.* Lexington: D. C. Heath, 1994.
LAWRENCE, D. H. *Studies in Classic American Literature.* New York: Viking Press, rpt. 1969.
LEE, Gus. *China Boy.* New York: E. P. Dutton, 1991.
LEE, Harper. *To Kill a Mockingbird.* Harmondsworth: Penguin Books, rpt. 1967.
LEMAY, J. A. Leo, ed. *An Early American Reader.* Washington, D.C.: United States Information Agency, 1988.
LENAU, Nikolaus. *Sämtliche Werke und Briefe,* ed. by Walter Dietze. Frankfurt: Insel Verlag, 1971.
LEONARD, Elmore. *City Primeval.* Harmondsworth: Penguin Books, 1988.
LESLEY, Craig, ed. *Talking Leaves: Contemporary Native American Short Stories.* New York: Dell, 1991.
LETTAU, Reinhard. *Täglicher Faschismus: Amerikanische Evidenz aus 6 Monaten.* München: Carl Hanser, 1971.
----. *Zerstreutes Hinausschaun: Vom Schreiben über Vorgänge in direkter Nähe oder in der Entfernung von Schreibtischen.* München: Carl Hanser, 1980.
LEVEN, Jeremy. *Creator.* Harmondsworth: Penguin Books, 1981.
LEVINE, Paul. *E. L. Doctorow.* London and New York: Methuen, 1985.
LEWIS, R. W. B. *The American Adam: Innocence, Tragedy and Tradition in the Nineteenth Century.* Chicago and London: University of Chicago Press, 1955.
----. *Trials of the Word: American Literature and the Humanistic Tradition.* New Haven and London: Yale University Press, 1965.
LEWIS, Sinclair. *Babbitt.* London: The Albatross, 1947.
LIEDTKE, Klaus. *Cowboys, Gott und Coca Cola: Was unsere Schutzmacht Amerika der Welt zu bieten hat.* Frankfurt: Eichborn, 1984.
LING, Amy. *Between Worlds: Women Writers of Chinese Ancestry.* New York: Pergamon Press, 1991.
LOCKE, Alain, ed. *The New Negro: An Interpretation.* New York: Alfred and Charles Boni, 1925.
LOCKE, John. *Two Treatises of Government,* ed. by Peter Laslett. Cambridge: Cambridge University Press, 1970.
LONDON, Jack. *The Call of the Wild and White Fang.* New York: Washington Square Press, rpt. 1964.

----. "The Mexican." In *The Chicano: From Caricature to Self-Portrait*, ed. by Edward Simmen. New York: Mentor Books, 1971. Pp. 89-112.
LONG, Elizabeth. *The American Dream and the Popular Novel*. Boston and London: Routledge & Kegan Paul, 1985.
LÜDDECKE, Theodor. "Amerikanismus als Schlagwort und als Tatsache." *Deutsche Rundschau*, 56 (March 1930), 214-221.
LÜFFE, Heinz Christian. *Zur Textkonstitution afro-amerikanischer Initiationsliteratur*. Frankfurt and Bern: Peter Lang, 1982.
LYNN, Kenneth S. *The Dream of Success: A Study of the Modern American Imagination*. Boston: Little, Brown & Co., 1955.
MACAULEY, Robie. "Let Me Tell You About the Rich ..." *Kenyon Review*, 27 (1965), 645-671.
MacLEISH, Archibald. *Collected Poems 1917 - 1952*. Boston: Houghton Mifflin, 1952.
----. *The Collected Poems of Archibald MacLeish*. Boston: Houghton Mifflin, no date [1962].
----. *Land of the Free*. New York: Da Capo Press, 1977.
MacLEOD, Celeste. *Horatio Alger, Farewell: The End of the American Dream*. New York: Seaview Books, 1980.
MADDEN, David, ed. *American Dreams, American Nightmares*. Carbondale, Illinois: Southern Illinois University Press, 1970.
MAHAN, Alfred Thayer. *The Interest of America in Sea Power, Present and Future*. Boston: Little, Brown and Company, 1897.
MAILER, Norman. *The Deer Park*. London: Corgi Books, rpt. 1967.
----. *Why Are We in Vietnam?* New York: Berkley Medallion Books, 1968.
MALAMUD, Bernard. *A New Life*. New York: Pocket Books, 1973.
----. *The Assistant*. Harmondsworth: Penguin Books, 1967.
----. *The Natural*. New York: Dell Books, 1965.
MANDEL, Ruth B. "Bernard Malamud's *The Assistant* and *A New Life*: Ironic Affirmation." *Critique: Studies in Modern Fiction*, 7 (1965), 110-121.
MARCHAND, Roland. *Advertising the American Dream: Making Way for Modernity, 1920 - 1940*. Berkeley, Los Angeles and London: University of California Press, 1985.
MARCUS, Greil. *Mystery Train: Images of America in Rock 'n' Roll Music*. New York: E. P. Dutton, 1975.
MAROVITZ, Sanford E. "The Lonely New Americans of Abraham Cahan." *American Quarterly*, 29 (1968), 196-210.
----. "The Secular Trinity of a Lonely Millionaire: Language, Sex, and Power in *The Rise of David Levinsky*." *Studies in Jewish American Literature*, 2 (1982), 20-35.
MARTINEZ, Julio A., and Francisco A. LOMELI, eds. *Chicano Literature: A Reference Guide*. Westport, Connecticut: Greenwood Press, 1985.
MARVELL, Andrew. *The Poems of Andrew Marvell*, ed. by Hugh MacDonald. London: Routledge and Kegan Paul, 1960.
MARX, Leo. *The Machine in the Garden: Technology and the Pastoral Ideal in America*. New York: Oxford University Press, 1964.
MARZIO, Peter C., ed. *A Nation of Nations: The People Who Came to America as Seen Through Objects and Documents Exhibited at the Smithsonian Institution*. New York: Harper & Row, 1976.
MASON, Peter. *Deconstructing America*. London: Routledge, 1990.
MATHER, Cotton. *Selections from Cotton Mather*, ed. by Kenneth B. Murdock. New York: Hafner Press, 1973. [Reprint of the edition New York: Harcourt, Brace, and Company, 1926].
MAYER-HAMMOND, Theresa. *American Paradise: German Travel Literature from Duden to Kisch*. Heidelberg: Carl Winter, 1980.

McCAFFERY, Larry. "A Spirit of Transgression." [Interview with E. L. Doctorow]. In *E. L. Doctorow: Essays and Conversations*, ed. by Richard Trenner. Princeton, New Jersey: Ontario Review Press, 1983. Pp. 31-47.
McCALLUM, Henry D., and Frances T. McCALLUM. *The Wire That Fenced the West*. Norman, Oklahoma: University of Oklahoma Press, 1965.
McCULLERS, Carson. *The Member of the Wedding*. Harmondsworth: Penguin Books, rpt. 1964.
McMURTRY, Larry. "The Winning of the West in Retrospect." *Dialogue*, No. 92 (1991), 34-39.
MELVILLE, Herman. *White-Jacket; or, The World in a Man-of-War*, ed. by Harrison Hayford, Hershel Parker, and G. Thomas Tanselle. Evanston and Chicago: Northwestern University Press and Newberry Library, 1970.
----. *Moby-Dick; or, The Whale*, ed. by Harrison Hayford and Hershel Parker. New York and London: W. W. Norton, 1967.
----. *The Confidence-Man: His Masquerade*, ed. by Hershel Parker. New York and London: W. W. Norton, 1971.
MERK, Frederick. *Manifest Destiny and Mission in American History*. New York: Alfred A. Knopf, 1963.
MERSEBURGER, Peter. *Die unberechenbare Vormacht: Wohin steuern die USA?* München: Bertelsmann, 1983.
MEYER, Hildegard. *Nord-Amerika im Urteil des Deutschen Schrifttums bis zur Mitte des 19. Jahrhunderts. Eine Untersuchung über Kürnbergers "Amerika-Müden."* Hamburg: Friederichsen, de Gruyter & Co., 1929.
MILLER, Arthur. *Collected Plays*. London: Secker & Warburg, rpt. 1978.
----. *Collected Plays*. Vol. II. London: Secker & Warburg, 1981.
MILLER, Henry. *The Air-Conditioned Nightmare*. London: Panther Books, rpt. 1973.
MILLS, C. Wright. *White Collar*. New York: Oxford University Press, 1951.
MÖLLENBERG, Holger. *Die Rhetorik amerikanischer Literatur: Gedankliche Voraussetzungen moderner Literatur der Indianer Nordamerikas und ihre rhetorische Verwendung zur Beeinflussung einer differenzierten Leserschaft*. Frankfurt: R. G. Fischer, 1982.
MOGEN, David. "Owen Wister's Cowboy Heroes." In *The Western: A Collection of Critical Essays*, ed. by James K. Folsom. Englewood Cliffs, New Jersey: Prentice-Hall, 1979. Pp. 57-72.
----, Paul BRYANT, and Marle BUSBY, eds. *The Frontier Experience and the American Dream: Essays on American Literature*. College Station: Texas A&M University Press, 1989.
MOORE, Thomas. *The Poetical Works of Thomas Moore, Collected by Himself*. London: Longman, Brown, Green, and Longmans, 1853.
MORE, Sir Thomas. *Utopia: A Fruteful and Pleasaunt Worke of the Beste State of a Publyque Weale*. Amsterdam: Theatrum Orbis Terrarum, and New York: Da Capo Press, 1969. [Reprint of the edition London, 1551].
MOREY-GAINES, Anne-Janine. *Apples and Ashes: Culture, Metaphor, and Morality in the American Dream*. Chicago: Scholars Press, 1982.
MÜLLER, Emil-Peter. *Antiamerikanismus in Deutschland: Zwischen Care-Paket und Cruise Missile*. Köln: Deutscher Instituts-Verlag, 1986.
MUNDEN, Kenneth J. "A Contribution to the Psychological Understanding of the Origin of the Cowboy and His Myth." *American Imago*, 15 (1958), 103-148.
MURAYAMA, Milton. *All I Asking for Is My Body*. San Francisco: Supra Press, rpt. 1981.
NACHBAR, Jack, ed. *Focus on the Western*. Englewood Cliffs, New Jersey: Prentice-Hall, 1974.
"The New Ellis Island." *Time*, June 13, 1983, pp. 10-17.

NIEBUHR, H. Richard. *The Kingdom of God in America.* Chicago and New York: Willett, Clark & Company, 1937.
NIETZSCHE, Friedrich. *Werke in drei Bänden,* ed. by Karl Schlechta. München: Karl Hanser Verlag, no date [1965].
NISBET, Robert. *History of the Idea of Progress.* New York: Basic Books, 1980.
NOVAK, Michael. *The Rise of the Unmeltable Ethnics: Politics and Culture in the Seventies.* New York: Macmillan, 1972.
NYE, Russel B. *The Unembarrassed Muse: The Popular Arts in America.* New York: Dial Press, 1970.
OATES, Joyce Carol. *The Wheel of Love.* Greenwich, Connecticut: Fawcett Crest Books, 1972.
----. *Where Are You Going, Where Have You Been? Stories of Young America.* Greenwich, Connecticut: Fawcett Premier Books, 1974.
----. "How I Contemplated the World from the Detroit House of Correction and Began My Life Over Again." In *The American Short Story I: Initiation,* ed. by Peter Freese. Paderborn: Ferdinand Schöningh, 2nd ed. 1989. Pp. 144-163.
OKUBO, Mine. *Citizen 13660.* Seattle: University of Washington Press, 1983.
ORTEGA Y GASSETT, José. *Der Aufstand der Massen.* Hamburg: Rowohlts Deutsche Enzyklopädie, 1956.
ORTIZ, Simon J. "Kaiser and the War." In *Growing up in a Multicultural Society: Nine American Stories,* ed. by Peter Freese. München: Langenscheidt-Longman, 1994. Pp. 141-159.
----, ed. *Earth Power Coming: Short Fiction in Native American Literature.* Tsaile, Arizona: Navajo Community College Press, 1983.
O'SULLIVAN, John L. "The Great Nation of Futurity." *Democratic Review,* 6 (November 1839), 426-430.
OSTENDORF, Bernhard. "Ralph Ellison, 'Flying Home.'" In *Die amerikanische Short Story der Gegenwart: Interpretationen.* Berlin: Erich Schmidt, 1976. Pp. 64-76.
OTT, Ulrich. *Amerika ist anders: Studien zum Amerika-Bild in deutschen Reiseberichten des 20. Jahrhunderts.* Frankfurt and New York: Peter Lang, 1991.
PACHTER, Marc, ed. *Travelers to the New Nation 1776 - 1914: An American Studies Reader.* Washington: United States International Communication Agency, 1982.
PAINE, Thomas. *The Life and Works of Thomas Paine,* ed. by William M. Van der Weyde. New Rochelle, New York: Thomas Paine National Historical Association, 1925.
PARK, Sue Simpson. "A Study in Counterpoint: Joyce Carol Oates's 'How I Contemplated the World from the Detroit House of Correction and Began My Life Over Again.'" *Modern Fiction Studies,* 22 (1976), 213-224.
PARRINGTON, Vernon Louis. *Main Currents in American Thought.* Vol. I, *1620 - 1800: The Colonial Mind.* New York: Harvest Books, no date.
PAYNE, William. "Recent Fiction." *The Dial,* 6 (1885).
PEALE, Norman Vincent. *The Power of Positive Thinking.* Kingswood: Cedar Books, rpt. 1968.
PEARCE, Roy Harvey. "Hawthorne and the Sense of the Past or, The Immortality of Major Molineux." *Journal of English Literary History,* 21 (1954), 327-349.
PERRY, Ruth. "A Short History of the Term *Politically Correct.*" In *Beyond P.C.: Toward a Politics of Understanding,* ed. by Patricia Aufderheide. Saint Paul, Minnesota: Graywolf Press, 1992. Pp. 71-79.
PIESMAN, Marissa, and Marilee HARTLEY. *The Yuppie Handbook: The State-of-the-Art Manual for Young Urban Professionals.* New York: Pocket Books, 1985.

PLACIDO, Beniamino. "Die Erfindung Amerikas." In Gian Paolo Ceserani, Umberto Eco and Beniamino Placido. *Modell Amerika: Die Wiederentdeckung eines Way of Life.* Münster: Englisch-Amerikanische Studien, 1985. Pp. 95-141.
PORTER, Cole. *Songs by ... Cole Porter.* New York: Harms Inc., 1954.
PRATT, Julius W. "The Origin of 'Manifest Destiny.'" *American Historical Review,* 32 (1927), 795-798.
PROTZMAN, Ferdinand. "To Germans, U.S. Past Is Mostly Blank." *International Herald Tribune.* February 2, 1989. P. 6.
PÜTZ, Manfred. "Max Webers und Ferdinand Kürnbergers Auseinandersetzung mit Benjamin Franklin: Zum Verständnis von Quellenverfälschung und Fehlinterpretation." *Amerikastudien - American Studies,* 29 (1984), 297-310.
----. "Max Webers These vom 'Geist des Kapitalismus' und der Fall Benjamin Franklin." *Jahrbuch der Universität Augsburg,* 1988, pp. 193-207.
PYNCHON, Thomas. *The Crying of Lot 49.* New York: Bantam Books, 1967.
----. *Gravity's Rainbow.* New York: Bantam Books, 1974.
QUINN, David B. *North America from Earliest Discovery to First Settlements: The Norse Voyages to 1612.* New York: Harper & Row, 1977.
RADDATZ, Fritz. Amerikanisches Alphabet." *Süddeutsche Zeitung,* December 5/6, 1964.
RAEITHEL, Gert et al. "Projektvorschlag: Europäische Amerika-Urteile im 20. Jahrhundert." *Sprache im technischen Zeitalter,* 56 (1975), 333-341.
----. "Antiamerikanismus als Funktion unterschiedlicher Objektbeziehungen." *Englisch-Amerikanische Studien,* 6 (1984), 8-21.
----. "What's Anti-Americanism Anyway?" *Englisch-Amerikanische Studien,* 10 (1988), 171-178.
RANDALL, Dudley. *Cities Burning.* Detroit: Broadside Press, 1968.
RAPF, Joanna. "'Some Fantasy on Earth': Doctorow's *Welcome to Hard Times* as Novel and Film." *Literature/Film Quarterly,* 13 (1985), 50-55.
RASCHE, Bernd. *Der Zwang zum Erfolg: Kulturgeschichtliche Untersuchungen eines modernen Leidens an amerikanischer Kurzprosa des 20. Jahrhunderts.* Stuttgart: M & P, 1991.
RAVITCH, Diane. "Multiculturalism: E Pluribus Plures." *The American Scholar,* 59, 3 (Summer 1990), 337-354.
REBOLLEDO, Tey Diana, and Eliana S. Rivero, eds. *Infinite Divisions: An Anthology of Chicana Literature.* Tuscon and London: The University of Arizona Press, 1993.
REICH, Charles A. *The Greening of America.* London: Allen Lane, 1971.
REICH, Robert B. *The Next American Frontier.* Harmondsworth: Penguin Books, 1984.
REESE, Michael, and Jennifer FOOTE. "The End of the Dream." *Newsweek,* July 31, 1989. pp. 27-33.
REESE, Lynn, Jean WILKINSON, and Phyllis Sheon KOPPELMAN, eds. *I'm on My Way Running: Women Speak on Coming of Age.* New York: Avon Books, 1983.
RICHMAN, Sidney. *Bernard Malamud.* New York: Twayne Publishers, 1966.
RICKENBACKER, William F. "60,000,000 Westerners Can't Be Wrong." *National Review,* 13 (October 23, 1962), 322-325.
RIDEOUT, Walter B. *The Radical Novel in the United States, 1900 - 1954: Some Interrelations of Literature and Society.* Cambridge, Massachusetts: Harvard University Press, 1956.
RIECK, Werner. "Poetische Bilder von Völkern als literaturwissenschaftliches Problem." *Weimarer Beiträge,* 32 (1986), 48-68.
RIESMAN, David, Nathan GLAZER, and Reuel DENNEY. *The Lonely Crowd: A Study of the Changing American Character.* New Haven and London: Yale University Press, 1950.
RIFKIN, Jeremy, with Ted HOWARD. *Entropy: A New World View.* London: Paladin Books, 1985.

RIIS, Jacob A. *How the Other Half Lives: Studies Among the Tenements of New York.* New York: Dover Publications, 1971.
RILEY, Patricia, ed. *Growing Up Native American: An Anthology.* New York: William Morrow, 1993.
RINGER, Robert J. *Winning Through Intimidation.* Los Angeles: Los Angeles Book Publishers Co., 1974.
----. *Looking Out for Number One.* New York: Funk & Wagnalls, 1977.
----. *Restoring the American Dream.* San Francisco: QED, 1979.
RITTER, Alexander, ed. *Deutschlands literarisches Amerikabild: Neuere Forschungen zur Amerikarezeption der deutschen Literatur.* Hildesheim and New York: Georg Olms, 1977.
RIVERA, Tomás. *"...y no se lo tragó la tierra" / And the Earth Did Not Part.* Engl. transl. by Herminio Ríos. Berkeley, CA: Quinto Sol Publications, 1971.
RODRIGUEZ DE MONTALVO, Garci. *Las Sergas de Esplandían* [1526], ed. and intr. by Pascal de Gayangos y Arce. Madrid: Ediciones Atlas, 1950. - Excerpts, transl. by Edward Everett Hale, in *The Atlantic Monthly,* 82 (March 1864), 266f.
ROMBERG, Sigmund, and Dorothy DONNELLY. *The Student Prince.* London: Chappell, and New York: Harms, 1932.
ROOSEVELT, Theodore. *The Winning of the West: An Account of the Exploration and Settlement of Our Country from the Alleghanies to the Pacific.* 4 vols. New York: G. P. Putnam's Sons, 1889 - 1896.
ROSEN, Kenneth, ed. *The Man to Send Rain Clouds: Contemporary Stories by Indians.* New York: Random House, 1975.
ROSENFELD, Isaac. "The Jew as American Millionaire." In *Jewish-American Literature: An Anthology,* ed. by Abraham Chapman. New York: Mentor Books, 1974. Pp. 618-625.
ROTH, Henry. *Call It Sleep.* New York: Avon Books, 1964.
ROTH, Philip. *Goodbye, Columbus.* London: Corgi Books, 1964.
----. "The Conversion of the Jews." In *The American Short Story I: Initiation,* ed. by Peter Freese. Paderborn: Ferdinand Schöningh, 2nd ed. 1989. Pp. 127-142.
----. *Reading Myself and Others.* New York: Bantam Books, 1977.
SALTZMAN, Arthur. "The Stylistic Energy of E. L. Doctorow." In *E. L. Doctorow: Essays and Conversations,* ed. by Richard Trenner. Princeton, New Jersey: Ontario Review Press, 1983. Pp. 73-108.
SANFORD, Charles L. *The Quest for Paradise: Europe and the American Moral Imagination.* Urbana, Illinois: University of Illinois Press, 1961.
SANTIAGO, Danny. "The Somebody." In *Growing up in a Multicultural Society: Nine American Stories,* ed. by Peter Freese. München: Langenscheidt-Longman, 1994. Pp. 81-95.
----. *Famous All Over Town.* New York: Plume Books, 1984.
SAUZAY, Brigitte. *Die rätselhaften Deutschen: Die Bundesrepublik von außen gesehen.* Stuttgart: Bonn Aktuell, 1986.
SCHAEFER, Jack. *Shane.* London: Corgi Books, rpt. 1979.
SCHARNHORST, Gary, with Jack BALES. *The Lost Life of Horatio Alger, Jr.* Bloomington, Indiana: Indiana University Press, 1985.
SCHEIBER, Jane L., and Robert C. ELLIOTT, eds. *In Search of the American Dream.* New York: North American Library, 1984.
SCHEIN, Harry. "The Olympian Cowboy." [Transl. from the Swedish by Ida M. Alcock]. *The American Scholar,* 24 (1955), 309-320.
SCHLESINGER, Arthur M., Jr. *The Disuniting of America: Reflections on a Multicultural Society.* New York and London: W. W. Norton, 1992.
SCHÜTT, Peter. "Amerika - jenseits des Ural: Anmerkungen zum USA-Bild bundesdeutscher Schüler." *Englisch-Amerikanische Studien,* 4 (1982), 397-399.

SCHULBERG, Budd. *What Makes Sammy Run?* London: Corgi Books, rpt. 1967.
SCHULLER, Robert H. *Tough Times Never Last, But Tough People Do!* Toronto: Bantam Books, 1984.
SCHWEIGLER, Gebhard L. "Anti-Americanism in Germany." *The Washington Quarterly*, Winter 1986, pp. 70-71.
SEE, Carolyn. "The Hollywood Novel: The American Dream Cheat." In *Tough Guy Writers of the Thirties*, ed. by David Madden. Carbondale and Edwardsville: Southern Illinois University Press, 1968. Pp. 199-217.
SENNETT, Richard. *The Fall of Public Man: On the Social Psychology of Capitalism.* Cambridge: Cambridge University Press, 1977.
SHAKESPEARE, William. *The Tempest*, ed. by Frank Kermode. London: Methuen, and Cambridge, Massachusetts, Harvard University Press, rpt. 1966. The Arden Shakespeare.
SHARPE, Tom. *The Great Pursuit.* London: Pan Books, 1979.
SHELTON, Frank W. "E. L. Doctorow's *Welcome to Hard Times*: The Western and the American Dream." *Midwest Quarterly*, 25 (1983), 7-17.
SHEPARD, Sam. *True West.* In his *Seven Plays.* London and Boston: Faber and Faber, 1985.
SHIRLEY, Carl R., and Paula W. SHIRLEY. *Understanding Chicano Literature.* Columbia: University of South Carolina Press, 1988.
SILKO, Leslie Marmon. *Ceremony.* New York: Viking Penguin Books, 1986.
SIMMEN, Edward, ed. *The Chicano: From Caricature to Self-Portrait.* New York: Mentor Books, 1971.
----, ed. *North of the Rio Grande: The Mexican-American Experience in Short Fiction.* New York: Mentor Books, 1992.
SIMMS, William Gilmore. *The Yemassee.* New York: Harper & Brothers, 1835.
SINGER, David. "David Levinsky's Fall: A Note on the Liebman Thesis." *American Quarterly*, 19 (1967), 696-706.
SKAGGS, Calvin, ed. *The American Short Story.* New York: Dell Books, 1979.
----, ed. *The American Short Story.* Vol. II. New York: Dell Books, 1980.
SLANSKY, Paul, ed. *The Clothes Have No Emperor: A Chronicle of the American 80s.* New York: Simon and Schuster, 1989.
SLATER, Peter Gregg. "Ethnicity in *The Great Gatsby*." *Twentieth Century Literature*, 19 (1973), 53-62.
SLOTKIN, Richard. *Regeneration Through Violence: The Mythology of the American Frontier, 1600 - 1860.* Middletown, Connecticut: Wesleyan University Press, 1973.
----. *The Fatal Environment: The Myth of the Frontier in the Age of Industrialization, 1800 - 1890.* Middletown, Connecticut: Wesleyan University Press, 1985.
----. *Gunfighter Nation: The Myth of the Frontier in Twentieth-Century America.* New York: Atheneum, 1992.
SMITH, Henry Nash. *Virgin Land: The American West as Symbol and Myth.* Cambridge, Massachusetts: Harvard University Press, rpt. 1982.
----. "The Search for a Capitalist Hero: Businessmen in American Fiction." In *The Business Establishment*, ed. by Earl F. Cheit. New York: Wiley and Sons, 1964. Pp. 77-112.
SMITH, Jean Wheeler. "Frankie Mae." In *Black Short Story Anthology*, ed. by Woodie King. New York: New American Library, 1972. Pp. 35-46; and in *Black-Eyed Susans: Classic Stories By and About Black Women*, ed. by Mary Helen Washington. Garden City, New York: Doubleday, 1975. Pp. 3-18.
SMITH, Lew, ed. *The American Dream.* Glenview, Illinois: Scott, Foresman and Company, 1977.

SOLLORS, Werner. "Literature and Ethnicity." In *Harvard Encyclopedia of American Ethnic Groups*, ed. by Stephan Thernstrom. Cambridge, Massachusetts, and London: The Belknap Press of Cambridge University Press, 1980. Pp. 647-665.
----. *Beyond Ethnicity: Consent and Descent in American Culture*. New York and Oxford: Oxford University Press, 1986.
----. "*E pluribus unum*; or, Matthew Arnold Meets George Orwell in the 'Multiculturalism' Debate." Working Paper No. 53 (1992) of the John F. Kennedy-Institut für Nordamerikastudien.
SONNICHSEN, Charles Leland. *From Hopalong to Hud: Thoughts on Western Fiction*. College Station and London: Texas A&M University Press, 1978.
SPENCER, Herbert. "A Theory of Population, Deduced from the General Law of Animal Fertility." *Westminster Review*, 57 (1852), 468-501.
----. *First Principles*. New York: D. Appleton and Company, 1864.
SPENGLER, Oswald. *Jahre der Entscheidung. Erster Teil, Deutschland und die weltgeschichtliche Entwicklung*. München: C. H. Beck, 1933.
SPICER, Edward H. "American Indians." In *Harvard Encyclopedia of American Ethnic Groups*, ed. by Stephan Thernstrom. Cambridge, Massachusetts, and London: The Belknap Press of Harvard University Press, 1980. Pp. 58-114.
SPILLER, Robert E. "The Verdict of Sidney Smith." *American Literature*, 1 (1929/30), 3-13.
STAISCH, Peter. *Mein Amerika: Innenansichten aus dem Land der Widersprüche*. München: Piper, 1991.
STAPF, Kurt H., Wolfgang STROEBE and Klaus JONAS. *Amerikaner über Deutschland und die Deutschen: Urteile und Vorurteile*. Opladen: Westdeutscher Verlag, 1986.
STAUFFER, Helen Winter, and Susan J. ROSOWSKI, eds. *Women and Western American Literature*. Troy, New York: The Whitston Publishing Company, 1982.
STEIN, Howard F., and Robert F. HILL. *The Ethnic Imperative: Examining the New White Ethnic Movement*. University Park and London: Pennsylvania State University, 1977.
STEINBECK, John. "Flight." In *The Long Valley*. London: Corgi Books, rpt. 1973. Pp. 32-52.
STONE, Albert E. *The Innocent Eye: Childhood and Mark Twain's Imagination*. New Haven: Yale University Press, 1961.
"Strangers in Paradise: Asians try to find their place on North America's West Coast." *Time*, March 5, 1990, pp. 34-41.
STONE, J. B., and Luther K. MASKET, eds. *Stories from the Black Experience*. Stuttgart: Ernst Klett, 1981.
STRONG, Josiah. *Our Country: Its Possible Future and Its Present Crisis*, ed. by Jurgen Herbst. Cambridge, Massachusetts: The Belknap Press of Harvard University Press, 1963. [Reprint of the rev. ed. New York: Baker and Taylor, 1891.]
TAKAKI, Ronald. *Strangers from a Different Shore: A History of Asian Americans*. Boston: Little, Brown and Company, 1989.
TAKUWA, Shinji. *The American Dream and Self-Examination*. Tokyo: Eihosha, 1978.
TAN, Amy. *The Joy Luck Club*. New York: G. P. Putnam's Sons, 1989.
----. *The Kitchen God's Wife*. New York: G. P. Putnam's Sons, 1991.
TANNER, Stephen L. "Rage and Order in Doctorow's *Welcome to Hard Times*." *South Dakota Quarterly*, 22 (1984), 79-85.
----. *The Reign of Wonder: Naivety and Reality in American Literature*. Cambridge: Cambridge University Press, 1965.
----. *City of Words: American Fiction 1950 - 1970*. London: Jonathan Cape, 1971.
TAWNEY, Richard Henry. *Religion and the Rise of Capitalism: A Historical Study*. Harmondsworth: Penguin Books, rpt. 1964.

TAYLOR, Lonn, and Ingrid MAAR, *The American Cowboy*. Washington: Library of Congress, 1983.
TAYLOR, Walter Fuller. *The Economic Novel in America*. Chapel Hill: University of North Carolina Press, 1952.
TEBBEL, John. *From Rags to Riches: Horatio Alger, Jr., and the American Dream*. New York: Macmillan, 1963.
TERKEL, Studs. *American Dreams Lost and Found*. New York: Ballantine Books, 1981.
----. *The Great Divide: Second Thoughts on the American Dream*. New York: Avon Books, 1989.
----. *Race: How Blacks and Whites Think and Feel about the American Obsession*. New York: Anchor Books, 1993.
THERNSTROM, Stephan, ed. *Harvard Encyclopedia of American Ethnic Groups*. Cambridge, Massachusetts, and London: The Belknap Press of Harvard University Press, 1980.
THOMAS, Piri. *Down These Mean Streets*. New York: Vintage Books, 1974.
THOREAU, Henry David. *The Writings of Henry David Thoreau*. Boston and New York: Houghton Mifflin, no date [1893 and 1906].
TONN, Horst. *Zeitgenössische Chicano-Erzählliteratur in englischer Sprache: Autobiographie und Roman*. Frankfurt: Peter Lang, 1988.
----, ed. *Hispanic Groups in the USA*. Berlin: Cornelsen, 1992.
TRACY, Brian, and Erwin HELMS, eds. *American Dreams, American Nightmares*. Paderborn: Ferdinand Schöningh, 1981; and TRACY, Brian, and Erwin HELMS. *American Dreams, American Nightmares - Interpretations and Suggestions for Teaching*. Paderborn: Ferdinand Schöningh, 1982.
TRAUTMANN, Korinna, ed. *Hispanic Americans*. Stuttgart: Ernst Klett Verlag, 1989.
TROMMLER, Frank. "Aufstieg und Fall des Amerikanismus in Deutschland." In *Amerika und die Deutschen: Bestandsaufnahme einer 300jährigen Geschichte*, ed. by Frank Trommler. Opladen: Westdeutscher Verlag, 1986. Pp. 666-676.
TRUETTNER, William H., ed. *The West as America: Reinterpreting Images of the Frontier, 1820 - 1920*. Washington and London: The Smithsonian Institute Press, 1991.
TUDYKA, Kurt. "Anti-Amerikanismus - Was ist das?" In *Amerika: Der Riskante Partner*, ed. by Anton-Andreas Guha and Sven Papcke. Königstein: Athenäum, 1984. Pp. 117-130.
TURNER, Donald Lloyd, ed. *God's Own Country: Religion in America*. Paderborn: Ferdinand Schöningh, 1987.
TURNER, Frederick Jackson. "The Significance of the Frontier in American History." In *An American Primer*, ed. by Daniel J. Boorstin. New York: New American Library, 1985. Pp. 542-570.
TURNER, Justin G. "Emanuel Leutze's Mural *Westward the Course of Empire Takes Its Way*." *Manuscripts*, 18, No. 2 (September 1966), 4-16.
TUVESON, Ernest Lee. *Redeemer Nation: The Idea of America's Millennial Role*. Chicago and London: University of Chicago Press. 1978.
TWAIN, Mark. *The Writings of Mark Twain*. St. Clair Shores: Scholarly Press, 1976. [Reprint of the Author's National Edition. New York and London: Harper and Brothers, 1897-1899].
----. *A Connecticut Yankee in King Arthur's Court*, ed. by Bernard L. Stein. Vol. IX of *The Works of Mark Twain*, ed. by Frederick Anderson. Berkeley: University of California Press, 1979.
----. *The Innocents Abroad; or, The New Pilgrims' Progress*. Hartford: American Publishing Company, 1869.

TYLER, Royall. *The Contrast*. In *The Norton Anthology of American Literature*, ed. by Nina Baym et al. New York and London: W. W. Norton, 3rd ed., 1989. Vol. I. Pp. 749-789.
ULICH, Michaela, Wolf STENGER, and Dietrich BÜSCHER, eds. *Language & Politics: Political Speeches in the U.S.A.* München: Langenscheidt-Longman, 1983.
UPDIKE, John. *Couples*. Greenwich, Connecticut: Fawcett Crest Books, 1969.
VASQUEZ, Richard. *Chicano*. New York: Avon Books, 1971.
VEBLEN, Thorstein. *The Theory of the Leisure Class: An Economic Study in the Evolution of Institutions*. New York and London: Macmillan & Co., 1899.
VILLAREAL, José Antonio. *Pocho*. Garden City, New York: Doubleday Anchor Books, 1970.
VONNEGUT, Kurt. *God Bless You, Mr. Rosewater, or Pearls Before Swine*. London: Panther Books, rpt. 1972.
----. *The Sirens of Titan*. New York: Dell Books, rpt. 1972.
----. *Cat's Cradle*. New York: Dell Books, rpt. 1970.
----. *Breakfast of Champions, or Goodbye Blue Monday!* New York: Dell Books, 1974.
----. *Wampeters, Foma & Granfalloons (Opinions)*. New York: Delta Books, 1974.
----. *Hocus Pocus*. New York: G. P. Putnam's Sons, 1990.
VONNEGUT, Mark. *The Eden Express*. New York: Bantam Books, 1976.
WALKER, Alice. *In Love and Trouble: Stories of Black Women*. London: The Women's Press, 1984.
----. "Everyday Use." In *Growing up in a Multicultural Society: Nine American Stories*, ed. by Peter Freese. München: Langenscheidt-Longman, 1994. Pp. 33-50.
WALKER, Scott, ed. *Stories from the American Mosaic*. Saint Paul, Minnesota: Graywolf Press, 1990.
WALSER, Martin. "Wo viel Schatten ist, ist auch viel Licht. Eindrücke eines verhinderten Einwanderers." In *Bilder von Amerika: Gespräche mit deutschen Schriftstellern*, ed. by Heinz D. Osterle. Münster: Englisch-Amerikanische Studien, 1987. Pp. 219-230.
WALZER, Michael. "Puritanism as a Revolutionary Ideology." In *Essays in Colonial American History*, ed. by Paul Goodman. New York: Holt, Rinehart and Winston, 1967. Pp. 33-48.
WANAMAKER, John. "The Evolution of Mercantile Business." In *An American Primer*, ed. by Daniel J. Boorstin. New York: New American Library, 1985. Pp. 654-664.
WARREN, Robert Penn. "Blackberry Winter." In *The Circus in the Attic and Other Stories*. New York: Harcourt, Brace & World, 1962. Pp. 63-87; and in *The American Short Story I: Initiation*, ed. by Peter Freese. Paderborn: Ferdinand Schöningh, 2nd ed., 1989. Pp. 94-116.
WATTS, Emily Stipes. *The Businessman in American Literature*. Athens, Georgia: University of Georgia Press, 1982.
WEBER, Max. *Die protestantische Ethik I: Eine Aufsatzsammlung*, ed. by Johannes Winckelmann. München and Hamburg: Siebenstern, 2nd rev. ed., 1969.
WEBER, Max. *The Protestant Ethic and the Spirit of Capitalism*, transl. by Talcott Parsons. London: Unwin Paperbacks, 1985.
----. *Gesammelte Aufsätze zur Religionssoziologie I*. Tübingen: J. C. B. Mohr, 9th ed., 1988.
WEHLER, Hans-Ulrich. *Preußen ist wieder chic ... Politik und Polemik in zwanzig Essays*. Frankfurt: edition suhrkamp, 1983.
WEINBERG, Albert K. *Manifest Destiny: A Study of Nationalistic Expansionism in American History*. Chicago: Quadrangle Books, no date [originally 1935].
WEISS, Richard. *The American Myth of Success: From Horatio Alger to Norman Vincent Peale*. New York: Basic Books, 1969.
WEST, Nathanael. *The Collected Works of Nathanael West*. Harmondsworth: Penguin Books, 1975.

"Westerns: The Six-Gun Galahad." *Time*, March 30, 1959. Pp. 36-43.
WHITE, G. Edward. *The Eastern Establishment and the Western Experience: The West of Frederic Remington, Theodore Roosevelt, and Owen Wister*. New Haven and London: Yale University Press, 1968.
WHITE, Hayden. *Metahistory: The Historical Imagination in Nineteenth-Century Europe*. Baltimore and London: Johns Hopkins University Press, 1975.
WHITFIELD, Raoul. *Death in a Bowl*. New York and London: A. A. Knopf, 1930.
WHITMAN, Walt. *The Complete Writings of Walt Whitman*, issued under the editorial supervision of His Literary Executors, Richard Maurice Bucke, Thomas B. Harned, and Horace L. Traubel. St. Clair Shores: Scholarly Press, 1977. [Reprint of the edition New York: G. P. Putnam's Sons, 1902].
WHYTE JR., William H. *The Organization Man*. New York: Simon & Schuster, 1956.
WINCKELMANN, Johannes, ed. *Die protestantische Ethik II: Kritiken und Antikritiken*. München and Hamburg: Siebenstern, 1968.
WINTER, Rolf. *Ami Go Home: Plädoyer für den Abschied von einem gewalttätigen Land*. Hamburg: Rasch und Röhring, 1989; München: Goldmann Paperback, 1990.
----. *Die amerikanische Zumutung: Plädoyers gegen das Land des real existierenden Kapitalismus*. München: Wilhelm Heyne, 1990.
WINTHROP, John. "A Modell of Christian Charity." In *An American Primer*, ed. by Daniel J. Boorstin. New York: New American Library, 1985. Pp. 26-43.
WISTER, Fanny Kemble, ed. *Owen Wister Out West: His Journals and Letters*. Chicago: University of Chicago Press, 1958.
WISTER, Owen. *The Writings of Owen Wister*. New York: Macmillan, 1928.
----. *The Virginian: A Horseman of the Plains*. New York: Harper & Row, 1965.
WITTKE, Gabriele. *Female Initiation in the American Novel*. Frankfurt: Peter Lang, 1991.
WOLFE, Tom. *The Bonfire of the Vanities*. London: Pan Books, 1988.
WRIGHT, Richard. *Native Son*. New York: New American Library, no date.
----. *Uncle Tom's Children*. New York: Harper & Row Perennial Library, 1965.
----. *Eight Men*. New York: Pyramid Books, 1969.
----. "Almost a Man." In *The American Short Story*, ed. by Calvin Skaggs. New York: Dell Books, 1979. Pp. 257-269.
WYLIE, Philip. *Generation of Vipers*. New York and Toronto: Farrar & Rinehart, 1942.
WYLLIE, Irvin G. *The Self-Made Man in America: The Myth of Rags to Riches*. New Brunswick, New Jersey: Rutgers University Press, 1954.
YAMAMOTO, Hisaye. "Writing." *American Journal*, 3 (1976), 126-133.
----. "Yoneko's Earthquake." In *Growing up in a Multicultural Society: Nine American Stories*, ed. by Peter Freese. München: Langenscheidt-Longman, 1994. Pp. 96-118.
ZACHARASIEWICZ, Waldemar. "National Stereotypes in Literature in the English Language: A Review of Research." *REAL: The Yearbook of Research in English and American Literature*, 1 (1983), 75-120.
ZANGER, Jules. "David Levinsky: Master of Pilpul." *Papers on Language and Literature*, 3 (1977), 283-294.
ZANGWILL, Israel. *The Works of Israel Zangwill*. New York: AMS Press, 1969. [Reprint of the edition London: Globe Publishing Company, 1925].
ZAPPA, Frank. *Plastic People: Songbuch*. Frankfurt: Zweitausendeins, 1977.
----, and Peter OCCHIOGROSSO. *Frank Zappa: I am the American Dream*. München: Goldmann, 1991.

Index

Abbey, Edward : 166, 357
Acosta, Oscar Zeta: 249
Adams, James Truslow: 93, 190
Adams, John: 89, 98, 100
Albee, Edward: 163
Aldrich, Thomas Bailey: 199, 200
Alger, Horatio: 85, 111-113, 136, 151, 275, 308, 313, 318
Ames, Nathaniel: 99, 100
Anaya, Rudolfo A.: 248
Anderson, Sherwood: 242
Astor, Johann Jacob: 316
Austen, Jane: 345
Autry, Gene: 350
Baldwin, James: 70, 77, 193f., 214, 251, 396
Bambara, Toni Cade: 252, 253ff., 271
Barlow, Joel: 115
Barth, John: 354
Barthelme, Donald: 166
Barton, Bruce: 281f.
Beadle, Erastus: 324
Beecher, Henry Ward: 124
Beecher, Lyman: 124f., 126, 331
Beecher-Stowe, Harriet: 124
Bellamy, Edward: 104
Bellow, Saul: 26, 71, 103, 249, 285
Berger, Thomas: 79, 354, 357
Berkeley, George: 35, 97f., 100, 125, 144f., 150, 349, 377
Beveridge, Albert J.: 139, 148, 150, 167, 332
Bierce, Ambrose: 318
Bierstadt, Albert: 378
Biggers, Earl Derr: 245
Bird, Montgomery: 321
Bloom, Allan: 222
Boone, Daniel: 120, 148, 176, 321, 323, 388
Boss Tweed: 201
Bradbury, Ray: 138

Bradford, William: 36, 102, 107
Brant, Sebastian: 94f.
Brautigan, Richard: 161, 166
Brendan: 95
Brinkmann, Carl: 61-63
Brown, Charles Brockden: 236, 321
Browne, Jackson: 160
Browning, Robert: 345
Bruce-Novoa: 248
Buntline, Ned: 327
Bush, George: 222
Byron, George Gordon: 392
Cahan, Abraham: 12, 167, 244, 294-306
Calamity Jane: 324, 359
Calvin, John: 109
Carnegie, Andrew: 112, 275, 279, 282, 283
Carter, Jimmy: 32, 34, 88, 175
Cather, Willa: 244
Chambers, Whittaker: 386
Chandler, Raymond: 137, 293
Channing, Ellery: 43
Chapman, Tracy: 161
Reich, Charles A.: 176
Chesnutt, Charles Waddell: 244
Chief Joseph: 378, 379, 380
Chin, Frank: 246, 264-266, 271
Chu, Louis: 245
Clark, John Hendrik: 192
Clark, William: 120, 145, 148
Cleaver, Eldridge: 251
Cody, Buffalo Bill: 176, 324, 327
Colt, Samuel: 364
Columbus, Christopher: 20, 35, 78, 94, 95, 96, 130, 148, 383
Conwell, Russell H.: 280
Cooke, Ebenezer: 354
Coolidge, Calvin: 310
Cooper, James Fenimore: 58, 120, 163, 242, 292, 321, 322, 323f., 328, 388, 389, 390, 391, 393

Coover, Robert: 151
Costner, Kevin: 172
Cotton, John: 102
Crane, Stephen: 170, 238, 270, 340
Crèvecoeur, J. Hector St. John: 36, 47, 100, 105, 107, 151, 153, 179, 194, 195, 197, 201, 300, 305, 342, 377
Crockett, Davy: 120
Currier & Ives: 148
Custer, George Armstrong: 138
D'Souza, Dinesh: 222
Dana, Richard Henry: 242
Dante Alighieri: 238
Darwin, Charles: 111, 283, 285, 301
Deadwood Dick: 324
Dickens, Charles: 47
Dickinson, Emily: 18
Dixon, Thomas W.: 155, 214
Doctorow, E. L.: 13, 19, 22, 47, 295, 355-375
Donne, John: 95
Donner Party: 127
Dos Passos, John: 319
Drayton, Michael: 96, 100, 107
Dreiser, Theodore: 112, 284f., 310
Duden, Gottfried: 36, 39, 43, 106, 395
Du Bois-Reymond, Emil: 60
Dukakis, Michael: 90f., 175, 274
Dunbar, Paul Lawrence: 244
Dwight, Timothy: 355
Earp, Wyatt: 137
Eastlake, William: 357
Eastwood, Clint: 137
Edwards, Jonathan: 102, 124
Eisenhower, Dwight D: 32
Eliot, George: 345
Ellis, Bret Easton: 165
Ellison, Ralph: 192, 250, 251, 252, 256, 271
Emerson, Ralph Waldo: 152, 191, 273, 381, 386, 390, 391, 393
Enzensberger, Hans Magnus: 47
Erasmus of Rotterdam: 95
Erdrich, Louise: 263f., 271
Farrell, James T.: 244

Faulkner, William: 174, 241, 243, 270, 304, 354
Faust, Frederick (alias Max Brand): 352
Ferlinghetti, Lawrence: 163
Fiedler, Leslie A.: 243, 320, 352, 353, 376
Filson, John: 323
Fiske, Jim: 316
Fitzgerald, F. Scott: 175f., 215, 240, 270, 293, 305, 307, 373, 390
Flint, Timothy: 323
Fonda, Henry: 358
Ford, Gerald R.: 32
Fourier, Charles: 104
Franklin, Benjamin: 43, 110, 114, 118, 127, 240, 273, 278, 279f., 305, 317, 392
Freneau, Philip: 115
Freud, Sigmund: 21, 47
Frost, Robert: 78, 79
Galle, Philippe: 36
Gast, John: 140, 142, 198
Gerstäcker: 47
Ginsberg, Allen: 164, 167
Glidden, Frederick (alias Luke Short): 352
Glidden, Joseph Farwell: 121
Goethe, Johann Wolfgang: 21, 30, 166
Goetz, Bernhard: 34
Gold, Michael: 294
Goldfish, Samuel: 295
Gonzales, Rodolfo: 168f., 257
Goodwin, Thomas: 102
Gould, Jay: 283
Granat, Robert: 257-259, 271
Grant, Madison: 155, 207-209, 214
Grant, Ulysses S.: 387
Greeley, Horace: 126f., 340, 375
Gregory, Dick: 294
Grey, Zane: 351
Griffith, D. W.: 214
Hailey, Alex: 66, 71, 193
Halfeld, Adolf: 63f., 395
Haliburton, Thomas Chandler: 286

Hall, Stanley: 190
Hammett, Dashiell: 137
Hardy, Thomas: 392
Haskin, Frederick J.: 197f.
Hawthorne, Nathaniel: 18, 26, 101, 104, 118, 236-238, 270, 317, 388, 393
Haycox, Ernest: 352
Hegel, Georg Wilhelm Friedrich: 58
Heller, Joseph: 249, 312
Hemingway, Ernest: 240, 270
Henry, Alexander: 243
Hercules: 148
Herrick, Robert: 308
Hiss, Alger: 386
Hitler, Adolf: 47, 67
Hochhuth, Rolf: 82
Holitscher, Arthur: 55, 60
Howells, William Dean: 118, 287-293, 295, 306, 307, 334, 384
Hughes, Langston: 174
Hunt, Thomas P.: 280
Hunter, Evan: 71
Huntington, Collis P.: 283
Huxley, Aldous: 95
Iacocca, Lee: 127, 175, 317
Ingraham, Prentiss: 327
Irving, Washington: 117f., 390
Jackson, Jesse: 88
James Brothers: 324
James, Henry: 26, 103, 193, 194
James, William: 113, 273, 292, 331, 383, 392
Jefferson, Thomas: 89, 104, 105, 106, 116, 120, 194, 205, 238, 392
Jiménez: 259f., 271
Johann, A. E,: 56
Johnson, Edward: 101
Johnson, James Weldon: 263
Johnson, Lyndon B.: 32, 47
Jones, Ernest: 21
Jong, Erica: 79
Joyce, James: 251, 379
Kallen, Horace: 155, 215, 219
Katsch, Bernhard: 69
Kearney, Dennis: 204

Kelley, William Melvin: 192
Kemble, Fanny: 331
Kennedy, Paul M.: 398
Kennedy, John F.: 32, 67, 136f., 138, 355, 356
Keppler, Joseph: 155
Kesey, Ken: 243, 354
Khrushchev, Nikita: 90
King, Martin Luther: 167, 188, 192
Kingston, Maxine Hong: 246
Kohl, Helmut: 67, 74
Korda, Michael: 314
Köttgen, Carl: 61, 63
Kunert, Günter: 23
Kürnberger, Ferdinand: 31, 43, 44, 45, 46, 56, 57, 106
L'Amour, Louis: 352
Lasch, Christopher: 313
Lathrop, John: 114
Lawrence, D. H.: 58, 278, 298, 323, 389
Lazarus, Emma: 195, 196, 271
Led Zeppelin: 165
Lee, Harper: 243
Lenau, Nikolaus: 43, 45f., 47, 57, 395
Leo XIII: 59
Leonard, Elmore: 137
Leone, Sergio: 172, 353
Lettau, Reinhard: 56
Leutze, Emanuel: 144f., 148
Leven, Jeremy: 151, 183, 184
Lewis, Sinclair: 191, 292, 308f. 310, 311
Lewis, Meriwether: 120, 148
Lincoln, Abraham: 383
Locke, Alain: 155
Locke, John: 104
Loew, Marcus: 295
London, Jack: 112, 245, 285
Lucas, George: 138
Machiavelli, Niccoló: 313
MacLeish, Archibald: 119, 134, 178, 320
Mahan, Alfred T.: 150
Mailer, Norman: 163, 249, 293, 354

Index

Malamud, Bernard: 13, 19, 103, 167, 249, 291, 355, 375-394
Malory, Thomas: 135, 332, 367
Marcuse, Herbert: 269
Marvell, Andrew: 256
Mather, Cotton: 98, 102
Mayer, Louis B.: 295
Maynard, Ken: 134
McCarthy, Joseph Raymond: 103, 354, 386, 393
McCullers, Carson: 243
McKinley, William: 131
McMurtry, Larry: 165, 357, 397
Mellon, Thomas: 283
Melville, Herman: 143f., 242, 286, 335, 391, 393
Mencken, H. L.: 309
Metternich, Klemens Fürst von: 36, 106
Miller, Arthur: 109, 166, 249, 311, 312
Miller, Henry: 118, 291f.
Moore, Thomas: 106
More, Thomas: 95, 103
Morgan, John Pierpont: 283, 316
Morton, Thomas: 101
Moses: 148
Nast, Thomas: 201
Newman, Paul: 134
Newport, Christopher: 96
Niebuhr, H. Richard: 139
Nietzsche, Friedrich: 284, 299
Nixon, Richard Milhous: 32, 87, 151, 175
Novak, Michael: 155, 219, 220, 271
Oates, Joyce Carol: 269, 270, 271
Okubo, Mine: 246
Ortega y Gasset: 58
Ortiz, Simon J.: 262-263, 271 [check, ob auch 264]
Orwell, George: 68
O'Sullivan, John L.: 116, 139, 143, 198
Owen, Robert: 103f.
Paine, Thomas: 36, 105, 115
Peale, Norman Vincent: 113, 282
Peck, Gregory: 137

Pericles: 207
Plato: 95, 176, 386, 392
Poe, Edgar Allan: 270
Polk, James Knox: 117, 120
Ponce de Leon, Juan: 101, 152
Porter, Cole: 121, 123
Presley, Elvis: 66
Pullman, George: 283
Pynchon, Thomas: 165, 311
Randall, Dudley: 169f., 197
Rapp, George: 103
Reagan, Ronald: 13, 32, 67, 72, 74, 88, 89, 103, 114, 175, 222, 352
Reich, Charles A.: 176
Remington, Frederic: 121, 131
Resnais, Alain: 78
Riesman, David: 309
Riis, Jacob August: 238,
Rilke, Rainer Maria: 257, 258
Ringer, Robert J.: 177, 249, 313
Rockefeller, John D.: 112, 283, 284, 316
Rodríguez de Montalvo, Garci: 35, 395
Rogers, Buck: 137
Rollo: 207
Romberg, Sigmung: 26
Roosevelt, Theodore: 130f., 328, 333
Rosenfeld, Isaac: 305
Roth, Henry: 244, 294
Roth, Philip: 249, 255ff., 271
Rush, Benjamin: 98
Salinger, Jerome David: 379
Santiago, Danny: 260-262, 271
Savage, Charles: 128
Schaefer, Jack: 172, 357
Schlesinger, Arthur M., Jr.: 222
Schulberg, Budd: 118, 293
Schuller, Robert: 114, 275, 282
Schütt, Peter: 26
Scott, Walter: 321, 328, 345
Seth Jones: 324
Sewall, Samuel: 278
Shakespeare, William: 95, 345, 392
Sharpe, Tom: 282
Shelley, Percy Bysshe: 386

Shepard, Sam: 166
Silko, Leslie Marmon: 236
Silver, Joan Micklin: 244
Simms, William Gilmore: 321
Sitting Bull: 359
Smith Brothers: 391
Smith, Sidney: 25
Spencer, Herbert: 111f., 283, 284, 301
Spengler, Oswald: 55, 64
Stanford, Leland: 283
Steinbeck, John: 245
Steven, George: 357
Strong, Josiah: 116f., 125f., 143, 331
Sumner, William Graham: 284
Tacitus: 17
Tawney, Richard Henry: 278
Taylor, Buck: 131
Taylor, Horace: 327
Terkel, Studs: 85
Thomas, Piri: 247
Thoreau, Henry David: 164, 165, 167, 244, 389, 391, 393
Tolstoy, Leo: 379
Tom Mix: 358
Trollope, Frances Milton: 107
Truman, Harry S.: 32
Tucholsky, Kurt: 57
Turner, Frederick Jackson: 129f. 170, 320, 322, 331, 338, 353, 358, 370, 378
Twain, Mark: 21, 25, 78, 82, 103, 113, 118, 242, 257, 270, 283, 322, 334
Tyler, Royall: 26, 103
Updike, John: 71, 103
Vanderbilt, Cornelius: 112, 283, 316

Vasquez, Richard: 247
Veblen, Thorstein: 308
Villarreal, José Antonio: 248
Vonnegut, Kurt: 66, 71, 77, 104, 166, 167, 174, 307, 314
Vonnegut, Mark: 104
Walker, Alice: 252f., 271
Walser, Martin: 27
Walton, Isaac: 382
Wanamaker, John: 279
Warner, Charles Dudley: 113
Warren, Robert Penn: 243
Washington, Booker T.: 250
Wayne, John: 134, 137, 351
Webb, Walter Prescott: 359
Weber, Max: 109, 130, 276-280, 286, 315
Weinberg, Albert K.: 140
Wells, H. G.: 273
West, Nathanael: 118, 293
Whitfield, Raoul: 293
Whitman, Walt: 100, 116, 143, 150, 164, 165, 381, 392
Wild Bill Hickok: 359
Winter, Rolf: 28, 316
Winthrop, John: 101
Wister, Owen: 19, 121, 131, 135, 170, 171, 172, 328, 330-355, 366, 378
Wolfe, Tom: 138
Wright, Richard: 192, 244
Wylie, Philip: 57
Yamamoto, Hisaye: 266-269, 271
Yerkes, Charles Tyson: 284
Young, Brigham: 120
Zangwill, Israel: 153-155, 179, 184, 197, 201
Zappa, Frank: 160

Arbeiten zur Amerikanistik
Herausgegeben von Prof. Dr. Peter Freese

Band 1 *Peter Freese (ed.)*
Religion and Philosophy in the United States of America
Proceedings of the German-American Conference at Paderborn,
July 29 - August 1, 1986
Essen 1987, 782 Seiten in zwei Teilbänden (das Werk wird nur
geschlossen abgegeben), DM 78,00/ÖS 608,00/SFr 78,00   ISBN 3-89206-149-1

Band 2 *Herwig Friedl / Dieter Schulz (eds.)*
E.L. Doctorow: A Democracy of Perception
A Symposium with and on E.L. Doctorow
Essen 1988, 203 Seiten, DM 42,00/ÖS 328,00/SFr 42,00   ISBN 3-89206-225-0

Band 3 *Peter Bischoff (ed. and introd.)*
Stories of the Early American West
Essen 1989, 211 Seiten, DM 36,00/ÖS/281,00/SFr 36,00   ISBN 3-89206-267-6

Band 4 *Peter Freese*
'America': Dream or Nightmare?
Reflections on a Composite Image
3rd, rev. and enl. ed. Essen 1994, 432 Seiten,
DM 56,00/ÖS 437,00/SFr 56,00   ISBN 3-89206-422-9

Band 5 *Klaus Benesch*
The Threat of History
Geschichte und Erzählung im afro-amerikanischen Roman
der Gegenwart
Essen 1990, 240 Seiten, DM 44,00/ÖS 343,00/SFr 44,00   ISBN 3-89206-377-X

Band 6 *Peter Freese (ed.)*
Germany and German Thought in American Literature
and Cultural Criticism
Proceedings of the German-American Conference in
Paderborn, May 16-19, 1990
Essen 1990, 522 Seiten, DM 68,00/ÖS 530,00/SFr 68,00   ISBN 3-89206-382-6

Band 7 *Sabine Wehner-Zott*
Radikale Religion in "The Radical"
Spättranszendentalismus in Neuengland
Essen 1991, 287 Seiten, DM 54,00/ÖS 421,00/SFr 54,00   ISBN 3-89206-397-4

Band 8 *Michael Porsche*
Der Meta-Western
Studien zu E.L. Doctorow, Thomas Berger und Larry McMurtry
Essen 1991, 210 Seiten, DM 44,00/ÖS 343,00/SFr 44,00   ISBN 3-89206-430-X

Band 9 *Randi Gunzenhäuser*
Horror at Home
Genre, Gender und das Gothic Sublime
Essen 1993, 313 Seiten, DM 64,00/ÖS 499,00/SFr 64,00   ISBN 3-89206-512-8

Band 10 *Peter Freese*
The Ethnic Detective
Chester Himes – Harry Kemelman – Tony Hillerman
Essen 1992, 254 Seiten, DM 48,00/ÖS 374,00/SFr 48,00   ISBN 3-89206-502-0

Band 11 *Achim Geldmacher*
Die Deutschen in Ann Arbor
Eine Studie über das Leben deutscher Einwanderer
in den USA, 1810-1918
Essen 1993, 444 Seiten, DM 86,00/ÖS 671,00/SFr 86,00   ISBN 3-89206-505-5

Band 12 *Peter Freese / Michael Porsche (eds.)*
Popular Culture in the United States
Proceedings of the German-American Conference in
Paderborn, 14-17 September 1993
Essen 1994, 460 Seiten, DM 96,00/ÖS 749,00/SFr 96,00   ISBN 3-89206-580-2

Band 13 *Horst Steur*
Bret Easton Ellis, *Less Than Zero*
Essen 1995, ca. 270 Seiten, DM 58,00/ÖS 452,00/SFr 58,00   ISBN 3-89206-639-6

Band 14 *Horst Tonn*
Wahre Geschichten
Dokumentarliteratur im 20. Jahrhundert
Essen 1995, ca. 300 Seiten, DM 78,00/ÖS 608,00/SFr 78,00   ISBN 3-89206-627-2